MAIN TRENDS
IN HISTORY

In the same series:

MAIN TRENDS IN HISTORY

GEOFFREY BARRACLOUGH

*Expanded and updated
by Michael Burns*

HM

HOLMES & MEIER

NEW YORK • LONDON

Published in the United States of America 1991 by
Holmes & Meier Publishers, Inc.
30 Irving Place, New York, NY 10003

First edition reprinted from MAIN TRENDS OF RESEARCH
IN THE SOCIAL AND HUMAN SCIENCES—Part II

Library of Congress Cataloging in Publication Data

Barraclough, Geoffrey, 1908–
    Main trends in history.

    (Main trends in the social and human sciences; 2)
    Originally published as chapter 3 of Main trends of
research in the social and human sciences, pt. 2.
    Bibliography: p. Includes index.
    1. Historiography.   2. History, Modern—20th cen-
tury—Historiography.   I. Title.   II. Series: Main
trends of research in the social and human sciences.
Selections; 2.
D.13.B332   1991   907'.2.
ISBN 0-8419-1287-4 (alk. paper)
ISBN 0-8419-1062-6 (pbk.) (alk. paper)

Manufactured in the United States of America

Contents

Editor's Acknowledgments

Geoffrey Barraclough could not examine thousands of titles on subjects ranging from pre-Columbian communities to cliometrics without assistance. So it went, on a more modest scale, for my contributions to this edition. I thank Sophie Moochhala for her meticulous work on the revised bibliography, and I am grateful to colleagues in the History Department at Mount Holyoke College who shared their thoughts on recent trends in their respective fields. Above all, I thank my wife, Elizabeth Kennan, for casting her well-trained eye over passages dealing with medieval history, and for editing the editor with patience and style.

Foreword

A Wandering Scholar

Across the five decades of his rich and varied career—from his first Fellowship at Merton College, Oxford, in the 1930s to his last post as visiting scholar at Munich University in 1983—Geoffrey Barraclough was a globe-trotter in body and soul. Early work on the medieval papacy took him to Italian, German, and British archives, and he returned to those and other international research centers for subsequent studies that, as time went by, broke the boundaries of Europe in the Middle Ages and moved toward sweeping syntheses which Barraclough called "universal" or "general" histories.[1] His first book, a meticulous monograph on aspects of church history in the thirteenth and fourteenth centuries, appeared when he was twenty-seven years old, and he completed his craft in his seventy-fifth year with a masterful new edition of a world historical atlas; the topics reveal the evolution of his interests and his expanding vision.[2] At the universities of Oxford, Cambridge, London, Liverpool, and Munich, at the University of California, at Williams College, and at Brandeis, generations of undergraduate and graduate students learned from Professor Barraclough the details of medieval German state systems and, later, the broad outlines of global trends and superpower politics in the twentieth century. Until his death on Boxing Day, 1984, in the old Oxfordshire wool town of Burford close by his first academic home, he remained his own sort of wandering scholar—erudite and distinguished, but a tireless, solitary traveler through historical time and space.

From the beginning his scholarship had a "social purpose," a keen sense of "relevance" which, he would insist, had nothing to do with ephemeral intellectual fashions or partisan political agendas.[3] In 1934, in a confident tone uncharacteristic of a fledgling historian, he announced that his book *Papal Provisions* would not be an analysis of a "technical and specialized and arid" topic but a study for the "general public . . . interested in the great historical movements of the past." Then and always, Barraclough aimed to explore "facts which belong as much to the present as to the past."[4] While he honored the fundamental rules of historical scholarship and demanded that students and colleagues do the same, he had no patience for soulless abstractions, for the rote memorization of dates and places and people. He believed, as his French contemporary Lucien Febvre put it, that facts should be "hooks on which we hang ideas."[5] The Papacy and the Reformation have "actuality today," Barraclough wrote in 1934; they "command present loyalties" and "direct present personalities." They "cannot be understood apart from their history."[6]

A decade later, prompted by the cataclysm of the Second World War, he again looked "back into the remote past" to achieve a better "sense of the present." Setting out on a "search for the original factors governing German history" from the Carolingian period to the Third Reich, he maintained that such a quest was essential "for all who wish to understand the German question of today."[7] Like his fellow historian across the Channel, Marc Bloch, who wrote his dramatic account of the fall of France while fighting with the Resistance, and like Bloch's comrade, Fernand Braudel, who outlined his magisterial study of the Mediterranean world in a German prison camp, Barraclough sketched the first draft of *The Origins of Modern Germany* in the midst of war, while still on active service with the Royal Air Force and far from archives and libraries.[8] Though very different in subject matter and method from the works of his *Annalistes* counterparts, Barraclough's survey of eleven-century German history also began as a reconstruction of the past through memory; it was informed by the contemporary state of the world and written with a passionate impatience to get the story told.

Shortly after the war, Barraclough exhibited his special blend of wit and sobriety when, addressing a World Affairs Lunch Hour Meeting in Sheffield, he reiterated the guiding principle of his scholarship: "As we sit here under the louring shadow of the atom bomb," he said in 1947, "well fed, with a conscientiously courageous smile on our faces, but with inward foreboding, like convicts on the morning of the day of execution—it is a good opportunity to take stock of human history, and see what it is all about."[9] With so many other scholars of his generation, Barraclough was reacting to a world in which morality had been "pitchforked out of politics" and in which the lessons of history had been either perverted for evil ends or ignored with tragic consequences. After Auschwitz, Dresden, Stalingrad, and Hiroshima, it was time, as Barraclough said later, "for reconsideration of . . . the fundamental postulates of historical thought."[10] As he reminds us in the pages that follow, he confronted the realization that "historical science was sunk in a deep rut churned by the ponderous cartwheels of nineteenth-century historiography;"[11] and, in response, he reoriented his view toward "the new perspectives in which the old Europe stands in a new age of global politics and global civilization."[12]

With the accomplished medievalist giving way to the generalist of universal history, it was appropriate that Barraclough succeed Arnold Toynbee as Stevenson Research Professor at the University of London in 1956. Aware of the immense problems with Toynbee's quasi-scientific notions of the cycles of civilization, Barraclough still defended his predecessor's courage to speculate, to reach with imagination and audacity beyond the horizons of Western history and to embrace the global view. Though criticized for abandoning the focused study of empirical evidence (a largely unwarranted attack against this highly professional scholar), Barraclough pressed on in his role as champion of a history which explores "humanity in all lands and ages." He showed a new interest in "extra-European" affairs and in those regions that would later be subsumed under the "Third World" rubric. And his comments on that score, expressed long before most Western historians broadened their own vision, have resonance today: "It is unfair and unprofitable to blame the Greeks and the Egyptians, the Chinese and the Indians, for having failed to achieve what *we* have achieved," he said in the late 1940s, "for there is no reason to suppose that they set out to achieve what seems to us desirable. What is profitable is to examine the reasons for their failure to achieve what *they* set out to achieve," he concluded, "for in that way, working by parallels, we may get some inkling of the causes underlying the rise and fall of civilizations, and of the process of civilization itself."[13] Born in the reign of Edward VII, when the sun, though descending, had not yet set on the British Empire, Barraclough attempted in the middle and late years of his career to understand Asian, African, Latin American, and other societies on their own terms. His sweeping approach to "universal systems" often worked against that goal; but, in the 1940s and 1950s especially, the quest was admirable and the point of view enlightened.

Formulated over the two decades following the Second World War, all of these concerns helped shape Barraclough's most widely read book, *An Introduction to Contemporary History,* first published in 1964 and still a mainstay in many college survey courses. Examining the changing environment of international relations, the rise of mass democracy, the twilight of European imperialism, the global challenges to Western hegemony, and other signposts of the new world in the decades between 1890 and 1960, the book imposed a strict periodization on "contemporary history." For some readers it was (and remains) a rich, provocative analysis of the "underlying structural changes" of the twentieth century, while for others it painted a vast landscape of problematic generalizations. But one thing was certain; it reconfirmed Barraclough's commitment to universal history—to what Emmanuel Le Roy Ladurie has called in another context the "parachutist's" perspective over the "truffle-hunter's"—and it carried a leitmotif that Barraclough would often repeat: "The European age . . . is over," he wrote, "and with it the predominance of the old European scale of values. Literature, like politics, has broken through its European bonds, and the civilization of the future . . . is taking shape as a world civilization in which all the continents will play their part."[14]

Barraclough never lost faith in the lessons of the past. In 1979, having just completed work on *Main Trends in History,* he began his last monograph in response to the "tensions and turmoil confronting the world today." The Shah of Iran had been deposed, Americans had been taken hostage in Teheran, the oil crisis had undermined world economies and Western confidence, and political leaders were behaving in bizarre, often perilous ways which put Barraclough in mind of another time and place. *From Agadir to Armageddon: Anatomy of a Crisis* is one of his most personal books, the last salvo of an *engagé* historian who hoped that the account of one international drama—the bellicose maneuvers of European powers at the Moroccan port of Agadir in 1911—would teach us something about the world of today. "To retell the story," he noted, "would be pointless if it had no bearing on our present predicament." Attacking "the false idol of the balance of power" and exposing the incessant "struggle for wealth and power which is rapidly developing into a struggle of all against all," he fashioned his book not as a traditional diplomatic history of the half decade prior to World War I but as an extended essay on "all the bungling, confusion and lack of coordination we have learned to associate with such actions in our own day." Too fine a historian to equate Agadir with the Persian Gulf or Moroccan rebels with Iranian mullahs ("I am aware," he wrote, "that no historical parallel fits neatly and tidily"), Barraclough was also aware that world leaders ignorant of world history were "pushing things to a head," much as their predecessors had done at the dawn of the century. The crucial difference is that now, at the century's end, "the stakes are higher."[15]

Though separated by nearly five decades, the preface of *From Agadir to Armageddon* has much in common with the opening pages of *Papal Provisions.* In 1934, the young medievalist from Merton College aimed to reach a general public "interested in the great historical movements of the past"; he wanted to avoid the perils of arid specialization and explore "historical facts which . . . have actuality today." In 1982, on the eve of his last trip home to Oxford, the distinguished seventy-four-year-old scholar implored his readers to broaden their horizons and learn from world history. It is still possible, he said, "even at this late date."[16]

Main Trends in History is, in some ways, the last panel of a scholarly triptych. Sharing the expansiveness and erudition of Barraclough's earlier synthetic works—*History in a Changing World* and *An Introduction to Contemporary History*—it explores nearly a century of historiographical trends, from the development of new methods and theoretical assumptions in Europe at the close of the nineteenth century, through the impact and application of Marxist models worldwide, to the immense broadening of the historian's "field of vision, both in time and space," in the 1960s and early 1970s.[17] Concentrating on the three decades following the Second World War, Barraclough surveys key trends in the principal research centers of Europe and North America; but, in his ambitious attempt to chart the methods and topics of interest to contemporary scholars, he also reaches out to the Soviet Union, China, Japan, India, Indonesia, Africa, and Latin America.

Though global in scope, the book is not a manifesto for a particular vision or interpretation of history. Barraclough knew how to take to the barricades in defense of his passionately held beliefs—he had done it many times—but he also knew how to chronicle events, or, in this case, historiographical trends, with as much objectivity as he could muster. This is not the time "to take sides," he tells us in his introductory chapter, but "to show, without passing judgment on the merits of different and often conflicting schools of thought, how the new impulses operative since 1945 have affected the study of history, and in particular to pick out those trends which, on present evidence, seem likely to achieve wider currency."[18] Only in his final pages does Barraclough enter the fray with a call for "integration . . . within the context of a larger pattern," with a general warning against the dangers of overspecialization. Historians should be wide open to the methods and findings of other disciplines, he says, but they must also avoid the corrosive problem of "fragmentation."[19]

Above all, Barraclough identifies the alignment of history with the social sciences—their critical "rapprochement"—as the central feature of modern scholarship. Like his fellow British historian E. P. Thompson, who noted how the social sciences had "thrust their seed" into Clio's womb, Barraclough describes the union and introduces the offspring. With clarity and insight, he shows how economics, sociology, psychology, anthropology, and other disciplines have, with varying degrees of success, intersected with history. And many of those "impulses" have indeed achieved "wider currency" in the years since Barraclough embarked on this study of history's main trends; a few, such as anthropology and sociology, have attracted even greater interest, while others, such as psychology and quantification, have lost some of the luster they enjoyed one and two decades ago. Historians, the most notorious scavengers in the scholarly world, continue to borrow, pilfer, purloin, and extract for their many recipes useful ingredients from the social sciences. But if that trend has continued in its general outlines, it has shifted in its specific concerns—partly because social scientists have moved down many new avenues over recent years, and partly because historians, at least good historians, are the beneficiaries of their imagination. They will, as they have always done, try anything.

While recognizing that one scholar's significant impulse is another scholar's irrelevant trend, the Epilogue of this new edition will attempt to update some of Barraclough's main themes and identify new topics and methodologies that currently engage historians. But a disclaimer is called for; Barraclough prepared much of his study using scores of detailed reports on worldwide historiographical trends compiled by the National Commissions of Unesco, the Council for Philosophy and Humanistic Studies, and other organizations. "Without these invaluable papers," he noted, "which supplement and bring up to date published information, it would be impossible to write this survey."[20] Without similar reports from the 1980s, it would, in turn, be impossible to reassess every trend outlined by Barraclough or to summarize recent publications on a global scale. Instead, the Epilogue will examine selected, though significant, topics and prognostications (for example, quantification, anthropological history, and the recent odyssey of psychohistory) and explore other issues uncharted by Barraclough (women's history, the concerns of "radical" historians, the "revival of the narrative," and more). For the most part, the principal focus will be on the work of historians practicing their craft in the research centers of Europe and the United States, including those scholars, though based in the West, whose interests reach out to Asia, Africa, and Latin America. In addition, to keep the gloss from overwhelming the text, the footnotes of the original edition have not been amended; but the general bibliography has been expanded to include a broad selection of recent books and articles.

As Barraclough understood so well, new trends, like awkward adolescents, move through early stages when mistakes are made and reductionism gets the best of common sense. So it went with the first applications of sociology and psychology to history; so it goes, as we shall see, with cultural anthropology and poststructuralism. If there is any safe rule in a discipline suspicious of regulation, it is that many of today's novel trends will be part of the historian's main arsenal of research tomorrow; and that new impulses, promising revolutionary discoveries, will emerge on the scene to spark renewed debates between the Ancients and Moderns of the historical profession.[21] It is also safe to imagine that Geoffrey Barraclough would have been keen to engage in that debate, and that he would have embraced those trends which open the cloistered precincts of specialization and broaden the historian's field of vision.

Notes

1. See, for example, Geoffrey Barraclough, *History in a Changing World* (Norman: University of Oklahoma Press, 1956), p. 19. For information on Barraclough's

career, see *The New York Times,* January 11, 1985; and Margot Levy, ed., *The Annual Obituary* (Chicago: St. James Press, 1985), pp. 628–29.

2. *Papal Provisions: Aspects of Church History, Constitutional, Legal and Administrative in the Later Middle Ages* (Oxford: Basil Blackwell, 1934); and *The Times Atlas of World History* (Maplewood: Hammond, 1984). Among Barraclough's major books, in addition to those cited above, are *The Origins of Modern Germany* (Oxford: Basil Blackwell, 1946); *The Medieval Empire: Idea and Reality* (London: G. Phillip, 1950); *An Introduction to Contemporary History* (New York: Penguin, 1964); and *From Agadir to Armageddon: Anatomy of a Crisis* (New York: Holmes and Meier, 1982).

3. Barraclough tells us below (p. 215) that history must be "approached in a scientific spirit and infused with a social purpose." An extended discussion of the problems and benefits of "relevance" in history is found in *History in a Changing World,* pp. 20–27.

4. *Papal Provisions,* p. vii.

5. The words are Febvre's, quoted in Roger Brunet, *Les Campagnes toulousaines: Etude géographique* (Toulouse: Faculté des Lettres et sciences humaines de Toulouse, 1965), p. 14.

6. *Papal Provisions,* p. vii.

7. *Origins of Modern Germany,* p. ix; see also p. 466.

8. Marc Bloch, *L'Etrange défaite: Témoignage écrit en 1940* (Paris: Michel, 1957); Fernand Braudel, *La Méditerranée et le Monde Méditerranéen à l'Epoque de Philippe II* (Paris: Armand Colin, 1966).

9. *History in a Changing World,* p. 221.

10. Ibid., p. 7.

11. See below, p. 206.

12. *History in a Changing World,* pp. 10–12.

13. Ibid., p. 231; see also p. 13. The emphasis is Barraclough's.

14. *An Introduction to Contemporary History* (Harmondsworth: Penguin, 1979 edition), p. 268.

15. *From Agadir to Armageddon,* pp. vii–4, 177–81.

16. Ibid., p. viii.

17. See below, p. 94.

18. See below, p. 4.

19. See below, p. 148.

20. See below, p. 178, note 763; see also p. 1, note 1.

21. For more on historiographical trends and the persistent battle between "Ancients and Moderns," see Lawrence Stone, *The Past and the Present* (Boston: Routledge and Kegan Paul, 1981), p. 30 and passim; and Gertrude Himmelfarb, *The New History and the Old: Critical Essays and Reappraisals* (Cambridge, Mass.: Harvard University Press, 1987). These (and opposing) views of the contemporary scene will be discussed in more detail in the Epilogue.

'Our civilization is the first to have for its past the past of the world, our history is the first to be world-history. [...] But besides that it is something more. A history adequate to our civilization can only be scientific history. [...] We cannot sacrifice the demand for scientific certainty without injury to the conscience of our civilization. Mythical and fictitious representations of the past may have literary value [...] but [...] they are not history.'

Jan HUIZINGA*

1. History in a Changing World: From the Close of the Nineteenth Century to the Second World War

It is evident today, after the lapse of a quarter of a century, that the Second World War inaugurated a new period in the conception of history and its functions and in historians' attitudes to their work. The present survey of current trends in the writing of history is accordingly concerned in the main with the course of development since 1945.[1] Prior to 1939 most historians followed without misgiving the guide-lines laid down by their predecessors at the turn of the nineteenth and twentieth centuries; after 1945 a sense of dissatisfaction with pre-war formulations gradually became apparent and from about 1955 the study of history entered a period of rapid change and reassessment.

The Second World War affected our conceptions of history in two main ways. Its most obvious consequence was a radical alteration of the environ-

---

* 'A definition of the concept of history', p. 8 in KLIBANSKY & PATON (eds.), *Philosophy and History* (1936).

1. To prevent misunderstanding, it is important to emphasize that the purpose of the following pages is to study contemporary trends which appear to be of universal significance, and not to present a survey of current historical writing in different countries or regions. Much historical work – perhaps as much as nine-tenths of the total output – is entirely conventional in approach, and while often adding considerably to knowledge, does not (and is not intended to) suggest new directions or methods. For this reason, however brilliant in some cases it may be, it is not specifically referred to here. Secondly, my concern has not been with special branches of history (e.g., history of science, history of law), though considerable progress has been made in some of these in recent years, but rather with general tendencies which affect the work of all historians in all areas and countries. It would be foolish to expect that the general scheme adopted, any more than the particular formulations and choice of subject-matter, are likely to satisfy historians everywhere, and I am only too well aware, in any case, of the immense gaps in my knowledge. I have nevertheless attempted to discuss the situation on a global scale, since I believe that an essential characteristic of historical work today is its globality. If I have been saved from errors, it is because of the comments and criticism provided both by individuals and by national committees. This work has benefited, in particular, from the national reports and materials supplied by, or on the initiative of the Unesco National Commissions of Australia, Belgium, Chile, Finland, Hungary, India, Indonesia, the Ukrainian SSR, the USSR, and Yugoslavia, and from the individual essays and comments collected by the international Council for Philosophy and Humanistic Studies in consultation with the International Com-

ment in which historians work. If we compare the world-situation before and after 1945 – still more, if we widen our vision and compare the world-situation in 1900 and in 1950 – four great changes are immediately apparent. The first is that nothing that happens in one part of the world is any longer without impact in the others; twentieth-century history is world-history in the fullest sense of the term. The second is the irresistible advance of science and technology, imposing everywhere a new social and intellectual pattern. The third is the declining importance of Europe, the contraction of Europe overseas, the rise to preponderance of the Soviet Union and the United States, and the resurgence of Asia and Africa. The fourth is the disintegration of the liberal synthesis and the rise of social and political institutions radically different from anything the nineteenth century had known. Whereas at the beginning of the twentieth century the liberal democratic order appeared to be advancing unchallenged, by 1960 the communist system – confined prior to 1939 to Soviet Russia – extended to one-third of the population of the inhabited world, and elsewhere, particularly in Africa, new forms of political organization were emerging, allied but not identical with either.

Confronted by changes as fundamental as these, it is not surprising that a new generation of historians was compelled to re-examine its inherited assumptions. Even before 1945 a sense of frustration and disillusionment was making itself felt. Speaking with all the authority of the Regius Professor in the University of Oxford, Sir Maurice Powicke referred feelingly

---

mittee of Historical Sciences. I have endeavoured to make proper acknowledgement of my special indebtedness, particularly for reports and papers submitted from various countries, at the appropriate place, but the number of obligations I have incurred is too great for all to be specifically acknowledged here. There are, however, a number of special obligations, first and foremost to the general rapporteur, Monsieur Jacques Havet, without whose indefatigable help and encouragement, in sometimes difficult circumstances, this report would almost certainly not have been completed, and secondly to the two Associate Rapporteurs, Professor I. S. Kon (Leningrad) and Professor K. O. Diké (Harvard). My obligation to all three is more considerable than I can express in a few words. I should also like to express my very great thanks to Dr. F. A. Fedorova, of the Institute for Scientific Information and Library of Fundamental Sciences of the Academy of Sciences of the USSR, whose help has far exceeded anything I had any right to expect, and also to Dr. Péter Hanák (Budapest), Professors Satish Chandra (New Delhi) and Sartono Kartodirdjo (as co-ordinator of the Indonesian National Committee), for reports and analyses which I have found unusually stimulating and suggestive. Finally, I owe warm thanks to Professor J. Dhont (Ghent), Professor N. A. Erofeev (Moscow), Professor J. R. T. Hughes (Northwestern University), Professor Henri-Irénée Marrou (Paris), Professor Charles Morazé (Paris), Monsieur Jean d'Ormesson (Paris), Professor Boyd C. Shafer (St. Paul, Minn.) and H. Exc. Professor Silvio Zavala, Mexican Ambassador in Paris, who have read the earlier versions of this paper and given me their frank and kind comments. On a more personal note, I should like also to acknowledge the stimulus I have had from many lively discussions with my former pupil, Marc Orlofsky (Brandeis University). The responsibility for the formulation and for errors and omissions naturally remains entirely mine.

to 'the malaise or discomfort which oppresses the thoughtful study of his-tory'.[2] Nor, of course, did he stand alone. A generation earlier, in the after-math of the First World War, Troeltsch and Karl Heussi had discussed at length the 'crisis' of historicism.[3] But the immediate effects of these mis-givings were limited. The stability of the old world had apparently been restored and even the great depression after 1929 did little to sap historians' belief in their inherited traditions. What destroyed their self-confidence was the course of events between 1939 and 1945. The extirpation of European Jewry, the Nazi bestialities in eastern Europe, the uprooting of tens and hundreds of thousands of men, women and children in a vast new *Völker-wanderung,* and finally the atomic holocaust at Hiroshima and Nagasaki, made it impossible for any sensitive person to view the course of history with the old complacency. 'When we are told that it is foolish to judge Charlemagne or Napoleon, or Genghis Khan or Hitler or Stalin for their massacres,' wrote Sir Isaiah Berlin – he might in fairness have added Crom-well to his list – when we are told that 'as historians our categories are neutral' and that our only task is 'to describe', 'we can only answer that to accept this doctrine is to do violence to the basic notions of our morality' and 'to misrepresent our sense of the past.'[4] A conception of history which led in this direction was no longer acceptable; the time had come for a re-consideration of the foundations and of the fundamental postulates of his-torical thought.

This is the background against which all attempts to review current trends in the study of history must be placed. Most, if not all, of the characteristic developments in historical writing and research today spring from one or other of the factors enumerated above. On the other hand, the exploration of new ways in history is still tentative. Conservative historians in both the liberal and the Marxist camps continue to wage a defensive battle against revisionism in all its forms, sometimes with cogent arguments, and it would be foolish to under-estimate the weight of conservative resistance. If a cen-sus were taken today, it would almost certainly show that the majority of professional historians is sceptical of, if not positively hostile to, the more recent trends. The conflict is, therefore, to some extent a conflict of gener-ations; for, as Professor Trevor-Roper has said,[5] a 'great gulf' has opened out between the older generation and the 'moderns', across which they view each other 'with incomprehension, almost disdain'. Its result is that history has become deeply involved in the much discussed 'crisis in the humanities' and that historians today find themselves in the thick of the struggle, so characteristic of the contemporary situation, to bring the study of man in all its ramifications into line with the widening horizons of human experi-

2. POWICKE, 'After fifty years' (1944, 1955).
3. TROELTSCH, *Der Historismus und seine Probleme* (1922); HEUSSI, *Die Krisis des Historismus* (1932); cf. IGGERS, *The German Conception of History* (1968), particularly Chap. 7.
4. BERLIN, *Historical Inevitability* (1954), pp. 76-77.
5. *Sunday Times,* 19 Feb. 1956.

ence and the new dimensions of cultural life which are the mark of the world in which we live.[6]

It would be quite wrong, in a survey such as this, to take sides in the conflict of views and interpretations which is going on in the historical world today. There can be no question here, even were I capable of it, of another profession of faith, such as Marc Bloch bequeathed to us in his famous *Apologie pour l'histoire*. My purpose is necessarily more modest – namely, to show, without passing judgement on the merits of different and often conflicting schools of thought, how the new impulses operative since 1945 have affected the study of history, and in particular to pick out those trends which, on present evidence, seem likely to achieve wider currency. No one can predict the future, and it may be that certain developments which appear promising at the present time will turn out on further examination to be unproductive and transitory. Nevertheless, sufficient time has now elapsed to make the character of the new trends apparent, and there is evidence that some have come to stay and have been accepted even by convinced adherents of the old methodology. In England, for example, Kitson Clark has made more than perfunctory obeissance to such modern techniques as quantification, conceding that 'there can be no clear frontier between what can be called "historical" and what "scientific",' and that 'scientific methods and techniques will almost certainly be extended into more and more fields of study';[7] and G. R. Elton, a hard-hitting defender of traditional ways, though polemicizing against the tendency 'to bring the social sciences into the working habits of English historians,' is well aware that sociology has taught historians to ask 'new questions.' As for German historicism, which for so long was the dominant philosophy outside the communist world, he has no hesitation in saying that it has been superseded 'because the progress of historical research itself called in question many of its confident conclusions'.[8]

Whatever view we may take of the controversies in the historical world today, it is clear that they have already had two significant results. First, and this is almost certainly an irreversible trend, history has become far more sophisticated; no one any longer supposes that all that is required of the historian is the practical application of common sense. Secondly, the challenge to traditional thinking has reinvigorated historical studies at a time when they appeared to be set in old ways. After a period of stability – some might even say, of rigidity – history is once again on the move; new impulses, trends and insights are propelling it in new directions. The present survey can only deal with these developments in general terms; considerations of space alone preclude any attempt to describe in all their fullness the particular undertakings of historians in particular countries. Such a survey, nevertheless, may serve a practical purpose, if it provides a back-

6. Cf. PLUMB, 'Introduction' and 'The historian's dilemma', pp. 9, 24-44 in PLUMB (ed.), *Crisis in the Humanities* (1964).

7. KITSON CLARK, *The Critical Historian* (1967), pp. 21, 193.

8. ELTON, *The Practice of History* (1967), pp. 23-24.

ground against which historians everywhere can appraise their more specialized programmes. The realization that the time has come for a new approach to the problems and materials of history transcends differences of ideology and environment; the new techniques and methods are a challenge to historians in every continent and in every political climate. It is not only that the answers of historians today are different from those of their predecessors; they also ask different questions. The scope of history, as they view it, has changed, and they are no longer satisfied with the formulations of thirty or fifty years ago.

History in the First Half of the Twentieth Century

The new trends in historical writing and research can only be properly appreciated when they are seen in the wider context of the development of historical theory and practice since the end of the nineteenth century. What we are witnessing today is a reaction, at least among the younger generation of historians, against the kind of history and the conceptions of history prevalent before 1945. Nothing is more characteristic of the present situation – and nothing, perhaps, of greater significance for the future development of historical studies – than the tendency to question the basic postulates which governed the work of historians in the first half of the twentieth century.

Historians in the first half of the twentieth century leaned heavily, so far as their methodology and theoretical assumptions were concerned, on their predecessors in the late nineteenth century. They stood in a continuous tradition, reaching back in Germany to Ranke and Waitz, in France to Michelet, Fustel de Coulanges and Sorel, in England to Stubbs and Gardiner, in Russia to Kluchevsky and, after the revolution of 1917, to Kluchevsky's pupil, Pokrovsky. Prior to 1917, when the impact of Marxism on the ideas of working historians was hardly more than peripheral, the great controversy was that between positivism, as represented by Comte and Buckle, and idealism, as represented by Droysen, Rickert and Windelband. In England this controversy flared up once again in the first decade of the new century in a lively, but ultimately sterile, debate between J. B. Bury and G. M. Trevelyan.[9] But this was the last flicker of old passions, and by the turn of the nineteenth and twentieth centuries a characteristic compromise had generally been reached. In theory most historians accepted the idealist position, with its sharp distinction between history and science and its emphasis on intuition (*Erlebnis*) as the historian's ultimate means of coming to terms with the past; but in practice their methodology was based on the positivist assumption that the two main objects of historical research are the discovery of 'new facts' and the elimination of error by the exer-

9. The Bury-Trevelyan controversy was summarized, with the main texts, by C. H. WILLIAMS, *The Modern Historian* (1938); cf. TREVELYAN, *Clio, A Muse, and Other Essays* (1913).

cise of 'historical criticism'. This uneasy synthesis was resolved, according to the manuals of historical method which now began to appear in considerable numbers, by dividing the historian's work into different phases: the collection and preparation of material, in which the positivist assumptions prevailed, and interpretation and presentation of results, in which the historian's intuitive faculties and individuality came into their own.

The appearance of manuals of instruction, setting down the established principles of critical research and handing them on virtually unchanged from generation to generation, was a characteristic feature of the situation at the turn of the nineteenth and twentieth centuries. It marked the emancipation of history and its emergence as a discipline in its own right. Of these manuals none was more famous nor more widely influential than that of Langlois and Seignobos which appeared in 1898.[10] The study of history was being organized on professional lines, and with this growing specialization it was perhaps natural that the techniques of research should become not only the subject of formal instruction in the universities but also the criterion of professional proficiency.

The second characteristic feature of the new situation was the attempt to garner the fruits of the new critical history which had taken hold in the decade following the death of Michelet in 1874, and so to provide a firm foundation of established knowledge for the coming generation. An early and distinguished example of this endeavour was the *Histoire générale* edited by Lavisse and Rambaud between 1893 and 1901. But the characteristic product of this phase of historical research and writing was the *Cambridge Modern History*. Planned by Lord Acton, though the first volume did not appear until after Acton's death in 1902, the *Cambridge Modern History* is significant not only because it was conceived as a co-operative international undertaking, but also because Acton, with his German education and background, was uniquely qualified to bridge the gap between idealism and positivism and bring together under one roof the results of German and western European historical thought and practice. The *Cambridge Modern History* was intended to set the seal on the progress achieved in the nineteenth century and at the same time, in Acton's own words, to 'chart and compass for the coming century'.[11]

Acton accepted with few reservations the basic tenets of the historicist position.[12] But at the same time he had no doubt that history was 'a progressive science'. The time for 'ultimate,' or definitive, history might

10. LANGLOIS & SEIGNOBOS, *Introduction aux études historiques* (1898). It was preceded in Germany by BERNHEIM, *Lehrbuch der historischen Methode* (1889). It is only necessary to compare recent works such as HALPHEN, *Introduction à l'histoire* (1948), NABHOLZ, *Einführung in das Studium der mittelalterlichen und der neueren Geschichte* (1948), or HALKIN, *Initiation à la critique historique* (1951), to see how little they differ in substance from their late nineteenth-century models.
11. *The Cambridge Modern History. Its Origin, Authorship and Production* (1907), p. 22.
12. KOCHAN, *Acton on History* (1954), Chap. 1; cf. STERN (ed.), *The Varieties of History* (1956), p. 246.

not yet have arrived; but it was just round the corner, for, as a result of the opening of the European archives, 'all information' was 'within reach' and 'every problem' had 'become capable of solution.' In Acton's view 'solidity of criticism' was the historian's essential quality. Granted this, he had no doubt about the feasibility (to quote his own example) of an account of the battle of Waterloo 'that satisfies French and English, Germans and Dutch alike'. Contributors to the *Cambridge Modern History* were exhorted to reveal neither their country, their religion nor their party; their sole object was to be 'the incease of accurate knowledge.' These observations reveal the mainsprings of Acton's philosophy of history. History, for him, was 'the record or truths revealed by experience', its purposes were 'eminently practical'; he saw it – and in this he spoke for his generation – as 'an instrument of action and a power that goes to the making of the future'.[13]

It would be easy, from the standpoint of the present, to criticize this robust, if simplistic, faith in history; it would also be unjust and shortsighted. We forget too easily how new the techniques of historical criticism were, how recent (as Acton's own experience showed) the victory over obscurantism, for how short a time the archives had been accessible to students. The 'increase of accurate knowledge' was no chimera in Acton's day; and in fact knowledge increased at unparalleled speed. In sheer quantity of output the early years of the twentieth century were a period of remarkable progress, and it would be grossly misleading to under-estimate their achievement. It was only in the next generation – the generation which survived the First World War – and in the second rather than in the first half of the period that extended from 1919 to 1939, that doubts arose; and, paradoxically, they arose less from philosophical questioning or from the changing circumstances of the post-war world – though these played some part– than from the speed and nature of the achievement itself.

It is only necessary to summarize briefly the main factors which weakened, if they did not entirely undermine, the faith in history which was so distinctive a feature of the opening years of the twentieth century. Most important in practice were the growing doubts within the historical profession itself about the direction in which its labours were taking it. Encouraged by Acton's successor at Cambridge, J. B. Bury, in the belief that 'a complete assemblage of the smallest facts of human history will tell in the end,'[14] historians of the following generation immersed themselves in abstruse research and meticulous detail, confident that their work, however specialized, would spontaneously lead to practical results. No one would question the high level of learning, industry and intelligence which went into these undertakings; but it is another question whether the gain was always commensurate with the effort. Too often the result appeared to be the ac-

13. For ACTON's views, cf. his 'Letter to contributors to the *Cambridge Modern History*' and his 'Inaugural Lecture on the study of history', both reprinted in *Lectures on Modern History* (1906).
14. BURY, *Selected Essays*, ed. Temperley (1930), p. 17.

cumulation of a mass of intractable material which defied synthesis. By the 1930's complaints were growing of 'arid professionalism' and an 'absence of vision', of historical research which was little more than 'a pedantic chase after the insignificant'.[15] Moreover, much of the work of historians of this generation consisted of criticism and modification or refutation of the work of their predecessors. Valuable though this may have been in itself, it accorded ill with Acton's vision of a gradual accretion of assured factual knowledge, and suggested instead that the writing of history was a circular process, reminiscent of a dog chasing its own tail. Certainly, it cast doubt on Acton's ideal of 'ultimate history'. Far from clarifying and stimulating, as had been the case at the turn of the nineteenth and twentieth centuries, the paradoxical result of the increase of historical knowledge was to complicate and perplex. It seemed that historians, carried away by one side of Bury's teaching, had forgotten the other side – namely, his warning that 'no collection of facts or sequence of facts' has 'the slightest theoretical importance' unless we can 'determine their vital connexion with the whole system of reality'.[16]

There were other reasons besides these practical considerations why Acton's belief in 'progressive' history wore thin. One was the storm-clouds of the First World War. After 1914, as they broke apart into warring factions, each interpreting the 'facts' of history in the light of its own national traditions, it was hard to think of historians as an international band of disinterested scholars, all striving for 'objective' truth. At the same time Tout's happy confidence that 'we are half-way towards solving a problem when we have traced it from stage to stage through the ages',[17] collapsed like a pricked balloon in the aftermath of the war, when, in the treaties of Versailles and Trianon, it was brought face to face with the intractable confusion of nationalities in eastern Europe. But more fundamentally important was the fact that the attempt to reconcile positivism and idealism by a division of labour was foredoomed to failure. The idealist assumptions of the German historicists, it was soon discovered, could not be confined to the later stages of the historian's work; but when applied to the materials and methodology of history, the idealist critique dealt the historian's vaunted factuality and objectivity a lethal blow. 'It is not I who speak,' Fustel de Coulanges had written, 'but history which speaks through me.' But the belief in the possibility – in Ranke's words – of 'extinguishing the self', which Acton clearly shared, was undermined by Dilthey's insistence on the necessary psychological involvement of the historian in any understanding of the past, just as Bury's famous pronouncement that 'history is a science, no less and no more,' was undermined by Rickert's critical analysis of the logical and methodological differences between history and the natural sciences. The 'facts' of history, it turned out, were not 'facts'

15. Powicke, *Modern Historians and the Study of History* (1955), p. 192.
16. Bury, *op. cit.*, p. 47.
17. Tout, 'The place of the Middle Ages in the teaching of history', p. 6 in *History*, Vol. VIII (1923).

at all, but a series of accepted judgements, and the very existence of truth in history, which the preceding generation had taken for granted, now appeared as an unresolved – and, for some, an insoluble – problem of epistemology.[18]

Another factor, to which we shall return, was the broadening scope of history. On the one hand, the new sciences of archaeology and anthropology pushed back the historian's horizons by centuries and forced him to broaden his sights and widen his perspectives. On the other hand, growing scepticism about the adequacy of the old 'factual' approach involved him in a series of characteristic refinements. From the time of Ranke to that of Acton, few historians had doubted that the main thread of history was political; since the state was the chief agent of historical change, the historian's business was to establish the facts of its evolution. After 1917, when Marxism became an important factor in historical thinking, the primacy of political history was no longer self-evident. Was not the action of governments, in reality, a response to, or reflection of, deeper economic undercurrents? Could the course of history be understood except in terms of the conflict of economic forces and the patterns imposed by economic systems? The other impulse came from the side of German historicism. If, as Simmel and Dilthey had demonstrated, there could be no question of the historian knowing 'facts' in an empirical way, if his only hope of understanding the past was to 're-live' it in his own mind, then why confine himself to political events? Did not the novels of Balzac, for example, throw as much light on social conditions in Restoration France as dry-as-dust documents from the archives? But, more important, was not the historian's central concern less the crude facts of history, the mere events of the past, than the ideas by which men lived, and particularly the climate of ideas in which statesmen and politicians operated? In Germany, Friedrich Meinecke became the founder of a powerful school of intellectual history, whose influence soon extended to England and the United States.

In this way, as emphasis shifted to the economic, social, cultural, intellectual and psychological aspects of history, the scope of the historian's work widened. But the result was to add to its complexity and to banish into a remote future the expectation of 'practical' results which had inspired historians of Acton's generation. Indeed, many historians at this time denied that history had any 'practical' use, claiming instead that their only task was to study the past 'for its own sake'. When the English historian, T. F. Tout, implicitly criticizing his predecessors, wrote in 1920 that 'we investigate the past not to deduce practical political lessons, but to find out what really happened',[19] he was only expressing the common belief of his generation.

The road which history travelled in the first half of the twentieth century, at least in western Europe, is best seen by comparing the *Cambridge*

18. Cf. STERN (ed.), *The Varieties of History* (1956), pp. 20-21, 25-26.
19. TOUT, *Chapters in the Administrative History of Medieval England*, Vol. I (1920), p. 7.

Modern History, published between 1902 and 1912, and the *New Cambridge Modern History*, the first volume of which appeared in 1957. What is immediately apparent is that, after five tempestuous decades, Acton's confidence and sense of purpose had evaporated. The spirit of the new editor's general introduction contrasts sharply with that of his predecessor. In his discussion of the problems which lie at the heart of the historian's work, the tone he adopts is one of resigned agnosticism. The central question of 'the purposes of the historian' is disposed of in a series of trite observations devoid of philosophical content;[20] and Acton's belief in 'definitive history' is dismissed as an illusion. 'Historians of a later generation,' Sir George Clark states,[21]

do not look forward to any such prospect. They expect their work to be superseded again and again. They consider that knowledge of the past has come down through one or more human minds, has been 'processed' by them, and therefore cannot consist of elemental and impersonal atoms which nothing can alter... The exploration seems to be endless, and some impatient scholars take refuge in scepticism, or at least in the doctrine that, since all historical judgments involve persons and points of view, one is as good as another and there is no 'objective' historical truth.

In so far as the *New Cambridge Modern History* may be taken as typical of the broad stream of historical writing and research, the impression it leaves is that, by the middle of the twentieth century, history had passed into an Alexandrian 'silver age', solid, responsible, productive – perhaps even over-productive – but garnering knowledge for its own sake with little sense of purpose or direction. Its revisions were subtle scholarly inflections rather than bold re-assessments; its ambition extended no further than 'simply to say what is known at present, to examine that knowledge from various standpoints, and to connect it with other knowledge'. This may be regarded as a respectable object, but it can hardly be described as challenging. By 1957 history was seen as a craft, rather than a science, and fifty years was marked out as the limit of any historian's competence.[22] The result was immersion in narrowly technical problems of a professional nature, of interest only to other professional historians. The critic who described the first half of the twentieth century as 'a time when most historians temporarily lost their bearings'[23] has been accused of exaggeration; but it would be hard to maintain that his criticism was irrelevant. It was at least a paradox worth pondering – as an English historian observed in 1964 – that, at the end of a period of such spectacular growth, 'doubt and discontent about the subject' among historians themselves were more widespread than at any previous time in the past.[24]

20. Cf. *The New Cambridge Modern History*, Vol. I (1957), pp. xxviii-xxix.
21. *Ibid.*, pp. xxiv-xxv.
22. POWICKE, *Modern Historians ...*, *op. cit.* (1955), p. 202.
23. Keith THOMAS, 'The tools and the job', p. 275 in *New Ways in History* (special issue of *The Times Literary Supplement*, 1966).
24. TAYLOR, *History in an Age of Growth* (1964), pp. 5-6.

The Crisis of Historicism

When we seek an explanation of the change of attitude which is so evident between 1900 and 1950, the factor which stands out above all others is the influence of the historicist school of thought which had its origins in Germany. As a body, it has often been said, historians are suspicious of philosophical argument; they do their work without preoccupying themselves greatly about the philosophical presuppositions of what they are doing. But philosophy, swept out of the door, is apt to fly back through the window; and as, in the 1920's, the views and writings of Dilthey and Croce found a wider audience, historicist ways of thinking increasingly affected the unconscious assumptions even of ordinary working historians who had no interest in philosophical questions and claimed that their research was entirely empirical.

Historicism was not, of course, the only school of historical thought in the 1920's and 1930's. After 1917 Marxism soon became dominant in the Soviet Union; it was also, as has already been observed, an increasingly powerful force outside it. In France and Belgium, the older positivist tradition was always strong and provided a counterpoise to German influences. Even in Germany Lamprecht and, at a later date, Eckart Kehr had struggled to break free from historicist assumptions, but their impact on the prevailing school of thought was minimal.[25] In the United States, where German influence was traditionally strong, American pragmatism brought about a reaction in favour of a more specifically sociological approach to history which set in before the First World War,[26] and in France a similar preoccupation underlay the work of Henri Berr and his collaborators in the *Revue de Synthèse historique*. Berr reacted against the emphasis of German historicism on the unique and individual; for him history was rather the natural co-ordinating point for the comparative study of society.[27] There is a direct connexion between Berr's efforts at reorientation and the new trends in French historiography inaugurated by Lucien Febvre and Marc Bloch during the 1930's.[28]

All these trends away from historicism were to be important in the future; but they did little – except in the Soviet Union – to offset its in-

---

25. For a summary of the notorious Lamprecht controversy, cf. SCHIEDER, Th., 'Die deutsche Geschichtswissenschaft im Spiegel der *Historischen Zeitschrift*' (1959), pp. 47-51 in SCHIEDER, Th. (ed.), *Hundert Jahre Historische Zeitschrift* (special centenary issue of that periodical, Vol. CLXXXIX); for the rejection of Kehr, cf. WEHLER's introduction to the collected edition of KEHR's essays, *Der Primat der Innenpolitik* (1965).

26. Cf. HERBST, *The German Historical School in American Scholarship* (1965), and STROUT, *The Pragmatic Revolt in American History* (1958).

27. Cf. BERR, *La synthèse en histoire* (1911); *L'histoire traditionnelle et la synthèse historique* (1935); and BERR's account of 'Les étapes de ma propre route depuis 1900' (1950).

28. Cf. GLÉNISSON, 'L'historiographie française contemporaine', pp. xi-xvi in *La recherche historique en France de 1949 à 1965* (1965).

fluence in the inter-war years. Even Bloch's new concern with 'structural' analysis, exemplified in the volumes he published on feudal society in 1939 and 1940, only made real impact after the end of the Second World War, by which time conditions and attitudes had undergone radical change. Historicism was not, of course, a single coherent doctrine; and a distinction has rightly been drawn between German historicism and the Italian historicism of Benedetto Croce.[29] Nevertheless, in one or other of its forms its influence was pervasive. Collingwood became its English step-father, and even in France, the native land of positivism, it made rapid progress through the influence of writers such as Raymond Aron and Henri Marrou.[30] In Spain, where the impact of German idealism had been strong ever since 1898, Dilthey's ideas helped to shape the thought of Ortega and of historians such as Amerigo Castro, and from Spain historicism made its way to Latin America.[31]

This is not the place to discuss the nature of historicism, nor its long history and evolution – nor, indeed, the undoubted achievements which stand to its credit.[32] That, in its greatest days, it represented a justifiable and healthy reaction against the exaggerated naturalism and scientism of positivist writing, no sensible person would deny.[33] But here we are concerned with its impact during the inter-war period; and this, it is now generally agreed, was negative, rather than positive. The German historicists were right in exposing the inadequacy of the empirical rules of thumb which masqueraded as 'historical science' in manuals such as the *Introduction* of Langlois and Seignobos. As E. H. Carr has said, this type of formal criticism and the accuracy it is meant to achieve are 'a duty, not a virtue', a 'necessary condition' of the historian's work 'but not his essential function', any more, for example, than they are the essential function of the geologist or petrologist.[34] It was when this had been achieved that the real problems began, and it was the merit of Simmel and Dilthey to draw attention to them. 'The central problems of a historical methodology or epistemology', it has been said, 'hinge upon the fact an objective knowledge of the past can only be attained through the subjective experience of

29. Cf. ANTONI, *Dallo storicismo alla sociologia* (1940); ROSSI, *Storia e storicismo nella filosofia contemporanea* (1960).

30. COLLINGWOOD, *The Idea of History* (1946); ARON, *Introduction à la philosophie de l'histoire* (1938) (English translation, *Introduction to the Philosophy of History*, 1961); MARROU, *De la connaissance historique* (1954).

31. Cf. ORTEGA y GASSET, *Historia como sistema*, and *Guillermo Dilthey y la idea de la vida*, both in *Obras completas*, Vol. VI (4th edn., 1958); cf. MARAVALL, *Teoria del saber historico* (1958).

32. The subject has been dealt with exhaustively in three recent books: KON, *Die Geschichtsphilosophie des 20. Jahrhunderts* (2 vols., 1964), BRANDS, *Historisme als Ideologie* (1965), and IGGERS, *The German Conception of History* (1968), and it is sufficient to refer to these authoritative treatments.

33. Cf. in general KON, *Der Positivismus in der Soziologie. Geschichtlicher Abriss* (1968).

34. CARR, E. H., *What is History?* (1961), p. 5.

the scholar.'[35] The failure of Simmel and Dilthey, and of their successors, Troeltsch and Meinecke, lay in their inability to resolve this fundamental dichotomy. If the earlier German historical school had been preserved from relativism by a firm belief in a metaphysical reality beyond, but accessible to, historical cognition, by the 1920's this faith had largely perished; and there is a curious irony in the fact that it was Dilthey, whose explicit purpose was to provide history with a firm philosophical foundation, who so decisively weakened the foundations of western historiography by casting doubt on the possibility of 'scientific' history and exalting intuition. It was certainly not his object, but it was the result of the critique which he and Rickert and Simmel exercised so vigorously.

Fundamental to the historicist outlook was the distinction between nature and spirit and in particular between what was called *die Welt als Natur* and *die Welt als Geschichte* – that is to say, between the world with which natural science deals and the world with which history deals. Natural science, it was held, was concerned with the consistent, the eternally recurrent, and the discovery of general prinriples; history was concerned with the realm of the unique, of the spirit, and of change. The one was 'nomothetic', the other 'idiographic'; and this basic difference imposed different methods. The abstract, classificatory methods of the natural sciences were unsuitable for the study of history, for the latter is confronted by individuals and groups who were once alive and whose unique personalities can only be grasped by the exercise of the historian's intuitive understanding.

The fundamental philosophical question raised by historicism – complicated by the further consideration that the historian himself is involved in history and cannot stand outside it and view it objectively – was, therefore, whether the historical world was intuitively accessible to human understanding in the way that Dilthey believed, or whether it must be assumed, as Kant had postulated in regard to the physical world, that the reality of things in themselves could never be known. But here we are concerned not with the philosophical problems involved in historicism, but with its practical consequences for the everyday work of the historian; and these may be summed up under five headings. First, by denying a systematic approach to history and putting a premium on intuition, historicism opened the door – in fact, if not perhaps necessarily in theory[36] – to subjectivism and relativism. Secondly, it encouraged a one-sided preoccupation with the particular and individual at the expense of generalization and of the attempt to discover common elements in the past. Thirdly, it meant – for how otherwise could the historian hope to catch every shade and tone of individuality? – immersion in ever more meticulous detail. Fourthly, it led to the study of the past 'for its own sake', or to the view – as expressed by a recent

35. Cf. STERN (ed.), *The Varieties of History* (1956), p. 25.

36. A number of German historians (e.g., HERZFELD in his introduction to MEINECKE's *Werke*, Vol. V, p. xvi) have sought to defend historicism against the charge of 'relativistic historical thought'. I do not find their arguments very convincing; but in any case, whatever the theoretical position, it can hardly be denied that in the majority of cases relativism was its practical outcome.

exponent of historicism[37] – that the historian's only purpose is 'to know and understand the past experience of man'. And, finally, it endorsed the belief that the essence of history is to narrate and relate events, and its corrollary, an obsession with causality, or what Marc Bloch once called the worship of 'the idol of origins.'[38]

The essential contradiction at the heart of historicism – and also the basic reason for its intellectual inadequacy – lay in its endeavour to base a positive faith in a meaningful universe on historical relativism.[39] This was an attempt to square the circle and as such it was foredoomed to failure. Troeltsch, above all others, was acutely aware of the dilemma, but unable to find a way out. The result was an ethical and philosophical nihilism which was the logical consequence of the claim that all values and cognitions are bound to the historical situation in which they arise. By insisting that the subject matter of history is the uniqueness of all human activity, the historicist school excluded the possibility of any real contribution by historians to a scientific approach to the questions of the nature of man or of the sense or direction of human history. Instead, it produced a vast progeny of 'historiens historisants', concerned only with history for its own sake – historians for whom, in Marc Bloch's phrase, the essence of history was 'la négation même de ses possibilités.'[40]

Few people today, looking back over the inter-war years, would deny that historicism seriously impoverished historical scholarship when it dismissed the great theoretical questions facing humanity as legitimate objects of historical study. The cult of the particular atomized history; the cult of the past 'for its own sake' cut the thread between history and life; the denial of the possibility of generalization from past experience and the emphasis on the uniqueness of events broke the link not only with science but also with philosophy. 'The more we try to sound the inexhaustible meaning of the particular,' one critic wrote,[41] 'the more devoid everything seems to be of any meaning in particular.' There was, of course, and still is, a lively popular demand for a story well told; and much of the output of historians in the form of biographies, narrative histories and accounts of battles and political campaigns, served chiefly to satisfy that demand. But, at a higher level, the charges levelled against historians by Buckle over a century ago still retained their cogency. 'In all the other great fields of enquiry,' Buckle wrote, 'the necessity of generalisation is universally admitted.'[42] Among historians, on the other hand, the 'strange idea' prevailed 'that their business is merely to relate events,' which they 'occasionally enliven' by 'moral and political reflections.' The result, Buckle concluded, was that 'for all the higher purposes of human thought' history was still 'miserably deficient.'

37. WOOD, *Freedom and Necessity in History* (1957), p. 15.
38. BLOCH, *Apologie pour l'histoire* (1949), p. 5.
39. For the following, cf. IGGERS, *op. cit.* (1968), pp. 13, 270, 285-286.
40. BLOCH, *op. cit.*, pp. xv-xvi.
41. LEON, 'The terror of history', p. 16 in *The Listener* (1955).
42. BUCKLE, *History of Civilisation* (new edn., 1857), Vol. I, pp. 3-5.

This deficiency was not the only consequence of the triumph of historicist thinking. No less important was its denial of objective truth, its assertion, in the words of an English historian, that 'history is "true" only in so far as it is the reflection of the past in the mirror of the writer's personality'.[43] The result of historicism was that everything was related, judged and evaluated in relation to time, place, context and environment. Hence it was 'impossible' for the historian 'to think one man essentially more wicked than another'[44] and Meinecke was able to justify 'the seeming immorality of the state's egoism' on the grounds that 'nothing can be immoral which comes from the innermost individual character of a being'.[45] The historian's function, it was argued, was simply to discover how a statesman's actions – be he a Napoleon or a Hitler – were 'historically conditioned'.[46] From this point it was not far to the view that historians 'teach and write that kind of history which is appropriate' to their own 'organization' and that they 'can scarcely help it if this kind of history is at the same time the one most adapted to the preservation of the existing régime.'[47]

Such an attitude clearly implied disbelief in objective history, and appeared to view it as merely a rather more sophisticated mythology, written to underpin the existing national and social order. Otherwise, the purposes of history, as conceived by the historicist school, were essentially personal and individual. 'It enlarges the area of individual experience by teaching about human behaviour, about man in relation to other men, about the interaction of circumstances and conditions in their effect upon individual and social fortunes.'[48] It widens our perspectives by opening our minds to the achievements of other ages and other peoples and thus helps us to appreciate the limitations of our own view of the world. It forces us, in short, 'to avoid parochialism'.[49] The study of history also shows that things are usually more complicated than they seem and therefore teaches us to eschew simplified judgements. And finally it provides insights and a new level of wisdom for the individual, which should help him to find his own values in a changing world.[50] 'If history had any didactic value at all,' an American historian concluded after a lengthy examination of its varieties, 'it lay in the value of teaching men their own capabilities.'[51]

No doubt these are useful lessons, but it is another question whether in themselves they are sufficient to justify the vast expenditure of money and

43. OGG, *Herbert Fisher* (1947), p. 176.
44. BUTTERFIELD, *History and Human Relations* (1951), p. 108.
45. MEINECKE, *Weltbürgertum und Nationalstaat* (6th ed., 1922), p. 92.
46. BUTTERFIELD, *op. cit.* (1951), p. 70.
47. BUTTERFIELD, *The Englishman and His History* (1944), p. 1.
48. ELTON, *The Practice of History* (1967), p. 48.
49. TREVOR-ROPER, *The Past and the Present. History and Sociology* (1969), p. 5.
50. Cf. RITTER, 'Betrachtungen über einige Gesamtergebnisse und Grundfragen moderner Historiographie', p. 330 in *Xo Congresso internazionale di Scienze storiche, Relazioni*, Vol. VI (1955): 'nicht klug für heute oder für morgen, sondern weise für immer'.
51. SAVELLE, 'Historian's progress', p. 25 in *Pacific Historical Review* (1958) or p. 201 in SAVELLE, *Is Liberalism Dead, and Other Essays* (1967).

learning which has gone into historical research during the past century. All science, from physics to psychology, is concerned with 'teaching men their capabilities,' but other sciences have a more positive content as well. The real value of history as a social activity', we are told, 'lies in the training it provides, the standards it sets.'[52] But, here again, this is not something peculiar to history, and it might plausibly be argued that other sciences – physics, for example, or mathematics – provide a far more rigorous training and set far more exacting standards of scientific precision. The question to be asked is, therefore, whether this is all the historian has to offer, and, if so, in what specific way it differentiates history from other intellectual pursuits.

It is not surprising that eventually considerations such as these led to frustration and disillusionment. Already before 1939 they were beginning to act as a solvent of complacency, particularly among French historians. Ranke's admonition to discover *wie es eigentlich gewesen* had become almost the first and last word of historical wisdom; but what was its value when the past 'as it really was' turned out to be a will-o'-the-wisp, darting ever beyond the historian's reach, just when the thought he had grasped the hem of its fleeting garment?

Nevertheless, down to 1939 only a small minority of historians were prepared to discard their inherited preconceptions, and even after the Second World War historicist assumptions went largely unchallenged during the first post-war decade. This was not entirely surprising. The desire to maintain or restore continuity, to carry on where one had broken off in 1939, was a natural reaction, and in western Germany, where the threads of continuity had been violently sundered, it was deliberately fostered by survivors of the older generation, such as Gerhard Ritter.[53] But by 1955 a new generation was coming to maturity which, even when not seeking consciously to break with the past, was ready to explore new methods and new lines of approach. The war had broken the historicist spell. In Germany itself it 'destroyed much of the institutional framework within which historicism had arisen' and led to a critical re-examination of historicist assumptions.[54] But, on the whole, historicism was not so much challenged and rejected as by-passed and side-tracked. The death in 1954 of Friedrich Meinecke – 'the last great master of neo-idealist history',[55] who nevertheless showed signs in his later years of revulsion against historicist doctrines[56] – may be regarded as the end of an epoch. 'The naive innocence

52. ELTON, *op. cit.* (1967), p. 49.

53. Cf. RITTER, 'Gegenwärtige Lage und Zukunftsaufgaben deutscher Geschichtswissenschaft' (1950); 'Betrachtungen über einige Gesamtergebnisse und Grundfragen moderner Historiographie', *op. cit.* (1955); 'Scientific history, contemporary history and political science' (1961).

54. IGGERS, *op. cit.* (1968), p. 27; cf. also W. J. MOMMSEN, *Die Geschichtswissenschaft jenseits des Historismus* (1971).

55. Von SRBIK, *Geist und Geschichte vom deutschen Humanismus*, Vol. II (1951), p. 293.

56. Cf. his lecture on *Ranke und Burckhardt* (Berlin, 1948). Already in 1942

of traditional historical thought' had perished,[57] and historians – tentatively but unambiguously – began the search for new ways.

Marxism and Marxist History

Among the factors preparing the way for this revulsion against idealist historiography the impact of Marxist thought was particularly important. As Charles Morazé has observed, Marx's system was the very antithesis of that which had arisen 'in the moral shelter of the false pretences of idealism.'[58] In the context of the history of history, the importance of Marxism lay first and foremost in the fact that it presented a convincing alternative to historicism, in its idealistic and relativistic acceptation, at a time when the latter, obsessed by its own internal problems, was losing its earlier vigour. Many other attempts – including Croce's interpretation of history as 'the story of liberty' and Toynbee's conception of history as the succession of higher religions[59] – were made during the years between the two world wars to establish a universal concept with which to refute H. A. L. Fisher's famous confession that he could see no 'rhythm' or 'pattern' in history but 'only one emergency following upon another as wave follows upon wave.'[60] None carried conviction because none could escape the charge of subjectivism and relativism.[61] The main reason for the growing influence of Marxism was the conviction that it offered the only really satisfactory basis for a rational ordering of the complex facts of human history.

Marxism as a philosophy and a general outlook affected the thinking of historians in five main ways. In the first place, it both reflected and stimulated a reorientation of historical research away from the description of isolated – mainly political – events towards the investigation of complex and long-term social and economic processes. Secondly, it made historians aware of the need to study the material conditions of people's lives and the history of technology and economics in the context of industrial relations as a whole, and not as isolated phenomena. Thirdly, Marxism stimulated enquiry into the part played by the masses in history, particularly during periods of social and political upheaval. Fourthly, Marx's concept of the class structure of society and his investigation of the class struggle not only exercised a wide general influence over historical studies but also directed

(*Aphorismen und Skizzen zur Geschichte*, p. 11) he had described 'the historicism which analyses itself and seeks understanding from a study of its genesis' as 'a snake that bites its own tail'.

57. SCHIEDER, Th., *Staat und Gesellschaft im Wandel unserer Zeit* (1958), p. 187 (English translation, *The State and Society in Our Times* (1962), p. 147).

58. MORAZÉ, *La logique de l'histoire* (1967), pp. 298-299.

59. CROCE, *La storia come pensiero e come azione* (1938), translated into English as *History as the Story of Liberty* (1941); TOYNBEE, *A Study of History* (1934-1961).

60. FISHER, *A History of Europe*, Vol. I (1935), p. vii.

61. Cf. HUGHES, H. Stuart, *Consciousness and Society* (1958), pp. 226-227.

attention specifically to the investigation of the formation of classes in early bourgeois society in the west and the analogous processes in other social systems, particularly slavery, serfdom and feudalism. And finally, Marxism was important because it aroused renewed interest in the theoretical premisses of historical study and in the theory of history in general. For Marx, history was both a natural process, subject to definite laws, and a universal drama, written and performed by man himself. While Marx and Engels emphasized that the historian should not simply record the chronological sequence of events, but should provide a theoretical explanation of them, employing for this purpose a complex set of concepts, they also declared categorically that 'such abstractions provide neither a programme nor a pattern into which we can fit the great periods of history'.[62] Marx, in short, never denied the specific nature of the historical process or of historical cognition. 'History,' he wrote,[63]

does not do anything, it is not the custodian of vast treasures, it fights no battles! All this is done not by history but by men: real, living men possess it and fight for it. History is no master mind, which uses mankind to achieve its own ends. History is nothing more nor less than the activities of man in pursuit of his ideals.

Within this framework, the essential postulates of Marx's philosophy of history are clear and logical. Instead of the 'chaos of subjectivistic conceptions' – freedom, individuality, the nation, religion – which idealist historians arbitrarily chose as their criteria, Marxist historiography took as its starting-point the primary function of all human societies, both primitive and advanced: namely, the satisfaction of man's physiological needs, the provision of food, dwellings, clothing, security and other basic necessities of life. 'Does it require deep intuition,' Marx asked, 'to comprehend that man's ideas, views and conceptions, in one word, man's consciousness, changes with every change in the conditions of his material existence, in his social relations and in his social life? What else does the history of ideas prove, than that intellectual production changes its character in proportion as material production is changed?'[64]

This approach to history received its classical formulation in Marx's preface to his *Critique of Political Economy*, where he laid down that it is 'in the social production which men carry on' that 'they enter into definite relations that are indispensable and independent of their will'. These relations are the 'relations of production' which in 'sum total' constitute 'the economic structure of society'; and this economic structure is 'the real foundation on which a legal and political superstructure arises and to which definite forms of social consciousness correspond'. Furthermore, the 'relations of production' themselves correspond to, and vary in accordance with, the different stages of development of the productive forces, and every

62. MARX & ENGELS, *The German Ideology*, ed. C. J. Arthur (London, 1970), p. 48.
63. MARX-ENGELS, *Werke*, Vol. II (Berlin, 1959), p. 98 (*Die Heilige Familie*).
64. *Communist Manifesto*, ed. H. J. Laski (London, 1948), p. 143; MARX-ENGELS, *Gesamtausgabe*, Abt. I, Bd. 6 (Moskau-Leningrad, 1933), p. 543.

change of the economic foundation brings about a 'more or less' radical transformation of the entire 'superstructure'. On this basis, Marx held, it was possible to distinguish 'in broad outline' the four main epochs of social development, characterized by 'the Asiatic, the ancient, the feudal and the modern bourgeois methods of production,' of which the last – namely, the epoch of capitalism – was destined to be succeeded, and was already in process of being superseded, by a fifth: the age of socialism and the socialist mode of production.[65]

This scheme, which Marx set out 'in broad outline,' must not, of course, be treated as a 'Procrustean bed of sociological patterns'.[66] As Marx and Engels never failed to emphasize, Marxism was a 'guide to study,' not a substitute for research.[67] Nor did they endorse a vulgar materialism. It was Engels who pointed out that 'the economic element,' although 'ultimately' the 'determining element,' was not 'the *only* determining one', and that political ideas, laws, religion and philosophy, once formulated in response to a particular economic situation, developed a logic of their own and exercised a retroactive influence over the economic substructure.[68] For Marx and Engels, the function of their conceptualization of history was essentially heuristic. Although they believed scientific (including sociological) concepts to be the reflection of particular facets or features of actual historical facts, they were opposed to any oversimplification of this process and particularly to the identification of the content of such concepts with the reality they denoted. As Engels wrote in a well-known letter in 1895, 'the concept of things and their reality are like two asymptotes, moving together, coming closer and closer to each other, but never meeting. The difference between them is this – that the concept is not the exact reality, and the reality is not the concept.' But if, he continued, the concept cannot of its very nature correspond directly to reality, of which it is essentially an abstraction, it is by the same token 'always something more than a mere fiction'.[69]

Marxism has therefore never reduced history to the status of abstract sociology or exaggerated the role of sociological concepts. On the other hand, it defended the 'sociologization' of history, in the sense that it held that historical studies should be directed towards the search for permanent or recurrent characteristics and patterns of historical development. The impact of this belief and of Marxism in general was already apparent by the end of the nineteenth century. The decade of the 1890's, following the

---

65. MARX-ENGELS, *Selected Works*, Vol. I (London, 1950), pp. 328-329.

66. Such a view was described by E. M. ZHUKOV (= ŽUKOV), *XIe Congrès international des Sciences historiques (Stockholm, 1960), Rapports*, Vol. I, p. 83, as 'a cartoon of Marxism . . . which has nothing in common with reality'.

67. Cf. GEFTER & MALKOV, 'Reply to a questionnaire on Soviet historiography', p. 192 in *History and Theory*, Vol. VI (1967).

68. ENGELS to J. Bloch, Sept. 21-22, 1890: *Selected Works*, Vol. II, p. 443; *Werke*, Vol. 37 (Berlin, 1967), p. 462.

69. ENGELS to Conrad Schmidt, 12 Mar., 1895: *Werke*, Vol. 39 (Berlin, 1968), p. 431.

abrogation of Bismarck's anti-socialist legislation in Germany, was the first great period of expansion in the history of European socialism, and with the growth of socialist parties went the spread of Marxist doctrines. The part played by their confrontation with Marxism in the intellectual development of Max Weber in Germany and Benedetto Croce in Italy is a matter of common knowledge. Like Croce, Weber granted a 'relative legitimacy to the materialist conception of history', understood 'as a heuristic principle'.[70] But if, in Stuart Hughes' words, 'the first and most obvious task' confronting the intellectuals of the 1890's should have been 'to come to terms with Marxism', in practice the majority of academic historians evaded the issue. As Sir Charles Webster has pointed out, Marx is not even mentioned in the standard survey of nineteenth-century historiography which G. P. Gooch published in 1913, and it was not until after the First World War that his real impact on historical thinking began.[71]

The reasons for this are many and varied, but basic to all was the hatred and fear of communism which had been widespread in continental Europe ever since 1848. In most countries, including Tsarist Russia, the organization of university teaching virtually excluded Marxists and socialists. Only France, with its long revolutionary tradition, was relatively more tolerant, and here the line of Marxist scholars stretches from Jaurès to Mathiez, Labrousse and Lefebvre. Elsewhere, particularly in imperial Germany, the majority of professional historians neither understood nor wished to understand the principles of Marxism or the materialistic interpretation of history, and the few Marxist historians (e.g., Mehring) were 'outsiders'. At the turn of the nineteenth and twentieth centuries, Marxism figured, if at all, 'as an aberrant, and peculiarly insidious form of the reigning cult of positivism',[72] and its numerous opponents, including such critics as Stammler and Rickert, contributed to the perpetuation of this false image. In the English universities down to 1918 – and, indeed, beyond[73] – Marx and Marxism were simply ignored so far as the study and teaching of history were concerned, and it was only the Russian revolution of 1917 that compelled historians outside Russia to take the Marxist interpretation of history seriously. Even so, the reaction was essentially hostile, conditioned by ideological rather than scientific or scholarly considerations. The event that really turned the scales was the worldwide depression of 1929–30 and the deepening crisis of capitalist society, which appeared to justify Marx's historical diagnosis.[74] The slump of 1929 brought the period of neglect or contemp-

70. HUGHES, H. S., *op. cit.* (1958), p. 316.
71. GOOCH, *History and Historians in the Nineteenth Century* (1913); cf. *The Historical Association, 1906-1956* (1957), p. 82.
72. HUGHES, H. S., *op. cit.*, p. 42.
73. The present writer does not recollect once having heard the name of Marx mentioned by his teachers at Oxford between 1926 and 1929; but Oxford was perhaps exceptional and the position at the London School of Economics was certainly different.
74. Cf. the remarks of Jean GLÉNISSON, pp. xxi-xxii in *La recherche historique en France de 1940 à 1965, op. cit.* (1965).

tuous dismissal of Marxism to an end. After 1930 its influence spread far and wide and even those historians (still, outside the Soviet Union, the overwhelming majority) who rejected the Marxist interpretation of history were forced to reconsider their position in the light of it. The task facing historians now, as Sir Charles Webster said, was to meet Marx's challenge, 'not by neglecting the contribution he has made to historical thinking', but by subjecting his interpretation of history 'to new analysis in the light of the immense amount of evidence about the past which we are gradually accumulating and which was entirely unknown to him'.[75]

The position in the Soviet Union after 1917 was, of course, very different.[76] From the beginning, the Soviet government devoted considerable attention to the development of historical studies, for history was seen to be 'a powerful weapon of communist education' and Marxist historians regarded their work 'as part of the revolutionary, organized, systematic activity of the people in the name of the victory of a new social system'.[77] The well-known Marxist historian, Pokrovsky, became Assistant Commissar for Education and head of the historical division in 1918, and when in the same year a Socialist Academy of Social Sciences was set up, Prokovsky was its first president. Following the adoption on 1 July 1918 of a decree

75. WEBSTER, 'Fifty years of change in historical teaching and research', p. 82 in *The Historical Association, op. cit.* (1957).

76. Owing to linguistic limitations, the following pages could not have been written without the bibliographical assistance and constructive criticism of Soviet and other Marxist historians. In this connexion I should like to express my great indebtedness to Professor I. S. Kon (Leningrad), one of the two associate rapporteurs of this study, and to Dr. F. A. Fedorova (Moscow) for their generous and time-consuming co-operation. I am also particularly grateful to Dr. Péter Hanák (Budapest) for a brilliant and illuminating commentary, as well as to Professors N. A. Erofeev (Moscow) and E. Engelberg (Berlin) and Mr. Christopher Hill (Oxford). I have tried in what follows to avoid the political and ideological overtones, which mar a good deal of the literature in western languages and are not very relevant in the present context, and instead to subject Soviet historiography between 1917 and 1955 to the same sort of critical appraisal as I have applied in the preceding sections to western historiography in the same period. It need hardly be said that I alone am responsible for the interpretation here advanced, from which, without doubt, both Soviet and western experts will demur, at least in part. It is also evident that a sketch of this scope cannot hope to do justice to the whole range of historical writing in the period concerned, but I have regarded it as my task, here as in other areas, not to provide 'coverage' but to pick out what seem to be significant trends and innovations.

77. Cf. ZINOVIEV, *Soviet Methods of Teaching History* (1952; original Russian edition, Moscow, 1948), p. 3; GEFTER & MALKOV, *op. cit.* (1967), p. 203. In this connexion it is important to bear in mind that, in the Soviet view, ideological neutrality in the social sciences is impossible, and that there is no contradiction between a progressive and conscious party-mindedness (*partijnost'*) and scientific objectivity. There is no need to pursue the much discussed question of *partijnost'* here, but simply to remind western writers who contest it, of Herbert BUTTERFIELD's observation (*History and Human Relations* (1951), p. 99) that those who imagine they are 'writing history without any presuppositions at all', are sometimes 'merely refusing to examine' their 'presuppositions'.

on the reorganization and centralization of archives in the RSFSR, the various state archives were brought together to form a single collection, and a considerable amount of previously inaccessible documentary material was placed at the disposal of historians. In 1919 a State Academy of the History of Material Civilization (GAIMK) was established, to be followed by a Russian Association of Social Science Research Institutes (RANION) in 1923. In 1920, the 'Istpart' Committee had been formed to study the history of the Russian Communist (Bolshevik) Party and the October revolution, and 1922 saw the launching of the journal *Krasny arhiv* (Red Archives), which has published a large amount of valuable source material for the history of the Communist Party and the revolutionary movement.

At this stage the most pressing task was to train a new generation of Marxist historians. Only a minority of the older historians (among others R. J. Vipper, V. P. Volgin and N. M. Rožkov) had become interested in Marxism before the revolution. The majority knew very little about it, while others were openly hostile, and the early phases of the reconstruction of Soviet historical studies took place in an atmosphere of lively ideological conflict between Marxists and representatives of the older, pre-Marxist schools of historiography. In the end a considerable number of the older historians (B. D. Grekov, S. V. Bahrušin, J. V. Got'e, S. A. Žebelev, E. V. Tarle, V. I. Pičeta, A. D. Udal'cov) and younger men such as E. A. Kosminsky, S. D. Skazkin, N. P. Gracianskij, V. V. Stoklickaja-Tereskovič and N. M. Družinin, went over to the Marxist camp, working side by side with party veterans like M. N. Pokrovsky, N. M. Lukin, E. M. Jaroslavsky and V. I. Nevsky. The foundation in 1925 under the auspices of the Socialist Academy of an Association of Marxist Historians, with Pokrovsky at its head, was particularly influential in encouraging a Marxist outlook among historians, and the holding of a first All-Union Conference of Marxist Historians from December 1928 to January 1929 marked a significant stage in the process of reconstruction.

The overall adoption of a Marxist outlook was nevertheless only a beginning. There can be no question here of tracing the stages in the development of Soviet historiography between 1929 and the death of Stalin in 1953, any more than we have followed in detail the evolution of western historiography in the same period. The course of events has been described at length, both by Soviet and by western writers, and it is sufficient to refer to some of the readily available literature on the subject.[78] The process

78. Developments in the earlier period were surveyed in VOLGIN, TARLE & PANKRATOVA (eds.), *Dvadcat' pjat' let istoričeskoj nauki v SSSR* (= Twenty-five Years of Historical Science in the USSR) (1942). The more important later writings include *Očerki istorii istoričeskoj nauki v SSSR* (= Essays on the History of Historical Science in the USSR) (4 vols., 1955-66); ILLERICKIJ & KUDRJAVCEV, *Istoriografija istorii SSSR* (= Historiography of the History of the USSR); ARCIHOVSKIJ (ed.), *Očerki po istorii sovetskoj nauki i kul'tury* (= Essays on the History of Soviet Science and Culture) (1968); IVANOVA, *U istokov sovetskoj istoričeskoj nauki, 1917-1929* (= On the Sources of Soviet Historical Science, 1917-1929) (1968); SAHAROV, *Izučenie otečestvennoj istorii za 50 let sovetskoj vlasti* (= The Study of National

of bringing Soviet historiography into conformity with Marxist doctrine proved, in fact, to be arduous and prolonged, and it was also complicated by external factors, including at first the bitter ideological hostility of the capitalist world, and later, particularly under Stalin, fluctuations in policy. While these external influences were real, western writers have tended until recently to dwell upon them unduly, to the neglect of the internal evolution of Soviet historiography.[79] The important point is that acceptance of the Marxist framework left room for refinement, change of emphasis, and development, particularly in methodology. Soviet evaluations of the early period, down approximately to the death of Pokrovsky in 1932, recognize its defects, but at the same time insist upon its positive qualities, particularly the opening of new fields and areas of study. Pokrovsky's own well known *History of Russia*, published at the end of 1920, marked the transition from descriptive political history, such as had been characteristic of pre-revolutionary Russian historiography, to a specifically socio-economic approach.[80] At the same time entirely new problems were opened up, such as the history of the revolutionary movement, in particular of the October revolution, and the history of the class struggle, with particular reference to the peasant wars in Russia and the struggle of the working class in western Europe. The debate which followed the publication in 1928 of Petrushevsky's essays on the economic history of medieval Europe opened up the whole question of feudalism.[81] At the same time the application of Marx's periodization of

History during 50 Years of Soviet Rule) (1968); VAJNŠTEJN, *Istorija sovetskoj medievistiki* (= History of Soviet Mediaeval Studies) (1968); ČEREPNIN, '50 let sovetskoj istoričeskoj nauki i nekotorye itogi eë razvitija' (= 50 years of Soviet historical science and some results of its development) (1967); ILLERICKIJ, 'Problemy otečestvennoj istoriografii v sovetskoj istoričeskoj nauke (1917-1967)' (= Problems of national historiography in Soviet historical science – 1917-1967) (1968). In western languages there is a statement of the Marxist position by E. ENGELBERG, 'Über Gegenstand und Ziel der marxistisch-leninistischen Geschichtswissenschaft' (1968), and the most readily available sources for the views and attitudes of Soviet historians are the Soviet contributions to the proceedings of the X-XIIIth International Historical Congresses, particularly SIDOROV, 'Hauptprobleme und einige Entwicklungsergebnisse der sowjetischen Geschichtswissenschaft', in Vol. VI of the *Relazioni* of the Xth Congress (1955), and ZHUKOV (= ŽUKOV), 'The periodization of world history', in Vol. I of the *Rapports* of the XIth Congress (1960). In addition, a number of important statements by Soviet historians have been made available in English translation in *Soviet Studies in History* (of which the first issue appeared in 1962) and, from time to time, in the *Current Digest of the Soviet Press*. Two introductory books in English are MAZOUR, *Modern Russian Historiography* (2nd edn., 1958), and BLACK (ed.), *Rewriting Russian History. Soviet Interpretations of Russia's Past* (1956), but more up-to-date, objective and useful for recent developments is KEEP & BRISBY (eds.), *Contemporary History in the Soviet Mirror* (1964). For a useful bibliography of the earlier literature, cf. STADTMÜLLER, pp. 380-384 in *Saeculum*, Vol. XI (1960).

79. This is emphasized, in my view correctly, by S. V. UTECHIN, pp. 117-154 in KEEP & BRISBY (eds.), *Contemporary History in the Soviet Mirror* (1964).

80. POKROVSKIJ, *Russkaja istorija v samom sžatom očerke* (1920) (English translation, *Brief History of Russia*, 1933).

81. Cf. PETRUŠEVSKIJ, *Očerki iz ėkonomičeskoj istorii srednevekovoj Evropi* (= Essays on the Economic History of Mediaeval Europe)) (1928).

history led to significant changes of emphasis in other areas, in the field of ancient history, for example, to closer examination of the problems of slavery.

In spite of these positive achievements, a number of shortcomings remained. The most serious of these, without doubt, was a crude sociological and economic approach to history which affected not only methodology and the understanding of the functions and aims of historical study but also the interpretation of the historical process itself. Too little attention was paid to the relatively independent rôle of the superstructure of ideas and institutions, and despite Engels' warning about 'making oneself ridiculous,' misleading attempts were made to relate all social and cultural processes directly to economics.[82] Pokrovsky himself made fun of Marxist writers who, carried away by a misconceived belief in economic determinism, sought to explain the origins of the war of 1914 in terms of fluctuations in the price of corn.[83] Too often, in the discussions which took place at this time, ideological considerations prevailed over factual argumentation, and interest in the investigation of specific facts and processes was at a low ebb. Many important periods of history, particularly those relating to the more or less distant past, were inadequately studied, if not entirely neglected, and history was largely submerged in ethnology and other social sciences.

There were, of course, considerations of a practical nature which, in part at least, explained this situation. Since a substantial *cadre* of Marxist historians was lacking, the first necessity was to train such a body at short notice, and it is not surprising that a temporary lowering of standards should have resulted. At the same time, the lack of adequate Marxist textbooks, both for schools and universities, meant a diversion of effort away from fundamental research to the preparation of general histories, usually on a collective basis, which contributed little if anything to knowledge but rather reinterpreted known facts from a Marxist point of view. Very few monographs were produced, and the concentration of attention on a limited range of topical problems, though perhaps inevitable in the circumstances, resulted in a failure to grasp the historical process as a whole.

These and other shortcomings without doubt hampered the development of historical studies, and in the early 1930's they were severely criticized in the Central Committee of the Communist Party. Among its decisions the most important were embodied in the well-known decree of 1 September 1934, restoring history to the curriculum of primary and secondary schools and re-opening the faculties of history in Moscow and Leningrad. In succeeding years, faculties were also opened in other universities, and an Institute of History was established as part of the Academy of Sciences of the U.S.S.R. after the amalgamation of the latter with the Communist

82. MARX-ENGELS, *Selected Works*, Vol. II, p. 443: 'Without making oneself ridiculous, it would be a difficult thing to explain in terms of economics the existence of every small state in Germany, past and present'.

83 Cf. POKROWSKI (= POKROVSKIJ), *Historische Aufsätze* (1928), p. 20.

Academy in 1936. With the foundation of the Institute of History, which quickly became the country's leading research institute, there was a marked improvement in facilities for the publication of historical research, which now began to cover a wider range of subjects. New periodicals, such as *Vestnik drevnej istorii* ('Bulletin of Ancient History'), *Istoričeskie zapiski* ('Historical Notes') and *Istoričeskij žurnal* ('Historical Journal'), made an appearance, and there was an improvement in the techniques and methods employed. Nevertheless Soviet historians still retained without serious question the canons of textual criticism and the techniques for handling historical evidence developed by positivist historians in western Europe in the second half of the nineteenth century. Methodologically, although work of great distinction was performed in the fields of archaeology and prehistory,[84] and some beginnings were made in the use of statistical analysis,[85] Soviet historians for the most part were slow and hesitant in their response to the more sophisticated techniques and lines of approach being explored in the west. The more progressive historians in western Europe – notably those grouped round Marc Bloch and Lucien Febvre in France – were far from hostile to Marxism; but their search for new methods and new techniques carried them into areas where Soviet historiography at this stage had hardly ventured.[86]

The progress of Soviet historiography also revealed new complexities. The impact of Marxism, though more pervasive, was less dramatic than Pokrovsky and historians of his generation had probably expected. Marx himself had insisted that 'our problems are only beginning when we start to examine our material, whether it concerns the past or the present, to put it in order, and get down to the task of portraying it as it really is'.[87] The adoption of a Marxist point of view, in other words, did not solve the concrete problems of historical research; it simply placed them in a new perspective. Nowhere was this more clearly revealed than in the great debate over periodization which was one of the main preoccupations of Soviet historians in the 1940's.[88] Probably the most significant feature of this debate, in retrospect, is its inconclusiveness. The broad framework set up by Marx and Lenin was not questioned, but within that broad framework little progress was made in establishing a precise and generally acceptable periodization either of Russian or of world history. On the contrary, one of the main conclusions was that 'no attempt to divide up history in accordance with strictly uniform and universally valid criteria could

84. This is dealt with in Professor S. J. De Laet's chapter on *Archaeology and Prehistory* in *Main Trends of Research in the Social and Human Sciences*, Part II, Vol. 1, (1978), pp. 186, 191, 193–194, 205.

85. For example, KOSMINSKY's *Studies in the Agrarian History of England in the Thirteenth Century* (1956), which originally appeared in Russian in 1935.

86. Cf. GLÉNISSON, 'L'historiographie française contemporaine', pp. xxii–xxiii in *La recherche historique en France de 1940 à 1965, op. cit.* (1965).

87. *German Ideology*, ed. Arthur, p. 48.

88. It is summarized in the useful selection of articles from *Voprosy istorii* reprinted in German under the title *Zur Periodisierung des Feudalismus und Kapitalismus in der geschichtlichen Entwicklung der UdSSR* (1952).

lead to positive results'.[89] In historical reality there were no such things, for example, as 'pure' slavery or 'pure' feudalism. What confronted the historian was an 'unequal combination', varying from country to country, in which there were residues from 'the preceding social-economic modes of life' and also 'the embryonic forms' of later social systems. 'The development of history,' Zhukov emphasized, 'is never schematic, uniform or straightforward. The life of separate countries or nations often reveals ... partial and temporary deviations from the general laws and from the logical course of events.'[90] The other main conclusion was the danger of relating the periodization of history exclusively to economic factors. 'If we wish to divide the history of a country into periods,' it was stated, 'we have no right to narrow artificially the area of facts and events which have to be taken into acount. [...] On the contrary, it is only after a penetrating and objective appraisal of all relevant events in the life of a people that we can draw the general conclusions from which a valid periodization can be constructed.'[91]

The results of the debate over periodization were important in so far as they emphasized the inherent difficulties and complexities of historical work and the immense variety (*Mannigfaltigkeit*) and apparent irreconcilability (*Widersprüchlichkeit*) of historical events.[92] Through this labyrinth Marxism provided a number of conspicuous guide-posts; but within the area thus charted out there were many different paths, and this left room for considerable differences of direction and varieties of interpretation. As the second period of Soviet historiography drew to a close, there was thus a reaction against the dogmatic and rigid interpretation of Marxist theory in the 1930's and 1940's, and historians were warned not to force events 'into a preconceived scheme, which may be logical but is not historically well-founded'.[93] The task of Soviet historians was now defined as 'the investigation of every social situation in all its aspects and its evaluation in the light of the concrete historical circumstances which called it forth'.[94] To the outsider, this does not sound very different from the way many 'bourgeois' historians would describe their work.

In view of these developments it is not surprising that, by 1955, when Soviet historians returned after a long interval to the International Congress of Historical Sciences, Soviet historiography was ready to move on into a new period. At the time of the Twentieth Party Congress in 1956, a mood of self-questioning was apparent among Soviet historians, parallel in many ways to that we have observed in western 'bourgeois' historio-

89. Reported in STADTMÜLLER, *Die neue sowjetische Weltgeschichte*, p. 309 in *Saeculum*, Vol. XI (1960).

90. ZHUKOV, 'The periodization ...', *op. cit.*, pp. 397, 456 in Vol. VI of the *Rapports, XIe Congrès international des Sciences historiques (Stockholm, 1960)*.

91. *Zur Periodisierung des Feudalismus und Kapitalismus*, pp. 330-331.

92. Cf. SIDOROV, 'Hauptprobleme ...', *op. cit.*, pp. 397, 456 in Vol. VI of the *Relazioni, Xo Congresso internazionale di Scienze storiche (Roma, 1955)*.

93. *Zur Periodisierung ...*, p. 330.

94. SIDOROV, *op. cit.*, p. 393.

graphy at the same period. In part, this sprang from the difficulty of re-conciling respect for historical reality with 'lines' or directives laid down from above and from 'the mistakes and distortions associated with Stalin's cult of personality.'[95] The editorial board of *Voprosy istorii KPSS*, the new journal of party history founded in 1957, pointed out that the adop-tion of Stalin's *Short Course* as a 'standard for party-historical investiga-tions' had 'significantly retarded the further scientific working out of prob-lems of the history of the party',[96] and the same applied in different de-grees to other periods and aspects of Russian history. More significant in the present context were the problems which became apparent as soon as the question arose of applying historical materialism to particular concrete historical situations. In particular, it was found that there were a number of 'blank areas' *(belye pjatna)* –among them the problems of recurrence *(povtorjaemost')*, typicalness *(tipičnost')*, socio-economic systems *(formacija)*, and historical epochs *(èpoha)* and stages *(ètap)* – which were in need of clarification, and the other requirement was the development of new methods and techniques.[97] As a result of the vast expansion of historical knowledge, historians were confronted, as M. I. Gefter pointed out, by 'new and un-usual' problems, which it was 'difficult or simply impossible to approach [. . .] with the old measuring tape'.[98] In short, by 1955 or 1956 Soviet historiography stood as much in need of new impulses as did the 'bourgeois' historiography of the west.

Another new factor in the situation was the rapid expansion of Marxist historiography after 1945. In the countries of eastern and south-eastern Europe – in Poland, East Germany, Hungary, Jugoslavia, Bulgaria, Ru-mania, and Czechoslovakia – the first ten years after the war saw the dis-placement of the old nationalist history and 'gentry historicism' by a Marx-ist interpretation which shifted the emphasis to peasant movements, the development of industrial capitalism and the formation of an industrial working class.[99] There was also a marked increase of Marxist influence in other parts of the world.[100] Among the younger English historians, a

95. Cf. GEFTER & MALKOV, p. 205 in *History and Theory*, Vol. VI (1967).

96. 'K novomu pod"emu istoriko-partijnoj nauki' (= For a new upsurge in the science of the history of the Party), pp. 3-20 in *Voprosy istorii KPSS*, 1960, No. 5.

97. Cf. PUNDEFF's review of the volume *Istorija i sociologija* (1964), p. 451 in *History and Theory* (1967).

98. *Ibid.*, p. 453.

99. This early phase is, for the most part, adequately described in the various reports presented by the delegates of the east European countries to the Tenth International Congress of Historical Sciences: cf. *La Pologne au Xe Congrès inter-national des sciences historiques* (Warsaw, 1955); *Ten Years of Yugoslav Histori-ography, 1945-1955* (Belgrade, 1955); *Etudes des délégués hongrois au Xe Congrès international des sciences historiques* (Budapest, 1955). For the German Democratic Republic, developments are best followed in the periodical, *Zeitschrift für Ge-schichtswissenschaft* (Berlin, 1952-   ). I have also benefitted greatly from a re-port, 'L'historiographie en Yougoslavie', prepared specially by Bogo Grafenauer, and should like to express my particular thanks to Péter Hanák for a stimulating paper on 'Trends in Historical Research in Hungary'.

100. For the position in Asia, cf. below, pp. 98, 122, 143.

flourishing and influential Marxist school took shape, including such well-known personalities as Eric Hobsbawm, Christopher Hill, John Saville and Edward Thompson. Not surprisingly, the active participation of English, French, Italian, Jugoslav and other Marxists contributed to the ferment of new ideas. Furthermore, as the Marxist interpretation of history took root in a variety of different historical environments, it found itself confronted not only by new source material, but also by divergent patterns of historical development – the fact, for example, that the model of capitalist transformation in east-central Europe differs markedly from that of western Europe[101] – which had to be assimilated and taken into acount. The result, once again, was the emergence of new questions and new problems, or at least the need to reconsider old problems in the light of a widening body of factual knowledge and an extended range of different socio-economic relationships. The more widely the Marxist interpretation came to prevail, the greater the need was felt for flexibility in its application to particular historical situations, clarity and precision in its basic concepts, and improvement in its methodology.

By 1955 few historians, even among its opponents, questioned the positive impact or the challenge which an intelligent Marxist approach to history represented; but it was increasingly felt that a system of thought formulated in the nineteenth century in response to nineteenth-century conditions had little beyond a general stimulus to offer to historians in the middle of the twentieth century. In the words of one of the younger English historians, 'sociological interests' had 'outgrown their original source of inspiration,' and 'the stereotyped social vocabulary of Marxism had been found increasingly inadequate to convey the complex realities of historical development.'[102] This observation implied in no sense a rejection of Marxism, but rather a demand for its refinement and elaboration in the context of new knowledge and the conditions of the rapidly changing world in which we live.

2. The Search for New Concepts and a New Methodology

The preceding sections will have served their purpose if they have indicated something of the ferment in the historical world which was coming to the surface, both among 'liberal' and among Marxist historians, around the year 1955. Such a survey, no doubt, almost necessarily emphasizes the critical and heterodox at the expense of the conventional and orthodox, and tends to exaggerate the amount of self-questioning current at the time among practising historians. Most historians resented – and still resent – any suggestion that their methods and attitudes are inadequate, and were

101. Cf. Hanák, Report on 'Trends in historical research in Hungary', p. 31 of manuscript.
102. Keith THOMAS, 'The tools and the job', p. 275 in *New Ways in History* (special issue of the *Times Literary Supplement*, 1966).

content to write narrative history of a traditional sort. This is a fact which it would be foolish to ignore or under-estimate. The continuing popularity of narrative history and its place in the historian's work are questions we shall have to come back to.[103] For the moment it is sufficient to say that the tendency after 1955 was to explore other, less traditional lines of approach. It is to these that we now turn.

The impetus behind the new developments was, of course, different in different countries and areas. This does not mean that there was not a continuous – indeed, a rapidly increasing – process of cross-fertilization. On the contrary, the ease of communications in an age of air-travel, the new mobility, frequent visits by historians from one country to another (particularly from western Europe to the United States), a multitude of conferences, and in the case of the Soviet Union and other countries in eastern Europe the relaxation of controls over contacts between communist and non-communist historians following Soviet participation in the Tenth International Congress of Historical Sciences in 1955, all contributed to a fruitful exchange of ideas. Nevertheless the search for new concepts and new methods followed different paths from different starting-points in different countries and regions. The United States, the Soviet Union, and western Europe were, to begin with, the main areas of renewal and advance;[104] and even if the most significant feature at the present stage is a process of fusion or convergence – as historians in different parts of the world absorb, explore and refine the new techniques and insights of their fellow-workers elsewhere – it is still important to consider briefly the different starting-points of new development.

The distinguishing feature in the United States was the steadily advancing alignment between history and the social or behavioural sciences.[105] This dates effectively from the 1940's and the Second World War which, like the 'new deàl' before it, opened up a wide range of new opportunities for political and social scientists, and was generally agreed to provide empirical evidence of the practical value of their survey research techniques and quantifying methods by comparison with traditional forms of historical analysis. There is little doubt that the practical achievements of social science and the prospects it held out of a more effective and more purposeful methodology were the main stimulus inducing historians in the United States to re-examine their inherited assumptions and methods. Tentative and reluctant at first, the progress and consolidation of this re-examination can be traced in the successive reports and publications of the Social Science

103. Cf. below, p. 210.

104. Asia and Africa entered into the picture at a somewhat later date – approximately from 1960, often known as 'Africa's year' – and their impact on historical study will be considered separately; cf. below, Section 4, pp. 141–147.

105. The following remarks are based on the brief general survey in SHAFER, FRANÇOIS, MOMMSEN and MILNE, *Historical Study in the West* (1968), pp. 175-189, supplemented by BOGUE, 'United States. The new political history' (1968); cf. also SAVETH (ed.), *American History and the Social Sciences* (1964), and CAHNMAN & BOSKOFF (eds.), *Sociology and History. Theory and Research* (1964).

Research Council;[106] and it is clear that this institution, through the purposeful deployment of its resources, has been a powerful influence in changing the outlook of American historians during the last quarter of a century.

Its success was due also to the fact that it could build on empirical and pragmatic currents which reached far back in American history. The conviction that history, like all other intellectual pursuits, is 'an instrument of practical adjustment'[107] and can only be justified as such, had deep roots in the United States. Temporarily weakened under the impact of German historicism and the doubts and self-questioning produced by the depression of the 1930's, this pragmatic tradition quickly re-asserted itself, as the United States resumed its phenomenal material progress after 1945. But it did so on new foundations and with new methods and techniques. If, to begin with, American historians had drawn heavily on the ideas of European scholars – particularly Max Weber's analytical approach and his use of 'models' – from the 1940's their work assumed a characteristically American stamp, as they adopted the 'heuristic concepts' and operational tools of sociologists such as Lazarsfeld, political scientists such as Lipset, and economists such as Kuznets and Leontieff.

The result was an 'inner revolution', the pioneers of which included James C. Malin, Merle Curti, Thomas C. Cochran and William O. Aydelotte.[108] Reacting against the 'flaccidity' of conventional historical analysis and convinced that it was 'so preoccupied with the outward and formal, the episodic, the unique and the individual' that it had 'failed to draw attention to some of the most significant developments of our political past', they set out to exploit the methods, results and implications of the measurement techniques developed by the social and behavioural sciences. Inevitably, the claims advanced on behalf of the new approach have been hotly contested;[109] but it remains the outstanding contribution of the United States to have demonstrated to the world at large the important part which data analysis, numerical techniques, ecological correlation, econometrics, and other more sophisticated conceptual tools are able to play in the historian's work.

If in the United States developments proceeded fairly steadily from the later years of the 'new deal' and the time of the Second World War, in the Soviet Union, as we have already seen,[110] the beginning of a new

---

106. *Theory and Practice in Historical Study* (1946); *The Social Sciences in Historical Study* (1954); *Generalization in the Writing of History*, ed. by L. GOTTSCHALK (1963); LANDES & TILLY (eds.), *History as Social Science* (1971).

107. Cf. STROUT, *The Pragmatic Revolt in American History* (1958), p. 159.

108. Cf. COCHRAN, *The Inner Revolution: Essays on the Social Sciences in History* (1964); MALIN, *On the Nature of History. Essays about History and Dissidence* (1954); AYDELOTTE, 'Quantification in history' (1966).

109. For an urbane and witty survey of conservative reactions, cf. WOODWARD, 'History and the Third Culture' (1968).

110. Cf. above, pp. 26–27.

phase of development can be observed around the years 1955–56.[111] Within a few months of the death of Stalin in March 1953 it was possible to detect a more critical note in the pages of *Voprosy Istorii*, and at the beginning of 1956, before the meeting of the Twentieth Party Congress, a frank and full discussion of the established pattern of Soviet historiography took place at a conference in Moscow.[112] But it was the Twentieth Party Congress that consolidated the new trends, and though doubts have been expressed about their lasting effects,[113] the claim that Soviet historiography embarked on 'a new stage of development'[114] after 1956 is amply borne out by the evidence.

The outward manifestations of the change – the appearance of new institutions, new journals, new centres of historical studies in the Ukraine, Transcaucasia, Central Asia, and other republics, the widening field of research, and the growing specialization evinced by the foundation of special institutes for the study of Latin America, Africa, Asia, and other regions – are evident enough, and do not need further consideration here. More difficult to assess are the underlying implications. Apart from a reaction

111. Apart from the more general literature referred to p. 22, n. 78 above, there is a full account of Soviet historiography between the Twentieth and the Twenty-Second Party Congresses in DRUŽYNIN (ed.), *Sovetskaja istoričeskaja nauka ot XX k XXII s'ezdu KPSS* (2 vols., 1962-63). For the contemporary situation cf. also the collective work, *Istoričeskaja nauka i nekotorye problemy sovremennosti* (= Historical Science and Some Contemporary Problems) (1969), and more particularly a number of articles covering the last decennium in *Voprosy istorii*: 1960, No. 5 ('Nekotorye itogi raboty Instituta Istorii Akademii Nauk SSSR za 1959' [= Some results of the work of the Historical Institute of the USSR Academy of Sciences since 1959]); 1963, No. 1 (PONOMAREV, 'Zadači istoričeskoj nauki' [= The tasks of historical science]); 1968, No. 1 ('Jubilejnoe obščee sobranie Otdelenija Istorii AN SSSR' [= Jubilee General Assembly of the Department of History of the USSR Academy of Sciences]); 1968, No. 5 ('Važnejšie dostiženija v oblasti istoričeskih nauk v 1967 g.' [= Outstanding achievements in historical science in 1967]); 1969, No. 8 ('Novye rubeži sovetskih istorikov' [= New frontiers for Soviet historians]); 1969, No. 9 (ČUBAR'JAN, 'Itogi meždunarodnogo soveščanija kommunističeskih i rabočih partij i zadači istoričeskoj nauki' [= Conclusions of the International Congress of Communist and Workers' Parties and the aims of historical science]); and TIHOMIROV, 'O značenii istoričeskoj nauki' (= The significance of historical science) (1969). Among western writing, cf. particularly UTECHIN, 'Soviet historiography after Stalin', in KEEP & BRISBY (eds.), *Contemporary History in the Soviet Mirror, op. cit.* (1964); MENDEL, 'Current Soviet theory of history' (1966), and the articles by PUNDEFF in *History and Theory*, Vol. IV (1964) and Vol. VI (1967).

112. Cf. the report, 'Osnovnye tečenija sovremennoj istoriografii na X Kongrese istoričeskih nauk' (= Main trends of contemporary historiography at the Xth Congress of Historical Sciences) (1956), and the comments in KEEP & BRISBY (eds.), *Contemporary History in the Soviet Mirror, op. cit.* (1964), pp. 123-124, and *Soviet Culture*, Nos. 4-5 (May-June 1956), p. 2.

113. Cf. PIROSCHKOW, 'Sowjetische Geschichtswissenschaft im inneren Widerstreit (1956-1959)' (1960).

114. This is the title of a leading article, 'Sovetskaja istoričeskaja nauka na novom ètape razvitija' (= Soviet historical science at a new stage of development), in *Vopr. ist.*, 1960, No. 8.

against the more exaggerated political trends of the Stalinist period – including the cult of personalities, such as Ivan IV, and the patriotic glorification of Russia's past – the main feature was the rejection of 'dogmatism' and 'quotationism' and the reassertion of the need for factuality. As a consequence of the 'cult of the individual', E. M. Zhukov asserted, Soviet historians were suffering from 'a psychological trauma'; instead of proceeding from facts to generalizations, they 'uncritically' repeated 'axiomatic formulas', and selected 'factual data to support this or that theoretical conclusion already drawn at some ealier date by the classics of Marxism-Leninism'.[115]

The reaction of historians was to assert that history, in the words of B. F. Porshnev, is 'concreteness at its maximum'.[116] Quoting Lenin, Mme Pankratova, at that time editor of *Voprosy istorii*, called upon Soviet historians to base their writing on 'exact and indisputable facts' and put an end to the suppression of unpalatable material, which, as V. G. Trukhanovsky, her successor as editor-in-chief of *Voprosy istorii* later said, could only 'impoverish history'. One result, voiced by Trukhanovsky himself but also by many others, was an urgent call to historians to write 'living, not schematic history' – that is to say, 'history with flesh, blood, emotions and passions' and with 'the richness of colours and gradations that one finds in real life'.[117] As A. Y. Gurevich reminded historians, the categories of historical materialism are mainly epistemological guides to research, not *a priori,* ontological descriptions of reality, and the business of the historian – though he may also legitimately concern himself with facts which 'play no rôle in the causal chain of past events' but were nevertheless significant for contemporaries – is to test their applicability in concrete cases and in this way to refine and, if necessary, modify or redefine them.[118]

Behind these limited, practical demands was a general principle of wider significance, namely, the reassertion of the autonomy of history and of historical research. What was required now, if history were to be able to perform its proper function, was a clearer delimitation between the philosophy of society (historical materialism), the theory of society (sociology), and the

115. Cf. 'Vsesojuznoe soveščanie istorikov' (report of the All-Union Conference of historians on measures to improve the training of historians and history teachers, held in Moscow in December 1962) in *Voprosy istorii*, 1963, No. 2, and B. N. PONO-MAREV's basic paper for that conference, 'Zadači istoričeskoj nauki i podgotovka naučno-pedagogičeskih kadrov v oblasti istorii', published in the preceding issue with an extensive English summary, 'The tasks confronting historical science and the training of historians and history teachers'.

116. *Istorija i sociologija* (1964), p. 313.

117. For Pankratova's statements, cf. *Pravda,* 22 Feb. 1956, and *XX S'ezd KPSS, Stenografičeskij otčët* (= XXth Congress of the Communist Party of the Soviet Union, Stenographic record) (Moscow, 1956), Vol. I; those of Trukhanovsky, Ponomarev, and others are reported in the article on the discussions of the methodology of history in the Academy of Sciences in January, 1964, published under the general title 'O metodologičeskih voprosah istoričeskoj nauki' (= About the methodological questions of historical science) in *Vopr. ist.,* 1964, No. 3, and also in *Istorija i sociologija, op. cit.*

118. Cf. GUREVIČ, 'Obščij zakon i konkretnaja zakonomernost' v istorii' (= General law and concrete regularity in history) (1965).

history of society (the historical sciences), and recognition of the relatively independent rôle of each.[119] Writing in 1962, the Bulgarian Marxist, N. Stefanov insisted that the history of the historical process must be clearly differentiated from the theory of the historical process;[120] otherwise there was a danger that Marx's thought, instead of continuing to be a powerful weapon of critical analysis, might shrink to a dogma devoid of explanatory power and insight into society. As M. T. Iovchuk pointed out, the 'general truths' of Marxism 'cannot be suited and applicable to any age unless they are developed, made concrete, and enriched by new data, and individual obsolescent propositions are replaced by new ones corresponding to the new historical circumstances.'[121]

The changes which Soviet historiography has undergone since 1956 have resulted, in the first place, in greater latitude regarding access to sources, choice of subject matter and presentation of facts. As a consequence, the work of Soviet historians now extends to a wide range of topics which previously were largely ignored, for example, the history of inter- and intra-class movements in the Soviet Union since 1917 and historical analysis of the structure of Soviet society.[122] Perhaps even more significant in the present context is the improvement which has taken place in the methods of historical research. This went with a new respect for and willingness to experiment with the methods of western, or 'bourgeois', historiography, but was due, more fundamentally, to the rehabilitation of sociology in the Soviet Union after its eclipse in the 1930's and to increasing collaboration between historians and social scientists.[123] Urged to explore the new methods of sociological analysis, Soviet historians have paid increasingly close attention since the early 1960's to cybernetics, computer techniques, statistics, structural analysis and the use of models.[124] Nor have their ef-

---

119. Cf. 'O metodologičeskih voprosah istoričeskoj nauki', *op. cit.*, and the paper by FEDOSEEV & FRANCEV, 'O razrabotke metodologičeskih voprosov istorii (= On the working out of the methodological questions of history) which served as a basis for that discussion, in *Vopr. ist.*, 1964, No. 3 and in *Istorija i sociologija*; see also PUNDEFF's analysis in *History and Theory*, Vol. IV (1964), pp. 75-77, and Vol. VI (1967), p. 451.

120. STEFANOV, *Vaprosi na metodologijata na istoričeskata nauka* (= Methodological Questions in Historical Science) (1962).

121. Cf. PUNDEFF, *op cit.* (1967), p. 454.

122. Cf. ROGAČEVSKAJA, *Iz istorii rab. klassa SSSR v pervye gody industrializacii, 1926-1927* (= History of the Labouring Class of the USSR in the First Years of Industrialization) (1959); ARUTJUNJAN, *Mehanizatory sel'skogo hozjaistva SSSR v 1929-1957 gg.* (= The Agents of the Mechanization of Agriculture in the USSR from 1929 to 1957) (1960); TRIFONOV, *Očerki istorii klassovoj bor'by v SSSR v gody NEP (1921-1937)* (= Essays on the History of the Class Struggle in the USSR during the Years of the NEP – 1921-1937) (1960).

123. Cf. KON, 'Istorija i sociologija' (1970) (French translation, 'Histoire et sociologie', 1971); RUMJANCEV, 'Obščestvennye nauki v SSSR i sovremennost'' (= The social sciences in the USSR and the present time) (1968).

124. Cf. GEL'MAN-VINOGRADOV & HROMČENKO, *Kibernetika i istoričeskaja nauka* (= Cybernetics and Historical Science) (1967); BARG, *O nekotoryh predposylkah formalizacii istoričeskogo issledovanija* (= Premises for the Formalization of His-

forts to win new insights stopped at that point. In addition, B. F. Porshnev has directed attention to social, or group, psychology,[125] and a major project of content analysis in progress at the University of Moscow is seeking to follow the evolution of moral values during the Renaissance by systematic examination of a corpus of literary texts of the period.[126] If, methodologically, Soviet historiography appeared to be hesitant in 1950 in the use of sophisticated modern techniques, twenty years later they had been fully assimilated. From the point of view of the evolution of historical science, this is probably the most important of the changes it has undergone since 1956.

There were, of course, other factors contributing to the changes of attitude and approach among Soviet historians. Prominent among them were the new perspectives which confronted Soviet historiography when – both before and after the setting up of an independent Institute of World History in 1969 – it turned more actively than previously from Russian and European to Asian and African history. As K. A. Antonova pointed out, it was not easy to subscribe to the view that 'the whole world follows one and the same series of stages' when 'before our very eyes the industrial development of new Asian and African nations is occurring in a manner so very unlike that of the classical European model.'[127] This is a question to which we shall return. For the moment it is sufficient to say that the challenge of world history was for practical purposes a new feature of the post-Stalin era, for it was the emphasis placed at the Twentieth Party Congress on the rôle of the 'third world' that directed the attention of Soviet historians in general to the history of Asia and Africa. By widening their horizons and forcing them to take into consideration situations which hitherto had received little attention, except at the hands of specialists, confrontation with the problems of world history played a considerable part in the process of reappraisal which was the mark of Soviet historiography after 1955. The result was to shake confidence both in traditional formulations and traditional methods, and to reinforce the search for new ways.

In western Europe, also, as we have already noted,[128] the year 1955 marked a turning-point, for it was then that the new ideas stemming, direct-

---

torical Research) (1967); *Metodologičeskie i istoriografičeskie voprosy istoričeskoj nauki* (= Methodological and Historiographical Questions of Historical Science) (collective work, 1964); STAERMAN, 'K probleme strukturnogo analiza v istorii' (= On the problem of structural analysis in history) (1968), and KAHK, 'Nužna li novaja istoričeskaja nauka?' (= Do we need a new historical science?) (1969). As specific Soviet contributions in special areas (e.g., computer techniques) will be noted later at the appropriate point, it is sufficient in addition to refer here to the list of books and articles cited by GEFTER & MALKOV in their 'Reply to a questionnaire on Soviet historiography', p. 207 in *History and Theory*, Vol. VI (1967).

125. PORŠNEV, *Social'naja psihologija i istorija* (= Social Psychology and History) (1966); PORŠNEV & ANCIFEROVA (eds.), *Istorija i psihologija* (= History and Psychology) (1970).

126. Cf. GARDIN, 'Une approche linguistique' (1969).

127. *Istorija i sociologija, op. cit.* (1964), p. 282.

128. Cf. above, pp. 16–17.

ly or indirectly, from Marc Bloch and Lucien Febvre made full impact. This is not the place to discuss the work of Bloch and Febvre in detail.[129] It is sufficient to say that the 'school' they gathered round them, and the journal *Annales*, which they founded in 1929 as a vehicle for propagating their new and challenging conceptions of history and its rôle, quickly became the main stimulus directing the thought of western European historians into unaccustomed channels and suggesting new methods and new lines of approach. Theirs was the dominant influence, but not, of course, the only one. In England, for example, Sir Louis Namier's analysis of the politico-social forces at play in eighteenth-century English politics, added another new dimension;[130] but Namier's influence, partly because he fought shy of general concepts, partly because his work dealt with the structure of politics at a time when emphasis was moving away from political history to the study of society as a whole, was far more restricted both in range and in duration, and by 1955 its force was spent. Naturally Bloch and Febvre exerted considerable influence even before 1939, outside as well as inside France;[131] but the consolidation of their position, interrupted by the war, took time, and 1955 stands out as the year in which the 'battles for history', to which Febvre devoted his life, were finally won.[132] The programme and methods of the 'school of the *Annales*' have not been accepted without demur, particularly from the side of German historicism;[133] but Momigliano summed up the position accurately enough when he stated in 1961 that it was 'taking the place in Europe of the German historical school as the central forge of future historians.'[134] Developments since that time have only confirmed his judgment.

At the heart of the programme of the school of the *Annales* is an in-

---

129. The whole subject is admirably treated in GLÉNISSON's brilliant essay, 'L'historiographie française contemporaine: tendances et réalisations', in *La recherche historique en France de 1940 à 1965* (1965); cf. also HUGHES, H. S., *The Obstructed Path* (1966), Pt. I, and (in addition to the literature listed by Glénisson, p. xvi) DAVIES's essay on Marc Bloch in *History*, Vol. LII (1967).

130. Cf. NAMIER, *The Structure of Politics at the Accession of George III* (2 vols., 1929), and *England in the Age of the American Revolution* (1930).

131. In England, for example, Bloch's characteristic attitude and approach influenced the work of M. M. Postan, and by an inverse process, POSTAN's writings – in particular, the seminal article, 'The chronology of labour services' (1937) – exercised a profound influence over the work of French medievalists.

132. Cf. GLÉNISSON, *op. cit.*, pp. l-li.

133. Cf. particularly RITTER, 'Betrachtungen . . .', pp. 296-315 in Vol. VI of the *Relazioni, Xo Congresso internazionale di Scienze storiche* (1955), together with the article 'Zur Problematik gegenwärtiger Geschichtsschreibung' in RITTER's *Lebendige Vergangenheit* (1958), and WAGNER, *Moderne Geschichtsschreibung* (1960), pp. 89-112. BORN, 'Neue Wege der Wirtschafts- und Sozialgeschichte in Frankreich' (1964), and WÜSTEMEYER, 'Die "Annales": Grundsätze und Methoden ihrer "neuen Geschichtswissenschaft"' (1967), though critical, are more sympathetic. For more recent and cogent criticism, cf. DE JONGE, 'Geschiedenisbeoefening in Frankrijk' (1969).

134. MOMIGLIANO, *Studies in Historiography* (1966), p. 233, reproduced in translation from *Revisto storia italiana* (1961).

sistent demand for a widening of the dimensions of history and an enlargement of the historian's vision. This demand was common not only to Bloch
and Febvre, but also to their followers of the second generation, particularly Fernand Braudel, who succeeded Febvre in 1956 as director of the
department of economic and social sciences at the Ecole pratique des
hautes Etudes,[135] and Charles Morazé.[136] The new history was, in
Febvre's famous phrase, to be *une histoire à part entière*; its concern, that
is to say, was to be the whole of human activity, 'tout ce qui, étant à
l'homme, dépend de l'homme, sert à l'homme, exprime l'homme, signifie
la présence, l'activité, les goûts et les façons d'être de l'homme'.[137] The
contrast with the conventional 'history of events' is obvious and was always
explicit. Febvre never tired of polemicizing against *l'histoire événementielle*
which, under the influence of German historicism, concentrated all its attention on the sequence of individual occurrences – largely the documented
occurrences of political history – seeking to explain and rationalize them by
a hypothetical chain of cause and effect. History so conceived was, in
Braudel's words, little more than 'a new sort of chronicle', which, because
of its shortness of view, failed to see the wood for the trees.

The new history, Febvre insisted, must emancipate itself from the documents and the limitations they imposed. It must use all the artefacts of
man – language, signs, the evidence of the countryside, field-systems,
necklets, bracelets – and every other available resource. It must, in short,
be wide open to the findings and methods of other disciplines – geography,
economics, sociology, psychology – and at the same time must resist the
temptation, so marked in the 1920's and 1930's, to divide itself into a
number of 'specialisms' (economic history, the history of ideas, etc.), each
going its own independent way. Economic history abstracted from its social
context was worse than useless; it was positively misleading.[138] In any
case, the value of specialized research in social or economic history lay
above all else in its ability to reveal new tasks and new ways of approach
for history as a whole.[139] For the historian's business, above all else, is to
ask questions. 'A document', wrote Bloch, 'is a witness, and like most
witnesses it rarely speaks until one begins to question it.' Therefore a 'questionnaire' is 'the first necessity of all well-conducted historical research',
and the relevance of a historian's work is directly related to the quality of
the questions asked.[140] No more than any other science can history pro-

---

135. For Braudel, cf. GLÉNISSON, *op. cit.*, pp. lvii-lxii, and WÜSTEMEYER, *op.
cit.*, pp. 27-37.

136. Cf. MORAZÉ, *Trois essais sur Histoire et Culture* (1948) and *La logique de
l'histoire* (1967).

137. FEBVRE, 'Vers une autre histoire' (1949, 1953), p. 428 in FEBVRE, *Combats
pour l'histoire* (1953).

138. How misleading was wittily indicated by Sidney POLLARD in 'Economic
history – A science of society', pp. 6-8 in *Past and Present*, No. 30 (1965).

139. Cf. BORN, *op. cit.* (1964), p. 308.

140. Cf. BLOCH, *Apologie pour l'histoire* (1949), p. 26, and DAVIES, 'Marc Bloch',
op. cit. (1967), p. 274. 'Toute recherche historique', Bloch continues, 'suppose, dès

ceed by a mere amassing of facts. The 'past' does not exist; the idea of restoring this 'collection of dead bodies' to life by a painstaking reconstruction of fragmentary survivals was the illusion on which conventional history had foundered. It is the historian who creates the 'object' of his studies, in exactly the same way as scientists do.[141] History, Bloch stoutly maintained, has no right to claim a place among the serious forms of knowledge unless it offers 'in place of a simple, disjointed and virtually unlimited enumeration ... a rational classification and progressive intelligibility.'[142]

The general programme outlined by Bloch and Febvre thus culminated in a reassertion of the scientific character of the historian's work, as contrasted with the intuitive, subjective and anti-scientific bias of German historicism. The belief in the scientific validity of history – even if it is still 'a science in its infancy' – is a recurrent theme from Bloch to Braudel.[143] It explains, without doubt, the impact of their ideas on a generation wearied of the flaccidity of conventional history, its rhetoric, its subjective 'explanations', its reliance on unverifiable 'insights', its concern with surface events, its spurious controversies, and its juggling with 'apophthegms of banal psychology which are no more and no less true than their opposites.'[144] Febvre's conception of history as 'une reconstitution des sociétés et des êtres humains d'autrefois par des hommes et pour des hommes engagés dans le réseau des réalités humaines d'aujourd'hui,'[145] had a resonance and immediacy for the post-war generation which conventional history totally lacked, and it is significant that Gerhard Ritter, for all his scepticism about the basic postulates of the 'Ecole des *Annales*', was forced to admit that they had steadily won adherents in Germany ever since 1948.[146]

---

ses premiers pas, que l'enquête ait déjà une direction. Au commencement est l'esprit. Jamais, dans aucune science, l'observation passive n'a rien donné de fécond'.

141. 'Il n'y a pas le Passé, ce donné – le Passé, cette collection de cadavres dont l'historien aurait pour fonction de retrouver tous les numéros pour les photographier un à un et les identifier. Il n'y a pas le Passé qui engendre l'historien. Il y a l'historien qui fait naître l'Histoire'. Such is FEBVRE's formulation in the famous programmatic introduction he contributed to MORAZÉ's *Trois essais sur Histoire et Culture* (1948), p. viii.

142. *Apologie*, p. xiii.

143. *Ibid.*, p. xiv: '... ce tard-venu dans le champ de la connaissance rationnelle. Ou, pour mieux dire, vieille sous la forme embryonnaire du récit, longtemps encombrée de fictions, plus longtemps encore attachée aux événements les plus immédiatement saisissables, elle est, comme entreprise raisonnée d'analyse, toute jeune.' With this, compare BRAUDEL's far more confident profession ('Stockholm 1960', p. 499 in *Annales*, Vol. XVI, 1961) – itself a measure of the ground gained in twenty years: '... je le répète, avec obstination, il peut y avoir des histoires diverses, mais *une seule* histoire scientifique.'

144. *Apologie*, p. 102. I have expressed my view about the spurious controversies in which professional historians are so apt to delight – 'the learned games about the rise of the gentry or the causes of the French Revolution' – in *History and the Common Man* (1967), p. 8, and do not need to repeat what is said there.

145. Introduction to MORAZÉ, *Trois essais* ..., p. viii.

146. 'Betrachtungen ...', p. 311 in *Relazioni, Xo Congresso* (1955), Vol. VI; specifically, a 'majority' of German historians had abandoned concern with 'devel-

Nevertheless, this admitted fact alone does not explain the triumphant advance of the 'new history' after 1955. Neither the insights of Bloch and Febvre nor their onslaught on the crudities and inadequacies of *histoire historisante* were essentially new. Their conception of history differed little in essentials from that of Henri Berr a generation earlier, and so far as general theory was concerned, there was little to be said that Berr had not already said in books – still eminently readable and instructive – such as *L'histoire traditionnelle et la synthèse historique*.[147] What was new about Bloch and Febvre was that they opened a road from the old history to the new. Their essential contribution was less their general concept of history than their triumphant demonstration not only that it *could* be realized, but also *how* it could be realized, in practice. The real change, in short, was methodological. Instead of being satisfied – as, by and large, Berr had been satisfied – with taking up a theoretical stand, they set a practical example by writing the sort of history in which they believed, working out in detail the practical implications of the new goals, and elaborating a methodology to put them into effect; and since their efforts, also, were fragmentary, and their formulations incomplete, their successors and disciples – Braudel, Vilar, Labrousse, Morazé, and others – carried on where they left off. In this way a new methodology, inspired by new insights, was gradually achieved – a methodology the potentialities of which were nowhere more brilliantly demonstrated than in Braudel's epoch-making book, published in 1949, on the Mediterranean world in the age of Philip II.[148]

The lines of evolution are not difficult to follow. Bloch, for example, had criticized historians 'de souffle un peu court', who 'regarded the current of human development as made up of a succession of brief but powerful thrusts, each of which lasted at most for the duration of a few lives', and had emphasized instead the 'immense continuum' of history.[149] It was left to Braudel to elaborate the concept of *la longue durée*,[150] and to emphasize, as the essential dialectic of history, the interplay between this long-term continuity – the history, 'almost immobile', of man's grappling with his enveloping environment[151] – and the short-term surges and sequences, which break against it as against a rock, but which sometimes, like the waves of the sea, break it down, producing (in Braudel's words) 'ce passage d'un monde à l'autre' which is 'le très grand drame humain sur lequel nous voudrions des lumières.'[152] But how was the *longue durée* to be made accessible to the historian's knowledge? What it revealed was the existence of stable social

---

opment' and 'origins' and turned instead to structural analysis, on the French model, of particular epochs or of concepts such as feudalism or the Renaissance.

147. Published in 1935; cf. above, p. 18.

148. BRAUDEL, *La Méditerranée et le monde méditerranéen à l'époque de Philippe II* (1949).

149. *Apologie pour l'histoire*, pp. xvi, 12.

150. 'La longue durée' (1958, reprinted in BRAUDEL, *Ecrits sur l'histoire*, 1969).

151. BRAUDEL, *La Méditerranée . . ., op. cit.,* Préface, p. xiii in the 1st edn. (1949); reproduced in *Ecrits sur l'histoire*, p. 11.

152. Cf. GLÉNISSON, *op. cit.* (1965), p. lx.

structures, capable of outlasting and withstanding the upheavals of political disturbance; what was needed, therefore, was a history of structures – *histoire structurelle* or *histoire structurale* – and this the old techniques of the historian, their attention focused on the transient, the unique and the individual, were unable to provide. Moreover, within the existing social structures it is possible to discern not merely an infinite series of fleeting individual events – 'flowers of a single day, fading so quickly that no one can grasp them twice' – but also recurrent rhythms, or cycles: cycles, particularly, of economic life, the rise and fall (for example) of prices and wages, but also cycles of cultural life; cycles which a few 'great men' might contrive to break through, but by which the actions even of those whom traditional history acclaims as among the greatest manipulators of events – Bismarck, for example – prove, on close inspection, to be almost entirely conditioned.[153] These are the 'conjunctures' – a term adopted from the vocabulary of economics – and once again they confront us with a phenomenon which the ordinary processes of historical research are ill-adapted to describe. And yet, of the three elements which go to make up history – structures, conjunctures, events, or (in Braudel's terminology) 'geographical time', 'social time', 'individual time' – it is the former with which the historian is (or should be) primarily concerned; for the structures and conjunctures are the essential framework within which the drama of events is confined, the stage on which the individual plays out his fleeting role. When the actor has gone, the stage is still there, to be occupied by other actors, as glittering and persuasive – and ephemeral – tomorrow and the day after.

History approached in this way required new methods. The mere enumeration of events, however skilfully interlocked in a chain of cause and effect, was quite incapable of meeting the new demands. Historians who thought they could explain the partition of Africa after 1882 as a series of piecemeal reactions without cause or purpose, and failed to see new impulses at play and a change of mood, offered a typical example of the myopia of *histoire événementielle*.[154] The facts they enumerated might be true, but they were not significant.[155] By keeping meticulously to the course of events, and the day-by-day decisions of politicians and administrators, they left out of account the larger cycle, or 'conjuncture', in which those events and decisions were embedded. The historian concerned with the conjuncture must proceed differently. The history of conjunctures is

153. Helmut Böhme, one of the new generation of German historians, who has absorbed the methodology of the *Ecole des Annales*, has shown convincingly and with great learning the way in which Bismarck's policies were conditioned by the cycle of boom and depression in Germany, beginning with the *Konjunktur* of the 1850's and ending with the slump of 1873; cf. Böhme, *Deutschlands Weg zur Grossmacht* (1966).

154. Cf. Robinson & Gallagher, *Africa and the Victorians* (1961), and, by the same writers, 'The imperialism of free trade' (1953); cf. my critique, *An Introduction to Contemporary History* (2nd edn., 1967), pp. 58-64.

155. Cf. Thornton, *Doctrines of Imperialism* (1965), p. 45

essentially an *histoire mathématisante*, a history of graphs and tables recording demographic change, movements of production and prices, and
similar series, which only figures can make explicit. Nor should it be thought
that this method is useful only in the economic sphere. On the contrary,
cultural history – particularly the history of popular culture – is also susceptible of numerical analysis. Instead of the subjective criterion of the
emergence of 'great artists' and 'great writers' – for who is to judge who
is 'great' and who is not, and by what standard, in a field where taste
changes so sharply and rapidly? – an analysis of what was printed and
what was read, and in what numbers and by whom, over a given period
of time – for example, from 1780 to 1850 – can provide significant results
which no other method is capable of providing.[156] The history of 'structures', on the other hand, requires different methods still. Its affiliations are
with geography, demography, ethnography, climatology and botany. There
were few matters about which Bloch and Febvre were more emphatic than
the links between history and geography; their subject-matter, Bloch maintained, was basically identical.[157] The unit of history was not the medieval
lordship, the administrative districts of the rising European monarchies, or
the modern national state – and here the contrast with the spatial divisions
used by conventional historians is quite as marked and deliberate as that
elsewhere with their chronological divisions – but the geographical region:
a conception to which Braudel gave palpable shape when he devoted the
first part of his book on the Mediterranean at the time of Philip II to a
géohistoire of the Mediterranean region as a cultural and historical unity.

The influence of the school of the *Annales* quickly spread through Europe.
In Italy it led to a 'gradual withdrawal from Crocean positions';[158] in Germany it affected – though with characteristic modifications – the attitude
towards history of Schieder, Conze and (almost alone of German medievalists) Bosl,[159] and still more the younger generation of historians (e.g.,
H.-U. Wehler) which grew up after 1945;[160] in England it is visible – to
take a random selection of names – in the work of Rudé, Hobsbawm, Laslett and E. P. Thompson.[161] But individual names and instances are a

156. As examples cf. Raymond WILLIAMS, *Culture and Society, 1780-1850*
(1958), or CIPOLLA, *Literacy and Development in the West* (1969). Unfortunately
CANTOR & WERTHMAN (eds.), *The History of Popular Culture* (1968), pay scant
attention to content analysis.
157. DAVIES, *op. cit.* (1967), p. 275.
158. MOMIGLIANO, *op. cit.* (1961), p. 237 in *Studies in Historiography* (1966).
159. Cf. SCHIEDER, Th., 'Strukturen und Persönlichkeiten in der Geschichte'
(1962); CONZE and SCHIEDER in *Geschichte in Wissenschaft und Unterricht*, Vol. III
(1952); BOSL, 'Geschichte und Soziologie' (1956) and 'Der "Soziologische Aspekt"
in der Geschichte. Wertfreie Geschichtswissenschaft und Idealtyp' (1965). Cf. also
SCHIEDER's volume of essays already referred to, *Staat und Gesellschaft im Wandel
unserer Zeit* (1958) (English translation, *The State and Society in our Times*, 1962).
160. Cf. WEHLER (ed.), *Moderne deutsche Sozialgeschichte* (1966).
161. Cf. RUDÉ, *The Crowd in History* (1965); HOBSBAWM, *Primitive Rebels*
(1959) and *Labouring Men* (1964); LASLETT, *The World We Have Lost* (1965);
THOMPSON, *The Making of the English Working Class* (1963).

totally inadequate index of an influence so pervasive. The essential point about the new history, the characteristic which made it so widely acceptable, was that it did not seek to enforce a new dogma or philosophy, but called for a new attitude and new methods; it did not tie the historian down in a rigid bed of theory, but opened out new horizons. It may be that neither Bloch nor Febvre had a consistent philosophy of history;[162] the fact would not have disturbed them greatly. The renewal of history, they believed, would come from practice rather than from theory. Hence, under the impact of the *Annales,* the old controversy whether history is an art or a science has fallen into oblivion. With good reason. The attempt of German neo-idealists to erect an 'iron curtain' between history and science, or between *die Welt als Geschichte* and *die Welt als Natur,* was always fallacious; it was built on conceptions of the character of scientific investigation and of historical investigation which have long since been refuted, and since the errors underlying this false dichotomy are now common knowledge, there is no need to recapitulate them here.[163] The point is rather that, once the neo-idealist balloon was pricked – once, in particular, it became clear that the traditional preoccupation of historians with descriptive narrative, and with the individual and unique, was a voluntary choice, not a logical necessity imposed upon them by their materials – the way was cleared for a vision of history and the historian's work which was far more responsive to the stimulus of the natural, social and human sciences. It was into the breach thus opened up that the historians of the *Annales* leapt with a new-found confidence in the potentialities of historical work which could not but awaken enthusiastic response.

History, seen from the angle of historians emancipated from the old antithesis between the 'nomothetic' and the 'idiographic', is as scientific as any other of the 'sciences': neither more nor less. 'Science des hommes', said Marc Bloch: not of the individual man, but of men, and not of men in general, but of men in society.[164] Significant was Bloch's approval of the dictum of Fustel de Coulanges: 'history is not an accumulation of events of all kinds which have happened in the past; it is the science of human communities.'[165] This was the key to the revolution which Bloch and Febvre inaugurated: the switch from the individual, the 'homme isolé', to the 'homme en groupe', to the society of which each individual, whether he likes it or not, is necessarily a part.[166] History which starts and ends with

162. Cf. KON, *Die Geschichtsphilosophie des 20. Jahrhunderts,* Vol. II (1964), pp. 50-54.

163. The refutation by Edgar WIND, 'Some points of contact between history and natural science' (1936), is exemplary; cf. also ANDERLE, 'Theoretische Geschichte' (1958), and BARRACLOUGH, 'Scientific method and the work of the historian' (1962). BLOCH, of course, had already made the main point: *Apologie,* p. xvi.

164. *Ibid.,* p. 4.

165. BLOCH, *Apologie,* p. 110, n. 4; cf. DAVIES, 'Marc Bloch', *op. cit.* (1967), p. 278.

166. Cf. WÜSTEMEYER, 'Die "Annales" ...', *op. cit.,* p. 26 in *Vierteljahrschrift für Sozial- und Wirtschaftsgeschichte,* Vol. LIV (1967).

the individual, which takes individual actions as its measure, may not need to be, may not even be capable of being, scientific; the history of man in society is, and cannot be otherwise. Its closest affiliations are with sociology. Bloch professed more than once to see no real distinction between history and sociology.[167] But he himself put his finger on the essential difference. If the social scientist is concerned above all with the analysis of a static society at a given moment, the distinguishing feature of the historian is his sense of time. History, says Bloch, is not merely 'science des hommes'; it is the science of men in time.[168] And, against the tendency of sociologists to dismiss history as irrelevant, he went on proudly to assert that the only way to understand the present was to turn away from it and see it as part of a continuing process.[169] It was the historical dimension, the ability to 'place' the present in context, to guard against the myopia of the 'short view', which afflicts economists and political scientists as much as *historiens historisants*, that was the historian's essential contribution to the science of society.[170]

In turning to the social sciences for new insights, as well as for models and methods, the school of the *Annales* was moving along lines similar to, and often converging with, those which historians in the United States were simultaneously following. There is certainly a close parallel between the two movements of renewal. The difference is the emphasis on the French side on the sense of time. This, no doubt, is the reason why, in their hands, the theoretical frameworks suggested by the social, economic and political sciences, are a more flexible tool than is usually the case in the United States. As Momigliano has said, 'the *Annales* have given France a model of the interchange between sociology and historiography' which is 'infinitely more subtle and varied than the American example'[171] –and therefore, no doubt, better adapted to winning adherents. On the other hand, their approach has much in common with that of the present generation of Soviet historians, with whom they seek an exchange of views.[172] Both are enemies of any form of economic determinism,[173] but both are convinced of the possibility – and necessity – of an approach to history which, in the best sense of the word, is scientific. By directing attention away from the unique and ineffable to structures and conjunctures which limit and condi-

167. *Ibid.*, p. 16; DAVIES, *op. cit.*, p. 278.

168. ' "Science des hommes", avons-nous dit. . . . Il faut ajouter: "des hommes dans le temps" ' - *Apologie*, p. 4.

169. WÜSTEMEYER, *op. cit.*, p. 14.

170. Braudel, for example, attacks economists for having 'pris l'habitude de courir au service de l'actuel, au service des gouvernements': cf. GLÉNISSON, *op. cit.*, p. lviii, and WÜSTEMEYER, *op. cit.*, p. 32.

171. MOMIGLIANO, *op. cit.* (1961), p. 233 in *Studies in Historiography* (1966).

172. Cf. BORN, *op. cit.* (1964), p. 307.

173. Compare, for example, BRAUDEL's remark (*La Méditerranée et le monde méditerranéen*, p. 307); 'L'économique façonne le politique, le social, le culturel, mais la réciproque est vraie', with the remarks of GEFTER & MALKOV in their 'Reply to a questionnaire on Soviet historiography', pp. 184, 187-188, 192 in *History and Theory*, Vol. VI (1967).

tion the individual's conscious choice – to the 'inconscient social' which is 'plus riche scientifiquement que la surface miroitante à laquelle nos yeux sont habitués'[174] – the historians working in the tradition of Bloch and Febvre have opened the way for a dialogue with the historians of the Soviet world; or at least they have provided them with insights and methodological innovations from which they can profit and are profiting.

If we try to sum up the new tendencies in historical study since 1955, we may say that they are marked by a convergence the main characteristic of which is a general repudiation of the basic presuppositions of the previous generation. This has been accompanied by a striking revival of interest in the theory of historical thinking and writing.[175] But since this theoretical discussion is for the most part concerned with the analysis, rather than with the criticism, of what the conventional historian does – since, in other words, it tends to accept the adequacy of the traditional framework – it is of greater interest to philosophers than to historians seeking new ways forward, and its contribution to the formulation of current trends has not been very considerable. For that reason it is sufficient, in the present context, to refer to it in passing.[176] The main feature of the current trends is the alignment of history, so long regarded as their antithesis, with the social sciences. Though there is still disagreement as to the precise nature of the relationship, practically no historian today – unless he is a self-proclaimed survivor from an older generation – would question their affiliation.[177] This, in the broadest sense, is the central achievement of the Ecole des *Annales*, to which many writers not directly associated with the school have attested. E. H. Carr, for example, had the unusual distinction of delivering, in 1961, a series of lectures on the nature of history without so much as mentioning Bloch or Febvre or the *Annales*. But when he said that 'scientists, social scientists and historians are all engaged in different branches of the same study: the study of man and his environment, of the effects of man on his environment and of his environment on man',[178] he was enunciating a doctrine which they, by precept and example, had

174. BRAUDEL, 'La longue duŕe', p. 740 in *Annales* (1958) or p. 63 in *Ecrits sur l'histoire*; cf. GLÉNISSON, *op. cit.*, p. lxii.

175. Cf., for example GARDINER, *The Nature of Historical Explanation* (1952), and GARDINER (ed.), *Theories of History* (1959); DRAY, *Laws and Explanation in Hisktory* (1957); GALLIE, *Philosophy and the Historical Understanding* (1964); DANTO, *Analytical Philosophy of History* (1965); WHITE, *Foundations of Historical Knowledge* (1965); GRUŠIN, *Očerki logiki istoričeskogo issledovanija* (= Essays on the Logic of Historical Research) (1961); BOBRINSKA, *Historyk, Fakt, Metoda* (1964); *Filosofskie problemy istoričeskoj nauki* (= Philosophical Problems of Historical Science) (1969); GUREVIČ, 'Obśčij zakon i konkretnaja zakonomernost' v istorii' (= General law and concrete regularity in history) (1965).

176. It is discussed more fully, and more appropriately, by Professor Paul Ricoeur in *Main Trends in Philosophy* (1979).

177. Cf. the discussion on 'History, sociology and social anthropology' reported in *Past and Present*, No. 27 (1964), pp. 102–108.

178. CARR, E. H., *What is History?* (1961), p. 80.

made the common conviction of historians everywhere.

What the changes amount to has perhaps been best summed up – or at least summed up in a form which most historians today will find acceptable – by the American historian, H. Stuart Hughes.[179] Stuart Hughes is only willing to accept the concepts and categories of social science as 'hypotheses of varying degrees of range and explanatory power', which are neither 'exhaustive' nor 'exclusive'; he rejects 'any mechanical superimposing of social science theory on traditional historical prose' and refuses to discard the inherited 'literary and discursive mould.' Nevertheless, there is, he maintains, 'no radical distinction' between history and science, and the social sciences offer 'a wide and varied range of hypotheses fully capable of historical application.' Their importance is that they enable historians 'to refine and to make more explicit their whole procedure of explanation' – or, as an English historian has put it, 'to be objective when the facts are available, and to refrain from unverifiable pronouncements when they are not.'[180] The significance of Bloch's vision of history, Hughes maintained, was that it 'released us from bondage to a type of study that had narrowed the aim of history.' This was his great achievement: under his inspiration 'we saw that if we turned the conventional prism of historical vision only a little, a whole new world of possibilities would come into view.'

However circumspect his approach to the 'new history' – perhaps precisely because he is so circumspect – the words of Stuart Hughes epitomize the change of attitude which historians have experienced in the past fifteen to twenty years. They are no longer satisfied with traditional history and its methods. It was always, Hughes says, 'an intellectually invertebrate affair' which 'had no clear concepts and no recognized canon of interpretation.'[181] And he concludes his survey with the prediction that 'the study of history today is entering a period of rapid change and advance such as characterized the science of physics in the first three decades of the twentieth century.'[182] What is significant about this advance is that the propelling force behind it derives from practice rather than theory. Just as the development of music was conditioned by improvements in the nature of musical instruments and developments in astronomy were dependent upon the ability to build more powerful and efficient telescopes, so the new trends in history are a response to new techniques and methods, which alone make them possible. 'C'est la méthode qui demeure au centre des préoccupations.'[183]

179. HUGHES, H. S., 'The historian and the social scientist' (1960), reprinted in RIASANOVSKY & RIZNIK (eds.), *Generalizations in Historical Writing* (1963); cf. also HUGHES, H. S., *History as Art and as Science* (1964), pp. 1-21.

180. THOMAS, K., 'The tools and the job', p. 276 in *New Ways in History* (special issue of *The Times Literary Supplement*, 1966).

181. HUGHES, H. S., 'The historian and the social scientist', *op. cit.* (1960), p. 20 in RIASANOVSKY & RIZNIK (eds.), *Generalizations in Historical Writing, op. cit.* (1963).

182. HUGHES, H. S., *History as Art and as Science, op. cit.* (1964), p. 20.

183. GLÉNISSON, *op. cit.*, p. liii.

It is, therefore, to the new methods, stemming in the main from sociology, economics and anthropology – but also owing something to the extension of the field of history to new areas, such as Africa, where traditional methods have been found wanting – that it is now necessary to turn. No doubt, in some cases, the new methodologies are still crude and leave much to be desired. But experimentation with them is the precondition of further progress – perhaps, indeed, of the future of history itself. For, as a Belgian writer recently said, history is at a parting of the ways. It may cross the threshold of the sciences, on which it stands, in which case it can become 'la science des sciences humaines'; but if it does not – if it shirks the challenge – it runs the risk of forfeiting its status as either a science or an art, and eking out a meagre existence as a 'hobby' – respected, no doubt, and popular, but bereft of real significance and of the ability to play any part in human affairs.[184]

3. The Impact of the Social Sciences

The impulse behind the 'new history' which emerged around 1955 came, as we have seen, in the main from the social sciences. There is nothing surprising, still less is there anything derogatory about this. Historians have spent much time defending the 'autonomy' of history.[185] To do so, as James Harvey Robinson observed many years ago, is 'to misapprehend the conditions of scientific advance.' Every science and every discipline is dependent on other sciences or disciplines; 'it draws its life from them, and to them it owes, consciously or unconsciously, a great part of its chances of progress.'[186] At the time of its first great advance in the days of Mabillon and the Bollandists, historical study consciously followed the example of the new science of biblical criticism; later, in the days of Niebuhr and Ranke, it borrowed and exploited the methods of classical philology. In turning to the social sciences for new insights and new techniques, historians today are only continuing a practice which has been followed at every turning-point in the development and refinement of historical studies in the past.

Nor is it surprising that historians should have seen much in the work of social scientists which reflects their own preoccupations. History and social science share common aims; and some at least of their roots spring from the same soil. Both claim to deal, at least in principle, with the whole range of social life, with 'the total situation as it is at any given point of time'; their purpose is a comprehensive understanding of human actions and rela-

---

184. Cf. LEBRUN, 'Développement et histoire quantitative', pp. 600, 605 in *Revue de l'Institut de Sociologie* (1967); cf. BARRACLOUGH, *History and the Common Man* (1967), p. 5: 'a form of entertainment [. . .] certainly high-class entertainment – entertainment for the tired boffin, relaxation for the intelligent scientist or technologist [. . .] but [. . .] entertainment nevertheless.'
185. Cf. ELTON, *The Practice of History* (1967), pp. 8 sqq., 47-48.
186. ROBINSON, *The New History* (1912), p. 73.

tionships.[187] And although history has many roots, some reaching back into the remote past and aligning it with religion and philosophy, as a rational enquiry it has its origins, like social science, in the same soil as nineteenth-century positivism. Both social science and history, in other words, claimed to be seeking for certain truth; both appealed to the example of natural scientists at loggerheads as adversaries, instead of allies; and it is not sur-and social improvement.[188] This, we have seen,[189] was the belief of historians such as Fustel de Coulanges, Acton or Bury, every bit as much as it was that of Marx and Engels, or Comte and Spencer. It was the impact of German historicism, reacting against positivist formulations, that destroyed this identity or semi-identity of purpose, setting historians and social scientists at loggerheads as adversaries, instead of allies; and it is not surprising that the collapse of German historicism during and after the Second World War should have opened the way for a reconciliation.

There were, of course, other more immediate reasons for the change of attitude. The very success of social scientists, measured both by the standard of public recognition and by the heuristic potentialities of their methods and concepts, was impressive; and it is not surprising that historians should have asked themselves whether these methods and concepts might not have something to contribute to their own studies. A second factor was the impact of the changed conditions of the post-war world. The years between 1940 and 1970 saw the emergence of a new set of problems – mass behaviour, acculturation, urbanization, the role of élites, to name but a few – with which the conventional methods of historical research were ill-adapted to deal. The result was a methodological gap – 'a serious gap between historiographic theory and practice' – and one main reason why historians turned to the techniques developed by social scientists was the belief that they offered a means of closing this methodological gap.[190]

This does not mean that historians have simply taken over the unprocessed terminology and categories of social science. For one thing, none of the social sciences is a single, self-contained unit with a logically integrated body of theory, which can be automatically transferred and assimilated in this way; all are in a state of growth and experimentation every bit as fluid as that of history itself, and there are as many sharp differences of opinion regarding theory and method between social scientists as there are between historians. Secondly, historians have approached the social sciences from different angles, seeking different things, and often under the influence of their own national traditions. Soviet historians naturally operate within a Marxist framework; French historians look for preference to Durkheim, Simiand, Lévi-Strauss and Gurvitch; in Germany the aura of Max

187. Cf. *The Social Sciences in Historical Study* (1954), pp. 41, 87.

188. Cf. EISENSTADT, A. S., 'American history and social science' (1963); reprinted in EISENSTADT (ed.), *The Craft of American History*, Vol. II (1966): see pp. 116, 119 in the latter edition.

189. Above, pp. 6-7.

190. Cf. BENSON, 'An approach to the scientific study of past public opinion', pp. 28-29 in ROWNEY & GRAHAM (eds.), *Quantitative History* (1969).

Weber still remains powerful; while in the United States, under the influence of social scientists such as Merton, Parsons, and Lazarsfeld, the emphasis almost from the beginning has been less upon large-scale theorization than upon the application of specific concepts or methods to limited historical problems and concrete historical situations. These differences, reflecting different national and historical traditions, have left their mark, and it is only necessary to compare the writings of Fogel, Aydelotte or Lee Benson in the United States, Braudel, Goubert or Morazé in France, and Brunner, Schieder or Conze in Germany, to perceive the salient distinguishing features.

No less important is the fact that the impact of the social sciences has occurred in two distinct, though overlapping phases. Even during the period when the influence of German historicism was at its height, there were always, as we have seen,[191] a certain number of historians, such as Henri Berr in France or James Harvey Robinson in the United States, who looked to the social sciences for new insights. But emphasis at this stage was on the more theoretical and speculative aspects of sociology, anthropology and psychology, and even those who were most dissatisfied with the old orthodoxies rarely set out to seek new evidence or more rigorous techniques.[192] This was the situation, by and large, from 1900 to 1950. Between 1950 and 1955 a new phase began, the essential characteristic of which was a shift of emphasis from the broad general concepts developed by social scientists to the question of methods. Not, of course, that interest in the concepts of social science ceased; but it was now realized as well that every new form of historical enquiry calls for a corresponding technical equipment, that new questions necessitate both the mobilization of a new documentation and the elaboration of an appropriate methodology. And this new methodology was provided by two developments of the period after 1940: first, the proliferation of new sociological techniques – numerical analysis, scaling techniques, multiple correlation and regression analysis, and other sophisticated statistical procedures – and, secondly, the breakthrough in computer technology which greatly expanded the feasibility of quantitative historical work. After 1950 the possibilities opened up to historians by the social sciences were not only far richer but also far more clearly delineated than before.[193]

The impact of the social sciences on historical study has, therefore, taken place at two different levels. First, there is the appeal to the broader categories of sociological thinking, which is now of fairly long standing and has

191. Above, p. 11.
192. My own book, *History in a Changing World* (1955) may be taken as a fairly typical example of the trend prevalent at this period: though critical of older viewpoints and insistent upon the necessity for new directions, its criticism was essentially negative and in accepting the adequacy of the traditional methodology, it failed (as I. S. KON, *Die Geschichtsphilosophie des 20. Jahrhunders*, Vol. I (1964), pp. 15-16, correctly observed) to indicate any positive way forward.
193. Cf. PRICE, pp. 4, 7 in *Studies in Quantitative History* (*History and Theory*, Beiheft 9, 1969).

won at least a grudging acceptance. Secondly, there is the use of new quantitative methods, which, in spite of the somewhat heady claims advanced on its behalf in the last nine or ten years, is still at a tentative and exploratory stage. In the following survey we shall deal first with the more general impact of social science concepts, and then with the new methodological trends generally subsumed under the heading of quantification or quantitative history. It is usual in such a survey to examine separately the impact of each of the main branches of social science – anthropology, ethnology, sociology, demography, economics, political science, psychology – but such a division exaggerates their autonomy. While some historians have paid particular attention to one branch of social science (for example, social anthropology) and others to another (for example, sociology), at least in the earlier stages their impact was never very clearly or exactly delimited. In addition, we must bear in mind the influence of concepts such as 'structure' and 'structuralism', which have invaded all the sciences from mathematics and linguistics to anthropology and sociology.[194] In the recent past the most pervasive influence of all has been that of economics, particularly econometrics. This not only changed the direction of economic history in one generation from description to analysis, but was also the factor mainly responsible for making historians in all branches and fields of history keenly aware of the importance of statistics and quantifiable data.[195] In general, however, what historians discovered in the social sciences was a series of concepts and a variety of new approaches, to which they were willing to turn because of their uneasiness about their own traditional methods. Whether these concepts derived from sociology, from anthropology, or from economics, was a secondary consideration; the important thing was to explore the possibility that they would enable them to add a new dimension to their work.

The Contribution of Sociology and Anthropology

If the fundamental reason why historians turned to the social sciences for new insights and perspectives was a sharp reaction against historicism and its postulates and preconceptions, it is not surprising that they should have looked in the first instance to anthropology and sociology for reorientation. Of all the social sciences these were nearest to their own preoccupations.

194. It is sufficient here to refer to the introduction by PIAGET, *Le structuralisme* (1968) (English translation, *Structuralism*, 1971).

195. Cf. DAVIS, R., *History and the Social Sciences* (1965), pp. 5-6. The turning-point in England, Davis suggests, came between the publication of LIPSON's *Economic History* (1915-31) and that of Sir John CLAPHAM (1926-38). What distinguished the latter was its recognition that the 'analytical power of Marshallian economics' provided a tool for 'fruitful dissection of our economic past'. In his preface Clapham specifically criticized 'historians who neglect quantities', and claimed that 'it is possible, all along the line, to make the story more nearly quantitative than it has yet been made'.

The boundary-line between contemporary and past society is tenuous, shifting and artificial; so also is that between 'primitive' and 'civilized' cultures. Moreover, there are many problems of vital importance – for example, acculturation or the changes consequent upon contacts between different (usually more primitive and more advanced) societies – which are matters of equal concern to anthropologists, historians and sociologists.

The difference between history, on the one side, and anthropology and sociology, on the other, is one of method, rather than of aim or subject matter.[196] It may be true, in strict logic, that the only evidence available to any social scientist, no matter what his special field may be, is historical evidence.[197] The fact remains that he handles that evidence in ways different from those which historians have traditionally been taught to use. The sheer bulk of material to be correlated, to say nothing of the complexity of relationships in contemporary society, means that the sociologist cannot hope to produce meaningful results by the simple process of assembling factual data in a descriptive narrative; he is compelled, whether he likes it or not, to turn to other methods – polls, sampling, statistical analysis, and the like – which offer better prospects of mastering a vast, amorphous body of information. As for the anthropologist, his problem is in a sense the very opposite: namely, the paucity, if not the total lack, of conventional historical records. But here again, the result is to enforce the need to devise alternative methods, in this case the collection of information in the field and the interrogation of living witnesses.

In both cases, however, what is significant is not so much the particular techniques as the fact that both anthropologists and sociologists approach their sources with specific questions. They do not seek random information, but specific information, answers to questions forced on them (it has been said) 'by the pressure of recurrent situations.'[198] And secondly, in order to evaluate the answers, they are compelled to place them in a theoretical framework. Before they can be made 'sociologically intelligible', they must be ranged against the 'structural order' of the society the anthropologist or sociologist is studying, the 'patterns which, once established, enable him to see it as a whole' or as 'a set of interrelated abstractions'; and having isolated these structural patterns in one society, he goes on to compare them with similar patterns in other societies, constructing a typology of forms and determining their essential features and the reasons for the variations between them.[199]

In principle, this may not be very different from the tasks the majority of historians also claim to perform. They also, like social scientists, use concepts and hypotheses as a basis for selection and interpretation, and

196. Cf. EVANS-PRITCHARD, 'Social anthropology. Past and present', p. 25 in EVANS-PRITCHARD, *Essays in Social Anthropology* (1962).

197. Cf. BRAUDEL, 'Histoire et sociologie' (1958, 1969), p. 104 in *Ecrits sur l'histoire* (1969); cf. also *The Social Sciences in Historical Study* (1954), p. 31.

198. EVANS–PRITCHARD, 'Anthropology and history' (1961, 1962), p. 59 in *Essays in Social Anthropology, op. cit.* (1962).

199. EVANS-PRITCHARD, 'Social anthropology. Past and present', *ibid.*, pp. 22-23.

cannot, in fact, proceed otherwise.[200] But in practice, there are two main differences. The first is that the historian's conceptualization tends to be implicit, arbitrary and unsystematic, whereas the social scientist's is explicit and systematic. The second is the historian's tendency, because his sources usually provide him with some sort of loose narrative pattern to which the facts can be related, to evade so far as possible the theoretical issues, and also to deal for preference less with the underlying structure than with events and personalities, which are usually far more sharply delineated in historical records than in the materials anthropologists and sociologists commonly use.

It is against this background that the contribution of sociology and anthropology must be evaluated. In the broadest sense it may be summed up as a recall to the ideal of scientific exactitude which historians (or at least non-Marxist historians) abandoned when, at the turn of the nineteenth and twentieth centuries, they turned their backs on their positivist inheritance, and, dismissing the hope of discovering objective laws governing the course of human history as a will-o'-the-wisp, they fell back instead on the less exacting task of providing society with a 'collective memory.'[201] The social sciences followed a different course. Whereas historians, their confidence undermined by historicists such as Rickert and Dilthey, were unable to make up their minds whether their investigations should be considered scientific or not, for sociologists and anthropologists science – defined by Einstein as the endeavour 'to make the chaotic diversity of our sense-experience correspond to a logically uniform system of thought' by correlating 'single experiences' with 'the theoretic structure'[202] – is the essence of their work. They cannot repudiate the goals and methods of scientific enquiry without at the same time cutting away the ground from under their own feet; if they cannot claim to be furnishing society with certain knowledge arrived at by certain methods, they can claim nothing at all.[203] Naturally, they have refined their positivist inheritance in a multitude of ways;[204] but they have never abandoned its basic tenet, the belief in the validity of a science of man.

It is this belief in the possibility of a scientific approach to the investigation of human society that is the main contribution of the social sciences in

---

200. Typical examples of organizing concepts used by historians are imperialism, capitalism, feudalism, revolution, democracy, the Russian peasant, the Renaissance humanist, the benevolent despot; cf. *The Social Sciences in Historical Study* (1954), p. 94.

201. This is the definition of the historian's function adopted, e.g., by RENIER, *History. Its Purpose and Method* (1950), pp. 19, 24.

202. Cf. ANDERLE, 'Theoretische Geschichte' (1958), p. 28 in *Historische Zeitschrift*, Vol. CLXXXV.

203. As A. S. EISENSTADT observes in 'American history and social science', *op. cit.* (1963): p. 120 in EISENSTADT, A. S. (ed.), *The Craft of American History*, Vol. II (1966).

204. It need hardly be said that it is none of my business to discuss them; but cf. for example MACRAE's remarks, pp. 126-130 in PLUMB (ed.), *Crisis in the Humanities* (1964).

general, and of sociology and anthropology in particular, to historians seeking a way out of the cul-de-sac into which a rigid adherence to historicist preconceptions had led them. As Tawney once pithily observed, 'There is no reason why savages should have all the science.'[205] If anthropologists using scientific methods could explain the working of primitive societies and sociologists using similar methods could cast light on the structure and functioning of contemporary society, it was not easy to find convincing reasons why historians should not approach the study of past societies in similar ways. The applicability of particular techniques or particular concepts might be open to question; but the example of the social sciences was undoubtedly the most important factor encouraging historians to re-open the question of the possibility of scientific history. 'History', wrote R. H. S. Crossman, 'need no longer remain either a story with a moral (Plutarch) or a bogus branch of physics, chemistry and biology (Herbert Spencer), if the historian, building on the discoveries of social science, seeks to observe those uniformities through which the patterns of human behaviour can be correlated – and ultimately predicted.'[206]

If we seek, therefore, to specify the ways in which the social sciences have affected the attitudes and presuppositions of historians, there is no doubt that the first and most general result was a major shift of focus, from the particular to the general, from events to uniformities, and from narrative to analysis. In this respect it is unnecessary to draw too firm a line between anthropology and sociology. Some writers, it is true, have placed particular emphasis on anthropology, often said to be the social science 'most congenial' to historians.[207] Thus Bagby has insisted that history, if it is ever to become more than a 'semi-rational activity', must 'rely heavily on anthropology' for concepts and methods;[208] and Evans-Pritchard has even asserted that 'history must choose between being social anthropology or being nothing.'[209] And it is, of course, evident that anthropology has exerted an independent influence in a number of ways. It has served, for example, as a corrective to the historian's inherent ethnocentrism, has shown that the writing of history is not dependent upon the availability of written records, and has provided tools for historians concerned with areas (e.g., Africa) where written records are rare or non-existent. These are points to which we shall return. It also needs no particular demonstration to perceive that historians dealing with such institutions as kingship can profitably make use of the work of anthropologists such as Vansina on African kingdoms or Evans-Pritchard on divine kingship among the Shilluk people of the Sudan;[210] and the same applies to

205. Cf. Keith THOMAS, 'History and anthropology', p. 12 in *Past and Present* (1963).
206. Cited by ANDERLE, *op. cit.* (1958), pp. 6-7.
207. Cf. *The Social Sciences in Historical Study* (1954), p. 35.
208. BAGBY, *Culture and History* (1958), pp. 20, 50.
209. *Op. cit.* (1962), p. 64; but it is only right to add that he also asserted the reverse.
210. Cf. VANSINA, 'A comparison of African kingdoms' (1962); EVANS-PRITCHARD,

many other aspects of social life from marriage and divorce to blood-feuds, rebellion and millenarian movements. It is not, as Keith Thomas has pointed out, that there is any shortage of historical material about these subjects, but rather that historians have never studied them in the way that anthropologists have learnt to do. Anthropological studies of primitive mentality, for example, can provide medievalists hampered by the paucity of evidence for the ideas and attitudes of the serf in medieval Europe with valuable insights, for it would be stretching probability too far to suppose that peasant societies everywhere did not have a number of features in common.[211]

When, however, we turn from such specific instances to the more general impact of anthropology and sociology, it is not easy to differentiate between them. The links between social anthropology and sociology are, after all, extremely close and growing steadily closer,[212] and it is not surprising that historians have been more interested in what they have in common than in their differences. If we survey the by now fairly extensive body of literature in which the impact of sociology and anthropology on the study of history is examined, we find a fair measure of agreement on a number of general propositions, and it is sufficient for present purposes to list them briefly.[213]

The Divine Kingship of the Shilluk of the Nilotic Sudan (1948, 1962).

211. Cf. THOMAS, K., *op. cit.* (1963), pp. 10, 16-17.

212. Cf. the remarks in SIEGEL (ed.), *Biennial Review of Anthropology, 1965*, pp. 182 sqq.

213. In addition to works already cited, the following are some of the more important studies: CAHNMAN & BOSKOFF (eds.), *Sociology and History. Theory and Research* (1964); LIPSET & HOFSTADTER (eds.), *Sociology and History. Methods* (1968); *Istorija i sociologija* (1964); SAVETH (ed.), *American History and the Social Sciences* (1964); DOVRING, *History as a Social Science* (1960); PERKIN, 'Social history' (1962); LEFF, *History and Social Theory* (1969); BENSON, *Toward the Scientific Study of History* (selected essays, 1971); KOMAROVSKY (ed.), *Common Frontiers of the Social Sciences* (1957); LEWIS, I. M. (ed.), *History and Social Anthropology* (1968); KRUITHOF, 'Qu'est ce qui est important dans l'histoire? Une approche socio-logique' (1963); COCHRAN, *The Inner Revolution. Essays on the Social Sciences in American History* (1964), collected papers among which two are particularly note-worthy: 'The social sciences and the problem of historical synthesis' (originally published as 'The "presidential synthesis" in American history', 1948), and 'History and the social sciences' (1955); *American Journal of Sociology*, Vols. LXIII (1957), pp. 1-16, and LXV (1959), pp. 32-38, articles by HALPERN, THRUPP and WOLFF; HOFSTADTER, 'History and the social sciences' (1956); LASLETT, 'History and the social sciences' (1968); BARRACLOUGH, 'Scientific method and the work of the his-torian' (1962); HOLLOWAY, 'History and sociology' (1967), and 'Sociology and his-tory' (1963); MORAZÉ, 'The application of the social sciences to history' (1968); COBBAN, 'History and sociology' (1961); AYDELOTTE, 'Geschichte und Sozialwissen-schaften' (1954); BOSL, 'Geschichte und Soziologie' (1956), and 'Der soziologische Aspekt in der Geschichte' (1965); SCHIEDER, Th., 'Strukturen und Persönlichkeiten in der Geschichte' (1962); PITZ, 'Strukturen. Betrachtungen zur angeblichen Grund-lagenkrise in der Geschichtswissenschaft' (1964); STAERMAN, 'K probleme struktur-nogo analiza v istorii' (= On the problem of structural analysis in history) (1968); BARG, 'Strukturnyj analiz v istoričeskom issledovanii' (= Structural analysis in historical research) (1964).

1. First, and basic to all else, is the realization that the 'model' of historical understanding constructed by neo-idealists such as Rickert, Dilthey, Croce and Collingwood, is not obligatory; or, as one writer puts it, 'if some historians see no generalities in their data, it is because they do not look for them', not because they are not there.[214] Philosophically, it was always possible to question the validity of the neo-idealist position.[215] The contribution of anthropologists and sociologists is to have demonstrated that these philosophic doubts are empirically justified; in other words, that meaningful results are obtainable by methods which, according to neo-idealist theory, are inapplicable to the study of human society.

2. In particular, anthropologists and sociologists have demonstrated that the alleged 'uniqueness' of historical facts, which is supposed to make the scientific study of history impracticable (and, if practised, misleading), is a myth. Even if historians are concerned for preference with the deviant rôles that induce change – the personality, for example, of Napoleon or Hitler – rather than with understanding the pattern of the normal ones, it still remains true, as has often been pointed out, that deviant rôles cannot be adequately understood without understanding of the norms from which deviation has taken place; or, as Huizinga put it, 'the concrete can be distinguished only by means of the abstract', the 'particular' only 'within a general frame'.[216] More than this, however, the individual who has played so central a part in traditional historical writing, is also an 'abstraction'; he 'is as much a construct as the concept of a group', can be 'observed only through a series of actions', and is 'a conceptual rather than a perceptual unity'.[217] Indeed, if the singular or individual is, as is often argued, 'ineffable', it follows that it is *ipso facto* unknowable.[218] Hence the paradox that knowledge of large-scale events is potentially more accurate than knowledge of the small-scale events which historians so carefully describe; or, as von Bertalanffy says, 'it is the statistical or mass model' – not the individual action – 'which is backed by empirical evidence.'[219]

3. One result of the reassessment of the role of the individual is to dispel the nightmare of historical determinism, which has proved so powerful an inhibition against any attempt to establish regularities in history. No one denies that the individual is free to choose among certain courses of action. It is also true that his freedom of choice is conditioned, both by concrete

214. CAHNMAN & BOSKOFF (eds.), *op. cit.* (1964), p. 5.

215. Cf. GARDINER, *The Nature of Historical Explanation* (1952), pp. 44, 64.

216. STERN (ed.), *Varieties of History* (1956), pp. 298-299; *The Social Sciences in Historical Study* (1954), p. 50.

217. KOMAROVSKY, Introduction, p. 16 in KOMAROVSKY (ed.), *Common Frontiers . . .*, *op. cit.* (1957); cf. BRAUDEL, 'Positions de l'histoire en 1950' (Leçon inaugurale, 1950), p. 21 in *Ecrits sur l'histoire* (1969).

218. *De singularibus non est cognoscendum*; cf. LEBRUN, 'Structure et quantification', pp. 41-42 in PERELMAN (ed.), *Raisonnement et démarches de l'historien* (1963).

219. Von BERTALANFFY, *General Systems*, Vol. VII (1962), p. 17; cf. BAGBY, *Culture and History* (1958), pp. 35-36; DOVRING, *History as a Social Science* (1960), p. 78.

external circumstances and also by ingrained attitudes and values, which 'are not simply distributed at random', but are 'interdependent, arranged in a pattern, and subject to reciprocal variation'.[220] In abstract that may be little more than a platitude. The contribution of sociology is to make it precise; that is to say, it shows that free choice or free will is not merely an arbitrary factor – a sort of *Deus ex machina* which precludes any rational ordering of human history – but that, on the contrary, it is susceptible of rational analysis and even of mathematical formulation.[221] In this way, it enables us, in Braudel's words, to 'transcend' the individual, to understand that history is not merely the unique and individual – 'that which is not seen twice' – but that individual events and episodes are parts of a more complex and durable reality, namely society.[222]

4. Sociology and anthropology have, therefore, opened the way – it always existed, but it was hidden beneath a thick historicist undergrowth – from the individual to the typical and from the single event (or chain of events) to the underlying structural framework within which events and personalities operate. This framework constitutes, in the words of Professor Forbes, 'the foundation of the whole social life of any continuing society',[223] and the new emphasis on structure, on the persistence of 'an organized system of actions that exhibits an appreciable degree of temporal continuity', is probably the most distinctive single contribution of sociology and anthropology to history. Its significance has already been briefly discussed.[224]

5. The social structure is not, of course, something which can be directly observed. Rather, it is a set of abstractions derived from analysis of observed behaviour; but by relating these abstractions logically, so that they present a pattern, we are able to see society in its essentials and as a single whole. Anthropologists and sociologists believe that 'an understanding of human behaviour can only be reached by viewing it in its full social setting'; they 'view every institution as a functioning part of a whole society', and their object is to disclose the structural patterns of that society.[225]

6. Concern with structural patterns, rather than with establishing a causally linked series of events, necessarily results in a shift of emphasis. The anthropologist is concerned first and foremost with domestic and community relationships, with family, kinship, law, and other determinants of social conduct (e.g., taboo); the sociologist is concerned mainly with the normative structure of contemporary society, e.g., the aspirations and mobility of different social groups, the quest of individuals for status and security, voting preferences and habits, shifting patterns of industrial enterprise and employment, the role and identity of minority groups. But these or similar

220. *The Social Sciences in Historical Study*, p. 43.
221. As pointed out, e.g., by von BERTALANFFY, *op. cit.*, p. 17.
222. Cf. BRAUDEL, 'Positions de l'histoire en 1950' and 'Histoire et sociologie' (1958), pp. 21, 102 in *Ecrits sur l'histoire* (1969).
223. Cited by Keith THOMAS, *op. cit.* (1963), p. 17.
224. Above, pp. 38-40.
225. Cf. EVANS-PRITCHARD, 'Social anthropology: past and present', pp. 19, 23, 24 in *Essays in Social Anthropology, op. cit.* (1962).

institutions and relationships manifestly played an equally important role in the societies about which historians write. Why, then, should they be left to sociologists and anthropologists? The simple answer is that traditional historical methods provided no satisfactory techniques for dealing with them. The importance of anthropology and sociology is, therefore, not merely that they directed the historian's attention to such matters, but also that they indicated how they could be handled and evaluated.

7. Hitherto historians, where they have dealt with society, have treated it for the most part as an impressionistic 'backcloth', roughly sketched in, against which the drama of political events was played out. Once the importance of the structural factors in history was admitted, it became evident that the structural patterns must be studied for themselves. The result was not merely a widening of subject matter, but a radical change in perspective. It meant, for example, the displacement of the state, the focus of traditional political history, by society, the realization that the predominance of the political unit is confined (and even then incompletely) to a relatively short phase of history (essentially the nineteenth and early twentieth centuries), and that the effective unities of social life may (and usually do) transcend, or alternatively cut across, political boundaries. Thus it is more intelligible to study the structure of Balkan civilisation as a whole than the separate histories of Bulgaria, Serbia, Rumania or Croatia,[226] and it is more intelligible, as Marc Bloch showed us, to study Berry, Brittany, Lorraine, Languedoc – regions 'of very profound human differences', whose structures 'differ more widely from each other than from their immediate political neighbours' – than it is to study medieval France.[227] 'These regional and linguistic groupings have a cohesion of their own, which corresponds with idiomatic ways of conducting life from birth to death, distinctions of class and status, forms of property tenure and modes of commercial life;' and it goes without saying that habits so deeply ingrained affected people's attitudes and responses, including their political responses.[228]

8. The further result of the new emphasis on structure was to shake the hitherto almost axiomatic belief in the primacy of political history. Contrary to common opinion, political history in the traditional sense of a narrative of political events has no appreciable practical or didactic value.[229] It continues to be written because there is an avid public demand for it, but most professional historians today would agree with Jaime Vicens Vives that it has nothing 'essentially new' to contribute.[230] Furthermore, the

226. Cf. STOIANOVICH, *A Study in Balkan Civilisation* (1967); it should hardly be necessary to add that BRAUDEL's work, *La Méditerranée et le monde méditerranéen à l'époque de Philippe II* (1949), exemplifies a similar approach to Mediterranean history.

227. BLOCH, *Les caractères originaux de l'histoire rurale française* (new edn., 1952), p. ix (English translation, *French Rural History*, 1966, pp. xxiv-xxv).

228. Cf. MORRISON, *Europe's Middle Ages* (1970), p. 13.

229. Cf. DOVRING, *op. cit.* (1960), pp. 54, 89.

230. Cf. VICENS VIVES, *Approaches to the History of Spain* (English translation, 1967), p. 176 (Spanish original, *Aproximación a la historia de España*, 1960).

habit of using political events as a criterion by which to group, order and correlate history may often be positively misleading. Braudel has written of the shortsightedness of historians who suppose that the course of events since 1945 was shaped by the Yalta or Potsdam agreements,[231] and T. C. Cochran, in a much cited article, showed how the American civil war, 'that great divide of American historiography,' shrinks in magnitude when viewed in the light of 'long-run social criteria.' To divide, arrange and categorize events in terms of reigns, wars, administrations – Louis XIV, the Second World War, the Truman administration – emphasizes the short-term at the expense of the long-term. 'While events are an indispensable part of the data of history, and even chance events ... may have strong repercussions on their environment, the use of social sciences approaches focuses attention on the aspects of the event that reveal the major dynamics of the culture.'[232]

9. The historian's central concern, says Cochran, should therefore 'be the material and psychological changes that have most affected ... such human conditioning factors as family life, physical living conditions ... and fundamental beliefs', and these factors should determine the 'topical and chronological divisions.' This, no doubt, is what Braudel meant when he urged historians to concentrate on 'les réalités sociales.' It is what Jaime Vicens Vives had in mind when he exhorted Spanish historians to abandon the old 'stereotypes and platitudes' and turn instead to 'the basic factors' – 'men, misery, and famine; epidemics and death; land ownership, the relations between a lord and his vassal ... between an employer and a worker ... between a priest and a believer ... '. This does not imply merely a preference for 'the structural basis' – in other words, another subjective and arbitrary choice. On the contrary, it is necessary because it is only when we know what is normal that we have any standard of measurement by which to evaluate the singular or accidental.[233]

10. But how are we to establish the social realities and the structural basis? As the poet Gray long ago observed, the annals of the poor are short and simple. Their place in historical records is extremely limited. Furthermore, historical materials have their own inherent bias. Any manuscript collection is at best an accidental historical accretion, pointing perhaps to conclusions that are completely different from those we would reach, if all the related manuscripts had been preserved. Nor, contrary to common belief, is the situation different if we turn from narrative sources to archaeological evidence.[234] In addition, the historian imports his own bias, not in this instance in the crude sense of imposing his prejudices in his interpretation of the evidence, but more directly in the very process of selecting

231. 'La longue durée' (1958, 1969), p. 63 in BRAUDEL, *Ecrits sur l'histoire* (1969).

232. *The Social Sciences in Historical Study*, pp. 163, 170.

233. *Ibid.*, p. 169; BRAUDEL, 'Positions de l'histoire en 1950', p. 23 in *Ecrits ...*, *op. cit.* (1969); VICENS VIVES, *op. cit.* (English translation, 1967), p. xxiv.

234. Cf. ROWNEY & GRAHAM (eds.), *Quantitative History* (1969), pp. 78, 122; DOVRING, *op. cit.*, p. 35.

the evidence which seems important. As Tilly has put it, 'the implicit structure of explanation', the formulation of the question to be answered, influences the search for data; and it is not surprising that historians interested in the rôle of individuals, their motivations and responsibilities, should ignore categories of evidence which apparently have little, if any, direct bearing on the questions with which they are immediately concerned.[235] In any case, they are led in this direction by the ordinary historical sources (chronicles, annals, memoirs, letters) which take the normal for granted, as something known and not requiring explanation, and concentrate instead on the exceptional events or personalities which strike the writer (naturally enough) as more interesting and therefore more worthy of being recorded. Thus one main reason, apart from curiosity, for the traditional historian's emphasis on outstanding personalities is the simple one that their actions are better recorded (to say nothing of often being deliberately magnified), whereas historical data on average people and everyday situations are hard to find. The conclusion is that the historian concerned not with single events but with social structures must 'generate' his own data from specific types of documents which 'idiographic' history, precisely because it is idiographic, has ignored. There can, in other words, be no question of simply revising our picture of the past by approaching the existing documentation from a different point of view. On the contrary, the historian who wishes to elucidate social structures and social relations cannot escape the enormous labour of compiling a new documentation which corresponds to the new questions.[236]

11. It is at this point that the 'alternative logic' of sociology has most to offer to historians. Sociology and anthropology provide alternative ways of looking at the evidence which practical experience has shown to be helpful; indeed, it has been pointed out with great cogency that if historians neglect them, they will 'miss many of the problems', fail to ask the right questions (i.e., 'questions which elicit replies'), and consequently be unable to provide satisfactory answers.[237] A sociological conception of what is to be explained, and how it is to be explained, leads to different ways of dividing up the material, the exploration of different types of data, different methods of handling the data, different criteria of the crucial issues, and new conclusions. At the same time, it also clarifies the traditional controversies, provides techniques to deal not only with the new subject-matter, but also with familiar historical problems.

12. It does this, above all else, by introducing greater precision of thought than is usually found in historical writing. At first sight this may seem paradoxical. Nothing is apparently more exact and definite than the his-

235. Cf. TILLY, 'The analysis of a counter-revolution', pp. 188-190, 196 in ROWNEY & GRAHAM (eds.), *op. cit.*

236. ROWNEY & GRAHAM (eds.), *op. cit.*, p. 63; BRAUDEL, 'Positions de l'histoire en 1950', p. 25 in *Ecrits . . ., op. cit.*

237. Cf. EVANS-PRITCHARD, 'Anthropology and history' (1961, 1962), p. 59 in *Essays in Social Anthropology* (1962).

torian's habitual concentration on concrete detail. But this appearance of exactitude is deceptive. The idea that history is a series of self-explanatory concrete facts is an assumption of the same order as Dr. Johnson's proof of the reality of a chair by kicking it, or the refutation of the Copernican system by pointing out that anyone can see the sun moving across the skies from morning to night. The common-sense assumptions on which historians rely amount, in fact, to vague, untested, unreliable generalizations, whose 'validity is frequently not much greater than the explanations of physical events given by primitive tribes.'[238] They assume that they know the laws of human behaviour and use them as yardsticks, instead of testing them by means of historical evidence, with results which are demonstrably false, as John Demos has shown, for example, in the field of family history.[239] But even where we may believe that their conclusions are valid, the impressionistic nature of their methods makes it impossible to test or confirm them. For example, 'historians use haphazard quotations from newspapers without any awareness of modern content analysis techniques'; they fail to make their assumptions explicit and are unsystematic in their generalizations.[240] One of the main practical contributions of sociology is to provide them with tools and techniques by which this lack of precision can be corrected; it enables the historian to replace inspired guesses by exact and rigorously constructed hypotheses.

13. Among these techniques there is no doubt that quantitative analysis holds the first place; indeed, it may be said that it is not so much a technique as the basic procedure underlying most other techniques. For this reason, and because of all current trends it is the most powerful, we shall discuss it separately.[241] All generalizations are inherently quantitative in character, and although they may not be aware of it, historians who use terms such as 'typical', 'representative', 'significant' or 'widespread', are making vague and indefinite quantitative statements, whether or not they present figures to justify their assertions. The principal value of quantification, in its broadest sense, is that it provides a means of verifying general statements of this sort; in other words, the issue raised by quantitative analysis is simply the extent to which historians are willing to substitute relatively precise quantitative statements for the imprecise ones they are in the habit of making.[242]

14. But quantification is not the only criterion of systematic methodology, and although it may be currently the most significant contribution of social science to the historian's technical equipment, it is not the only one. The requirement that data should be compiled, classified and analysed compre-

238. Cf. BAGBY, *Culture and History* (1958), p. 37.

239. DEMOS's article, 'Families in colonial Bristol' (1968), is reprinted in ROWNEY & GRAHAM (eds.), *op. cit.*, pp. 293-307.

240. *Ibid.*, p. 121; KOMAROVSKY, Introduction (quoting LAZARSFELD, unpublished paper), p. 29 in KOMAROVSKY (ed.), *Common Frontiers . . .*, *op. cit.* (1957).

241. Cf. below, pp. 84-94.

242. Cf. BENSON, p. 117 in KOMAROVSKY (ed.), *op. cit.* (1957); ROWNEY & GRAHAM (eds.), *op. cit.* (1969), pp. vii, 4.

hensively and rigorously, not partially or in an haphazard fashion, may lead to mathematical formulations, but it does not necessarily do so, and perhaps in some instances it cannot do so. Thus anthropologists have succeeded, without recourse to quantification, in establishing certain propositions of universal validity (e.g., every culture includes some form of religion, or every culture includes prohibitions of incest).[243] And, more significantly, sociologists have formulated what may be called 'organizing concepts', or 'conceptual images', of which Max Weber's 'ideal types' (e.g., bureaucracy, status groups, charismatic leadership) are the best known examples. The theories advanced by sociologists to account for and establish patterns of social change are another example of systematic analysis which, of its nature, is not and cannot be quantitative.[244]

15. Max Weber regarded the formation of typological concepts as the major contribution of sociology to history. The essential quality of such types, or models, is that, though derived from empirical (frequently historical) data, they seek to go beyond the data and establish abstract concepts or correlations. Such models may claim universal validity (in which case they are usually designated 'ideal types'); but in practice they usually apply to particular societies at particular times. This is true, for example, of Weber's concepts of the city and of bureaucracy, which are seen as elements in an historical configuration called 'modern capitalism', although it is also true (as Weber pointed out) that what is specifically characteristic of the European (or western) city can only be ascertained through considering what is lacking in other (e.g., ancient Chinese or Islamic) cities, and is therefore (or may therefore be seen as) a stage towards the construction of an 'ideal type' of the city, relevant to all times and places.[245] In either case, the essential purpose is to abstract from the complexity of historical events the predominant traits of at least relatively stable structures. The value of such theoretical models lies in their ability to give organization and meaning to otherwise diffuse data; they help historians to escape from the limitations of particularity.

16. The importance of models for the historian is not that they offer him solutions, but that they indicate relationships and patterns which he can profitably employ in interpreting historical evidence. Elements and lines of investigation that would not occur to the empiricist relying on ordinary 'common sense' may often be suggested by the results of logical theorizing. Clearly, the use of models can be abused and misused, like any other method; in particular, it is dangerously easy to fit facts to theory, instead of using them to test theory. But it is important to note that a theoretical model does not necessarily have to be true to be useful, nor does the fact

243. BAGBY, *op. cit.*, p. 135; cf. BRAUDEL, 'La longue durée' (1958, 1969), p. 70 in *Ecrits . . ., op. cit.*

244. Cf. BOSKOFF's article, 'Recent theories of social change' (1964), and HAGEN, *On the Theory of Social Change* (1962).

245. Max WEBER, *The City* (English translation, 1958); cf. CAHNMAN & BOSKOFF (eds.), *Sociology and History, op. cit.* (1964), pp. 118-119, 127.

that the historian can dredge up a few random examples which appear to discredit it necessarily destroy its validity. Types are meant to be conceptual images, not descriptions of actual events or situations. It is possible that confrontation with factual situations will bring to light flaws or ambiguities which may require the conceptual image to be remodelled or sometimes even discarded. But the resulting recognition of reality nevertheless rests upon the classificatory scaffolding which has been erected, and almost inevitably the process of confrontation will have called attention to previously unnoticed characteristics of the evidence.[246]

17. Although it cannot be our purpose here to discuss in detail the different models used by sociologists, a few examples will help to clarify the way in which they have affected historical study. Such models can obviously be of various scales of magnitude, varying from the small-scale particularized concepts which are the historian's ordinary stock-in-trade (the battle of Stalingrad, the anti-Hitler plot, the Second World War) to what Braudel has called 'immense Weberian abstractions',[247] i.e., attempts to construct single generalized systems comprehending the whole range of social phenomena. Experience has shown that neither of these is a satisfactory conceptual tool, and the tendency today is to concentrate instead on the 'middle range' of conceptual models, i.e., to analyse significant clusters of facts with a view to establishing correlations, configurations and coherent patterns which explain, in part or in whole, the actual working of particular societies at particular times. Thus, to take a few simple examples, much effort has gone into the analysis of voting patterns and voting behaviour, of public opinion, and of social mobility, all subjects of evident interest and importance to the historian.[248] On a larger scale, one may instance Schumpeter's famous concept of the entrepreneur as the architect of innovation and economic progress, which was the starting-point for a long series of empirical studies, or the attempt of Sigmund Diamond, on the basis of a study of American businessmen, to set up a model of the reactions of all dominant classes when they feel that their privileges and status are threatened.[249] Similarly, it is easy to see that the concepts used by social scientists in their studies of urban sociology and urbanization – beginning with the famous *Middletown* studies of the Lynds – provide

246. *Ibid.*, p .11; cf. COCHRAN, in EISENSTADT, A. S. (ed.), *The Craft of American History*, Vol. II (1966), p. 101.

247. Cf. BRAUDEL, *op. cit.*, p. 184.

248. Cf. on voting behaviour, the papers by HEBERLE and BENSON in CAHNMAN & BOSKOFF (eds.), *op. cit.*, pp. 407-421 (the latter an excerpt from BENSON's *The Concept of Jacksonian Democracy*, 1961), and McCORMICK in ROWNEY & GRAHAM (eds.), *op. cit.*, pp. 372-384; on public opinion, BENSON, *ibid.*, pp. 23-63, and the discussion between LAZARSFELD, STRAYER and DAVID in KOMAROVSKY (ed.), *op. cit.*, pp. 242-274; on social mobility, the contributions of THERNSTROM, SMITH and STONE in ROWNEY & GRAHAM (eds.), *op. cit.*, pp. 99-108, 209-216, and 238-271.

249. SCHUMPETER, *The Theory of Economic Development* (1934) and *Capitalism, Socialism and Democracy* (1942); DIAMOND, *The Reputation of the American Businessman* (1955), particularly p. 182.

useful lines of approach for historians investigating the history of the city at different times and places in the past.[250]

18. No less important for historians than the models set up by sociologists are the methods used in creating these models. Their essential characteristic is the substitution of systematic analysis for narrative description. If we are concerned, for example, with such groups as the holders of earldoms in twelfth-century England, south German entrepreneurs in the sixteenth century, or American railroad leaders between 1845 and 1890 – that is to say, with a cluster of individuals with similar outlooks and ways of life, sharing common interests – how are we to gauge their attitudes and responses? Mere enumeration of a few individual instances and generalization therefrom – the historian's ordinary procedure – is clearly unlikely (except by a lucky guess) to produce a satisfactory answer; complete enumeration is, in practice, impossible, and if attempted only too likely to lead to the trite conclusion that 'things hang together in a perplexing tangle of causation beyond possibility of unravelment.'[251] What historians have begun to learn from sociologists, in short, is that a descriptive synthesis of events – even worse, a few impressionistically gathered examples, such as G. M. Trevelyan was content to string together in his *English Social History* – is no substitute for a theoretical integration of them, and that there are whole sectors (for example, public opinion) which cannot be made intelligible by traditional historical methods, but which do yield to sociological analysis.

19. It is clearly impossible here to enumerate all the specific forms of analysis which sociologists have brought to bear (in any case they are continually being refined and modified); but a few examples may indicate their significance. The historian, for instance, confronted by categories such as 'aristocracy' and 'bourgeoisie', is apt to conclude that they are so vague and indeterminate as to be unusable, and to reject them altogether.[252] The sociologist, on the other hand, attempts to make them precise and usable by the procedure known as 'group analysis' – that is to say, by analysing the bases of group formation, the processes of group cohesion, the condi-

250. LYND & LYND, *Middletown: A Study in Contemporary American Culture* (1929) and *Middletown in Transition* (1937); cf. HANDLIN & BURCHARD (eds.), *The Historian and the City* (1963); DYOS (ed.), *The Study of Urban History* (1968); CALLOW (ed.), *American Urban History* (1969).

251. This was the conclusion of Charles BOOTH after completing the seventeen volumes of his monumental work, *Life and Labour of the People in London* (3rd edn., 1902-1903) – a classical example of the intellectual sterility resulting from the separation of theory and empirical research, as S. W. F. HOLLOWAY points out in *History*, Vol. XLVIII, pp. 176-179.

252. 'No two people can agree on who the bourgeois and the aristocrats were; no one can formulate ... a criterion for distinguishing between them that can be followed consistently, and every argument is thus liable to be at variance with easily ascertainable facts.' – BEHRENS, ' "Straight history" and "history in depth" ', p. 125 in *Historical Journal* (1965). This scepticism was carried further, as is well known, by A. B. COBBAN in his book, *The Social Interpretation of the French Revolution* (1964).

tions of group action, and the structure and patterns of inter-group relations.[253] He seeks to discover what attitudes and ideas, or social or economic interests, the individual members of any politically or socially active
group (e.g., the Jacobins, the Farmers Grain Dealers Association of Iowa)
have in common, and to use these 'regularities' to establish the basis of
group cohesion and the structure of the group. Rather than accepting articulated beliefs (expressed, for example, in public statements, speeches,
pamphlets) as explanations of collective activities, sociologists see such beliefs as strongly influenced and limited by social structure, and therefore
concentrate on analysis of the composition of the group and, more generally, of the conditions under which a group of men will fight in the name
of a set of beliefs. This is the way in which historians such as Brinton,
Soboul and Rudé have sought to analyse such groups as the Jacobins and
the *sans-culottes,* asking first who were the participants, how they differed
from other people, how they were organized, what were their relations to
other similar groups, and only after this detailed analysis turning to the
question of their motives.[254] Meanwhile, in the analysis of the group, other
more specific techniques and concepts have been devised: e.g., rôle analysis, defined as 'anticipated uniformities in response or behaviour when a
given type of person, such as a middle-aged railroad executive, is confronted with a specific social situation', and reference group analysis, i.e.,
the concept that each individual belongs to a number of groups (church,
family, club, business or profession), whose standards of conduct he will
be expected (and usually will strive) to fulfil and which can exert varying
degrees of pressure forcing him to conform. Such correlations are evidently
an important factor in the analysis of voting behaviour and voting
patterns.[255]

20. If, in conclusion, we wish to measure the influence of sociological
conceptions on historical attitudes, we may think that it is nowhere better
expressed than in Alexander Gerschenkron's definition of the purposes of
history. 'Historical research,' says Gerschenkron, 'consists essentially in application to empirical material of various sets of empirically derived hypothetical generalizations and in testing the closeness of the resulting fit,
in the hope that in this way certain uniformities, certain typical situations,
and certain typical relationships among individual factors in these situations
can be ascertained.'[256] Such a definition would have been unthinkable for
most historians a generation ago, and is a measure of the impact of the
social sciences on historical thinking. What it signifies is the discovery by

253. Cf. *The Social Sciences in Historical Study,* pp. 44-47.
254. Cf. BRINTON, *The Jacobins* (1930); SOBOUL, *Les sans-culottes parisiens en
l'an II* (1958); RUDÉ, *The Crowd in the French Revolution* (1959); cf. HAYS in
EISENSTADT, A. S. (ed.), *The Craft of American History,* Vol. II (1966), pp. 132 sqq.,
and TILLY in ROMNEY & GRAHAM (eds.), *Quantitative History* (1969), p. 207.
255. Cf. COCHRAN, *Railroad Leaders* (1953), p. 13; on reference group theory,
cf. KOMAROVSKY (ed.), *Common Frontiers of the Social Sciences* (1957), pp. 394 sqq.
256. Cf. GERSCHENKRON, *Economic Backwardness in Historical Perspective*
(1962), pp. 5-6.

historians that a descriptive synthesis – a synthesis in terms of great men and a sequence of important or unique events – is no substitute for a theoretical integration.[257] Evans-Pritchard uses as an illustration the struggle between King John of England and the English barons, leading up to Magna Carta. This struggle, he says,[258] is meaningful only when the relations between the barons and John's predecessors on the English throne are also known, and also when the relations between kings and barons in other countries with feudal institutions are known – 'in other words, where the struggle is seen as a phenomenon typical of, or common to, societies of a certain kind'.

The specificity of King John and Robert FitzWalter as individuals loses much of its importance when they are viewed in their rôles as representatives of a characteristic set of social relations. Of course, things would have been in some respects different if someone else had been in John's place, but they would have been in other, and more fundamental, respects the same. An historical fact thus shorn of its unique features escapes also temporality. It is no longer a passing incident, a sort of accident, but is, as it were, taken out of the flux of time and achieves conceptual stability as a sociological proposition.

21. 'History', says the distinguished French historian, Frédéric Mauro, 'is the projection of the social sciences into the past.'[259] This programmatic statement sums up the changes of the last twenty years. No doubt, it is a formulation which many members of the historical profession, even today, would be reluctant to endorse; but it is at least indicative of what has been the most powerful contemporary trend in historical studies. It should, of course, be emphasized that the traffic is not all in one direction, and that if historians are increasingly aware of the contribution which sociology and anthropology can make to their work, they also believe that history can add a new, and vitally important, dimension to sociology and anthropology – namely the dimension of time, to which, it is generally admitted, sociologists and anthropologists have paid too little attention.[260]

It is also true that the impact of the social sciences – with the sole exception of economics[261] – has been more in the nature of a general stimulus than the specific assimilation of new techniques. Historians have not yet, for example, in their treatment of developing societies, reached anything like the degree of precision that anthropologists have attained in the study of primitive societies, nor have they derived much benefit from the progress of modern linguistics.[262] Much, therefore, remains to be done to bring the methodology of history up to the level of that of the other social

257. THOMAS, K., 'History and anthropology', *op. cit.* (1963), p. 6.
258. EVANS-PRITCHARD, 'Anthropology and history' (1961, 1962), p. 49 in *Essays in Social Anthropology* (1962).
259. Cited by DAVIS, R., *History and the Social Sciences* (1965), p. 3.
260. Cf. KON, 'Istorija i sociologija' (1970) (French translation, 'Histoire et sociologie', 1971).
261. Cf. below, pp. 72-77.
262. Cf. the criticisms of KOSELLECK, 'Wozu noch Historie?' (1971), pp. 1-8 in *Historische Zeitschrift*, Vol. CCXII (on linguistics, p. 15).

sciences. The reason, fundamentally, is that, in spite of all that has been written on the subject, only a handful of historians have more than a smattering of sociology, political theory or psychology, and less than one per cent even an elementary statistical and mathematical training.[263] As if in reply to Mauro, many historians prefer to think of themselves as 'having contacts with the social sciences', rather than as being social scientists; what they envisage, as Vann Woodward wittily observes, is not a marriage but a liaison, an *entente cordiale* rather than an *Anschluss*.[264] But there is also a strong tendency in other quarters to emphasize the unity of the 'human sciences', of which history is one.[265] If there is little intrinsic difference between the areas of cultural or social anthropology and sociology, and both interlock with psychology, in the sense that psychological considerations enter implicitly or explicitly into all considerations of human action, the same is true of history. Having outlined, with specific reference to sociology, the more general results of the new contacts between the social sciences and history, it is therefore necessary to turn, more briefly, to the impact of other branches, beginning with psychology.

Psychology and History

Concern with the psychological aspects of history is, of course, in itself nothing new. For Thucydides the ultimate key to all historical explanation lay in human nature, and historians, as disciples of Thucydides, have habitually thought of themselves as psychologists in their own right. What has changed is the place of psychology in historical research. First of all, emphasis has shifted from individual to social psychology. Secondly, the way historians make use of psychological knowledge is different: instead of treating human psychology as constant, unchanging and universal, and therefore as a fixed basis for interpreting human action, it is seen as one aspect in any social situation, which has to be explained like all others in its historical context. And finally, the progress of psychology itself since Freud published his first epoch-making works some seventy years ago, and particularly since the beginnings of active empirical research in social psychology in the 1930's, has laid the foundations for a much more rigorous and sophisticated use of psychological concepts in history than was previously the case.[266]

263. Cf. LEBRUN, 'Développement et histoire quantitative. Vers une historiométrie?', p. 600 in *Revue de l'Institut de Sociologie*, 1957, No. 4.

264. WOODWARD, 'History and the Third Culture', pp. 25-27 in *Journal of Contemporary History* III (2), 1968.

265. This is, of course, a central theme of the work of F. Braudel, as GLÉNISSON emphasizes: cf. *La recherche historique en France de 1940 à 1965* (1965), pp. lvi-lvii.

266. For the following cf. WEHLER, 'Zum Verhältnis von Geschichtswissenschaft und Psychoanalyse' (1969) (with full bibliographical references); also LANGER, 'The next assignment' (1958), reprinted in his *Explorations in Crisis* (1969); GRUHLE, *Geschichtsschreibung und Psychologie* (1953); PORŠNEV, *Social'naja psihologija i*

Not surprisingly, it was the field of individual psychology that first attracted historians' attention. For historians of an older generation this interest requires no explanation. Convinced of the pre-eminent role in history of 'great men', and believing that their primary task was to analyse their motives and actions, they had no hesitation in making use, where necessary, of psychological (and, in the post-Freudian generation, of psychoanalytical) explanations. More significant is the recent revival of what has come to be called 'psychohistory'. E. H. Erikson's studies of Luther and Gandhi are early and well known examples of this genre,[267] but since 1970 it has had a considerable vogue, though the signs are that it may now have passed its peak. The reasons are not difficult to perceive.[268] Essentially, they turn on the question whether individual psychology, with its inherent emphasis on the individual personality as the key to historical events, has any substantive contribution to make to the work of the historian; and this question is equally valid whether we are discussing Freud's own forays into historical psychology, the now totally discredited popular or semipopular psychoanalytical biographies of the 1920's (e.g., Emil Ludwig's *Bismarck*), or the more sophisticated writing of contemporary psychoanalytical historians.

This is a complicated question, involving as it does the further question of the relationship between history and biography, and it must suffice here to note the views of contemporary writers. These are, in general, sceptical. For most historians today, recent attempts to reactivate psychoanalytic biography seem at once irrelevant and reactionary.[269] Having learnt from sociology the limits of individual action, they view with suspicion the inherent tendency in writing of this sort to emphasize the decisive importance of the actions and decisions of individual personalities and their psychical preconditions. Psychoanalysis, it is conceded, may help to explain the importance of an historical event for an individual; it does not explain the

---

istorija (1966); PORŠNEV & ANCIFEROVA (eds.), *Istorija i psihologija* (1970); *The Social Sciences in Historical Study* (1954), pp. 58-68; MAZLISH (ed.), *Psychoanalysis and History* (1963), where LANGER is also reprinted; MAZLISH, 'Group psychology and problems of contemporary history' (1968); BESANÇON, 'Histoire et psychanalyse' (1964), 'Psychoanalysis: auxiliary science or historical method?' (1968), and 'Vers une histoire psychanalytique' (1969); DUPRONT, 'Problèmes et méthodes d'une histoire de la psychologie collective' (1961) and 'L'histoire après Freud' (1969); VERNANT, 'Histoire et psychologie' (1965); KAKAR, 'The logic of psychohistory' (1970); LIFTON, 'On psychology and history' (1964) and his collected papers, *History and Human Survival* (1969).

267. ERIKSON, *Young Man Luther* (1958); *Gandhi's Truth* (1969).

268. They are discussed by (among others) J. BARZUN, *Clio and the Doctors* (Chicago, 1973); H. GATZKE, 'Hitler and psychohistory', *American Historial Review*, Vol. LXXVIII (1973), pp. 394-401; and G. HIMMELFARB, 'The "New History"', *Commentary*, Vol. LIX (1975), pp. 72-78. Here also will be found reference to more recent forays by psycho-historians such as Binion, Waite and Mazlish, which it would be otiose to cite in detail here.

269. Cf. WEHLER, 'Zum Verhältnis ...', *op. cit.* (1969), p. 552 in *Historische Zeitschrift*, Vol. CCVIII; BESANÇON, 'Psychoanalysis ...', *op. cit.*, p. 150 in *Journal of Contemporary History* (1968).

event. Hitler's individual psychology is not the real question for the historian, but the state of German society which enabled him to rise to power and to retain it until April 1945.[270] And if it is replied that the two are somehow connected, the answer is that this is a matter of faith, rather than of demonstrable proof. The distinctive feature of Erikson's studies of Luther and Gandhi, it is sometimes said, is that they transcend the individual; Luther's crisis of identity was paradigmatic of the identity-crisis of sixteenth-century Germans, Gandhi's of that of twentieth-century Indians.[271] But this congenial theory, though it reflects what common sense would tell us, is more easily asserted than demonstrated; and reviewers have not been slow to point out the inherent difficulties.[272] The fact is that individual psychology has not been satisfactorily integrated with group psychology, the links between personality factors and the public arena, or between private motivations and public acts, have not been made clear. As Morazé has said, 'however brilliant their results', recent attempts to apply psychoanalysis to history 'never completely dispel the methodological doubt to which from the outset they give rise.'[273]

When we turn from individual psychology to social psychology the situation is different. Many years ago Henri Berr insisted that historical synthesis 'must lead ultimately ... to social psychology' – 'to a knowledge of the basic needs to which institutions and their changing manifestations are the response' – and from Berr's time forward historians have been increasingly aware of the importance of social psychology in the analysis of historical questions.[274] Both Bloch and Febvre had a deep interest in collective psychology, as seen in the case of the former in his book *Les rois thaumaturges* (1924), in the case of the latter in *Le problème de l'incroyance au XVIe siècle* (1942). The original stimulus without much doubt came from the studies of group behaviour, mass hysteria, collective consciousness and the irrational forces in history published by Gustave Le Bon, Graham Wallas and William McDougall at the turn of the nineteenth and twentieth centuries.[275] But the current concern with social psychology is more closely related to the active empirical research before and during the Second World War, and to the attempts to explain and analyse charac-

---

270. WEHLER, *op. cit.*, p. 549; the same point is made by BESANÇON, *op. cit.*, p. 153, when he writes that 'the neurosis of Tsar Ivan or of Dostoevsky is not a historical problem, nor does it solve any historical problem'.

271. WEHLER, *op. cit.*, pp. 544, 546; BESANÇON, *op. cit.*, p. 151; MAZLISH, 'Group psychology ...', *op. cit.*, pp. 168-169 in *Journal of Contemporary History* (1968); KAKAR, 'The logic ...', *op. cit.*, p. 194 in *Journal of Interdisciplinary History* (1970).

272. Cf. GEERTZ, p. 4 in *New York Review* XIII (9), 1969; POMPER, pp. 204, 206 in *History and Theory*, Vol. IX (1970).

273. MORAZÉ, 'The application of the social sciences to history', p. 210 in *Journal of Contemporary History* (1968); cf. also MAZLISH, *op. cit., ibid.*, pp. 163, 172.

274. BERR, 'Sur notre programme', p. 6 in *Revue de Synthèse historique*, No. 1 (1900). BERR's statement is reproduced in English translation in STERN (ed.), *The Varieties of History* (1956): cf. p. 253.

275. LE BON, *La psychologie des foules* (1895); WALLAS, *Human Nature in Politics* (1908); McDOUGALL, *An Introduction to Social Psychology* (1908).

teristic problems and phenomena of the contemporary world, such as violence, totalitarianism, racial confrontation, anti-Semitism, aggression, revolution, in terms of group psychology.[276] The events of recent history, as Mazlish has said, beg for explanation in terms of group psychology and group behaviour;[277] and if this is true of recent history, it is obviously true of other periods also. Devereux's investigation of classical Sparta, William Langer's analysis of the 'prolonged and widespread emotional strain' resulting from the epidemics of late medieval Europe, and Lefebvre's classical study of the mass hysteria of 1789 in France, are examples of the insights which psychology has to offer to the historian.[278]

As these examples show, the field in which psychology has made most impact on history, is the analysis of collective actions and reactions. And since the impact of irrational, subconscious forces is most clearly visible in times of disturbance and stress, following some particularly shattering experience – in fourteenth-century Europe, for example, the plague, in Germany after 1918 defeat in war, in the United States after 1968 the traumatic experience of the failure in Vietnam – historians have tended to concentrate on such periods. If every society has 'a unique psychological fabric', deriving at least in part from common experiences and attitudes, it seems reasonable (as William Langer has said) 'to suppose that any great crisis, such as famine, pestilence, natural disaster, or war, should leave its mark . . ., the intensity and duration of the impact depending, of course, on the nature and magnitude of the crisis.'[279] But, however justified in itself it may be, this emphasis on periods of crisis, and on the changes which they bring about, is only one particular application of group psychology, and one, moreover, which tends to single out the morbid and pathological elements at the expense of more normal reactions. Though normally submerged, the basic human drives and impulses are continuously at work in every society, and every sudden crisis is the outcome of a long silent process of maturing in the gestation of the collective psyche.[280]

The historian is not only confronted at every turn by what Vicens Vives called 'the indelible and irreversible stamp of collective personalities;[281] he has also a continuous need to penetrate 'the secrets of the collective forces' which shape the life of a society and of the individuals composing

---

276. E.g. ARENDT, *The Origins of Totalitarianism* (3 vols., 1951); LORENZ, *Das sogenannte Böse. Zur Naturgeschichte der Aggression* (1963) (English translation, *On Aggression*, 1966); ADORNO et al., *The Authoritarian Personality* (1950); JOHNSON, *Revolution and the Social System* (1964); ACKERMAN & JAHODA, *Anti-Semitism and Emotional Disorder* (1950); SIMMEL (ed.), *Anti-Semitism* (1946).

277. MAZLISH, *op. cit.* (1968), p. 163.

278. DEVEREUX, 'La psychanalyse et l'histoire: une application à l'histoire de Sparte' (1965); LANGER, *Explorations in Crisis, op. cit.* (1969), pp. 418-430; LEFEBVRE, *La grande peur de 1789* (1932).

279. LANGER, *op. cit.*, p. 416.

280. DUPRONT, 'L'histoire après Freud', *op. cit.*, p. 48 in *Revue de l'Enseignement supérieur*, Nos. 44-45 (1969).

281. VICENS VIVES, *Approaches to the History of Spain, op. cit.* (1967), p. 168.

that society at any moment in history. No one any longer supposes that these can be explained simply as a rational pursuit of well-defined interests, and much of the historiography of a phenomenon such as imperialism is vitiated by the fact that it takes the rationalizations of imperialists at face value instead of seeking to penetrate to their unconscious foundations. No historian concerned with imperialism or nationalism or totalitarianism can afford to ignore their psychological roots; and every historian, no matter what society he is dealing with nor what period, must take account of the psychological tensions – the tensions between the forces of stability and the forces of change, but particularly the inescapable tension, operative at all times, between the rational superstructure of the social order, necessary to ensure society's continued functioning, and the instinctive mass reactions of its members – which are the fabric and substance of history.

Unfortunately, as Alphonse Dupront has pointed out, these aspects of the past are rarely illuminated by ordinary historical evidence.[282] Testifying to particular events, it takes for granted the continuities between these events, the ceaseless flow of daily life beneath the surface of recorded history, which is like the ground bass in a modern concert, a constantly repeated muffled rhythm above which is heard the ever-changing melody of historic events. Behind the written word there is another language, a language of words spoken and forgotten in the course of daily life; behind conscious, recorded history there is an unconscious, or subconscious, history which is unrecorded; behind the noisy life of the market-place or the political platform there is a silent life, going on all the time, which is as much a part of reality as the 'great events' which catch the headlines.

The practical problem, for the historian, is how to come to terms with this 'silent life,' how to grasp anything so intangible, and yet so real, as a 'collective mentality.' It is a problem with which historians are only just beginning to come to grips, and all that can be said at present is that, if the programme is ambitious, it is one which proposes no short-cuts. Alphonse Dupront, who has drawn up an outline of the problems and methods, specifically disclaims quick solutions or 'brilliant generalisations.'[283] The first requirement, still far from satisfied, is an 'inventory of the forms, creations, images, values, and all other expressions, healthy as well as morbid, in which, through historical times, the collective mentality is manifested';[284] among which Dupront specifically singles out symbols, myths, cosmologies, 'representations of space and time'.[285] In practice, as Dupront makes clear, such studies will have to concentrate for long on particular manifestations of collective psychology. Examples, in addition to Dupront's own investigations of crusading ideology and of the psychological motivations of pilgrimages, are Philippe Ariès's distinguished study of families and children under the *Ancien Régime,* and of changing attitudes to death, and the writings of

---

282. For the following cf. DUPRONT, 'L'histoire après Freud', *op. cit.,* pp. 29-34.
283. Cf. DUPRONT, 'Problèmes et méthodes . . .', *op. cit.,* p. 10 in *Annales* (1961).
284. *Ibid.,* p. 4.
285. *Ibid.,* p. 10.

Robert Mandrou.[286] On a different level, but no less important, are studies of the 'collective mentality' of different social groups, e.g., the Prussian officer corps, French notables between 1840 and 1849, the Russian nobility in the eighteenth century.[287] The undeniable fact that individual members of such groups will not all react in identical ways in the same situation in no way diminishes the value of establishing the 'dominant attitudinal pattern'; on the contrary, it provides the only standard by which deviations can be appraised and classified. And socially, as the history of the German resistance to Hitler makes only too clear, the 'collective mentality' nearly always prevails over the wish of individuals to break free from its entangling psychological coils.

But, although it would be flying in the face of the evidence to deny that groups such as the Prussian officer corps or the Kwantung army developed some sort of 'collective mentality', it is less easy to establish the precise ways in which historians can usefully turn to psychology in describing and analysing such phenomena. Common sense would suggest, for example, that the experience of the Long March must have had profound psychological effects on the surviving Chinese communists. But when we are told that the sense of mission and dedication which infused the Chinese Communist Party under Mao was a consequence of 'the survivor's characteristically guilt-laden need to contrast his own continuing life with others' deaths',[288] we may well wonder how much, if anything, this statement contributes to historical understanding. Not merely, as one commentator has said,[289] that Mao does not seem to have been 'tormented with an overriding sense of guilt'; more important, for the historian's purposes this sort of information, even if true, is irrelevant. In fact, if we examine most exercises in social psychology – Langer's study of the effects of epidemics in medieval Europe, or Ariès's study of childhood in eighteenth-century France, for example – recourse to specific psychoanalytical techniques is conspicuously absent; and though the borderline between social psychology and sociology is shadowy, it would seem that, of the two components, it is sociology which has more to offer the historian. This is true, for example, of such a group as the Prussian officer corps, and explains why analysis to date has been in

286. Cf. Ariès, *L'enfant et la vie familiale sous l'Ancien Régime* (1960) (English translation, *Centuries of Childhood*, 1962) and 'La mort inversée. Le changement des attitudes devant la mort dans les sociétés occidentales' (1967); Mandrou, *Introduction à la France moderne, 1500-1640. Essai de psychologie historique* (1961), *De la culture populaire aux XVIIe et XVIIIe siècles* (1964), and *Magistrats et sorciers en France au XVIIe siècle* (1968).

287. Cf. Confino, 'Histoire et psychologie. A propos de la noblesse russe au XVIIIe siècle' (1967); Tudesq, *Les grands notables en France (1840-1849). Etude historique d'une psychologie sociale* (1964); Endres, 'Soziologische Struktur und ihr entsprechende Ideologien des deutschen Offizierkorps vor dem Weltkriege' (1927); Zapf, *Wandlungen der deutschen Elite, 1919-1961* (1965).

288. Lifton, *Revolutionary Immortality. Mao Tse-tung and the Chinese Cultural Revolution* (1968), p. 14.

289. Cf. Crowley (ed.), *Modern East Asia. Essays in Interpretation* (1970), p. 273.

sociological rather than in psychological terms. Too often, as Ralf Dahrendorf has said, psychoanalysis tends to be 'converted into an imprecise metaphor of sociology.'[290]

There are, of course, specific reasons why this should be the case. First and foremost, there is the much commented upon difficulty in constructing a bridge between individual and collective psychology.[291] When we are told, for example, that 'the fears and rages of mass movements' are 'the residue of childish emotions', this observation may be interesting, but does not get us much further in analysing any particular mass movement, and particularly in comparing its manifestations in one place with those in another. When it is suggested that 'Luther's trials were typical of his time', this is an assumption, not a scientifically validated fact, and not even a very plausible assumption at that. It may be 'perfectly clear that disaster and death threatening the entire community will bring on a mass emotional disturbance', but what form that disturbance will take and what effects it will have is another question.[292] As Trevor-Roper has observed, such 'disasters no doubt helped ... they do not explain.'[293] Too often, in Dahrendorf's words, 'the social dimension of socio-psychoanalysis' is 'dealt with in terms of unproved, at times implicit assertions.'[294] The reason is, of course, that the techniques of psychoanalysis cannot be applied at first hand to historical material, and attempts to do this at second hand can therefore, as Alain Besançon correctly observes, never 'be a psychoanalysis, properly speaking, but simply a judgement made by the psychoanalyst by analogy with other cases in his immediate experience.'[295] Such judgements may or may not be interesting and informative; but they remain subjective insights, no different in quality (though different in content) from the insights which historians obtain by looking at the material from another angle. 'Knowledge of the interrelations of culture and personality,' in short, 'is closer to the level of clinical insight than of systematic validation.'[296]

There are, therefore, at least at the present stage of psychological knowledge, fairly narrow limits to the contribution which psychology can make to history. In spite of all that has been written on the psychological origins of anti-Semitism and authoritarian personalities, Mazlish's reluctant conclusion is that such studies 'do not shed much light on the phenomena of contemporary history.'[297] Psychoanalysis adds to other explanations in history; it is no substitute for them. Methodologically, there is general

290. DAHRENDORF, *Society and Democracy in Germany* (1968), p. 375.

291. Cf. LANGER, *Explorations in Crisis, op. cit.* (1969), p. 414; DUPRONT, 'L'histoire après Freud', *op. cit.*, pp. 37, 39; DAHRENDORF, *op. cit.*, p. 372.

292. The examples are taken from LANGER, *op. cit.*, pp. 415, 426, 429.

293. Cf. TREVOR-ROPER, *Religion, the Reformation and Social Change* (1967), p. 99.

294. DAHRENDORF, *op. cit.*, p. 377.

295. BESANÇON, 'Psychoanalysis . . .', *op. cit.*, p. 151 in *Journal of Contemporary History* (1968).

296. *The Social Sciences in Historical Study*, p. 65.

297. MAZLISH, 'Group psychology . . .', *op. cit.*, pp. 172, 174 in *Journal of Contemporary History* (1968).

agreement, it must be handled with great caution, so much so that the principle has been adumbrated that there should be no recourse to psychological explanations so long as other convincing explanations (e.g., economic explanations) are available.[298] One particular danger is the 'generalization of micro-data without reference to a macro-model', e.g., the explanation of revolution in terms of the psychology of one or more individual revolutionaries.[299] This directly contravenes a basic principle of sociological and anthropological research, which we have already discussed – namely, that we must look at the whole problem before venturing general conclusions. No less dangerous is the temptation to use vulgar psychological concepts – inferiority complex, repression, subconscious, introversion, and the like – out of context, as explanatory principles. As Besançon has said, it is a 'useless and dubious' intellectual exercise to 'try to discover psychoanalytical concepts within the historical material'; rather, 'one should consider the material from the psychoanalytic standpoint . . . and then bring to light relations between facts which appear accidental or which had not previously been accorded the dignity of facts.'[300]

This cautious approach does not, of course, imply that psychology or even psychoanalysis is useless to the historian. It simply means that their impact is less direct than is sometimes supposed. What they offer the historian is not so much a new technical equipment as a stimulus to look at historical situations in a new light. Devereux, for example, has pointed out that it was only after the anthropological work of Frazer and the psychological discoveries of Freud that historians began to understand the irrational element in Greek religion and culture, the reason being that, although not a single new fact had come to light in the meantime, they now had a theoretical framework through which the isolated and disparate facts could be scientifically co-ordinated.[301] Such examples could be multiplied. Mannoni's study of the psychology of colonization, for instance, opens up a new perspective by placing the colonists and the natives in a direct psychological confrontation, and Stanley Elkins has brought similar psychological insights to bear on the question of race and slavery in the United States of America.[302]

This is what is meant by saying that group psychology is 'neither a substitute for history, nor a cosmetic to be applied externally to Clio, but an intrinsic and meaningful part of historical explanation.'[303] Every rational

298. Cf. DEVEREUX, 'La psychanalyse et l'histoire: une application . . .', *op. cit.*, p. 23 in *Annales* (1965).

299. Cf. JOHNSON, *Revolution and the Social System, op .cit.* (1964), p. 25.

300. BESANÇON, 'Psychoanalysis . . .', *op. cit.*, p. 152 in *Journal of Contemporary History* (1968).

301. DEVEREUX, 'La psychanalyse et l'histoire . . .', *op. cit.*, p. 23 in *Annales* (1965).

302. Cf. MANNONI, *Psychologie de la colonisation* (1950) (English translation, *Prospero and Caliban: The Psychology of Colonization*, 1956); ELKINS, *Slavery. A Problem in American Institutional and Intellectual Life* (1959).

303. MAZLISH, 'Group psychology . . .', *op. cit.*, p. 177 in *Journal of Contemporary History* (1968).

analysis of historical decisions and events leaves an unexplained residue. In so far as psychology helps him to decipher this residuary matter, no historian is likely to refuse its aid. It is more likely, perhaps, to help him to clarify his mind by posing new questions than to provide him with new answers; but used circumspectly, there is no reason why it should not widen the horizons of historical understanding.

Economics and the Demographic Setting

When we turn from sociology and social psychology to economics, we arrive on firmer ground.[304] The question is no longer one of a subtle but rather indeterminate re-shaping of the historian's general attitude and approach, a new openness towards and awareness of the findings and methods of scholars in other, closely related branches of 'human studies', but of a precise and deliberate application of well-defined theories. Indeed, it has even been suggested that economics is the only one of the social sciences which has as yet made a serious contribution to history.[305]

It is not difficult to understand why historians should believe that economics has a particularly significant contribution to make to their work. Economic facts impinge upon the historian at every turn, and every historian, no matter what his particular ideological standpoint may be, is aware of their importance in the human story. He is aware also that if he is to understand man's economic development, he must be equipped with the necessary theoretical and statistical tools. No historian, for example, would try to explain the rise of prices in sixteenth-century England without some knowledge of the quantity theory of money; no historian would presume to write about the slump of 1929, the policies of the New Deal, or the world trading structure established after 1945, without recourse to the relevant

304. For the following cf. COLE, *Economic History as a Social Science* (1967); POLLARD, 'Economic history: a science of society' (1965); COURT, 'Economic history' (1963); BRAUDEL, 'Pour une économie historique' (1950, reprinted in *Ecrits sur l'histoire*, 1969); MEYER & CONRAD, 'Economic theory, statistical inference and economic history' (1957, reprinted in CONRAD & MEYER, *The Economics of Slavery and other Studies in Econometric History*, 1964); REDLICH, 'New and traditional approaches to economic history' (1965) and 'Potentialities and pitfalls in economic history' (1968); MURPHY, 'The "new" history' (1965); DAVIS, L. E., 'The New Economic History: a critique' (1968); HACKER, 'The new revolution in economic history' (1966); HUGHES, J. R. T., 'Fact and theory in economic history' (1966, reprinted with other relevant papers in ANDREANO (ed.), *The New Economic History: Recent Papers in Methodology*, 1970); FOGEL, 'The New Economic History, its findings and methods' (1966, reprinted in ROWNEY & GRAHAM (eds.), *Quantitative History*, 1969); FOGEL, 'The reunification of economic history with economic theory' (1965) and 'The specification problem in economic history' (1967); HUNT, 'The New Economic History' (1968) (with a 'Comment' by G. R. HAWKE); SLICHER VAN BATH, 'Nieuwe wegen in de amerikaanse economische en sociale geschiedenis' (1969); LÉVY-LEBOYER, 'La "New Economic History"' (1969); NORTH, 'The state of economic history' (1965).
305. Cf. DAVIS, R., *History and the Social Sciences* (1965), p. 5.

economic theory. The links between history and theory are very much closer in the analysis of economic changes than they are in other branches of historical study. Ever since the days of Adam Smith, Ricardo and Marx, historians have been acutely aware of the importance of economic factors in shaping the course of historical change. But it is not only that economics was far in advance of the other social sciences in developing a coherent body of theory. In addition, it seemed to most historians that economic data were far more susceptible of precise statistical and theoretical analysis than the less tangible data of sociology. For their own practical purposes, governments and other agencies had compiled tax-lists, records of prices and wages, census-returns, customs and excise levies, etc., which provided economists and historians with a solid substratum of exact factual knowledge, capable of arrangement in serial form. Hence it seemed possible to deal with the economic aspects of history at a far higher level of sophistication and assurance than was possible in any other area.

These long-standing links between history and economics have been reinforced by recent developments. At the turn of the nineteenth and twentieth centuries the tendency had been for the two branches of knowledge to draw apart, in the same way as history and sociology were drawing apart. Economists (or at least non-Marxist economists) concerned themselves with the construction of an allegedly timeless system of economic relations considered to be of universal application. Historians concerned with change in time replied, with rare exceptions, by ignoring economic theory. This trend was reversed in the 1930's with the decline, under the impact of world events, of neo-classical economics. As the world succumbed to slump and depression, the focus of economic theory swung sharply from the study of short-term equilibrium problems to trade cycles and trade-cycle theory, a preoccupation which lasted until the 1950's, when – again under the impact of world events – it was succeeded by concern with the problems of development and long-term economic growth.[306]

These changes in the basic trends of economic thought brought about a reconciliation between history and economics and were without doubt the main explanation of the rapid growth of economic history which is a characteristic of the period.[307] Concern with long-term trends and with the dynamics of economic growth almost necessarily emphasized the historical factor. It gave moral support to historians working on the more quantitative aspects of economic history and at the same time suggested new lines of research to historians. Particularly significant was the growing interest in price history, as an essential component of any study of business cycles; and the work undertaken in this field under the auspices of the International Scientific Committee on Price History was the first significant

306. For a brilliant short account of these changes cf. ROBINSON, *Economic Philosophy* (1962); cf. also COLE, *Economic History . . ., op. cit.* (1967), pp. 7-8.

307. Cf. CHAUNU, 'L'histoire sérielle. Bilan et perspectives' (1970), pp. 302, 309 in *Revue historique*, Vol. CCXLIII.

breakthrough in historical quantification.[308] The next advance came in 1950 when, as a result of the initiative of Simon Kuznets, the International Association for Research in Income and Wealth embarked on a large-scale reconstitution of the national revenues of the advanced industrial countries. The results, whatever doubts may be entertained as to the reliability of some of the data, make possible a comparison of changing economic structures, and thus provide the elements of a typology.[309]

Economic history has, of course, always had a quantitative orientation. But the quantitative data employed down to this time were almost entirely those made available by governments or similar agencies, and economic historians were satisfied to classify such statistical information and use it descriptively to illustrate the course of historical development. The position for the historians of prices was different. Beginning with the pioneering work of Thorald Rogers, they had to put together their own data series, and were thus the first to make use of massive statistical reconstructions, organizing their information in ways which shed light on 'rigorously defined concepts of economic analysis'.[310] In doing so they paved the way for what has come to be called the 'new economic history'.

The 'new' economic history is a product of the very recent past, its first specific formulation occurring in the writings of A. H. Conrad and J. R. Meyer in 1957 and 1958, and of Davis, Hughes and McDougall in 1960 and 1961.[311] High claims have been made on its behalf. Its appearance has been said to have marked a 'revolution', a complete break with traditional economic history. Whether or not this is true, is perhaps a matter of no great importance. Even so outstanding an exponent of the new school as R. W. Fogel recognizes a 'clear line of continuity between the old and new economic history.'[312] What is beyond doubt is that a greater emphasis on theory and a more systematic use of rigorous statistical analysis have become the hallmarks of economic history since roughly 1955, and are likely to remain so in the future. The point is simply that many unresolved questions in economic history are such that the only intellectually satisfying answers are, by definition, quantitative.

The impact of the new approach is not, however, confined to economic history in a limited and technical sense, but affects historical work generally. The questions, for example, whether or not slavery was profitable in the United States before the Civil War, or whether railways had a major impact on the development of the American economy, are of importance for the general historian as well as for the economic historian, and are bound to influence any interpretation or evaluation of the course of Amer-

308. Cf. PRICE, 'Recent quantitative work in history', p. 5 in *Studies in Quantitative History* (*History and Theory*, Beiheift 9, 1969).

309. Cf. MATHIAS, 'Economic history, direct and oblique', p. 81 in BALLARD (ed.), *New Movements in the Study and Teaching of History* (1970).

310. ROWNEY & GRAHAM (eds.), *Quantitative History* (1969), p. 330.

311. Cf. DAVIS, L. E., HUGHES, J. R. T. & McDOUGALL, *American Economic History: The Development of a National Economy* (1961).

312. *American Economic Review*, Vol. LIV (1964), Suppl., pp. 377-378.

ican history.[313] Furthermore, the 'new' economic history directly challenges one of the central assumptions of the idealist school of historians – namely, that history can never be 'scientific' in its demonstrations of proof, because, owing to the uniqueness of historical events, a control experiment is never possible. The answer of the new school of economic historians is that, on the contrary, it is possible, at least in favourable cases, to construct a 'counterfactual' situation by means of which the gap between what actually happened and what might, in different circumstances, have happened, can be measured. This general methodological point is perhaps the most important single contribution of the new economic history so far as non-specialist historians are concerned.[314]

The 'methodological hallmarks' of the new economic history have been set out by R. W. Fogel. As basic he picks out 'its emphasis on measurement and its recognition of the intimate relationship between measurement and theory.'[315] But there is no doubt that it is the second rather than the first of these characteristics that is distinctive. Measurement alone, unless accompanied by statistical processing and systematic quantitative analysis, is likely to result in nothing more than a different form of narrative. It substitutes figures for words and is (at least in common practice) more precise and accurate; but it introduces no new factor. So far as techniques of measurement are concerned, including indirect measurement ('reconstructing measurements which might have existed in the past but are no longer extant') the 'new' economic history is more subtle and sophisticated than the old; but the difference is one of degree rather than of kind.[316] Where the two part company is, in Fogel's words, in the endeavour of the new economic historians 'to cast all explanations of past economic development in the form of valid hypothetico-deductive models.'[317]

The essential characteristic of the 'new economic history' is the use of such hypothetico-deductive models, which exploit to the full the elaborate techniques of econometrics, the point being to establish in mathematical terms the way in which the variables in a given situation interact. It is unnecessary on this occasion to discuss these techniques in detail, but a few examples cited by Fogel indicate their nature.[318] In general, the aim is to construct a model which represents the various constituent elements contributing to economic change and shows (in most cases by the use of

313. Cf. ENGERMAN, 'The economic impact of the Civil War' (1966).

314. Cf. MATHIAS, *op. cit.* (1970), pp. 82-83.

315. FOGEL, 'The New Economic History, its findings and methods', p. 330 in ROWNEY & GRAHAM (eds.), *op. cit.* (1969).

316. HUNT, 'The New Economic History', p. 5 in *History* (1968).

317. FOGEL, 'The New Economic History . . .', *op. cit.*, pp. 334-335 in ROWNEY & GRAHAM (eds.), *op. cit.* (1969).

318. They include regression analysis ('perhaps the most frequently used tool'), input-output analysis, and the hypergeometric distribution (used, for example, by Kindahl to estimate the total number of state banks in operation in the United States immediately after the Civil War); cf. FOGEL, 'The New Economic History . . .', *op. cit.*, pp. 330-331 in ROWNEY & GRAHAM (eds.), *op. cit.* (1969).

algebraic formulae) the way they interact. In this way correlations can be made to measure the relative importance of each over a period of time.

The main purpose for which hypothetico-deductive models have so far been used is to establish the effect of innovations (e.g., the introduction of railways), institutions (e.g., banks) or processes (e.g., of steel-making) on the course of economic development. Since what would have happened if the particular innovations had not occurred, or the particular factors had not been present, is not recorded, this can only be done by the creation of a hypothetical model, from which a so-called 'counterfactual situation' (i.e., the situation which would have existed in the absence of the specified circumstances) can be inferred. Counterfactual propositions are not, of course, new in themselves. They are implicit in a whole variety of judgements, some specifically economic and others not, such as the effect of the Norman Conquest on England or what would have happened if Hitler's remilitarization of the Rhineland had been resisted in 1936; and the main effort of the new economic historians so far has been to test and make explicit specific counterfactual propositions of an economic sort currently found in traditional historical writing, e.g., that tariffs accelerated the growth of manufacturing.

The use of counterfactual propositions has not escaped criticism. Redlich, in particular, has objected that the use of hypotheses which cannot be verified produces not history but 'quasi-history'. The answer, of course, is that hypotheses are involved anyhow, and that it is better to make them explicit than to leave them implicit. In fact, as Hawke has pointed out, a good deal of the criticism proves on examination to be beside the point.[319] The fact nevertheless remains that the net gain from the more sophisticated extensions of the new economic history has been less decisive than many of its proponents believed. Hacker is surely right when he concludes that 'economic analysis, using the tools of econometrics, is not ... by itself capable of explaining causatively the process and structure of change and development.'[320] As Hughes points out, there are 'non-systematic disruptions of normal economic life' – wars, harvest failures, mob psychoses during stock-market panics – which 'must somehow be handled in colligated analyses,' but which are too often brushed aside as extrinsic in favour of '*a priori* formulations of theoretic assumptions.'[321] Furthermore, as the inherent difficulty of constructing adequate large-scale models has become increasingly apparent, economic historians have succumbed to the temptation to concentrate on 'micro-studies', avoiding the major problems which concern historians, such as economic growth or 'take off'.[322] In-

319. Cf. HAWKE, Mr. Hunt's study of the Fogel thesis. A comment' (1968); cf. also the judicious survey by MURPHY, 'On counterfactual propositions', in *Studies in Quantitative History, op. cit.* (1969).

320. HACKER, 'The new revolution in economic history', *op. cit.*, p. 175 in *Explorations in Entrepreneurial History*, 2nd ser., Vol. III (1966).

321. HUGHES, J. R. T., 'Fact and theory in economic history', *op. cit., ibid.*, p. 93.

322. LÉVY-LEBOYER, 'La "New Economic History"', *op. cit.*, p. 1064 in *Annales* (1969).

deed, the more the central problems of modern economic history have been analysed, the less clear it has become whether they are questions to which economic historians, using exclusively econometric hypotheses, can provide satisfactory answers.

Nevertheless, in spite of a certain disenchantment with some of its more extreme manifestations, the achievement of the new economic history is immense, and even so thorough-going a critic as Redlich has no doubt that it is 'here to stay.' The danger lies in allowing economic theory to circumscribe research and in this way to pass over the empirical material through which our knowledge of the realities of economic life can be enriched. But it is also true, as Hughes is careful to emphasize, that 'there *are* regularities which theory can help to elucidate,' and that only mastery of theory makes it possible to discriminate between the regular and the irregular, and between the expected and the unexpected. The main achievement of the new economic history is, on the one side, the slow but steady development of a settled body of economic analysis of historical change, and, on the other side, the emphasis it has placed on measurement and theory. Historians have learnt that there is no substitute for rigorous statistical analysis, based upon systematically organized data, and impressionistic judgements, derived from haphazard figures, eked out by the subjective impressions of contemporaries, are discredited among serious historians today. Economic history, in particular, has been transformed from a narrative supplying factual information about the material apparatus of life at different times into a search for answers to specific questions, and it is generally accepted that 'the more completely the problems dominate the search for facts, the nearer is the study to the true function of history in social science.'[323]

No less important is the way this change of orientation has spread from economic history to cognate subjects, which have undergone a similar transformation. Among these the new school of historical demography, which emerged in France around 1950, is outstanding.[324] In this case the initiative came both from historians (Labrousse, Meuvret, Reinhard), who hoped by linking economic and demographic problems to explain economic growth by reference to demographic circumstances, and from professional demographers and statisticians (Sauvy, Henry, Fleury), who saw the need to extend the time-span of the available statistical material, or (as has been said) to move from 'transversal' to 'longitudinal' analysis.[325] The construction of a new methodology was the work of Louis Henry, outlined in 1953

323. POSTAN, *Historical Method in Social Science* (1939), p. 14; reproduced in POSTAN, *Fact and Relevance. Essays on Historical Method* (1971), p. 25.

324. For a good general survey, cf. REVELLE (ed.), *Historical Population Studies* (*Daedalus*, Spring 1968); cf. also van der WOUDE, 'De historische demografie in de ontwikkeling van de geschiedwetenschap' (1969).

325. Cf. GOUBERT, 'Historical demography and the reinterpretation of early modern French history', pp. 37-39 in *Journal of Interdisciplinary History* (1970); VANN, 'History and demography', p. 75 in *Studies in Quantitative History, op. cit.* (1969).

and elaborated in 1956;[326] and from 1959, when the first study using the new methods was published,[327] progress has been rapid, and some 500 monographs have been produced or are in preparation in France alone. In England a parallel development occurred in 1964 with the foundation of the Cambridge Group for the History of Population and Social Structure.[328]

The difference between historical demography, as practised today, and population history of a traditional sort is similar to that between the 'new' economic history ('cliometrics') and the older forms of narrative economic history of a descriptive or illustrative character. In fact, little attention was paid to demographic questions by nineteenth-century historians, who treated population as a given condition, or parameter, rather than as a matter for critical analysis, and in any case were satisfied with gross aggregate figures of births and deaths and overall estimates on a national scale.[329] The obvious drawback of such figures, all questions of accuracy apart, is their inability to cast light on the dynamics of population growth, and therefore to answer the questions about long-term demographic trends which social scientists are asking; and the essential purpose of the new historical demography is to remedy this weakness.

It has been defined as 'the numerical study of society over time', its objects being 'to recover the facts about numbers of persons, their propensity to be born, to marry and to die, their arrangement in families, villages, towns, regions, classes and so on, as accurately as we can and as far back as we can go.' Once these facts have been assembled, it is claimed, they will 'constitute an anatomy of social structure', and introduce 'rigour and precision' into that 'hitherto exasperatingly vague subject, the history of society'. More specifically, they can be expected to establish the demographic characteristics of pre-industrial society and thus to cast light on the social causes both of pre-industrial stagnation and of the beginnings of industrial growth. Eventually, they should make it possible to draw useful comparisons between French or English society in pre-Malthusian times and pre-industrial, or developing, societies in the contemporary world.[330]

---

326. Cf. HENRY, 'Une richesse démographique en friche: les registres paroissiaux' (1953); FLEURY & HENRY, *Des registres paroissiaux à l'histoire de la population* (1956), of which *Nouveau manuel de dépouillement et d'exploitation de l'état civil ancien* (1965), is a revised and extended edition; cf. also HENRY, *Manuel de démographie historique* (1967), and HENRY's contribution on 'Historical demography' in the issue of *Daedalus* (1968) devoted to *Historical Population Studies*.
327. GAUTIER & HENRY, *La population de Crulai, paroisse normande* (1959).
328. Cf. LASLETT, 'The history of population and social structure' (1965). Cf. also WRIGLEY, EVERSLEY & LASLETT (eds.), *An Introduction to English Historical Demography* (1966); WRIGLEY, 'Population, family and household', in BALLARD (ed.), *New Movements in the Study and Teaching of History* (1970); GLASS & EVERSLEY (eds.), *Population in History* (1965); LASLETT, *The World We Have Lost* (1965).
329. Cf. CHAUNU, 'L'histoire sérielle. Bilan et perspectives' (1970), p. 302 in *Revue historique*, Vol. CCXLIII.
330. LASLETT, 'The history of population and social structure', pp. 583, 592-593 in *International Social Science Journal* (1965).

Such results can only be secured by intensive micro-analysis, and the efforts of Henry and his successors in England and elsewhere have been concentrated on the creation of a suitable micro-analytical methodology. The technique they have developed is known as 'family reconstitution', and has been described in detail by Henry himself and by others. Briefly, it requires the abstraction under appropriate headings of the information which is available in parish registers in France from the late seventeenth century, in England from 1538. The essential difference from older demography is that the classification is 'nominative', not 'aggregative'; that is to say, the basis is the individual family and the consolidation of all the documentary evidence relating to the births, deaths and marriages of a single family into one record. Whereas aggregative work is not concerned with men, women and children as individuals, nominative work is only possible where they can be individually identified. Instead of being directed towards producing vital statistics for a whole population, family reconstruction operates at the level of the single village or township and is primarily concerned to determine at what age people were getting married, having babies, and dying. Once the basic facts about the constituent families have been reconstituted, fertility and mortality can be investigated in great detail and very intricate demographic analysis becomes possible.[331]

The results obtained in this way by historical demography are very impressive.[332] Impressionistic treatment of population records inevitably tends to be accompanied by impressionistic analysis. Only when a society in a given period has been described in detail, so that the nature of the differences between it and other societies is known with precision, can we expect to understand the processes of historical change. In this respect, historical demography is a necessary complement to economic history. Economists today are aware, for example, that more is involved in the process of industrialisation than the economic co-efficients, and study of the family, which reflects a wide range of social and economic experience and activity, provides essential information which a purely economic analysis cannot accurately reflect.[333] Already the study of population and the family has unearthed significant differences between early modern Europe and other pre-industrial societies which cast new light upon this central topic: for example, the practice of late marriage which, by reducing fertility, may be regarded as a factor helping to preserve a relatively favourable ratio of

331. Cf. WRIGLEY, 'Population, family and household', *op. cit.* (1970), p. 95.

332. Most are listed by GOUBERT in his article 'Historical demography . . .', *op. cit.* (1970). They include his own work, *Beauvais et le Beauvaisis* (1960), and HENRY, *Anciennes familles genevoises* (1956). In England a notable study is CHAMBERS, *The Vale of Trent, 1670-1800* (1957). For the United States, cf. GREVEN, 'Historical demography and colonial America' (1967) and DEMOS, 'Families in colonial Bristol' (1968) (the latter reprinted in ROWNEY & GRAHAM (eds.), *Quantitative History, op. cit.*, 1969). Cf. also GIEYSZTOROWA, 'Research into demographic history in Poland' (1968).

333. It can, of course, be introduced into an economic model, but – failing demographic research – only as an 'exogenous variable'.

resources to population, while at the same time inducing a propensity to saving favourable to economic growth. If, as seems to be fairly well established, marriage was normally postponed until the means were available to set up a new household, the result was likely to be the formation of a pattern of saving and expenditure which would encourage capital accumulation.

Family reconstitution may be regarded in many ways as the historian's equivalent of the social survey. Just as the survey enables the social scientist to answer fundamental questions about the structure of contemporary society, so family reconstitution enables the historian to answer similar questions about societies in the past. There are, of course, many topics in which historians are legitimately interested, which need take no notice of demography; but in so far as society is the focus of the historian's activity, there are few which the micro-analytical methods of family reconstitution cannot clarify. Among these the relationship between population and economic growth is outstanding, and it would be generally agreed that historical demography has already shed new light on the factors enabling western Europeans to accumulate the economic and political power which underpinned their imperial expansion in the nineteenth century. Only with the aid of historical demography can we hope to find a satisfactory answer to the question why Western Europe was able to escape the cycle of events which, in other pre-industrial societies, has habitually frustrated sustained expansion.[334]

It must suffice to list briefly other topics upon which historical demography has shed new light. They include the impact of epidemics and famine, the effect of changes in the environment on the family policies of peasant populations, the incidence of infant mortality, the nature and extent of social mobility (indicated by the frequency with which a bride and her groom came from different socio-economic groups), class structure, the social consequences of such well-known phenomena as land-enclosure, migration and population mobility, the relations of towns and countryside. But the most remarkable, in view of its revolutionary long-term consequences, is the new light cast on the rise and spread of the practice of contraception, or family limitation.[335] The establishment through statistical means of the existence of family limitation in the past, Vann rightly insists, is one of the most striking tributes to the effectiveness of the new

334. Cf. LASLETT, 'The history of population and social structure', p. 590 in *International Social Science Journal* (1965); WRIGLEY, 'Population, family and household', p. 99 in BALLARD (ed.), *New Movements . . ., op. cit.* (1970); VANN, 'History and demography', p. 77 in *Studies in Quantitative History, op. cit.* (1969).

335. The literature on contraception is already considerable. Cf. DUPÂQUIER & LACHIVER, 'Sur les débuts de la contraception en France' (1969); CHAMOUX & DAUPHIN, 'La contraception avant la Révolution française' (1969); WRIGLEY, 'Family limitation in pre-industrial England' (1966). As VANN points out (*op. cit.*, p. 72), BERGUES, *La prévention des naissances dans la famille: ses origines dans les temps modernes* (1960), is still largely dependent on literary sources and consequently is not very enlightening about the extent or intensity of family limitation.

techniques of historical demography. It 'is an extraordinary example of how the most intimate details in the private lives of quite obscure people, who produced no literary evidence at all, can nevertheless become the object of our knowledge'. It shows also how the techniques of the quantitative social sciences provide new evidence of human behaviour, and enable us to answer questions which, because of the reticence and vagueness of the usual sources, are outside the range of historians using traditional historiographical methods. Such fragmentary literary evidence as exists tells us little about the extent or intensity of family limitation; but the evidence of behaviour, when quantitatively analysed, is clear and precise.[336]

Chaunu has written of the 'almost unlimited possibilities' of the new demographic history,[337] and there are already impressive examples of its value in building regional analysis around a solid demographic core.[338] It is nevertheless important to be aware of the practical limitations. The first necessity, obviously, is the availability of the basic vital statistics, and it was perhaps a happy accident that these happened to be available for a period (seventeenth and eighteenth centuries) and in countries (France and England) of particular interest to historians, economists and social scientists concerned with the problems of industrial growth and 'take off.' But for many other areas and for earlier periods (before the sixteenth century) the necessary statistical data are not normally available, and it is hard to see how the techniques elaborated by Louis Henry and his successors can be generalized. Moreover, micro-analytic studies of single parishes – such as Colyton in Devon and Crulai in Normandy – are both expensive and time-consuming. In the case of Colyton (for the period 1538–1837) it involved some 30,000 separate extraction slips (one for each entry over the 300 years of the parish registers) and the transfer of this material to 5,000 family reconstitution forms, before demographic and social analysis could begin.

These disadvantages can, perhaps, be overcome in part. Once the techniques of analysis have been established, it is not unreasonable to hope that they will make it possible to make use of less perfect documentation (e.g., taxation lists, hearth-tax returns) and in this way to carry back the analysis of social structure to dates considerably earlier than the time when parish registration started, e.g., to the thirteenth century.[339] Secondly, it is obvious that much time and effort can be saved if the information from parish registers can be processed by computer, instead of by hand.[340] Sampling

336. Vann, *op. cit.*, p. 74.

337. Chaunu, 'L'histoire sérielle. Bilan et perspectives' (1970), p. 315 in *Revue historique*, Vol. CCXLIII.

338. Cf. Braun, *Industrialisierung und Volksleben. Die Veränderung der Lebensformen in einem ländlichen Industriegebiet vor 1800* (1960); Le Roy Ladurie, *Les paysans de Languedoc* (1966).

339. As suggested by Laslett, *op. cit.*, p. 591.

340. Cf. Schofield, 'Population in the past. Computer linking of vital records' (1970); Winchester, 'The linkage of historical records by man and computer' (1970). For the use of computers by historians in general, cf. below, in Section 6,

methods have also been proposed.[341] But though they may be mitigated in this way, the inherent limitations of family reconstitution techniques remain, and it has already been suggested that they represent 'a stage which we are in the process of passing' in favour of a more refined use of aggregative methods, using such fragmentary evidence from earlier periods as exists.[342] The obvious advantage of such methods – used, wherever possible, in combination with those of Henry – is that they require less in the way of completeness and continuity and can be applied on a vastly wider scale.[343]

All in all, the increase in knowledge and understanding brought about by historical demography and the new economic history has been very considerable. In both cases, micro-analysis has made it possible to test familiar hypotheses of working historians and demonstrate their inadequacy, if not their falsity. Fogel's work has made it necessary at least to reconsider the glib generalizations advanced without due analysis about the economic effects of railway building in the United States; analysis of population structure has definitely discredited the views about the pre-industrial family and the effects of industrialization and urbanization on the family nexus prevalent among social scientists. These are significant results, particularly since in the latter instance we are dealing with a hypothesis which has implications for social policy as well as for social science. On the other hand it must also be said that some of the confident predictions about the revolutionary effects of the new economic and demographic history have not been borne out. The marked tendency in both fields to stick to more manageable, short-span issues, in which the number of variables is limited, the preference for small-scale investigations at the 'grass-roots' level and the concentration on micro-studies (a single parish, a single firm, a particular occupational group) may be judicious at a practical level. But they tend to leave the larger issues of history out of the picture, and the assumption that, as the numbers of local case studies build up into representative samples, they will provide the basis for wider generalizations (for example, on a national level) is not necessarily correct.

Just as the old positivist assumption that the 'facts of history', once historians had collected them, would somehow fit into a valid and generally accepted pattern, proved to be deceptive in practice, so there is a real danger that the efforts of the historical demographers and the 'cliometricians' will be dissipated in a vast series of fragmented studies with no generalized or final results. It is fair to say, for example, that the controversies

---

'The organization of historical work', 'The impact of new techniques', pp.192–197.

341. Cf. BALLARD (ed.), *New Movements in the Study and Teaching of History*, *op. cit.* (1970), p. 101.

342. CHAUNU, *op. cit.* (1970), pp. 317-318.

343. Cf. DUPÂQUIER, 'Sur la population française au XVIIe et au XVIIIe siècle' (1968). Examples of the more extensive methods are GOUBERT's two books, *Louis XIV et vingt millions de Français* (1966) and *Cent mille provinciaux au XVIIe siècle* (1968).

initiated in the United States by Fogel and Benson have generated more heat than light. They have complicated rather than clarified; and the same is true at another level of historical demography. The progress of demographic studies, far from confirming, has made it necessary to modify the conclusions derived from Henry's pioneering study of Crulai and Wrigley's equally fundamental survey of the parish of Colyton. We now find startling local differences in female fertility and child mortality rates; and though the result may be to create a picture with greater historical verisimilitude, the tendency is evidently to confirm the old historicist principle of the complexity, uniqueness and variety of historical experience, rather than to reduce this complexity – as the new methodology implicitly promised to do – to socially significant patterns based on incontrovertible quantitative data.

For these reasons the claims of historical demographers, like those of cliometricians, have become more modest and tentative as time has passed. Neither, it is now evident, is a short-cut to definitive solutions, such as were confidently predicted as short a time ago as 1966.[344] On the contrary, their tendency is to introduce new complications, which traditional historiography had overlooked, and so to complicate and to postpone solutions. This does not mean that the benefits which historical demography and the new economic history have introduced are not real, or that their impact will not endure; but it is likely to be less direct and more subtle than at one time seemed possible. However scientific its intentions, the limitations of data and the multiplicity of influences upon change condemn economic history – as one economic historian has said – 'to remain a depressingly inexact science'.[345]

What the new economic and demographic history has achieved so far – and it is a considerable achievement – is to force historians to reconsider and revise, and often to abandon, a whole series of generalizations and presuppositions which previously held sway. It has, in other words, widened the historian's field of vision, by opening doors which seemed to be closed. It has also provided him with new strategies of research. It is inconceivable that economic history or historical demography in future will proceed otherwise than on a basis of quantitative analysis; and it seems likely that quantitative methods, because of their proven value, will increasingly influence historians working in other fields. Economic history and historical demography have provided the most convincing evidence of the value of quantification as a tool of historical analysis; the question now is how far this tool is applicable in areas where measurable quantitative data are less readily available.

344. GOUBERT, for example, concludes his review ('Historical demography . . .', *op. cit.*, p. 48 in *Journal of Interdisciplinary History*, 1970) with the admission that historical demographers 'do not really understand' the facts they have detected; he emphasizes the 'great variety' of the 'demographic characteristics of pre-industrial society' and that 'we shall have much to learn about fertility.'

345. MATHIAS, 'Economic history, direct and oblique', p. 86 in BALLARD (ed.), *New Movements . . ., op. cit.* (1970).

Quantification in History

Behind the recent methodological advances in historical writing and research, there lies a new preoccupation, evidently derived from the social sciences, with measurement. It is this preoccupation which distinguishes the new history, as it has developed since around 1955, from the older historiography. Even in the Soviet Union and other countries where history followed a Marxist tradition, history down to that date was largely descriptive and narrative in character. Elsewhere, under the persistent influence of historicist and historico-genetical assumptions, belief in the specificity and individuality of historical events set up an almost insuperable psychological barrier against quantitative measurement and theoretical generalization.

The outstanding characteristic of recent historiography, from the point of view of methodology, has therefore been what, without exaggeration, may be called a 'quantitative revolution'. Measurement and quantification, as we have seen, have affected practically every branch of historical research during the last one or two decades. Paradoxically, however, the character and significance of the quantitative revolution are matters of controversy. For some, quantitative history signifies, in the most general terms, the historical study of any measurable series of phenomena; it is, in Pierre Chaunu's words, 'a history interested less in the individual facts [. . .] than in the elements which can be integrated in a homogeneous series.'[346] Others, in particular Jean Marczewski, have demanded a narrower and more rigorous definition.[347] In Marczewski's opinion, to make use of statistics, or of 'vertical chronological series', may produce interesting results; but it is merely an 'improvement' of traditional historical methods, which does not change or modify them in any fundamental way. Before we can speak of quantitative history *stricto sensu*, it is necessary in his view for the 'vertical' series, which represent no more than the evolution of a single category of phenomena (e.g., prices) over a period of time, to be supplemented and completed by 'horizontal' analysis of the 'structures' formed by all the relevant phenomena ('the totality of economic events') operating, and interacting, at the same period of time. The model for this is the system of national accounting, which permits precise description and evaluation of all the elements of economic activity from primary production to savings and investment, and which (not incidentally) can be reduced to a series of algebraic equations representing a more or less complex series of variables.[348]

Thus defined, quantitative history is an attempt 'to evaluate global eco-

346. CHAUNU, 'L'histoire sérielle', *op. cit.* (1970), p. 297.

347. Cf. MARCZEWSKI, *Introduction à l'histoire quantitative* (1965), where his earlier statements are collected and reprinted. No less important and programmatic are the articles of P. LEBRUN, 'Structure et quantification. Réflexions sur la science historique', in PERELMAN (ed.), *Raisonnement et démarches de l'historien* (1963) and 'Développement et histoire quantitative. Vers une historiométrie?', in *Revue de l'Institut de Sociologie* (1967).

348. Cf. MARCZEWSKI, *op. cit.*, pp. 12, 14, 48. MARCZEWSKI himself (p. 26) and LEBRUN, *op. cit.* (1967), pp. 591-596, offer examples of appropriate algebraic models.

nomic quantities in the rigid framework of national accounting, through which binding relationships between these quantities are established.'[349] But historians have objected that such a definition is unduly restrictive. They have also objected that quantitative history defined in this way is more concerned with the needs of theoretical economists than with those of historians. This is not the place to follow in detail the course of the controversy which has arisen.[350] Chaunu has attempted to resolve it by proposing a distinction between 'quantitative history' and 'serial history', the former term to be used in the restrictive sense employed by Marczewski (i.e., 'when the results can be cast in a mould in the form of national accounting'),[351] the latter for all other forms of measurement which set out to reinforce the critique of isolated facts by the requirement of coherent series.[352] At the time of writing, however, there is little evidence, at least outside France, that historians are prepared to observe this semantic distinction, and all indications suggest that the term 'quantitative history' will continue to be used in the broadest sense as a description of all types of historical writing in which emphasis falls on the measurement and analysis of quantitative information, as contrasted with the historian's traditional emphasis on qualitative evaluation.

For historians, therefore, the type of analysis proposed by Marczewski is one, but only one, application of the quantitative approach.[353] In their eyes it has – criticism in detail apart – three limitations which, if rigorously applied, would narrow the field of quantitative history in ways they cannot accept. First, it is limited, quite deliberately, to the economic substructure; the only quantitative history is therefore quantitative economic history. Secondly, it is applicable only in the period (not much further back than 1780) in which adequate statistical data are available; and this means, thirdly, that it can only be used for the history of those parts of the world – namely, Europe and North America – where concern with the statistics of national accounting developed at a (relatively) early date. Moreover, with its emphasis on the national unit, it is inherently unsuitable, as Chaunu has pointed out,[354] for periods – comprising, in fact, by far the greater part of historical time – when economic and political frontiers did not coincide.

These are substantial limitations. Within its self-appointed field, on the other hand, for the rather limited periods and regions in which it is appli-

349. LEBRUN, *op. cit.* (1967), p. 589.

350. It is sufficient to refer to VILAR, 'Pour une meilleure compréhension entre économistes et historiens' (1965), and CHAUNU, 'L'histoire sérielle. Bilan et perspectives', *op. cit.* (1970).

351. CHAUNU, 'L'histoire sérielle', *op. cit.* (1970), p. 300.

352. CHAUNU, 'Histoire quantitative ou histoire sérielle' (1964).

353. The same, it should be added, applies to some of the more specialized forms of econometric history devised by American economic historians, which are discussed above, pp. 75-76.

354. CHAUNU, 'Histoire quantitative ou histoire sérielle', p. 174 in *Cahiers Vilfredo Pareto*, Vol. 3, 1964.

cable, the type of quantitative analysis proposed by Marczewski and Lebrun has much to offer. Its main contribution, from the historian's point of view, is probably the emphasis it throws upon the 'non-spectacular events' of history, upon the evolution of the underlying economic structure of any given society, abstracted from the 'breaks' ('coupures' or 'ruptures') induced by momentary political events. In this sense it corresponds to, and may almost be regarded as, a precise statistico-mathematical representation of Braudel's concept of the *longue durée*.[355] Its other claim is to 'greater objectivity', by comparison with the usual procedures of the historian;[356] that is to say, the criterion of what is important in a particular economic situation is not simply the historian's own judgement, but the place of a particular factor in the whole 'constellation' of quantifiable factors, or the coherence of the 'system of reference' ('the relations of interdependence between the different components of the model') of which each variable is a part.[357]

Nevertheless it is important not to gloss over, or to minimize, the limitations of the quantitative approach. Marczewski himself emphasizes that, even in the best possible case (i.e., where all the necessary data are available), quantitative history can never, and does not in fact seek to, replace other forms of history. Precisely because it is concerned with 'the masses considered in terms of their continuous, long-range evolution', it ignores exceptional individuals ('heroes'), exceptional facts, and 'major discontinuities provoked by qualitative change'.[358] These exclusions, as Pierre Vilar was quick to point out,[359] are disconcerting if not fatal. What is the value, for example, of an account which deliberately ignores the First World War, because it was a 'distortion' so 'brutal' that it produced a 'structural discontinuity'?[360] Some historical events, no doubt, are insignificant and can be brushed aside as random complications which do not appreciably affect the economic structure; but others, equally clearly, are not. And since they cannot be quantitatively assessed, their existence and the way they impinge on the course of development impose radical limits on the scope of quantitative analysis. It can explain the 'normal' functioning of a society; but it cannot explain the major discontinuities resulting from qualitative changes or the process by which one type of society gives place to another. By itself, in short, it is unable to provide a complete or adequate expla-

355. Cf. above, p. 38.

356. Cf. MARCZEWSKI, *op. cit.* (1965), p. 15.

357. *Ibid.*, p. 14; cf. LEBRUN, 'Structure et quantification', *op. cit.* (1963), p. 30 in PERELMAN (ed.), *Raisonnement et démarches* ... ('remplacer le choix, dans l'ensemble des facteurs d'importance, d'un ou de plusieurs facteurs par la constellation, elle-même, des facteurs quantitativement pondérés'); LEBRUN, 'Developpement et histoire quantitative', *op. cit.* (1967), p. 598 in *Revue de l'Institut de Sociologie.*

358. MARCZEWSKI, *op. cit.* (1965), pp. 33, 36.

359. VILAR, 'Pour une meilleure compréhension ...' (1965), p. 302 in *Revue historique*, Vol. CCXXXIII.

360. MARCZEWSKI, *op. cit.*, p. 35. As VILAR remarks (*op. cit.*, p. 312), 'pour l'historien la guerre n'est pas "exogène". Il ne *peut* pas l'éliminer.'

nation of the social processes it relates.[361] Faced by 'the exogenous variables which, since they cannot be explained, can only be registered in all their historical singularity,' it has, like other types of history, to fall back in the last analysis on 'the complex totality of the human and the historical.'[362]

These considerations do not invalidate the quantitative approach; they only mean that we must accept its limitations and not ask too much of it. It is, in Marczewski's words, only one weapon in 'an arsenal of converging methods,' which can only operate 'within a fairly narrow range of conditions'.[363] Its contribution, however valuable it may be in itself, can never be more than 'partial' and 'preliminary'.[364] The question, of course, is whether this partial analysis, applicable in the first instance to economic data, is capable of extension to other, non-economic spheres. If we adopt Marczewski's narrow definition of quantitative history, this is evidently not the case, and that, no doubt, is one reason why most historians have rejected his definition as too restrictive. But quantification, as Lebrun points out,[365] is not simply a device for handling a particular limited range of questions ('the evaluation of global economic quantities in the rigid framework of national accounting'); it is also a form of analysis which opens up new ways of thought, and new procedures. It suggests, for example, that in the evaluation of historical evidence statistical criteria are as important as the traditional methods of historical criticism.[366] Both are necessary; but the historian who dispenses with quantifiable statistical information is as likely to present a partial, one-sided view as the historian who believes that only the quantifiable data are relevant.

The applicability of quantitative techniques is nevertheless far less limited in scope than is often supposed. Most historians are prepared to concede that quantification and statistical methods have a legitimate place in economic and even in social history, but they are still unwilling to accept their use in legal, constitutional and intellectual history. Like Hume in the eighteenth century, they take the view that 'controversies concerning the degree of any quality or circumstance' can never 'reach a reasonable certainty or precision' – that there is no standard, for example, to decide how great a general Hannibal was, or how good a historian Thucydides.[367] This, no doubt, is true absolutely; but it is also true that we can measure opinion, which is all we have to go on anyway, and the measurement of opinion – for example, about Macchiavelli or about Hobbes – gives us significant,

---

361. MARCZEWSKI, 'Quantitative history', pp. 190-191 in *Journal of Contemporary History* (1968).

362. MARCZEWSKI, *Introduction, op. cit.* (1965), p. 36; LEBRUN, 'Développement et histoire quantitative', *op. cit.* (1967), p. 584.

363. MARCZEWSKI, *Introduction*, p. 51; 'Quantitative history', p. 190.

364. Cf. LEBRUN, *op. cit.* (1967), p. 598.

365. *Ibid.*, p. 599.

366. *Ibid.*, p. 601.

367. Cf. AYDELOTTE, 'Quantification in history', p. 13 in ROWNEY & GRAHAM (eds.), *Quantitative History, op. cit.* (1969).

if not final, results. Moreover, this is not the only way in which so-called 'intangibles' or 'imponderables' can be statistically evaluated. If we know what people were reading, or what books were coming off the presses in what numbers, we have an index – perhaps imperfect, but certainly not valueless – of a climate of opinion, which is at any rate more satisfactory than a purely intuitive judgement of who were the influential writers. Finally, there are the techniques of content analysis – that is to say, the systematic and quantitative investigation of recurrent words or ideas or themes in a given body of material.[368] A recent example is an attempt to measure the development of American self-consciousness by counting the uses of certain symbolic terms in the colonial press of the mid-eighteenth century,[369] but it is easy to see many other areas – for example, Renaissance studies[370] – where similar methods might produce valuable results.

The effect of this quantitative approach is to add a new dimension – and, many historians would argue, a greater depth – to the study of areas which hitherto have largely been treated unsystematically. This applies, for example, to legal and constitutional history, in which, traditionally, historians have picked out specific cases or documents (Magna Carta, The Bill of Rights, *Rex v. Hampden*) which have, for one reason or another, been found particularly striking or important. It is evident that this approach may be misleading, unless such cases are seen against the background of the total pattern of litigation; and in the end only systematic quantitative analysis can provide such a background. Hence one scholar is engaged on a quantitative survey of all the cases heard in the court of Exchequer in England during the reign of Henry VII, while another is preparing a similar analysis of more than a century of litigation in the court of Star Chamber.[371]

The results of these attempts to extend the area of quantitative history have not always been entirely convincing. The further historians proceed from the 'hard', numerical data – prices, census figures, savings investment, and the like – of the economic historian and the demographer (and these also, it goes without saying, will often require processing before they become statistically usable), the larger is the part played by the statistical quality of the data inputs. If, for example, the terms or symbols selected for analysis do not really bear the connotations attributed to them, the exercise, however technically proficient, is unlikely to have much value. Sometimes the object proposed may be over-ambitious, sometimes the standards of measurement too crude. As an example one may cite David C. McClelland's well-known attempt to measure the strength in different

---

368. For a brief introductory exposition, cf. T. F. CARNEY, 'Content analysis', in *Journal of the Manitoba History Teachers' Association* (1969), and in *Bulletin de l'Association canadienne des humanités* (1969). I am also personally indebted to Professor Carney for discussing the subject with me.

369. It is referred to by PRICE in 'Recent quantitative work in history. A survey of the main trends', p. 11 in *Studies in Quantitative History, op. cit.* (1969).

370. Cf. above, p. 34.

371. Cf. PRICE, *op. cit.*, p. 11.

societies of men's ambition for achievement, and in this way to elucidate the factors accounting for the rise and fall of civilizations.[372] This is a remarkably stimulating book, and the fact that McClelland's handling of data is sometimes less than convincing[373] does not invalidate his aims. When one considers – to take one of McClelland's examples[374] – the remarkable diversity of judgements, by informed and responsible scholars from Gibbon to Baynes, on the vitality and cultural achievements, the growth and decline, of the Byzantine Empire, the need for an objective standard of measurement is unlikely to be disputed. After reading McClelland's book, one is left, as one historian has commented, with 'a haunting feeling ... that something important is being discussed which better techniques may one day see defined more clearly and measured more precisely'.[375]

The Present Situation

The search for quantity is beyond all doubt the most powerful of the new trends in history, the factor above all others which distinguishes historical attitudes in the 1970's from historical attitudes in the 1930's. This would be admitted even by those historians who, like the present writer, have not been involved actively in quantitative research, and is tacitly conceded by the vehemence of its opponents' attacks. No question has given rise to greater ferment in the historical profession, and this was strikingly confirmed by the place of honour assigned to it in the programme of the XIIIth International Congress of Historical Sciences held in Moscow in August 1970.[376]

This concern with the potentialities of quantitative measurement and numerical analysis should cause no surprise. One of the basic facts in the world today is the invasion of the so-called 'humanities' by a generation whose intellectual equipment is far more profoundly influenced by science

372. McCLELLAND, *The Achieving Society* (1st edn., 1961, paperback edn., 1967).
373. Despite McClelland's arguments to the contrary, few people will accept, for example, his contention (p. 112) that 'a sample of the thoughts of 15 men will give us an adequate measure of the level of achievement motivation in the Greek population from roughly 900 to 500 B.C.'; and the same doubts apply to his Spanish and English samples (pp. 130, 134). But the question is too large and technical to be discussed here.
374. *Ibid.*, p. 21.
375. Cf. DAVIS, R., *History and the Social Sciences* (1965), p. 15.
376. Among the papers dealing with the subject (all published by Nauka, Moscow, in 1970) the following are particularly relevant: PAPADOPOULLOS, *La méthode des sciences sociales dans la recherche historique*; DUBUC, *L'histoire au carrefour des sciences humaines*; SCHIEDER, *Unterschiede zwischen historischer und sozialwissenschaftlicher Methode*; SESTAN, *Storia degli avvenimenti e storia delle strutture*; HEXTER, *History, the Social Sciences and Quantification*; and DUPRONT, *Langage et histoire* (important for all questions concerning content analysis). – These papers appeared after the preceding section had been written, and these concluding pages have been added to take account of them and of other recent literature.

and a scientific outlook than their predecessors. In an age which has seen the emergence of the new science of cybernetics, the electronic revolution, the construction and exploitation of the resources of analogue and digital computers, it is not surprising that the younger generation of historians should have lost patience with the fumbling methodology of traditional historiography, and sought to build their work on less amateur foundations. History, as a result, is in the process of becoming far more sophisticated, and it is not easy to believe that this is a trend which will be reversed. If the general public is still impressed by art, rhetoric and verbal skill, the professional historian is more likely to be suspicious, and the qualities which enabled G. M. Trevelyan to sell over two million copies of his *English Social History* are at a discount.

It is, of course, true that many historians – perhaps a majority of historians – have not yet come to terms with the new trends. The most recent survey of the situation in the United States[377] reveals – not unexpectedly – a 'generation gap', and it is reasonable to assume that that gap is wider in Europe and (so far as the available evidence allows one to judge) in Asia than it is on the American continent. Its existence became fully apparent at the meeting of the American Historical Association in Washington in December 1969 and again at Boston a year later.[378] Though predominantly political, the attack on the older generation was directed also against the methodological deficiencies and the lack of theoretical sophistication which make so much traditional history a facile defence of the *status quo*. The charge levelled against 'history as currently written' was, in the words of C. Vann Woodward (himself a former president of the American Historical Association) that it is 'bland, banal or Philistine, [. . .] morally obtuse, aesthetically archaic and intellectually insipid.' The object of the new generation is to eradicate these defects by a more sophisticated methodology and new, scientific standards of conceptual clarity.

As we have had ample opportunity to observe, the search for 'objectively tested generalizations' rather than 'literary narrative' is not new. It reaches back at least to Buckle and Comte and, on another level, to Marx. What is new, and what accounts for the new emphasis on the quantitative approach, is the emergence of a number of sophisticated techniques which seem, at last, to have brought the realization of objectively tested history within reach. It is natural, and salutary, that historians should wish to explore the possibilities of these techniques. History has always borrowed from other disciplines, just as they have borrowed from it, and there is no reason why historians should not make use of the arsenal of weapons which mathematicians, statisticians and social scientists have fabricated and refined. Neither history nor the social sciences form self-contained systems, and experience shows that much of the most interesting and productive

377. LANDES & TILLY (eds.), *History as Social Science* (The Behavioral and Social Sciences Survey, 1971).
378. Cf. DONALD, 'Radical historians on the move' (1970), *New York Times Book Review*, LXXV (29), and *New York Times*, 17 Feb.

work occurs at and across the self-imposed frontiers between different disciplines.

It is also true that the attempt to explore the ideas and methods of social science carries with it certain inherent risks. This is something of which experienced exponents of quantitative history are well aware.[379] One danger, much commented upon, is the pursuit of technology for its own sake. 'The greatest hazard in quantitative research,' Aydelotte has said,[380] 'is not that of neglecting techniques, but that of becoming too much absorbed in them.' If some conventional historians can be accused of 'mindless confrontation of the documents',[381] it is equally possible to accuse some quantitative historians of mindless confrontation of the computer. The satisfaction of having mastered a sophisticated technique may become obsessive, and a particular methodology may be selected without reference to its appropriateness.[382] It is sometimes forgotten that there is no automatic defence in numbers alone, and that the question whether quantitative methods will be helpful on a given problem is a matter not of rule, but of the strategy of research; 'quantities without structural and critical evaluation are as analytically disorientated as opinions without evidence'.[383]

There is also a danger that the concepts and terminology of social science may be used as a substitute for systematic analysis. If there is no defence in numbers, there is no magic in vocabulary. As Vilar has pointed out, nothing is gained – and a great deal may be lost – by describing one of Du Guesclin's campaigns in the Hundred Years War as 'a defensive operational strategy associated with a para-military liberatory impulse'.[384] Besides being anachronistic, the use in this way of a pseudo-scientific terminology creates an impression of exactness and objectivity which is false.[385] More fundamental is the tendency to adopt social science concepts such as 'structure', without critical examination. Recent historical writing has been deeply involved with 'structures', particularly quantitative history which has been defined as the analysis of 'structures formed by phenomena belonging to the same period'.[386] And yet the concept of 'structures' and the theory of 'structuralism' are not something which can be taken for granted, and

---

379. Cf. LEBRUN, 'Développement et histoire quantitative', *op. cit.* (1967), p. 602.

380. 'Quantification in history', p. 21 in ROWNEY & GRAHAM (eds.), *Quantitative History, op. cit.* (1969).

381. DONALD, *op. cit.* (1970), p. 26 in *New York Times Book Review*.

382. Cf. PRICE, *op. cit.* (1969), p. 13.

383. AYDELOTTE, *op. cit.* (1969), p. 12; MATHIAS, 'Economic history, direct and oblique', pp. 78-79 in BALLARD (ed.), *New Movements in the Study and Teaching of History, op. cit.* (1970).

384. 'Stratégie opérationnelle défensive conjuguée à une pulsion libératrice extra-militaire'; cf. VILAR, 'Pour une meilleure compréhension ...', *op. cit.* (1965), p. 298 in *Revue historique*, Vol. CCXXXIII.

385. As HEXTER remarks (*op. cit.*, p. 27), 'one does not change pigliver sausage into *pâté de foie gras* by relabelling the tin.'

386. MARCZEWSKI, *Introduction, op. cit.* (1965), p. 48. Cf. CRAEYBECKX, 'La notion d'"importance"', p. 74 in PERELMAN (ed.), *Raisonnement et démarches de l'historien* (1963) ('Dégager d'abord les grandes structures du passé, voilà à quoi

sociologists have been much concerned with their inherent ambiguities.[387] This is not the place to discuss the problems, but Schieder is surely right in pointing out how disconcerting it is to find that historians have made no serious attempt to come to terms with them.[388] The difficulties they pose for the historian are by no means trivial. The concept of a social structure implies, for example, the concepts of the 'normal' (i.e., whatever fits the structure) and the 'pathological' (i.e., any deviation from the normal).[389] But by what objective standard we are justified in dismissing a series of attested historical facts as 'pathological' and at what stage in the process of historical change the 'pathological' becomes the 'normal' and the 'normal' becomes the 'pathological', are questions to which the answers are by no means self-evident.[390] They are nevertheless not insignificant, as anyone who has followed the long and tedious controversies between Marxist and non-Marxist historians about feudalism — the questions when feudalism began, what are the structural characteristics of feudal society, and when it was superseded by a non-feudal, bourgeois social structure — can attest.

The more historians have sought to make use of quantitative techniques, the more aware they have become of the obduracy of historical materials. It is surely significant that the most sophisticated of all attempts to bring historical data within a quantifiable framework, should have been constrained in the end to concede — with admirable honesty — not merely the existence of non-quantifiable historical variables, but that these independent variables operate in such a way as to preclude a complete explanation by quantitative methods.[391] If this is true of Marczewski's circumscribed field of study, it is hardly necessary to demonstrate that it applies even more drastically to broader and more loosely articulated studies. This does not mean that such studies are useless, but it does mean that the expectations of precise, finite and objective results which early enthusiasts for quantification entertained have largely been disappointed. As we have had more than one occasion to observe, instead of clarifying, quantification has frequently complicated and postponed solutions by drawing attention to factors which traditional historiography had overlooked. It has made the field of history more complex and unmanageable, rather than simpler and more coherent. The interplay between the individual — let us say, a Bismarck —

---

doivent s'attacher en premier lieu les historiens voulant participer à l'élaboration d'une vaste science du social'), and P. LEBRUN, 'Structure et quantification', *op. cit., ibid.*, pp. 43-47.

387. Cf. DUBUC, *op. cit.* (1970), p. 6; SESTAN, *op. cit.* (1970), pp. 19-20. Cf. also MACHLUP, 'Structure and structural change: weaselwords and jargon' (1958), and BASTIDE, 'Colloque sur le mot structure', pp. 351-352 in *Annales* (1959).

388. SCHIEDER, Th., 'Strukturen und Persönlichkeiten in der Geschichte' (1962), p. 273 in *Historische Zeitschrift*, Vol. CXCV.

389. *Ibid.*, pp. 275-276.

390. LEBRUN, *op. cit.* (1963), p. 44: 'Nous ne possédons pas encore d'authentique théorie des passages de structure à structure.'

391. Cf. above, p. 87.

and the society in which he works remains as mysterious are ever.[392]

That does not mean that quantitative history has not made, and will not continue to make, an important positive contribution.[393] By carefully measuring the framework of events it has narrowed the range of possibilities, and no one ever again is likely, for example, to attribute German unification to Bismarck's unaided efforts or his statesmanlike genius. It is also likely to enable us to pinpoint more exactly those great 'leaps in the dark' which it cannot explain. If it is true that we can only evaluate the abnormal when we have a standard of normality by which to measure it, there is no better way of establishing the norm than quantitative measurement. And if, to use Marczewski's terms,[394] historians today are more interested in 'masses' than in 'heroes', quantification is certainly the key unlocking the door through which we can approach the secrets of those anonymous, unwritten millions.

These are, taken all in all, substantive gains; but they also explain why, when we look in detail, the impact of social science methodologies has been less direct than many people at one stage expected. It should never be forgotten that 'the general conclusions of a quantitative investigation are not proved by the figures', that 'they are merely propositions that appear to explain what is known in a plausible fashion'.[395] Much of the impact of quantitative history has been negative. It has destroyed generalizations and categories which previously held sway, and no one would suggest that this is useless.[396] As Hughes rightly emphasizes, 'falsification increases our knowledge'.[397] But the result, inevitably, has been to force historians to retrace their steps, to re-examine their evidence and often to go back to the sources in search of new evidence. We are as far as ever – perhaps further than ever – from solutions, and the often expressed hope that history may cross the threshold of the sciences, in which the results of research are cumulative or additive, has not so far been fulfilled. Some of the findings of quantitative history may, as Marczewski asserts, be commensurable and additive 'in principle';[398] but in practice, owing to the impingement of unquantifiable variables, this is rarely, if ever, the case.

Nevertheless, no one comparing the character of historical research today and thirty years ago can possibly doubt the impact of the new methodology, nor that it is destined to increase. As the most recent survey has established, 'the very fields that involve their practitioners most heavily

392. This is what KRUITHOF ('Qu'est-ce qui est important dans l'histoire? Une approche sociologique', p. 113 in PERELMAN (ed.), *Raisonnement et démarches . . .*, *op. cit.*, 1963) calls the problem of 'the right man in the right place.'

393. CRAEYBECKX, *ibid.*, pp. 65-81, presents a very fair assessment.

394. *Introduction*, p. 33.

395. AYDELOTTE, *op. cit.*, p. 15 in ROWNEY & GRAHAM (eds.), *Quantitative History* (1969).

396. *Ibid.*, p. 19.

397. HUGHES, J. R. T., 'Fact and theory in economic history', p. 92 in *Explorations in Entrepreneurial History*, 2nd ser., Vol. III (1966).

398. *Introduction*, p. 14.

in the behavioral and social sciences are the ones which are growing and are currently staffed with junior men', whose outlook on their profession is basically different from that of their seniors.[399] Most of the younger generation of historians regard themselves as social scientists, but at the same time they are prepared to admit that the application of the methods of social science by historians differs from that, for example, of sociologists or anthropologists. Moreover, except perhaps in the field of economic history, this application is still tentative and experimental, and has done more to reveal the problems and difficulties than to garner a bright new crop of appetising fruit. The main result to date, it would seem, has been to give new directions to historians' interests, and in particular to concentrate their attention on analytical themes such as war, growth, population or urbanization. It has also shown that such themes require new tools, and if these tools are not yet particularly efficient and may need sharpening and adapting before they can effectively serve historians' purposes, it would be defeatist to suppose that the problems and difficulties cannot be overcome. The use of quantification and other social science techniques is still very recent. For the moment, the amount of talk and critical comment, and the proliferation of discussion-groups and conferences seem sometimes to outweigh the volume of genuinely new work being turned out.[400] But these are the familiar symptoms of a new ferment, and the important thing is that a new start has been made.

History has lingered too long in a twilight zone between myth and reality. Around 1950 it seemed, as Anderle pointed out, to have arrived, conceptually and methodologically, at a 'dead end'.[401] It may be that historians looking back from the twenty-first century will see the development of new aims and methods as a turning-point, comparable in scale and importance – as has sometimes been suggested – with the Copernican revolution which heralded the birth of modern physics. If history is ever to cross the threshold from pseudo-science to science, few people today would doubt that the decisive impulse will be the application and refinement of generalizing concepts and quantitative methods. But the victory has not yet been won.

4.　New Dimensions in History

If, as we have seen, the most powerful of the new trends in historical research is the shift from the idiographic to the nomothetic, and the attempt to range history with the social sciences as the science of man in time, there is no doubt that the second most significant change is the widening of the historian's field of vision, both in time and in space. This is, of course, not new in principle. Every historian with an alert mind must, sooner or later,

399.　Landes & Tilly (eds.), *History as Social Science, op. cit.* (1971), p. 30.
400.　Price, *op. cit.* (1969), p. 1.
401.　Cf. Anderle, 'Theoretische Geschichte' (1958), p. 13 in *Historische Zeitschrift*, Vol. CLXXXV.

be curious about the history of other peoples than his own; and among European historians we can trace back interest in events outside their immediate range of vision at least as far as Voltaire. What has given a new urgency to this widening of vision, and made it one of the significant contemporary trends, is the great change in the whole world-situation since 1945 and particularly since the rapid advance between 1957 and 1960 of the process of decolonization. Nothing is more certain in the contemporary epoch, as I . Elekec has said, than that 'a living history demands a concrete revision of the contents of the notion of universality and a more consequential and far-reaching application of it in historical research'.[402]

This means not only, as Elekec also points out, a displacement of the much criticized 'Eurocentric' view of history. Important as this is, and much as has been written about it,[403] this is only one side of the problem; and it must be matched by a similar effort by historians elsewhere to transcend their national and ethnographic limitations, if it is to produce worthwhile results. Not unnaturally, the work of historians in Asia – for example, in India and Indonesia[404] – since independence has been concentrated upon discovering their own past, and particularly in combatting the 'colonialist' interpretations of European scholars of a previous generation. No one would deny that this reaction was necessary and salutary, so far as it went. But it must also be recognized that, in the longer term, little is to be gained by replacing a European-centred 'colonialist' myth by a nationalist Indian or Indonesian myth. In the words of Satish Chandra, 'we should abandon the concept of centre and periphery', whether the centre is located in Europe or the Middle Kingdom.[405] Instead, it should be our aim to obtain – what hitherto has been lacking – a universal perspective on the central problems of human history and its 'dialectical antinomies': continuity and discontinuity, unity and differentiation, stagnation and progress, the alternation of revolutionary and static phases of social evolution, of acceleration and deceleration. This is only possible by means of comparison between divergent trends; and such a comparison will remain superficial, if not impossible, until we know more of areas of history which, for one reason or another, have hitherto been neglected.[406]

The great civilisations of Asia have, of course, a historical tradition of their own, as old as, and in most cases far older than, that of Europe. No

402. Cf. ELEKEC, *Connaissances historiques – conscience sociale* (XIIIth International Congress of Historical Sciences, Moscow, 1970), p. 10.

403. Cf. LOCHER, *Die Überwindung des europäozentrischen Geschichtsbildes* (1954); DANCE, *History the Betrayer* (1962). As is well known, one of the major projects of Unesco has been to combat the 'Eurocentric' view of the past, and restore a better balance. The relative publications are listed by Dance, p. 154.

404. I acknowledge with gratitude two admirable reports prepared by committees of Indian and Indonesian historians, which have been of great help to me in preparing this section. They will be referred to frequently in what follows.

405. The quotation is taken from a stimulating paper on 'The decentring of history', which Professor Chandra was good enough to prepare for the purposes of this study, and for which I am most grateful.

406. Cf. ELEKEC, *op. cit.* (1970), p. 11.

one today would entertain the old theory, so long prevalent in the West, of the unhistorical (or even ahistorical or anti-historical) Orient.[407] Interest in history stems from the same roots in east and west. Its remote origins in China or India or in western Asia were broadly similar to, the motivation for concern with the past more or less identical with, those in Europe.[408] Everywhere, in the beginning, its purpose was quasi-magical, its affiliations were with cults and religion, its object to placate the gods, the awe-inspiring divinities whose actions shaped human destinies. Everywhere, at a somewhat later stage, it recorded the acts of kings, who were regarded as gods, or the descendants of gods, or near to gods, and history became a form of propaganda, 'whereby the nobility and great deeds of kings were sung by priests and warrior musicians'.[409] Classical Chinese historiography has been succinctly described as 'history written by bureaucrats for bureaucrats';[410] it was concerned, in other words, not to record the past as it really had been, but to create a self-image by minimizing or glossing over, in the interests of the ruling dynasty and the prevalent social order, 'the cracks, the fissures, the tensions and deviations which were as characteristic of China as of any other society in the continuous process of development'.[411]

In all these respects the development of oriental and of western historiography long ran on parallel lines. Like classical Chinese historiography, the official chronicles of medieval France or England were compiled as an instrument of government, and English historiography in the sixteenth century was written in the interests of the Tudor dynasty. Nor was the position greatly different in the nineteenth century, as the writings of Sybel and Treitschke and other members of the Prussian school of political historiography attest. But the nineteenth century also saw in Europe the beginnings of the first serious attempt to put history on a new basis of factual objectivity. Both the school of Ranke, with its attempt to discover the past 'as it really was', and the school of Marx, with its attempt to penetrate the dialectical processes of history, reflected this great change, which had no parallel elsewhere. Historiography in its modern sense, as Majumdar has pointed out, 'was practically unknown to the Hindus at the beginning of the nineteenth century',[412] and what was true of India was true of other countries in the oriental world. As late as 1935, when the First Modern Historical Congress met in India, the president, Sir Shafaat Ahmed Khan, adjured Indian historians to adopt the critical methods of German histori-

407. Cf. PHILIPS (ed.), *Historians of India, Pakistan and Ceylon* (*Historical Writing on the Peoples of Asia*, Vol. I, 1961), p. 4.

408. Cf. VOEGELIN, 'Historiogenesis' (1960); BRUNDAGE, 'The birth of Clio' (1954); BUTTERFIELD, *History and Man's Attitude to the Past* (1961).

409. Cf. MAJUMDAR, in *Historical Writing on the Peoples of Asia*, Vol. I (1961), p. 13.

410. BALAZS, *ibid.*, Vol. III (1961), p. 82.

411. Cf. WRIGHT, 'The study of Chinese civilization' (1960), p. 235 in *Journal of the History of Ideas*, Vol. XXI.

412. *Historical Writing on the Peoples of Asia*, Vol. I (1961), p. 416.

ography, 'which have made history in the West almost an exact science'.[413]
In Japan it was the arrival in Tokyo in 1887 of Ludwig Riess, a devoted
disciple of Ranke, which inaugurated the new trend, and in China the reorientation of historical studies on the basis of methods and concepts developed by western historical and social science is exemplified in the person
of Ku Chieh-kang.[414]

No one objectively examining the facts can seriously doubt that the revival and modernization of historical studies in the countries of Asia – and,
indeed, the whole revitalization of the study of Asian civilization, among
western as well as eastern scholars – owes a very substantial debt to the
assimilation of western methods and concepts. It is also true, of course,
particularly in the earlier phases, when much of the historical writing and
teaching was in the hands of Europeans, that the introduction of western
methodology was often accompanied by European preconceptions and prejudices and by the adoption, conscious or unconscious, of a 'Eurocentric'
point of view which stood in the way of an objective appraisal of the place
of the great civilizations of the Orient in world history. Nor, secondly, does
it alter the fact that the Asian countries had their own indigenous traditions
of historiography – in India, for example, the so-called *itihas-purana* tradition – which constitute an important element in the indigenous culture.
But although attempts have been made to maintain indigenous traditions
and use them, rather than western models, as the basis of the new historiography, it is fair, on the whole, to say that demands for the revival of
traditional historiography have met with little response.[415] As the Committee set up by the Indonesian Institute of History has observed, the
modern approach to the study of history, which was 'brought in from the
West', is 'alien' to the traditional forms of historical writing and the latter
under present-day circumstances can only be considered 'irrelevant'. The
outstanding works of modern Indonesian historiography, beginning with
Djajadiningrat and Purbatjaraka, are 'written in a style which is essentially
different from that of traditional historiography', and their appearance marks
'a new epoch.' For this reason, and since we are here concerned only with
current trends, we may safely leave the traditional forms of historiography
out of account.[416]

The impact of western historiography occurred in three phases. To begin
with, the main concern was to adopt and assimilate the methods of internal

413. His remarks are quoted on p. 5 of the report referred to above, p. 95, n. 404.
414. Cf. WRIGHT, *op. cit.* (1960), pp. 248, 251, and GRAY in *Historical Writing*,
Vol. III (1961), pp. 202-203. KU's *The Autobiography of a Chinese Historian* (1931)
was translated by A. W. Hummel.
415. Such, at least, is the impression left by the Indian and Indonesian reports
referred to above. According to the former (p. 4) the result was 'a narrow attitude
in tracing India's social and cultural development'; according to the latter (p. 19)
'confusion in the picture of the past'.
416. Cf. the Indonesian report, p. 4. This does not mean, of course, that the texts
of traditional historiography cannot be used as a historical source. This was the
method of Djajadiningrat, at the same time as he 'demonstrated in detail the non-
historical basis of Indonesian traditional historiography' (*ibid.*, p. 28).

and external criticism, of painstaking factual research and careful accurate scholarship, elaborated by the German historical school in the nineteenth century. The German influence remained strong throughout the inter-war years, in China particularly after the revolution of 1911 and during the period of the Kuomintang. It was gradually superseded, from the 1920's onwards, by the influence of Marxism and of historical materialism, and a great controversy ensued which, in the case of China, was only resolved by the communist victory of 1949, though Marxism had been steadily gaining ground long before.[417] In India, as elsewhere in the Asian continent, Marxist categories – particularly Marx's concept of the Asian mode of production – continue to provide fruitful topics of debate, and the work of Marxist historians, such as D. D. Kosambi, exerts a powerful influence over the thinking of Indian historians of the younger generation.[418] But latterly interest has turned in a new direction, and the current trend is towards the assimilation and adaptation of the sophisticated techniques of analysis developed in the west during the past fifteen or twenty years.[419] A similar evolution, it will later be seen, took place in Latin America.

Whereas in Latin America historiography has always followed a European pattern, the new trends in Asian historiography are everywhere relatively recent. They have also proceeded unevenly and at different speeds. Whereas in India the assimilation of western concepts and methods has made steady progress since independence, historical studies in Indonesia are still in a transitional stage, and Indonesian historians still have some way to go before even the basic techniques of documentary criticism are generally accepted. Interest in methodology is lacking, and only a few historians, among whom Sartono Kartodirdjo is outstanding, are aware of the need for methodological refinement.[420] The fact is, of course, that 'historical study and writing in the modern sense of the word, is only a recent development' in Indonesia, as elsewhere. It was only shortly before the outbreak of the Second World War that the first department of history was established in Djakarta, and in India also it was only 'from about the middle of the fifties' that the stream of historical publications by Indian scholars began to swell, and historical studies entered a new phase. This date, as will be observed, corresponds closely with that which we have picked out as marking the inception of contemporary trends in the west.[421]

Writing in 1961, Bambang Oetomo observed that Indonesian historiography had 'not yet produced new contributions to the science of history'.[422] If by 'the science of history', we mean the methodological approaches used

417. Cf. GRAY, *op. cit.* (1961), pp. 208-209.
418. KOSAMBI's two books, *An Introduction to the Study of Indian History* (1956) and *Culture and Civilization of Ancient India* (1965), are described in the Indian report (p. 18) as 'a landmark'.
419. *Ibid.*, p. 31.
420. The conclusion of the extremely candid Indonesian report (p. 54) is that 'Indonesian historical studies have not yet reached the stage of take-off.'
421. Indian report, p. 12; cf. above, pp. 28-29.
422. *Historical Writing on the Peoples of Asia*, Vol. II, 78.

by historians, this still remains true, not only of Indonesia but of Asian historiography as a whole. Not surprisingly in the circumstances, historians in the 'third world' have been concerned mainly to explore the new techniques developed in the west, and apply them to the study of their own past. They realize, as western historians realize, that many of the most important questions cannot be answered with the type of documentary material which has been the mainstay of historians in the past, and are experimenting with new approaches derived from anthropology and the social sciences. They approach the subject, naturally, from their own point of view and on the basis of their own tradition, which is necessarily different from that of Europeans, and this freedom from Eurocentric preconceptions enables them to see the problems in a new light and gives a positive content to their results; but the box of tools they carry with them is of European (or North American) manufacture, and is perhaps likely to remain so for some time to come. Nor is there inherently any reason why this should not be so. Technical and technological innovations are the preserve of no one people, and if British or Russian historians can draw on the experience and methodology of the French school of *Annales* or of American 'cliometricians', there is nothing derogatory in Indian, or Japanese, or other Asian scholars doing likewise. Indeed, unless historians everywhere feel free to experiment with new techniques and concepts, rejecting them if necessary where they prove less than satisfactory, the study of universal history is unlikely to make great progress.

Meanwhile, a characteristic feature of the contemporary scene has been a great upsurge of interest in the history of the non-European world, not only among Asian and African historians, but also in Europe, in the United States and in Australia. It is only necessary to compare the reports and communications at the international historical congresses of 1960, 1965 and 1970 to perceive the change of focus, though it must also be said that even today the balance is still heavily weighted on the European side.[423] Nevertheless there has been a marked intensification of the study of oriental and

423. A rough calculation shows that, at the XIth Congress in Stockholm in 1960, out of a total of 125 recorded communications – if we leave out of account six papers by ancient historians on various aspects of ancient history in Asia Minor, which has traditionally been treated as part of Greek and Roman antiquity – only five communications, all in the section 'Moyen Age', relate to China (1), Japan (3) and Islam (1). Unless a paper on feudalism in the Ottoman empire is regarded as an exception, the sections 'Histoire moderne' and 'Histoire contemporaine' are exclusively devoted to Europe. Of 25 reports (excluding those in Vol. I on general historical problems), all but two (Yamamoto on the transition from T'ang to Sung in China, and Brown on traditional culture and modernization in india) are Eurocentric. At the XIIth Congress in Vienna in 1965, though the predominance of Europe was still marked – even in themes such as nationalism in the nineteenth and twentieth centuries, or the history of ruling classes, to both of which oriental history has material of fundamental importance to contribute – the introduction of a whole section on 'Histoire des continents' and the selection of 'Acculturation' as one of the central themes, marked a substantial change for the better, though here again the opportunity was missed to discuss the great work of acculturation of the Middle Kingdom.

African history by scholars in the west since approximately 1960, as the reports presented to the XIIIth International Congress by Soviet historians amply indicate.[424]

This upsurge of interest in the history of the countries of Asia and Africa by historians in the west, including historians in the Soviet Union and eastern Europe, is certainly partly conditioned by current political considerations. It reflects, in other words, awareness of the growing importance of the 'third world' in contemporary politics, and realization of the practical importance, from the point of view of everyday affairs, of a better understanding of their traditions and historical evolution. This preoccupation lies behind the insistent demand, in the United States and elsewhere, for 'orientation courses' on Asian civilizations.[425] As W. T. de Bary, among others, has pointed out, this pragmatical approach, tending as it does to evaluate Asian and African history in relation to its importance for the west, is not necessarily the best;[426] but there is no doubt that the broadening of the historian's field of vision which it denotes has had salutary effects. First of all, it has made European historians far more conscious of the limitations of their Eurocentric view of the world and far more willing to make the effort to transcend the limitations of space and time. Secondly and more specifically, it has resulted in a far more open and critical attitude to the questions of imperialism and colonialism, in a willingness to examine their impact from the point of view not simply of the colonial power, but also, to an equal or even greater extent, of the peoples affected, and particularly to treat the whole history of colonial expansion as a process of confrontation, in which all parties participated.[427]

The ideal to which historians are moving under the impact of recent world events is a view of history in which every people and every civilization in every part of the world has an equal place and an equal claim to consideration, and in which the experience of none is brushed aside as peripheral or insignificant. It needs scarcely be said that this ideal is far from realization, and that progress will remain slow and hesitant until far more is known of the history of neglected areas. At a time when European historians are increasingly aware of the limitations of the national framework of history which predominated for so long in Europe, it is easy to

424. Cf. KIM & NIKIFOROV, *Researches in the History of the Countries of the East (1965-1969)*, and NERSESOV, *Soviet Literature on the History of the African Countries for the Period 1965-69*. Other relevant papers include MARKOV, *Wege und Formen der Staatsbildung in Asien und Afrika seit dem zweiten Weltkrieg*; GEISS, *Das Entstehen der modernen Eliten in Afrika seit der Mitte des 18. Jahrhunderts*; PALLAT, *Qualitative Change in the Development of Asian Countries after World War II* (all Moscow, 1970).

425. Cf. LIU, J. T. C., 'An orientation course on Asian civilisations' (1957); LEWIS, M. D., 'How many histories should we teach? Asia and Africa in a liberal arts education' (1962); STAVRIANOS, 'The teaching of world history' (1959).

426. Cf. DE BARY & EMBREE (eds.), *Approaches to Asian Civilizations* (1964), pp. ix, xiii.

427. This change of attitude is admirably summarized in the introduction to von ALBERTINI, *Das Ende des Kolonialismus* (1970).

be impatient of the preoccupation of historians in the newly emancipated countries of Asia and Africa with the history of their own country. This tendency, in part a reflection of strong nationalistic impulses, can all too easily result, as Indonesian historians have candidly pointed out, in narrow mental horizons.[428] But it must also be borne in mind that in many areas the basic research, which is taken for granted in Europe, still remains to be done, and until this has been taken in hand at the local level by specialists with local knowledge, the foundations for broader generalization will remain shaky.

The great need today, over most of the newly emancipated 'third world', is for accurate, dispassionate, critical sifting and sorting of the evidence in conformity with the best available techniques of historical research. This is particularly true of 'black' or sub-Saharan Africa, where historians – or at least those historians dealing with the period before the coming of the Europeans – have had to start off from almost nothing during the last twenty years, and at the same time to devise appropriate tools and methods.[429] Their achievement in so short a time is remarkable; but the fact remains that an immense amount remains to be done before we can claim to possess an adequate framework of African history. And in Asia also, as a French scholar has recently pointed out, the amount of basic material that still remains hidden in largely unexamined manuscript collections is phenomenal. 'The State Library of Outer Mongolia at Ulan-Bator [. . .] alone has 98,000 different Tibetan titles, and there is no reason to suppose that the collection is complete. Recently, an Indian scholar was able to draw up a list of 1,500 important existing Indonesian works, of which only forty-five have been printed. In Asia Minor today documents are being unearthed so fast that in order to decipher them a hundred times as many specialists would be needed as are available.'[430]

Although the change in historical perspective is only at its beginning and the broadening of the field of vision still tentative, the shift in basic attitudes is nevertheless of fundamental importance. As analysis takes the place of description, historians have become increasingly aware that effective analysis requires a broader substructure of factual information than any single area or civilization can provide. Meaningful discussion of feudalism must extend to Japanese and Indian as well as European experience; to understand the process of urbanization it is necessary to take into account the history of the city in China, Latin America and the Islamic countries of the Middle East, as well as the towns of black Africa; the study of peasant movements involves the evaluation of a broad spectrum of comparable material reaching from pre-revolutionary Russia via Bohemia, the Rhinelands, Ireland and the Antilles, to Vietnam and China; and no examination of imperialism as a historical phenomenon is likely to be satisfactory

428. Cf. the report referred to above (p. 95, n. 404), p. 70.
429. The position of historical study in Africa is discussed below, pp. 109-114.
430. Cf. HERBERT, *Introduction à l'Asie* (1960), p. 15 (English translation, *An Introduction to Asia*, 1968, p. 13).

so long as it is confined to the European imperialisms of modern times and ignores the traditional imperialisms of the ancient world or the example of the Middle Kingdom.[431] The same applies to other basic concepts, such as the frontier.[432]

All this implies a new conception of world history and its potentialities. It also implies a new attitude to oriental history. If historians are to achieve a global perspective, the study of the Asian civilizations can no longer be treated as a specialized field which only Arabists, Indologists, Sinologists, and other Orientalists can safely tread. No one would wish to decry the contribution of earlier generations of oriental scholars; to them we owe most of the existing groundwork. But the fact remains that their interests in the main were literary and philological; they were rarely trained in historical method or fully aware of the sort of problems with which historians are primarily concerned. For this reason there has been a tendency recently among historians to speak of 'the incubus of Orientalism'.[433] This reaction may be exaggerated; but it is also true – not only in Europe, but also in the countries directly concerned – that oriental history is only beginning to emerge from isolation, as a specialized discipline, and take its place in the mainstream of historical thought. In Indonesia, for example, a philological approach to history, inherited from the Dutch, was predominant until very recently, and in Europe – both in east and in west – the history of the eastern countries is still more commonly associated with departments of oriental studies than with the faculty of history.[434] The results are twofold. The first is a concentration upon literary sources to the detriment of the social reality; the second is a marked tendency to adopt the self-image which those sources – the Zend Avesta, the Vedas, the Confucian classics

431. The much criticized, but pioneering book edited by R. COULBORN, *Feudalism in History* (1956), pointed the way. For other aspects, cf. the report prepared for the XIIIth Congress of Historical Sciences, *Enquête sur les mouvements paysans dans le monde contemporain* (1970); WOLF, *Peasant Wars of the Twentieth Century* (1965); Chap. I ('The new towns') in HODGKIN, *Nationalism in Colonial Africa* (1956); WRIGHT, 'Viewpoints on a city' (1963) and 'Symbolism and function. Reflections on Changon and other great cities' (1963); MORSE, 'Some characteristics of Latin American urban history' (1962); EISENSTADT, S. N., *The Political Systems of Empires* (1963) and *The Decline of Empires* (1967).

432. Cf. LATTIMORE, 'The frontier in history' (*Relazioni* of the Xth International Congress of Historical Sciences, 1955) and *Inner Asian Frontiers of China* (3rd edn., 1962); WEBB, *The Great Frontier* (1951); WYMAN & KROEBER, C. B. (eds.), *The Frontier in Perspective* (1957); LEWIS, A. R. & McGANN (eds.), *The New World Looks at Its History* (1963); GERHARD, 'Neusiedlung und institutionelles Erbe' (1962); KELLY, *Eastern Arabian Frontiers* (1964).

433. Cf. WRIGHT, 'The study of Chinese civilisation' (1960), pp. 245, 253 in *Journal of the History of Ideas*, Vol. XXI.

434. This is the position, for example, in the University of Oxford; for London, where there has recently been some change, cf. COWAN, *South East Asian History in London* (1963). In Leningrad in 1960 (according to G. A. LENSEN, p. 263 in DE BARY & EMBREE (eds.), *Approaches to Asian Civilisations*, 1961) out of 78 faculty members in the School of Asian Studies, 37 were linguists, 20 concerned with literature and philology, and only 21 were historians. Even so, it may be remarked, by most European standards this is a respectable total.

– propagated. In the case of India, for example, the result was a reconstruction of India's past 'based upon the high intellectual tradition and upon the formal codes for Indian life found in the classical writings.' It provided a picture of 'the leading ideas of the priestly and intellectual élite', but ignored the fact that, in India as in all other societies, 'the gap between the codes of the lawgivers and the life of the people was substantial.' The study of India's past, in other words, 'was tied too closely to one level of Indian experience', just as the history of China was cast in the mould of the Confucian classics.[435]

The current trend in extra-European history – more advanced in some areas than in others – is to correct this bias. For this, the first prerequisite is the emancipation of history from its subordination to 'philological orientalism', and its integration into the mainstream of historical research. This has now been accomplished almost everywhere, and is one of the first results of independence, which was followed in all countries by the creation of new universities and the establishment in them of separate departments of history. Although the results are only beginning to be felt, there is no doubt that the training thus made available has provided the essential impetus for the growth of historical studies. It has also, in some cases at least, deflected them on to nationalist lines. The motive of the newly independent governments in setting up new departments of history was, naturally enough, to provide 'a new historical image to its own people and to the world', and sometimes – as Oetomo has observed – 'the desire to produce nationalistic literature' has proved 'stronger than the desire to conform to scientific standards'.[436] This nationalistic phase, strong in the years immediately following independence, has now perhaps passed its peak. It still remains true that the second prerequisite – for European historians as well as for historians in the third world – is to transcend nationalist historiography and concentrate instead on problems which all historians have in common.[437] 'Indonesia-centric' history is no less partial and out-of-date than 'Eurocentric' history, and neither is an adequate substitute for a universal point of view.

Considering how much of the basic groundwork still remains to be done, it may be natural for historians in the 'third world' to concentrate at the present stage on the history of their own country, but this can be stultifying if that history is not viewed in a larger framework. Too often courses on a particular country or region of Asia ignore the general trends of development in Asia as a whole.[438] The third prerequisite is therefore, as Pulleyblank has said, to avoid the pitfalls of specialization, 'to read other oriental history and non-oriental history' and in this way to 'illuminate our special

---

435. Cf. CRANE, p. 29 in DE BARY & EMBREE (eds.), *Approaches to Asian Civilisations* (1961); for Islam, cf. ISSAWI, *ibid.*, p. 61.

436. OETOMO, p. 78 in *Historical Writing on the Peoples of Asia*, Vol. II (1961).

437. As is specifically stated in the Indonesian report, p. 71; cf. *ibid.*, pp. 23, 60, 64, on the so-called 'Indonesia-centric point of view'.

438. Cf. *The Treatment of Asia in Western Textbooks and Teaching Materials* (Unesco publication ED/147, Nov. 1956), p. 4.

problems from outside so that they in turn throw light on happenings in other times and places'.[439] This is an admonition that applies to western and eastern historians alike. So long as historians ignore the wider perspectives of world history, they run the risk of falling back into an intellectual isolationism, which is bound to stand in the way of any deeper understanding of the processes of historical development in both the western and the non-western world.

It would be absurd to deny, on a practical level, that it is the course of events since 1947 and 1949, since Indian independence and the communist victory in China, that has led to an increasingly active concern with the history of the non-western world. These events, as Panikkar was quick to point out,[440] marked the end of the European epoch and the advent of a new stage in world history, and it is evident in this new stage that the civilizations of China and India and Islam – in interplay, of course, with impulses coming from Europe – are as much a part of the historical background of our times as is the civilization of the west. But it is no less important to emphasize that the new concern with universal history is also a consequence of the development of historical study itself. So long as historians accepted the traditional linear and evolutionary approach, the single national or ethnic community seemed to be the natural unit of historical study, and the vast majority of historians were content to play their traditional rôle as guardians and exponents of their own community's cultural heritage. Even the great Ibn Khaldûn confined himself to the Maghreb, its tribes, peoples, kingdoms and dynasties, because (he said) he lacked 'the necessary knowledge of the East and its peoples'.[441] With the transition to a scientific and analytical history, it has become evident how stultifying such limitations are. What historians require today is a wider spectrum of comparative material, enabling them to probe and analyse the similarities and diversities of historical development and social patterns in all parts of the world, to understand the regularities in the structure of human societies and at the same time to seek out the deeper reasons for apparent irregularities and deviations from the expected. 'Without world history', as Reinhard Wittram has written, 'there is no sense in history.'[442]

Against this background we may turn to a brief and rapid review of contemporary trends and developments in different areas and regions. The inherent difficulties of such a review – particularly, the difficulty of seeing the wood for the trees – are too obvious to require emphasis. In particular, there are great disparities, and it would be misleading to generalize about all regions of the so-called 'third world', as though the situation everywhere were identical. If, after some hesitation, Latin American historiography has been included at this point, the reason is the tendency among

439. Cf. SINOR (ed.), *Orientalism and History* (1954), p. 79.

440. Cf. PANIKKAR, *Asia and Western Dominance* (1953), p. 11.

441. IBN KHALDÛN, *Discours sur l'històire universelle (al-Muqaddima)*, translation Vincent Monteil, Vol. I (Beirut 1967), Introduction, p. 62.

442. WITTRAM, *Das Interesse an der Geschichte* (1958), p. 135.

Latin Americans today – in marked contrast to their attitude in the nineteenth and earlier twentieth centuries – to emphasize the links, historical as well as contemporary, between their countries and those of Asia and Africa.[443] But, though it is instructive to compare the development of Latin American historiography with that of Asia and Africa, the dissimilarities are as conspicuous as the similarities, and it would stretch parallels too far, if it were regarded simply as a variant of a common pattern.[444] For this reason, the concluding observations at the end of this section[445] will be confined largely to the current situation in Asia and Africa.

The main impression, at the present stage, is of a gathering swell of publications on a world-wide scale, so numerous and so varied as to defy classification. Much of the work of historians in Asia and Africa, as well as in Latin America – like similar work by European historians, both in the west and in the east – is on traditional lines. Welcome as it is as an addition to knowledge, it reveals no distinctively new trends, and therefore falls outside the scope of the present survey. The two developments which appear to mark historical studies at the present time are an inter-disciplinary approach and the extension of the historian's field of vision both in time and in space. The former implies the search for new research mechanisms which possess greater heuristic and explanatory potency than those upon which historians have traditionally relied; the latter implies a willingness to look beyond the areas which have hitherto occupied the most prominent place in historical writing. So far as European historians are concerned, this means abandoning the 'Eurocentric' view of history. But it also means abandoning the view, which goes back to Ranke and Hegel, that the subject-matter of history is simply the succession of the 'higher civilizations', each related (in Lord Acton's words) 'according to the time and degree in which they contribute to the common fortunes of mankind'.[446] World history is not only the history of the 'higher' civilizations. The great civilizations of China, India and Islam are obviously as significant, for anyone wanting to understand the nature of civilization and its problems, as the history of Europe. But universal history requires a wider and longer vision still. It embraces also the peoples traditionally regarded as 'outside history' – not only the peoples of Africa but the tribes, some long forgotten, of the steppe-lands of central Asia, the mountain-peoples of Burma, Thailand and Vietnam, and the inhabitants of pre-Columbian America.[447] 'Civilization' is only a part, not even the larger part, of historical time. If we are to achieve any deeper understanding of it, it must be seen against the wider background

443. Cf. particularly RODRIGUES, *Brasil e Africa* (2nd edn., 1964) (English translation, *Brazil and Africa*, 1965).
444. Cf. below, p. 121.
445. Below, pp. 141-147.
446. *Lectures on Modern History* (1906), p. 317; cf. SCHULIN, *Die weltgeschichtliche Erfassung des Orients bei Hegel und Ranke* (1958).
447. This point was forcibly made by A. W. MACDONALD (*Historical Writing on the Peoples of Asia*, Vol. II (1961), pp. 326-328) regarding 'the historical role of the Karens, Kachins, Chins, Nagas, Kukis'.

of a history which covers impartially the whole of mankind. At this level history can only progress if it joins hands with archaeology and anthropology.

Pre-history

The first extension of the domain of history – its extension in time – came from the side of pre-historic archaeology. In some ways, it is the most important of all, for it has affected historians in all parts of the world, transforming their vision of the human past. In India, for example, the rapid growth of archaeology during the past twenty to twenty-five years has played an important part in establishing a cultural sequence, both in north and south India. Archaeological evidence has compelled historians to re-examine the pattern of Aryan settlements in India and the stages of the growth of Aryan society. At the same time, the discovery of neolithic and chalcolithic cultures in the Ganga valley, east India, the Narbada valley and south India, has thrown ligĥt on the pre-Aryan cultures in these areas. With the definite dating of the use of iron in north India, it has became possible to relate the clearing of forests in the valley of the Ganges with the help of the iron axe, and the cultivation of rain-watered lands with the help of the iron-tipped plough, to the rise of urban centres and large territorial empires in east India, and these facts have opened the way for a new approach to the question of the rise of Buddhism.[448]

The current state of archaeological research is surveyed in another section of this Study,[449] and we are concerned here only with its consequences for general history. These may be summed up as an immense widening of the historian's field of vision. In scarcely more than a hundred years archaeologists have unearthed half a dozen extinct civilizations whose very existence had been forgotten, and deciphered some of the scripts in which the representatives of these extinct civilizations kept their records and wrote their literature. As Gordon Childe has said, 'prehistoric archaeology has effected a revolution in man's knowledge of his own past comparable in scale to the revolutions achieved by modern physics and astronomy. Instead of the beggarly five thousand years patchily and fitfully illumined by written records, archaeology now offers the historian a vista of two hundred and fifty thousand years; like a new optical instrument it has already extended

448. I quote here from the Indian report referred to above p. 95, n. 404; cf. ALLCHIN, *The Birth of Indian Civilization* (1968); PIGGOTT, *Prehistoric India* (1961); WHEELER, *The Indus Civilization* (1953).

449. See the chapter on *Archaeology and Prehistory,* by Professor Sigfried J. DE LAET in *Main Trends of Research in the Social and Human Sciences*, Part 2, vol. 1, (1979); cf. particularly his remarks (p. 208) on the influence of prehistory on historical research. Professor De Laet's contribution has been of great help to me in formulating this short section; but it goes without saying that I have no intention of trespassing into his domain, and for all questions regarding methodology, classification and interpretation the reader is referred to his lucid account.

our range of backward vision fiftyfold and is every year expanding the field surveyed with the new perspective.'[450]

The impact of pre-history and pre-historic archaeology is so ubiquitous and well known that it is scarcely necessary to comment upon it at length. One of its first effects, so far as western historians were concerned, was to destroy the conception of ancient history as a unity dominated by Greece and Rome.[451] In works such as Mortimer Wheeler's *Rome beyond the Imperial Frontiers,* archaeology became the key to a universal view of history, linking Europe, Asia and Africa.[452] The most significaꞮt and lasting result of archaeological discovery, however, is to have broken the historian's traditional reliance upon written records, and, in some instances at least, to have demonstrated the unreliability and mythical character of the information those records convey. Both in Anglo-Saxon England and in India, for example, archaeological evidence indicates a radically different pattern of settlement from that put forward in popular tradition and literary texts.[453]

The characteristic feature of archaeological research is, of course, its reliance upon information derived from the artefacts of man's material culture – from flints, axes, stone, glass, pottery, and the like. This use of new material has opened up whole areas of history which were a closed book, and, moreover, offers concrete and tangible evidence which can be used with a high degree of statistical probability. Already it has demonstrated a network of communications extending from the Atlantic to the Oxus and the Indus by the third millennium before the Christian era, and there is no reason to doubt that the network will be extended, as systematic investigations in Siberia, China, India and North Africa get under way. It has brought within the historian's purview peoples without a written history, and in the case of the so-called 'historical' peoples has cast light on social and economic aspects of their history which the written records usually pass over in silence. Whereas Greek and Roman literary sources emphasize political events and the impact of great men, the archaeological evidence tilts the balance by revealing how people lived, what they produced, the patterns of commercial exchange, standards of living, and the technologies in use.

If, for obvious reasons, pre-history is the main domain of archaeology, it must be emphasized that its importance for the historian does not stop at that point. Wherever written records remain sparse, archaeological evidence provides a necessary, and in some cases the only available, source for reconstituting the past. In this respect it is perhaps sufficient, so far as Europe is concerned, to instance Salin's use of archaeological evidence from burial

450. Gordon CHILDE, 'A prehistorian's interpretation of diffusion' (1937), reprinted in STAVRIANOS (ed.), *The Epic of Man to 1500* (2nd edn., 1970): cf. p. 17.
451. Cf. VOGT, *Geschichte des Altertums und Universalgeschichte* (1957), p. 21.
452. WHEELER, *Rome beyond the Imperial Frontiers* (1954).
453. The pioneering work on Anglo-Saxon England was LEEDS, *The Archaeology of the Anglo-Saxon Settlements* (1913); for India, cf. for example BASHAM, 'Modern historians of ancient India', p. 291 in *Historical Writing on the Peoples of Asia,* Vol. I (1961). ALLCHIN, *op. cit.* (1968), p. 330, also draws attention to the limitations of 'text-based assessments of early Indian history'.

sites to reconstruct a picture of Merovingian civilization far fuller and more varied than we can obtain from written sources alone;[454] but it is obvious that there are many other areas (e.g., urban history) in which historians cannot advance without the aid of archaeology, and this even in modern times. Since 1955, industrial archaeology has been developed as a new discipline, with the aim of recording and interpreting the sites and structures of early industrial society, roughly of the period 1760–1860.[455]

The most significant result of archaeology, in its broadest terms, is the reinforcement it has given to the view that the central theme of human history is man's struggle with his environment. It is a theme the historian can only deal with if he is prepared to widen his vision beyond his traditional source material. Until very recent times – until, in fact, governments became concerned with planning and with the problems and processes of social change, which in many cases was not until the middle of the twentieth century – the written records told us little, if anything, of this perennial struggle, in which the energies of the world's teeming millions were continuously absorbed. Down at least to the seventeenth or eighteenth century, and in many parts of the world until much later, the only useful evidence the historian has comes from archaeology and social anthropology. This provides the concrete, factual knowledge – the knowledge of tools, techniques, crops, land use, and surviving artefacts – which enables him to reconstitute social forms, such as the village community and its economy, and trace the succeeding phases of social change. In this respect the new sociological orientation of history is heavily dependent on archaeology, and much of the best work is a result of the interplay between sociological insights and the evidence provided by archaeology – physical objects, field surveys of ancient trade routes, ethnography, and the like. This is the method, for example, Kosambi has used in India, and the reason why his work marks the beginning of what 'promises to be one of the most fruitful and productive trends of history writing in India'.[456]

Like the other social sciences, with which it is commonly grouped, archaeology can open up new perspectives for the historian in any area and at any time-point in the past. It corrects the distortions which are bound to arise from allowing one particular type of source – in particular, the written evidence – to dominate historical interpretation. But its specific contribution is the immense extension, in time and space, it has given to the historian's vision. It has opened up fields which were entirely closed, and forced him to take a far broader and more ecumenical view of his task. It is not only that it has captured the immense vista of pre-history; it has also, like anthropology, but with different methods and in different ways, directed him away from his almost exclusive preoccupation with the so-called 'historic' peoples – in particular, with the great civilizations of the

---

454. Cf. SALIN, *La civilisation mérovingienne d'après les sépultures, les textes et le laboratoire* (2 vols., 1950-52).
455. For a brief survey, cf. RIX, *Industrial Archaeology* (1967).
456. Cf. Indian report, p. 19.

past – to peoples whose history archaeology alone can bring to light but which is nevertheless an integral part of the epic of man. Wherever the written records are lacking or inadequate, it is the historian's main source of concrete, tangible evidence, and for this reason it is particularly important in the study of the history of Asia, Africa and Latin America. As historians embark on the task of establishing a really universal view of human history, as they seek to fill in the gaps, catch up on neglected areas, and complete what is still a very sketchy picture, it is increasingly to archaeology and the facts provided by archaeology that they will have to turn.

African History

Among the areas in which archaeology has a big part to play, but in which so far relatively little has been done, the history of Africa is one.[457] But Africa has its own particular problem for the archaeologist, in particular the disparate character of the terrain. For obvious reasons archaeological evidence has survived far better in the dry zones of the north than in the humid and torrid climate of equatorial Africa; indeed, there are areas – for example, the Ivory Coast – where metallic objects are totally lost in rust in less than a century and archaeological excavation is for all practical purposes 'futile'.[458]

These differences must be taken into account.[459] Like Asia and Europe, the continent of Africa comprises a number of very disparate areas, and it would be a mistake to treat it as a single historical unity. The extreme variations in climate and vegetation, and the different environments they

457. The position is summarized by R. MAUNY in the *Reports* of the *XIIth International Congress of Historical Sciences*, Vol. II (1965), pp. 208-213.

458. Cf. MONTEIL, 'La décolonisation de l'histoire' (1962), p. 10 in *Preuves*, No. 142 (English translation in WALLERSTEIN, *Social Change. The Colonial Situation* (1966): see p. 603).

459. For the following, cf. DIKE & AJAYI, 'African historiography', in *International Encyclopedia of the Social Sciences*, Vol. VI (1968); 'Le problème des sources de l'histoire de l'Afrique noire jusqu'à la colonisation européenne', in *Reports* of the *XIIth International Congress of Historical Sciences (Vienna, 1965)*, Vol. II, *History of the Continents* (1965), and the discussion, *ibid.*, Vol. V, *Proceedings* (1968; VANSINA, MAUNY & THOMAS, L. V. (eds.), *The Historian in Tropical Africa* (1964); CORNEVIN, *Histoire des peuples de l'Afrique noire* (1960), pp. 21-73 (on sources and methodology); *History and Archaeology in Africa*, ed. HAMILTON (1955) and ed. JONES (1959), being the proceedings of the conferences on African history organized by the School of Oriental and African Studies in 1953 and 1957; BLAKE, 'The study of African history' (1950); MONIOT, 'Pour une histoire de l'Afrique noire' (1962); DIKE, 'African history and self-government' (1953), pp. 177-178, 225-226, 251 in *West Africa*, Vol. XXXVII; HODGKIN, 'New openings: Africa', in *New Ways in History* (*Times Literary Supplement*, 1966). For Soviet work, cf. NERSESOV, *Soviet Literature on the History of African Countries* (XIIIth International Congress of Historical Sciences, Moscow, 1970). I am also greatly indebted to Professor K. O. Dike (Harvard) for his valuable comments and criticism.

created, have produced a large variety of different cultures, which – at least initially – are better treated separately than as a whole. The basic, but not the only, division in African history is between the lands north and south of the Sahara, and when we speak of African history today it is primarily to the history of tropical, or equatorial, or 'black' Africa that we are referring. This does not mean, of course, that significant cultural inter-connexions between north and south are lacking; on the contrary, the Sahara, particularly in Islamic times, formed a link, rather than a barrier, and there were continuing links, as well, not only between the different areas of Africa but between them and other continents.

Nevertheless, north Africa, with its long historic connexion with other areas bordering the Mediterranean, has a different history from sub-Saharan Africa. It came under the influence and within the political bound-aries of Rome and then of Islam, and thus became in some ways as much a part of the Islamic as of the African world. Nevertheless it retained its own imprint. The Berbers of north-west Africa reacted against both Roman Christianity and Arabic Islam and sought to maintain their own historical traditions, and Islam in the western Sudan, where after nearly nine cen-turies it has become indigenous to most Sudanese, differs in many respects from Islam in the Middle East.[460] Ethiopia, on the other hand, has all the marks of a people wedged in between two distinct cultures. Under the Solomonid dynasty, it produced its own particular amalgam of African and Judaeo-Christian constituents, but most historians would probably accept that Ethiopian ethnography is basically African, though greatly modified by continuous Asian and other intrusions.

In sub-Saharan Africa, also, regional differences are marked. There is a big difference between the coastal areas open to external contacts with Asia and Europe, and the interior, where the dense forest belt produced a restrictive environment which encouraged tribal isolation and segmentation. But this fragmentation was offset, from an early date, by the rise of king-doms and empires – such as the empires of Ghana (c. 300–1270), Mali (1285–1468) and Songhai (1355–1591) – seeking to control trade routes and to protect the prosperous black trading towns of the western Sudan from the perennial raids of desert nomads. Under the influence of Selig-man, western historians have habitually attributed the origins of these states to the impact of Mediterranean civilization, percolating from the Nile valley 'through the Meroitic filter',[461] but African historians have produced evi-dence that they were the product of indigenous cultures, and the same is true of the west African forest civilizations characterized by the kingdom

---

460. This is the reason why the many attempts to 'purify' Sudanese Islam through the jihads of the nineteenth century failed to 'reform' the faith. That the Christian churches also developed specific characteristics of their own, and often broke off into distinct sects, in an African environment, is also well known; cf. HODGKIN, *Nationalism in Colonial Africa* (1956), pp. 98-114.

461. Cf. OLIVER & FAGE, *A Short History of Africa* (1962), p. 50; see also SELIGMAN, *Races of Africa* (3rd edn., 1975).

of Benin, the kingdoms of the Yorubas, and, in more recent times, the Ashanti confederacy.

Nevertheless, it is not surprising that differences in historical structure have resulted also in considerable inequalities in both the quantity and quality of the historical records. Before the arrival of Europeans on the west coast, conventionally dated from 1434, virtually the only written sources are Islamic, and these cast little, if any, light on areas outside the Islamic sphere. 'The bigger part of the continent', as one specialist has pointed out, 'is not even touched by the Arabic sources', and the same, of course, is even more true of the early European (particularly Portuguese) accounts, which rarely provide information outside the coastal areas.[462]

Because of this relative paucity of written records historians of Africa are greatly dependent on archaeological and artistic materials, e.g., the classical *terra cotta* heads of Ife and the celebrated bronzes of Benin, which are now generally admitted to be the product of African hands. The fact that African historical traditions were for the most part transmitted orally and were rarely written down also accounts for the prominent rôle of the study of oral tradition in African history. But when we turn to the oral sources, we find a similar disparity or unevenness in their distribution. They are distinctly richer in structurally articulated kingdoms with established institutions, such as Rwanda, than in areas such as Burundi with a fluid and changeable political structure, and they decrease rapidly the further one goes back in time.[463] Though the old view that black Africa had no history before the European conquests of the nineteenth century – or that such history and civilization as it has was derived via the Arabs from north Africa and the Near East – is grotesquely ill-informed and has long been discarded by serious historians, it is still true that the documentation of all sorts for the nineteenth and twentieth centuries is incomparably richer and the coverage far more extensive than for the preceding periods. For much of African history the main work remains to be done.[464]

The stimulus to undertake a new African historiography came with the movement towards independence which gathered pace in Africa during and immediately after the Second World War. As in Asia, it led at an early stage to sometimes gross nationalist exaggeration in reaction against European interpretations of the African past, but from around 1960, under the influence of African historians such as K. O. Dike, speculative hypothesis based on slender evidence has increasingly given way to scientific enquiry. Dike's own early work marked in some ways a watershed.[465] Whereas European historians had viewed African history from outside, writing either of Europeans in Africa or of their impact on African society,

462. *Reports* of the *XIIth International Congress, Vienna, 1965*, Vol. V, *Proceedings* (1968), p. 312; cf. *ibid.*, Vol. II (1965), p. 181 ('Le problème des sources de l'histoire de l'Afrique noire ...", *op. cit.*).

463. *Ibid.*, Vol. II, p. 204, and Vol. V, p. 324.

464. *Ibid.*, Vol. II, p. 229.

465. Cf. DIKE, *Trade and Politics in the Niger Delta, 1830-1885* (1956).

Dike changed the focus from the Europeans to the Africans themselves, bringing out the interplay between the native societies of west Africa, which had maintained their identity in spite of four centuries of European contact, and the European traders, and insisting that the only valid African history must be a history of Africans. The outcome of this new trend, and its present culmination, may be seen in the volume of essays presented to Thomas Hodgkin on his sixtieth birthday.[466] What is remarkable about this volume is the fact that, though it covers a broad range of religious, nationalist, social, economic and political developments, the writers scarcely find it necessary to mention the rôle of European colonialists; indeed, as one contributor observes, the assumption that European conquest and rule was a formative influence in African history is definitely misleading.[467] Through all the successive stages in the evolution of African society, as Blake points out, 'the one permanent element is the Negro people in all their various tribal and confederate branches,' and the habit of looking at Africa primarily in terms of the exterior forces which have influenced it obscures 'such main trends in the pattern of African history as the structure of native society, tribal wars, tribal migrations, native land tenure, and the reaction of native cultures to alien cultures.'[468]

The central problem of the new African historiography is sources. It is true that written sources are not by any means as meagre as was at one time supposed, and much effort is currently being given to collecting, classifying and editing them. The problem still remains that these sources, both Islamic and European, reflect with rare exceptions the interests and point of view of outsiders and only cast an oblique light on the activities and attitudes of the African peoples themselves. Moslem historians, it is true, sometimes recorded African traditions, mostly in Arabic but sometimes in Arabic transcriptions of the vernacular, and after the sixteenth century there is an increasing number of Arabic sources written by Africans for Africans.[469] But on the whole, Moslem writers were mainly interested in the spread of Islam, and their accounts tend to be one-sided; they concentrate, for example, on leading personalities of the Moslem community, rather than the traditional states and their rulers. For a history of Africa which is a history of Africans the written records, in short, are unsatisfactory and insufficient. They pay too little account to the indigenous culture, to the historical legends, the genealogies, lists of kings, accounts of a community's origins and notable events in its history, which were embedded in oral tradition, and transmitted orally. Because of the importance of oral tradition in a society where indigenous written records are few, because it is far more widely spread throughout Africa than the

---

466. ALLEN & JOHNSON (eds.), *African Perspectives* (1970); cf. also RANGER (ed.), *Emerging Themes in African History* (1968).

467. ALLEN & JOHNSON (eds.), *op. cit.*, p. 85.

468. Cf. BLAKE, *op. cit.* (1950), pp. 51, 63 in the *Transactions of the Royal Historical Society*, 4th ser., Vol. XXXII.

469. Cf. the remarks of I. HRBEK, pp. 314-315 in Vol. V, *Proceedings* (1968), of the *Reports* of the *XIIth International Congress*.

written evidence, and because it casts light on many subjects which the latter ignores, oral tradition has a larger and more important place in African history than in that of any other continent. Only in the history of the native populations of America can it be said to play a comparable rôle.

A great deal of effort has, therefore, been devoted in recent years to the collection and recording of oral tradition. It has, says Dike, 'become a major preoccupation,' particularly as the rapid changes now taking place in modern African society are rapidly resulting in its disappearance.[470] Equally important is the problem of its evaluation and of the elaboration of critical rules and methods for its use. This is a highly technical question which has given rise to much controversy and cannot be discussed in this place.[471] It is sufficient to say that the pioneer of modern analysis is Jan Vansina, and that enough has been accomplished for the original scepticism about the value of oral evidence to be overcome. Nevertheless there is no doubt that the use of oral tradition involves great difficulties, among which the problem of chronology is outstanding. The traditional history of Africa is for the most part synchronic; accurate chronology and causation were of little, if any, account, and even where there are specific references to years, generations and periods, they may relate to 'structural' and not to chronological time.[472] The establishment of acceptable chronological landmarks is therefore a major task which is only possible by calling upon the resources and techniques of archaeology, linguistics, ethnology, zoology and botany – in short, by an inter-disciplinary approach.[473] Where Africa is concerned, the conventional methodology of European historiography, and particularly its assumption that only documentary history is real history, are largely inapplicable. In Europe itself, as we have seen, reliance upon the written document and the neglect of other forms of historical tradition have come increasingly under attack in recent years. But it is in Africa that the deficiencies of the traditional methodology are most plainly evident. African history can only progress by breaking through its bonds, and it has rightly been said that 'the most fruitful trend in African historiography in the last decade' is the development of an inter-disciplinary approach.[474] Only in this way can the traditional African historical material be processed and made available for the writing of history.

This is not the place for a detailed survey of the specific products of

470. *International Encyclopedia of the Social Sciences*, Vol. VI, p. 399.

471. The classical work is VANSINA, *De la tradition orale. Essai de méthode historique* (1961) (English translation, *The Oral Tradition. A Study in Historical Methodology*, 1965); cf. also PERSON, 'Tradition orale et chronologie' (1962); McCALL, *Africa in Time-Perspective. A Discussion on Historical Reconstruction from Unwritten Sources* (1964).

472. Cf. the remarks of A. DELUZ-CHIVA, 'Anthropologie, histoire et historiographie' (1965), pp. 617-620 in *Revue internationale des Sciences sociales*, XVII (4) (parallel English version, 'Anthropology, history and historiography', pp. 574-576 in *International Social Science Journal*, same ref.).

473. Cf. BLAKE, *op. cit.* (1950), p. 64.

474. *International Encyclopedia of the Social Sciences*, Vol. VI, p. 398 (DIKE).

the African historiography, but two general observations may be made. The first is that the bulk of the work, at least for the earlier periods, is almost of necessity local and particular. What is important at the present stage, in other words, is exact, detailed and scientific examination of 'case histories', rather than broad sweeping generalizations.[475] Secondly, and perhaps not surprisingly, the larger part of current writing is concerned with the history of the nineteenth and twentieth centuries. This is in part because of the incomparably greater quantity of available material, both written and oral, but it is also because of the need African historians feel to correct the conventional European view of the African past, and particularly of the European impact on Africa. The era of European conquest, it is now evident, coincided and interacted with a great upheaval and a vigorous upsurge in African society, so great that one can speak of an 'African repartition of Africa' in the nineteenth century. It is not difficult to understand why African historians should be concerned with this last 'era of independent African development', which only ended when 'the last resistance of Africans [. . .] was broken'.[476] It indicates the persistence, throughout the period of European dominance, of an independent African culture and history, which lay at the roots of the African nationalist revival. Although increasing attention has been paid in the last fifteen or twenty years to such questions as the indigenous origins of African culture, the transition from traditional tribal to industrial society, and the internal development and consolidation of particular African communities,[477] it is therefore not surprising that the colonial period and the African nationalist reaction to colonialism still loom large.[478] The difference is that they are now viewed from an internal standpoint, as they were seen and experienced by African themselves.

New Patterns in Latin American History

When we turn to Latin America, another continent with a long and pervasive colonial past, similar tendencies are apparent. In spite of the fact that its political emancipation occurred a century and a half ago, many characteristic features of the history of ex-colonial territories in the old world –

475. As MONTEIL emphasizes in 'La décolonisation de l'histoire' (1962), p. 12 in *Preuves*, No. 142 (cf. p. 605 in WALLERSTEIN, *Social Change, op. cit.*, 1966).

476. *Reports* of the *XIIth International Congress*, Vol. V, *Proceedings* (1968), pp. 314, 323.

477. POTEHIN, *Formirovanie nacional'noj obščnosti južnoafrikanskih Bantu* (1956), has written, for example, on the Bantu community of South Africa.

478. In addition to general works on the rise of nationalism in Africa as a whole and in different areas, there has been a great deal of specialized work on individual resistance leaders and on the history of particular rebellions. This cannot be cited in detail here, but reference should be made to the pioneering study of SHEPPERSON & PRICE, *Independent African* (1958). ROTBERG, 'Resistance and rebellion in British Nyasaland and German East Africa, 1885-1915' (1967) is a good example of recent specialized work on particular areas of African resistance.

the interaction, for example, between the colonizing and the indigenous peoples, and colonial forms of landholding – are enduring themes in Latin American history. More recently the insistent problems of neo-colonialism and under-development, as well as the revolutionary unrest in many Latin American countries since the Cuban revolution of 1959, have served to emphasize the points of contact between the historical inheritance of the peoples of Latin America and those of Asia and Africa. Not surprisingly, the result has been a re-appraisal of the content and methodology of Latin American history.[479] As Richard Graham has written with reference to Brazil, 'the grinding pressures of modern change' and 'the resulting conflicts and uncertainties' have driven the younger generation of historians to look at the past 'with new questions' and 'evaluate old answers by new criteria.'[480]

It is a paradox of Latin American history that it is, in one sense, 'one of the oldest and best established divisions of modern history', and in other ways 'a new and struggling field of study.'[481] Its roots, from the beginning, lay in Europe, its models derived from European historiography.[482] In view of the strength of European cultural traditions among the early creole élite, this is not perhaps, surprising. The long and heated controversy between 'Hispanists' and 'Indianists' over the rôle of Spain in the new world – the 'black legend' of Spanish inhumanity and brutality towards the indigenous population, and the 'white legend' of Spain's beneficent civilizing mission – shows the awakening of the realization that Latin American history could not be written simply from the point of view of the colonizing

---

479. For the current state of research cf. GRIFFIN (ed.), *Latin America. A Guide to the Historical Literature* (1971); CLINE (ed.), *Latin American History. Essays on its Study and Teaching, 1898-1965* (2 vols., 1967); AL'PEROVIČ, *Sovetskaja istoriografija stran Latinskoj Ameriki* (= Soviet Historiography of the Countries of Latin America) (1968); DABAGJAN, '50 let sovetskoj latinoamerikanistiki. Bibliografičeskij očerk' (= Fifty years of Soviet Latin American studies. Bibliographical essay) (1967); CARLTON (ed.), *Soviet Image of Contemporary Latin America* (1970); ESQUENAZI-MAYO & MEYER (eds.), *Latin American Scholarship since World War II* (1971). I am greatly indebted to the USSR National Commission for Unesco for placing at my disposal a most informative report by Dr. S. Dabagjan on 'The main trends of Soviet Latin American studies', to Professor Milton Vanger (Brandeis University) for advice and help in the preparation of this sub-section, and to H. Exc. Professor Silvio Zavala for his valuable comments.

480. GRAHAM, 'Brazil: the national period' (1971), p. 51 in ESQUENAZI-MAYO & MEYER (eds.), *Latin American Scholarship*.

481. GRIFFIN, pp. xxv, xxvii in GRIFFIN (ed.), *op. cit.* (1971).

482. There is, so far as I am aware, no general account of the development of historiography in Latin America as a whole. The following cover part of the ground: RODRIGUES, *Teoria da história do Brasil* (2nd edn., 1957), and *História e historiadores do Brasil* (1965); CARBÍA, *Historia crítica de la historiografía argentina desde sus orígenes* (1940); *Veinticinco años de investigación história en México* (1966); Cosío VILLEGAS, *Nueva historiografía política del México moderno* (1965); FELIÚ CRUZ, *Historiografía colonial de Chile* (1968); PÉREZ CABRERA, *Fundamentos de una historia de la historiografía cubana* (1959); and (critical) O'GORMAN, *Crisis y porvenir de la ciencia histórica* (1947).

power.[483] But no living native historiographical tradition survived, as it did in Asia,[484] to counterbalance that of Europe, and from the time of independence, if not before, Latin American historiography – even when seeking to establish an authentic Latin American tradition – closely followed prevalent European trends: first (and most pervasive of all) nineteenth-century European positivism;[485] then, after the First World War, German historicism;[486] and finally, at the end of the 1950's, the example of the French school of the *Annales*, as transmitted by Latin American historians like Jara, Florescano and Romano, who studied in Paris, and, in a masterly way, by the great Spanish historian, Jaime Vicens Vives.[487] Though it was not, of course, the only factor, the appearance between 1957 and 1959 of the social and economic history of Spain and America, which Vicens Vives planned and directed, may be taken as marking both the rejection of German historicism and the beginning of the modern period in Latin American historiography.[488] It not only set new objectives but also provided a striking example of the potentialities of new methods.

The influence of the French school of the *Annales* came at a time when, in any event, the pressure of contemporary problems was forcing Latin American historians in new directions. The old historiography, with its pervasive nationalist ethos, its cult of the heroes of the national independence movements, its preoccupation with the political and military aspects of history, and its 'endless recitation of undifferentiated detail', was of little use for understanding the contemporary situation and how it came about. In particular, the arid tradition of biographical narrative history, inherited from nineteenth-century Europe, was rejected by the younger generation of Latin American historians, who realized, as Raymond Carr has written, how inadequate a basis it was 'for the elaboration of an historically conditioned sociology of change.'[489] Not a few turned instead to Marxist and quasi-Marxist hypotheses; others applied the models of social science; all recognized the need for new questions and new methods. It is in this sense that Latin American history, in spite of its long traditions, can be termed 'a creation of the present century', and for most practical purposes of the second half of the present century.[490]

483. For the present state of the question, cf. KEEN, 'The black legend revisited' (1969); HANKE, 'A modest proposal for a moratorium on grand generalizations: some thoughts on the black legend' (1971); KEEN, 'The white legend revisited' (1971).

484. Cf. below, pp. 123-124.

485. Cf. ZEA, *El positivismo en México* (1943), and *Apogeo y decadencia del positivismo en México* (1945).

486. The intermediary was Ortega y Gasset; cf. above, p. 12, n. 31.

487. VICENS VIVES, *Historia social y económica de España y América* (5 vols., 1957-59); the sections on Latin America were contributed by Guillermo CÉSPEDES DEL CASTILLO and Hernández SÁNCHEZ-BARBA.

488. For the rejection of historicism, cf. REYES HEROLES, 'La historia y la acción' (1968).

489. Cf. CARR, R., 'New openings: Latin America', p. 299 in *New Ways in History* (*Times Literary Supplement*, 1966).

490. Cf. GRIFFIN, p. xxvii in GRIFFIN (ed.), *op. cit.* (1971).

The most obvious result was the updating of Latin American history, which had remained obdurately stuck in the colonial period and the stirring days of independence, and a new emphasis on the recent past.[491] But more fundamental was the shift of focus from periods to problems, e.g., race relations, the acculturation of disparate peoples, the decline and growth of population and of different sectors of the population, the relations of town and countryside and the progress of urbanization, industrialization and the rôle of foreign capital, agrarian systems and land-hunger, and above all the tenacity of conservatism and traditionalism and the obstacles to change.[492]

As elsewhere, what has become obvious with this change of emphasis is that the sources and materials used by earlier historians rarely provide the sort of information required for dealing with socio-economic questions. General books, such as those of Celso Furtado, covering the whole range of Latin American economic history or even that of one country, are valuable in providing working hypotheses;[493] but at the present stage the first necessity is detailed, archival study of particular areas, regions, cities or industries, from which eventually a veracious picture can be built up.[494] The predominant impression left is the weakness of the basis for generalization, and the need to review the broad issues and test them against the primary materials at the level of the village, municipality, state, province and department.[495] Furthermore, all generalizations must take account of the extreme diversity of the twenty Latin American republics in history, racial composition, social structure and economic development. Only in the broadest sense are the historical questions confronting them comparable. And, finally, the danger of treating their history by analogy with European or Asian models is very real. As Claudio Veliz has observed, 'models of development based on the historical experience of the more advanced countries of Europe are not applicable in Latin America.'[496] On the other hand, it is generally agreed that, by comparison with most areas of Asia and Africa, Latin America cannot be classified as backward.[497] Though there is every justification for treating it as part of the 'under-developed world',

---

491. Cf. CLINE (ed.), *op. cit.* (1967), pp. 398, 542, 574-575; but the facts are well known and scarcely need documenting.

492. Perhaps the best survey of these changes and of the new trends is in the papers of Stanley STEIN, 'The tasks ahead for Latin American historians', and 'Latin American historiography: status and research opportunities', reprinted in CLINE (ed.), *Latin American History, op. cit.* (1967).

493. Cf. FURTADO, *The Economic Development of Latin America* (1970) and *The Economic Growth of Brazil* (1963); for Chile, cf. PINTO SANTA CRUZ, *Chile: un caso de desarrollo frustrado* (1959).

494. E.g., S. STEIN's study of the Brazilian cotton industry (*The Brazilian Cotton Manufacture, 1850-1950*, 1957), or M. T. SCHORER PETRONE's study of the Brazilian sugar production (*A lavoura canavieira em São Paulo. Expansão e declinio, 1765-1871*, 1968).

495. Cf. CLINE (ed.), *Latin American History, op. cit.* (1967), pp. 549, 591.

496. VELIZ, *Obstacles to Change in Latin America* (1965), p. 1.

497. Cf. CARLTON (ed.), *Soviet Image of Contemporary Latin America, op. cit.* (1970), p. 201.

the specific character of its problems is in many ways different from those of other ex-colonial territories and their explanation must be sought in Latin American history itself.

These and other factors notwithstanding, the progress of Latin American studies in the last ten or fifteen years, both in the perception and formulation of the relevant problems and in the actual results achieved, has reached a new level of sophistication. To a very considerable extent this is due not only to meticulous local research providing the necessary substratum of concrete data, but also to the adoption of an inter-disciplinary approach, involving ethnography and the new disciplines of ethno-history, demography, social psychology, as well as economics and sociology. It must suffice here to instance a few of the more striking results, beginning with the much discussed population studies of W. W. Borah, S. F. Cook and L. B. Simpson, which have cast a grim and forbidding light on the fate of the Amerindian population under Spanish rule.[498] By substituting exact facts for the polemics of the 'black legend' and the 'white legend', this careful demographic work has provided a solid basis not only for a far-reaching reassessment of the colonial era,[499] but also – in combination with independent studies on the exploitation of land, soil erosion, and density of settlement – for the reconstruction of the social and cultural history of the American Indians after the Spanish conquest.[500]

Parallel with this concern with the native population went an intensified interest in slavery – particularly, but by no means exclusively, in Brazil (where the well known works of Gilberto Freyre provided a starting-point for criticism and further study)[501] – and more generally in the complicated process of the acculturation of the Negro in the new world.[502] In both cases progress and deeper understanding were due to co-operation between

498. Cf. Cook & Simpson, *The Population of Central Mexico in the Sixteenth Century* (1948); Borah & Cook, *The Population of Central Mexico in 1548* (1960), *The Aboriginal Population of Central Mexico on the Eve of the Spanish Conquest* (1963) and *Essays in Population History* (Vol. I, 1971). The estimates of Borah and Cook have been challenged by Rosenblat, *La población de América en 1492* (1967), but on the whole have found general acceptance, and their work for (Central)

487. Vicens Vives, *Historia social y económica de España y América* (5 vols., Mexico has provided a model for other areas, e.g., Sánchez-Albornoz, 'Perfil y proyecciones de la demografia histórica en la Argentina' (1965).

499. Cf. Stein, S. & B., *The Colonial Heritage of Latin America* (1970); Gibson, *Spain in America* (1966).

500. The outstanding study to date is Gibson, *The Aztecs under Spanish Rule* (1964); cf. more generally Spaulding, 'The colonial Indian. Past and future research perspectives' (1972) and Wachtel, 'La vision des vaincus: la conquête espagnole dans le folklore indigène' (1967) (prolegomena to a full-scale work not yet published).

501. For Freyre and subsequent work, cf. in summary Esquenazi-Mayo & Meyer (eds.), *Latin American Scholarship since World War II, op. cit.* (1971), pp. 15, 37-38, 54-55. Perhaps the best assessment of Freyre is by T. E. Skidmore, 'Gilberto Freyre and the early Brazilian Republic' (1964).

502. Cf. Bowser, 'The African in colonial Spanish America' (1972); Mörner, 'The history of race relations in Latin America' (1966); King, 'Negro history in continental Spanish America' (1944).

historians, anthropologists and archaeologists who began to a far greater degree than in the past to turn their attention to the period after the Spanish conquest.[503] More fundamental, however, was a shift, visible also in the history of institutions, from the point of view of the government to that of the governed – in other words, from the policies laid down in imperial laws and edicts to the way they were implemented (or not implemented) at a local or provincial level.[504] The result has been to emphasize the wide gap between precept and practice, and to create a clearer perception of the realities of colonial rule, as it was experienced by all sectors of the population, from the white creole upper stratum of *beneméritos* to the exploited Indian masses. It has also opened the way for a new approach to the basic questions of social structure and social change.[505]

For other historians – perhaps today the majority of historians – the starting-point is the search for a satisfactory explanation of the relative stagnation of Latin American society and the obstacles to modernization. Economists, political scientists and sociologists have sought the answer in an analysis of the current situation, emphasizing in particular the unfavorable impact of international capitalism.[506] Historians, on the other hand, have emphasized the stubborn long-term factors. What is almost unique to Latin America is the slowness of change. As Gibson has pointed out, the progress of industrialization – elsewhere (for example, in the English industrial revolution) a solvent of pre-industrial social stratification – has not liberated Latin America from 'the rigid class system' which it inherited from its colonial past.[507] Equally significant is the fact, pointed out by Stein in 1961, that, down to that time, in the century and a half since independence, there had only been two major social upheavals, the Mexican revolution and the Cuban revolution.[508] Historians, not surprisingly, are increasingly making it their business to probe these anomalies.

Among the long-term obstacles to change Claudio Veliz picked out 'the existence in Latin America of a sophisticated pre-industrial urban civilization'.[509] Morse's brilliant investigations of Latin American urban history are a major contribution to understanding of this phenomenon.[510] Others have pointed out that the 'hard bedrock' of Latin American history is still – as it always has been – the land, and that the current tendency to emphasize

503. Cf. SPAULDING, *op. cit.* (1972), p. 50.

504. Cf. GRIFFIN (ed.), *Latin America: A Guide ...*, *op. cit.* (1971), p. 189, and ESQUENAZI-MAYO & MEYER (eds.), *op. cit.* (1971), p. 8.

505. Cf. MCALISTER, 'Social structure and social change in New Spain' (1963) (reprinted in CLINE (ed.), *Latin American History, op. cit.*, 1967).

506. Cf. FRANK, *Capitalism and Underdevelopment in Latin America* (1969), and, from a different angle, the well known work of R. PREBISCH, *The Economic Development of Latin America and its Principal Problems* (1950).

507. GIBSON, 'Colonial institutions and contemporary Latin America' (1963), p. 389 in *Hisp. Am. Hist. Review*, Vol. XLIII.

508. STEIN, S., 'The tasks ahead ...', *op. cit.*, p. 548 in CLINE (ed.), *op. cit.* (1967).

509. VELIZ, *Obstacles to Change ...*, *op. cit.* (1965), p. 2.

510. Cf. MORSE, 'Some characteristics of Latin American urban history' (1962) and 'Trends and issues in Latin American urban research' (1970).

industrialization and the related questions of international trade may easily result in diverting attention from the dominant factor, namely the 'landed estate and its labour force.'[511] On the other hand, in spite of much discussion of the 'crumbling of the traditional order' and the 'rising pressure of hitherto submerged, unrecognized and neglected classes', and in spite of some intelligent and stimulating diagnoses of the current revolutionary situation,[512] historians have so far done little to analyse the revolutionary changes in the Latin American scene since 1930. Nothing is clearer than the fact that the great depression of 1930 opened a new era in Latin American history; but we are still without satisfactory accounts, e.g., of the Vargas régime in Brazil or of the mainsprings of Peronism in Argentina.[513] Though it is recognized that the modern type of authoritarianism differs fundamentally from the dictatorship of the earlier *caudillos*, it still remains true, as Whitaker wrote in 1965, that 'no comprehensive study has yet appeared' of 'the emergence of the modern type of Latin American dictatorship.'[514]

Latin American history has traditionally been studied from a nationalist point of view.[515] While there is justification for this approach in the marked differences in history and social structure of the different regions and republics, it is also a moot question whether the emphasis placed on national history may not have led historians to neglect the broader socio-economic forces which affect the whole continent.[516] As Griffin has written, nationalism in Latin America has 'tended to be a divisive force'.[517] Moreover, 'as soon as we go beyond narrative and attempt to explain how and why changes have taken place, the national basis for history seems insufficient.' Perhaps, in the long run, one of the most significant trends of Latin American historiography today is the tendency to emphasize the features which unite, rather than divide, the peoples of the sub-continent; even conventional biographical accounts of the leaders in the struggle for independence – Bolívar, for example, or San Martín – see them no longer primarily as national heroes but rather as the precursors of Latin American unity.[518] The effects so far on the conceptualization of Latin American history have not been great; most existing histories are compilations of the histories of the

511. Cf. CLINE (ed.), *op. cit.* (1967), p. 544.

512. E.g., RUIZ GARCÍA, *América latina: anatomía de una revolución* (1966); RAMOS, *Revolución y contrarrevolución en la Argentina: las masas en nuestra historia* (2nd edn., 1961). On the more recent revolutionary situation, GOTT, *Guerrilla Movements in Latin America* (1970) is particularly noteworthy.

513. As is pointed out in ESQUENAZI-MAYO & MEYER (eds.), *op. cit.* (1971), p. 61; but cf. LEVINE, *The Vargas Regime: The Crucial Years, 1934-1938* (1970), which, however, covers only part of the field.

514. Cf. CLINE (ed.), *op. cit.* (1967), p. 620.

515. Cf. WHITAKER, *Nationalism in Latin America* (1962), and WHITAKER & JORDAN, *Nationalism in Contemporary Latin America* (1966).

516. Cf. CLINE (ed.), *op. cit.* (1967), p. 542.

517. Cf. GRIFFIN, 'An essay on regionalism and nationalism in Latin America' (1964).

518. Cf. BUSHNELL (ed.), *The Liberator: Simón Bolívar. Man and Image* (1970).

different republics or at best of the different republics grouped in regions, and there is nothing to set beside Braudel's study of Mediterranean civilization or Stoianovich's study of Balkan civilization.[519] Nevertheless there is ample evidence of the existence of a sense of common Latin American nationality, coexisting with and overriding the traditional nationalisms of the separate republics; and its influence on historical thinking is already visible, for example, in the work of Silvio Zavala.[520]

When we compare the present position of historical studies in Latin America with that in other parts of the 'under-developed world', the differences are perhaps more striking than the similarities. This is at least partly due to the fact that it gained its independence a century and a half ago, and its historiography is not dominated, in the way that Asian and African historiography is dominated, by the theme of imperialism and of relations with the imperial power. In other ways, however, the new generation of Latin American historians has similar preoccupations, which arise not only from similarities in the current situation – the common experience of 'neo-colonialism', the population explosion, revolutionary internal stresses, and military governments – but also from long-standing historical causes. Like Asians and Africans, Latin Americans are seeking in history a key to the present, but they are also seeking – as the thoughtful and original works of Leopoldo Zea show[521] – a sense of their own identity and place in the world.

Contemporary Trends in the History of Asia

In Asia, the immediate occasion for the new interest in historical studies was the movement for national liberation.[522] Here, as in Africa, the

519. Cf. above, pp. 38, 55.

520. Cf. ZAVALA, *El mundo americano en la época colonial* (2 vols., 1967). It is unnecessary here to discuss how far this work revives, on new foundations, the (at one time much criticized) theses of H. E. Bolton (for which it is sufficient to refer to CLINE (ed.), *Latin American History . . ., op. cit.* (1967), pp. 528-529).

521. Cf. ZEA, *América como conciencia* (1953), *América latina y el mundo* (1965) (English translation, *Latin America and the World*, 1969), and *The Latin American Mind* (1963).

522. Among the general sources for the following survey the four volumes (1961-62) of *Historical Writing on the Peoples of Asia* (Vol. I: *Historians of India, Pakistan and Ceylon*, ed. C. H. PHILIPS; Vol. II: *Historians of South-East Asia*, ed. D. G. E. HALL; Vol. III: *Historians of China and Japan*, eds. W. G. BEASLEY & E. G. PULLEYBLANK; Vol. IV: *Historians of the Middle East*, eds. B. LEWIS & P. M. HOLT), although now a little dated, are outstanding. More up-to-date, and also extremely valuable, are the articles on 'Chinese historiography' (by A. F. WRIGHT), 'Islamic historiography' (by F. ROSENTHAL), 'Japanese historiography' (by J. W. HALL), and 'South and Southeast Asian historiography' (by WANG Gungwu), in *International Encyclopedia of the Social Sciences*, Vol. VI (1968), pp. 400-428. I am also particularly grateful for the special reports, referred to above, p. 323, n. 404, prepared by committees of Indian and Indonesian historians. Cf. also MAJUMDAR, *Historiography in Modern India* (1970); SOEDJATMOKO (ed.), *An Introduction to Indonesian*

growth of nationalism gave a stimulus to independent enquiry. In India, nationalist history emerged, broadly speaking, as a reaction against the British histories of India. As K. M. Panikkar wrote in 1947, once 'India became conscious of her past ... there was a growing demand for a history of India which would try and reconstruct the past in a way that would give us an idea of our heritage.' The true history of India during the British period, he insisted, 'does not consist of the activities of the East India Company or of its successor, the British Crown, but of the upheaval which led to the transformation of Indian society, through the activities of India's own sons.'[523] The political leaders in the other new nations also looked to the past to vindicate claims to status and respect. In Indonesia, Soekarno was acutely aware of the need to inculcate the image of 'a glorious past',[524] and after liberation departments and faculties of history were built up in all the newly emancipated countries. This was, of course, slow work, which is only now coming to fruition. In Vietnam and Burma, as in Indonesia, modern historiography is 'still in its very early beginning'.[525]

For this reason, if for no other, it would be misleading to discuss Asian history in general. Each country has its own particular problems and concerns, and each should be considered independently. Nevertheless, there are certain common tendencies, besides the reaction against the European interpretation of the Asian past. Of these five may be picked out. The first is the very real impact of Marxism. This, for obvious reasons, is strongest in China, and will be considered later;[526] but Marxism is a powerful influence throughout the Asian continent, particularly in Japan, where it 'continues to provide the most widely accepted historical world view,' and in South-East Asia, where 'Marxist thinking seems destined to play an ever-increasing role in the formation of concepts of history'.[527] The second is the emphasis on the inter-connexion between history and archaeology, and, indeed, more generally upon the importance of an inter-disciplinary approach. 'The development of historical studies,' it has been said, 'will necessarily be bound up with the progress of archaeological work';[528] and though this judgement refers specifically to Vietnam and Cambodia, it is certainly of wider application. Equally important is the liaison between history and anthropology. As C. C. Berg has insisted, in his seminal studies of Indonesian history, it is necessary to see a people's history-writing as an element of its

Historiography (1965); *Le Japon au XIe Congrès international des Sciences historiques à Stockholm: l'état actuel et les tendances des études historiques au Japon* (1960); and the article by R. F. WALL, 'New openings: Asia', in *New Ways in History* (*Times Literary Supplement*, 1966).

523. PANIKKAR, *A Survey of Indian History* (1947) – quoted by MAJUMDAR in *Historical Writing ...*, *op. cit.*, Vol. I (1961), pp. 417, 427-428.

524. *Historical Writing ...*, Vol. II (1961), p. 75.

525. *Ibid.*, pp. 78-79, 93, 98, 103.

526. Cf. below, pp. 136-140.

527. *International Encyclopedia ...*, Vol. VI, *op. cit.* (1968), p. 420; *Historical Writing ...*, *op. cit.*, Vol. II (1961), p. 331.

528. *Ibid.*, p. 309.

culture pattern,[529] and this requires techniques which the ordinary canons of historical criticism are unable to provide, particularly – this is the third characteristic feature of the new phase of Asian historiography – as the focus of historical research switches from the political to the social and cultural aspects of the people's history.[530] Fourthly, there is 'a desire to base new research upon the direct and critical exploitation of native sources', a growing awareness – as has been said of Indonesia – that, however much 'useful work remains to be done by delving into European archives, [. . .] for a real understanding of Indonesia's past attention must mainly be directed towards the manifold activities of the Indonesians themselves, notwithstanding the inherent difficulties of such a study'.[531] But with this goes, fifthly, an almost automatic acceptance of European methods and techniques. 'The recent historical writings of Vietnamese scholars,' as Honey pointed out in 1961, 'have one feature in common: they are all written in a style which is very different from that of the traditional Vietnamese histories.'[532] That this statement is true of other countries in Asia scarcely needs saying: the European concept of history, whether in its western or in its Marxist form, and European methods of conducting historical research, appear to have come to stay. Even when the history actually written represents a reaction against an alleged 'Eurocentric' approach, the methodology used is European in character and origin.

There is one further feature of contemporary Asian historiography which distinguishes it from that of Africa, and that is its ability to draw upon a lively consciousness of a great historical past. Whereas African historians today are confronted with the formidable task of virtually rediscovering and re-creating their early history, in Asia there are historical traditions of great antiquity, sustained and underpinned by a literary inheritance of high quality and renown. This is true not only of the great oriental civilizations of India, China and Islam, but also of South-East Asia, where the cultures of Mon, Khmer, Cham, Java, Bali and Burma, contemporary with the so-called 'middle ages' in Europe, flourished over a period of roughly a thousand years and produced art and architecture and a vernacular literature of striking individuality. These facts, naturally, have played a significant part in the direction of modern historical research and writing in the areas concerned. In Asia, as Margery Perham has pointed out,[533] 'there are great areas of cultural and religious unity and of common pride based on the inheritance of ancient civilizations,' and much of the effort of historians today is concentrated upon exploring this inheritance and freeing it from the alleged distortions of western writers. If one pole of historical

---

529. For Berg, whose influence would be hard to exaggerate, see HALL, D. G. E., *A History of South-East Asia* (1955), p. vi, and *Historical Writing* . . ., Vol. II, pp. 4-5; cf. also BERG's contribution, 'The Javanese picture of the past', to SOEDJAT-MOKO (ed.), *An Introduction* . . ., *op. cit.* (1965), pp. 87-117.

530. Cf. *Historical Writing* . . ., Vol. I, pp. 455, 457.

531. *Ibid.,* Vol. II, pp. 310, 323.

532. *Ibid.,* p. 102 .

533. *Foreign Affairs*, Vol. XXIX (1951), p. 638.

writing is the colonial period and the growth of the movements of national liberation, the other is the ancient past and its achievements. In India, the latter preoccupation was implanted at an early date by the Arya Samaj, which invoked the spirit of Vedic learning and civilization, and contrasted its magnificent achievements with those of the west.

Preoccupation with the ancient past is common throughout Asia. Characteristically, by far the largest part of historical writing in Hindi since 1947 relates to the cultural history of ancient India.[534] No doubt it was true, in the early period, that much of this writing gave too flattering a picture of the past. Moreover, since its object was reinterpretation of known facts in accordance with nationalist tenets, it rarely made a new contribution to factual knowledge. This was true also, in the same period, of historical writing in Urdu, and the position in Indonesia, as we have seen, was little different.[535] From the point of view of tangible accretions to historical knowledge, the ten or fifteen years after 1945 were largely unproductive. Since about 1960, on the other hand, there has been a distinct change. Asian historians with a sound training in historical method have reacted against the excessive and uncritical nationalism of their predecessors, and a new 'note of objectivity' is discernible.[536] In part, this may be attributed to the setting up of university departments of history, and to the higher standards they have introduced, as well as to greater awareness, which the universities have inculcated, of universal trends in historical research. If in the past historical writing in Asia has been isolated and consequently has tended to be parochial-minded, it is now rapidly entering the mainstream, with results which can only be applauded and encouraged. Secondly, the change is due to a turning-away from sweeping works of interpretation, for which the groundwork at this stage is largely inadequate, to the more fruitful field of regional history. It is not only, as has rightly been emphasized,[537] that sources can be handled more conveniently and intensively on a regional than on a national level; it is also a fact, as historians studying the European middle ages have found,[538] that regional studies often reflect a more accurate picture of historical reality. In a country, for example, of India's size and complexity, there are bound to be significant regional variations, and a study of regional variations is essential before meaningful generalizations can be made about India as a whole.[539]

These facts account for the new importance attached to regional studies, such as Tapan Raychaudhuri's study of society in Bengal in the fifteenth and sixteenth centuries.[540] They also account for the emphasis, in all Asian

---

534. Cf. *Historical Writing* . . ., Vol. I, pp. 469-471.

535. *Ibid.*, p. 495; for Indonesia, cf. above, p. 326.

536. Cf. *Historical Writing* . . ., Vol. I, p. 468.

537. *Ibid.*, pp. 471, 479.

538. Cf. above, p. 283.

539. This is pointed out in the report of the committee of Indian historians, pp. 29-30.

540. RAYCHAUDHURI, *Bengal under Akbar and Jahangir* (1966; 2nd edn., 1969).

countries, on the overriding need for intensive investigation and publication of the source materials hidden away in local archives. Until these sources have been made available on a scale far in excess of anything obtaining today, the greater part of current historical writing can scarcely be regarded as more than a series of interim reports challenging further investigation. Surveying Asia as a whole, the overall impression left is of the enormous amount of work remaining to be done before we can expect satisfactory answers to the major questions. That, no doubt, is why Unesco, at an earlier stage, put forward the suggestion that, while western historians should concentrate on making Asian history better known and understood in the west, Asian historians should concentrate first and foremost on writing their own history. This proposal may seem unbalanced or, as E. H. Dance has said,[541] 'topsy-turvy'; but its explanation is the current state of historical knowledge, and particularly the need for the sort of intensive investigation of Asian history which only trained and knowledgeable historians with local roots and the necessary linguistic equipment can undertake.

Nevertheless, it would be mistaken to underestimate the progress already made. As Wang Gungwu has said,[542] 'the key concepts' are now fully accepted by Asian historians: namely, 'that time and place must be accurate, that knowledge about man's past must be secular and humanistic, and that historical fact and interpretation must always be tested by the best scientific methods.' Development is, of course, uneven. Japanese historiography, ahead of that in other countries, 'came of age as a modern discipline' during the period between 1890 and 1930.[543] In India, modern historiography may be said to have begun – if only because of the reactions it produced among Indian historians – with the publication of the *Cambridge History of India* in six volumes between 1922 and 1932, and Ceylon did not lag far behind.[544] In South-East Asia, on the other hand, the British, Dutch and French made no effort to train local historians until just before the Second World War. In these circumstances, it is not surprising (China apart) that Japanese and Indian historiography are the most impressive, both in volume and in critical standards. In the Islamic countries, including both the Near and Middle East and Pakistan, the transition from the traditional historiography, centred on religion and the life of the Moslem religious community, to a secular and scientific view of history has proved more difficult to make.[545] The number of professional historians, though growing, is also still less than adequate, at least by comparison with Japan or with India, where there is now an ample body of trained historians to cover every period and every type of problem in Indian history. In particular, far more attention is now being given, both here and to a lesser extent

541. Cf. Dance, *History the Betrayer* (1960), p. 79.
542. Cf. *International Encyclopedia of the Social Sciences*, Vol. VI (1968), p. 427.
543. *Ibid.*, p. 418 (J. W. Hall).
544. *Ibid.*, p. 424 (Wang Gungwu).
545. Cf. *ibid.*, pp. 412 (Rosenthal), 425 (Wang Gungwu).

in South-East Asia, to the 'middle period' – i.e., the centuries between antiquity and the age of European colonialism – which tended to be neglected in the immediate post-independence years. As Panikkar pointed out,
the tendency to glorify the ancient past, to jump from British rule to the
age of the Vedas, involved a denial of the intervening centuries.[546] The
current tendency – which can only be welcomed – is to retrieve this
neglected period, and to emphasize its importance in the development of
the Asian peoples.

This is the general background which must be borne in mind when we
turn to consider particular trends and problems in different areas and
countries. Of some, there is little, if anything, further to be said. **Japan**, in
particular, is in many respects exceptional, so much so that it is at least
questionable how far it is appropriate to consider Japanese historiography
in an Asian pattern. The whole history of Japan in the last century, ever
since the Meiji restoration, has followed a different path from that of other
Asian countries. One has only to recall the salient features of modern Japanese history – its success in withstanding colonialist pressures, its ability to
deal on equal terms with the European powers and the United States, the
maintenance of its national identity even in defeat, and later its emergence
as one of the world's leading industrial countries – to realize that the intellectual heritage of Japanese historians is very different from that of most
other Asian historians.

Modernization came early to Japan and went ahead with great rapidity.
Western techniques for the collection and investigation of historical data
were introduced into the imperial university at Tokyo about 1890, and by
the 1920's at latest – that is to say, a generation ahead of most other Asian
countries – had completely displaced the traditional forms of historiography.
At the same time, Japan was being transformed into a modern industrial
state. This also created conditions very different from those elsewhere in
Asia. Supported by the resources of a wealthy industrialized country, with
a highly developed university system and well organized libraries and archives, Japanese historians enjoy advantages which few historians in other
Asian countries possess. Not surprisingly, Japan far outdistances any other
country in Asia in the sheer quantity of historical work produced, and in
no other country are western standards and western models held in higher
esteem. Translations of western historical literature appear in large numbers
and keep Japanese historians abreast of western scholarship and research.

In all these ways the position of historians in Japan is closer to that of
their colleagues in Europe and America than to that of historians in other
parts of Asia. At the same time, the fact that their own historical experience
has been so different from that of other Asian countries means that their
interests and preoccupations are also different. Because their country was
never reduced to colonial or semi-colonial status, Japanese historians have
escaped the preoccupation with colonialism which is so prominent a feature

546. PANIKKAR, *Asia and Western Dominance* (1953), p. 323.

of contemporary historical writing elsewhere in Asia. Furthermore, whereas most Asian historians at the present stage are preoccupied almost exclusively with their own national history, Japanese historians have a wider vision. Their contributions to Chinese history are well known, and are explained by Japan's long historic connexion with the mainland. And, finally, the active rôle played by Japan in international politics ever since the end of the nineteenth century has accustomed them to look at Japanese history in an international framework, rather than in isolation. Japanese imperialism and aggression, the rise of militarism and fascism in the 1930's, and the antecedents of the disastrous Pacific war are, understandably, a central preoccupation of Japanese historians today;[547] but they are questions which can only be examined and understood in relation to the policies of the other great powers, and the attempt to find out why and how Japan took this fateful turning strengthens the links between Japanese historians and western historians concerned with the same problems. On the other hand, the preoccupation with national identity, which is so powerful in the emergent nations of Asia and Africa today, plays little part in Japanese historical writing. The nationalist impulse was strong in Japanese historical circles in the 1930's; but the traumatic experience of war, defeat, atomic annihilation and foreign occupation brought nationalist history into disrepute, and it has not revived in any substantial degree.

In this respect the trends of Japanese historiography today contrast sharply with those elsewhere in Asia. It may be true that the question of Japan's national identity, of its place in the world between east and west, cannot so easily be brushed aside;[548] but once Japan became a great industrial nation, with all the tensions that industrialization implies, this problem lost its urgency, and Japanese historians prefer to leave it in abeyance. Like historians in the west, they are more concerned with social and economic history, particularly with the question how Japan's economic modernization should be interpreted and what were its effects on Japanese society, and for this purpose the historical experience of the west is more relevant than that of the under-developed countries of Asia. Indeed, it is hardly too much to say that Japan, as it has taken its place among the world's great industrial nations, has drawn apart from the rest of Asia. Japanese historians look to Europe and North America for their concepts and methodology. Though Marxist influence is strong, the bulk of historical writing is strictly empirical in character, and the strong nationalist and ideological overtones which we find in so much Asian historical writing, are lacking.

When we turn from Japan to the Arab countries of the **Near and Middle East** the situation that confronts us is far less clear-cut.[549] Here also, of course, there are strong western influences; but, as in Pakistan, they have

547. Cf. IRIYE, 'Japanese imperialism and aggression' (1963-64) and 'Japan's foreign policies between the World Wars' (1966-67).
548. Cf. *International Encyclopedia . . .*, Vol. VI, pp. 414, 420 (J. W. HALL).
549. In addition to the literature referred to above, p. 349, n. 522, cf. ZIADAH, 'Modern Egyptian historiography' (1953); INALCIK, 'Some remarks on the study of

not gone unchallenged. Though the younger generation of Middle Eastern historians, many of whom were trained in English, French and German universities, have adopted the standards of western scholarship and approach history in a positivist and empirical spirit, there are also conservative and orthodox historians, who reject western methodology and seek to keep the traditional Islamic historiography alive. G. E. von Grunebaum believes that historians in the Middle East must still contend with 'the absence in contemporary Islam of a positive secularist ideology.'[550] This may be an exaggeration; but it is certainly true that historiography in the Moslem and Arab world is caught in the cross-currents of a society in the throes of modernization, and has yet to find a satisfactory solution. So far, the impact of western historiography has been indecisive though some Arab historians not only use western methods of historical criticism but are also turning to 'neglected social and economic factors', there is still a 'preference for compilation rather than analysis', and much writing is 'no more than a continuation of medieval patterns' and 'devoid of any scientific approach'.[551]

The main reason for this failure to make the transition from traditional to modern forms of historiography is a very genuine ambiguity as to what the framework of Middle Eastern history should be. Historians in the Arab world are engrossed, in a way Japanese historians are not, by the search for their identity. The history of the countries of the Near and Middle East moves in three concentric circles: Islamic, Arab, and national, and it is a controversial question which of these provides the most appropriate framework for the understanding of the past. If traditionally the framework has been Islamic – if, in other words, Islam was treated as the unity of which the different countries of the Middle East were merely parts – the whole tendency since the rise of Middle Eastern nationalism has been to shift the emphasis from the religious to the political unit and from an eschatological to a secularist and nationalist approach. This occurred first in Turkey, where, after the revolution of 1908, a demarcation line was drawn between Turkish national history and Islamic history.[552] It spread to other lands – to Persia, to Egypt, to Syria and the Lebanon – as they asserted their independence. As in other parts of Asia, a nationalist interpretation of history was encouraged and nurtured by governments, beginning with Mustafa Kemal in Turkey, which hoped in this way to build up a sense of national cohesion and solidarity. In the Lebanon and Syria government decrees laid down specifically that the purpose of history was 'to strengthen the nationalist and patriotic sentiments in the hearts of the people.'[553] The result of this new nationalist impulse was a repudiation of the Islamic and Arab past. Just as the Turks turned for national inspiration to the ancient

---

history in Islamic countries' (1953); CHEJNE, 'The use of history by modern Arab writers' (1960); HADDAD, 'Modern Arab historians and world history' (1961).

550. *Historical Writing on the Peoples of Asia, op. cit.*, Vol. IV (1962), p. 471.
551. *Ibid.*, pp. 15, 438; CHEJNE, *op. cit.* (1960), p. 391.
552. Cf. LEWIS, B., 'History writing and the national revival in Turkey' (1953).
553. CHEJNE, *op. cit.* (1960), p. 392; cf. DANCE, *op. cit.* (1960), p. 75.

history of the Turkic peoples in their central and east Asian homelands, so Egyptian historians sought out the pre-Islamic roots of their nation in the Egypt of the Pharaohs, Iraqis evoked the Assyrian past, Lebanese traced their history back to the Phoenicians, while Iranian historians inveighed against the 'ignorance and superstition' of the mullahs and accused the Arabs of ruining the glorious Sassanid civilization.[554]

About this nationalist history, in which the contemporary political rivalries between the different peoples of the Middle East are only too plainly mirrored, it is perhaps sufficient to say, with Halil Inalcik, that 'national prejudices' too often 'overshadow historical realities'.[555] Moreover, it was not long before the inadequacy and artificiality of a purely national framework became apparent. In Turkey, after 1950, the extreme nationalism of the preceding period was abandoned. Instead, it was recognized that the most important epoch of Turkish history was the one that took place in Islam, and that Turkish and Islamic history constitute an 'organic whole'.[556] What is significant about this change is the evidence it provides of the resilience of the traditional Islamic view of history. In this view, the Quran, the Sharia and the institutions of Islam together constitute the unifying element in the history of the Near and Middle East, and it is a hopeless task to try to write or understand the history of any individual Islamic country except within the general framework of Islamic history. The other factor in the reaction against exaggerated nationalist interpretations is provided by pan-Arabism, with its concept of the Arab world as a single and indivisible entity throughout the ages. Here again we are confronted by a reaction against fragmentation and by the search for a common denominator; but unlike Islamic interpretations, the pan-Arabist perspective is secular. For historians of this school, the Islamic elements are not the most important; the unifying factor is rather the history of the Arab nation. By contrast with Islamic historians such as Nabih Amin Faris, for whom Islam is the bond uniting the history of Moslems everywhere, 'from Morocco to Indonesia'[557], they are concerned only with the Near and Middle East and the possibility of finding a satisfactory overall view of the common factors in its history.

Which of these conflicting interpretations provides the most satisfactory framework for the history of the Near and Middle East? The question is perhaps unanswerable; but it remains the most insistent preoccupation of historians in the Arab world. If an earlier generation, of which Muhammad Husayn Haykal was the representative figure, turned to the Islamic past as a defence against the west, contrasting the spiritual history of the Arab

---

554. Cf. CHEJNE, *op. cit.*, p. 384; *Historical Writing . . .*, Vol. IV (1962), p. 431.

555. *Op. cit.* (1953), p. 454. LEWIS, B., *The Middle East and the West* (1964), p. 93, is more caustic. 'Nationalist historiography', he says, 'is generally worthless to the historian – except the historian of nationalism, for whom it can be very instructive indeed.'

556. Cf. INALCIK, *op. cit.* (1953), p. 453.

557. For Nabih Amin Faris, cf. LEWIS, B., *op. cit.* (1964), p. 114.

peoples with that of Europe, the present generation is more concerned to establish its cultural identity in terms of its own history and the overlapping and sometimes conflicting allegiances of Islam, the Arab nation and the homeland. This preoccupation is entirely comprehensible, but it is also true that it may easily divert historians from their primary function, which is the systematic and objective investigation of the past. It has also narrowed the range of Arab history. With few exceptions, Middle Eastern historians are only interested in the origins of modern nationalisms, in medieval Islam or in the ancient history of the Middle East, to which they look for their pre-Islamic roots. 'To this day', as Rosenthal observes, 'interest in all non-Islamic history has remained limited, and nothing of first-rate importance appears to have been produced in the field.'[558] This does not mean that modern standards of historiography and modern techniques are absent. As already indicated, there is a growing body of Arab historians with a western training and a grasp of modern methodology, who have begun to publish serious monographs on the social and economic history of particular Islamic countries. But progress is hesitant and the scope of such work, or the areas covered, still very circumscribed. In spite of the introduction of western methods, Firuz Kazemzadeh concludes, 'modern Iranian historiography is undistinguished and contributes little that is of scholarly importance.'[559] Much of the best work continues to be written by western scholars, and historians in the Near and Middle East have so far produced little to compare with the excellent Soviet work on the Islamic peoples of central Asia.[560]

In **South-East Asia**, also, historians are confronted by a problem of cultural identity.[561] What, in the first place, is the validity of the concept of South-East Asian history? It is certain that the area does not present an integral civilization in the way that India, China, Korea or Japan may be termed integral civilizations. Are we to conclude that South-East Asia is merely a geographic grouping, or do the countries in the area share a common history, in the same way as the Arab (or Arabicized) countries of the Middle East? The religious and cultural differences between the Islamic and Buddhist areas and the regions of Chinese and Indian influence are common knowledge, but it is also true that even the Islamic tradition was not homogeneous, and that in each of the different traditions strong indi-

558. *International Encyclopedia* . . ., Vol. VI (1968), p. 412.

559. *Historical Writing on the Peoples of Asia*, Vol. IV (1962), p. 431.

560. There is a brief account of Soviet writing and research in FRYE's contribution, *ibid.*, pp. 367-374. Cf. also WHEELER, G. & FOOTMAN, *Bibliography of Recent Soviet Source Material on Soviet Central Asia*, No. 1, pp. 23-29 and No. 2, pp. 24-35 (1960), for historical work published in 1959 and 1960.

561. In addition to the literature referred to above, p. 349, n. 522, cf. HALL, D. G. E., *East Asian History Today* (1959); COWAN, *South East Asian History in London* (1963); WAHID (ed.), *History Teaching: Its Problems in Malaya* (1964); VAN DER KROEF, 'On the writing of Indonesian history' (1958); KARTODIRDJO, 'Historical study and historians in Indonesia today' (1963); BENDA, 'The structure of Southeast Asian history' (1962); SMAIL, 'On the possibility of an autonomous history of modern Southeast Asia' (1961).

genous features can be discerned, which were peculiar to the different peoples of the area. Already before the war, the Dutch historian J. C. van Leur, who died in 1942, picked out these indigenous elements as the key factor in South-East Asian history.562 Van Leur, it has been said, 'summoned into life a whole dead world, the historically autonomous world of South-East Asia up to the early colonial period',563 and his brilliant pioneering work remains a powerful influence. It is visible, for example, in the work of Resink, and is the basic hypothesis underlying Hall's attempt to treat South-East Asia as a single intelligible unit throughout the whole span of its history.564

As a reaction against the Eurocentric views which prevailed in the colonial period, this work performed an important task. It was important to insist that South-East Asian history must be written 'from within', in terms of the area's own internal development, and not simply in relation to its contacts with China, India or the West. The peoples of South-East Asia were not merely passive recipients, but had their own highly developed and well integrated culture, and their history, as Hall emphasizes, 'cannot be safely viewed from any other perspective until seen from its own'.565 But it is also true that the concept of an autonomous South-East Asian history is no more than a 'methodological proposition', which remains 'tentative and hypothetical',566 and in fact the trend of historical thinking since independence has been nationalist rather than regional.567 For Indonesian historians, for example, the central problem is 'the identity of the Indonesian people'; they are concerned not with the question whether South-East Asia as a whole is a single entity, but with the 'organic unity of Indonesian culture and history.'568 The same, it need hardly be added, is true of other countries, such as Burma or Vietnam.

After the Second World War and the attainment of independence, it was obvious that the day of colonialist historiography was past. European and Asian historians found no difficulty in agreeing about the dangers and misconceptions arising from an over-estimation of European influence before the twentieth century and the need, for a real understanding of South-East Asia's past, to concentrate attention primarily on the activities of South-East Asians themselves. But once the colonialist framework had been rejected, the question immediately arose what new frame of reference was to be put in its place. As in the Near and Middle East, this question

562. Cf. van LEUR, *Indonesian Trade and Society: Essays in Asian Social and Economic History* (1955), particularly the essay (pp. 147-156) on 'The study of Indonesian history'.
563. SMAIL, *op. cit.* (1961), p. 101.
564. Cf. RESINK, *Indonesia's History between the Myths* (1967); HALL, D. G. E., *A History of South-East Asia* (1955).
565. *Ibid.*, p. vii.
566. Cf. SMAIL, *op. cit.* (1961), p. 85; BENDA, *op. cit.* (1962), p. 107.
567. Cf. *Historical Writing on the Peoples of Asia, op. cit.*, Vol. II (1961), p. 327.
568. This is emphasized in the Indonesian report to which reference is made above, p. 95, n. 404; cf. in particular, *ibid.*, pp. 57-59.

remains unresolved, and it is still a matter for debate whether national history is an adequate basis for the new South-East Asian historiography.[569] The obvious difficulty is that few of the newly constituted states of South-East Asia represent an historic nation or national society. If the historic unity of South-East Asia is an hypothesis, so also is the historic unity of Indonesia. In the period immediately following independence, it was simply assumed that Indonesia was a cultural unit, which retained its national identity through the ages in spite of foreign influences, and an 'Indonesia-centric' point of view prevailed. But this approach was 'more successful in conception than in execution,' and from around 1965, or perhaps a little earlier, a reaction against the historiography of the 1950's set in, and a new phase began.[570]

Among the historians who represent the new trend in Indonesian historical writing Sartono Kartodirdjo is in many ways outstanding.[571] It is not that Sartono Kartodirdjo rejects an Indonesia-centric point of view; on the contrary, it underlies the whole content of his work. But, unlike an earlier generation of Indonesian historians, he is acutely aware that it is not enough simply to postulate the existence of an autonomous Indonesian history, but that it has to be substantiated by concrete research. He is also aware that it cannot be substantiated on the level of political developments and 'grand events' on a national scale. The Dutch may have regarded their East Indian colonies as an administrative unity, but from an Indonesian point of view each island, each district, each of the peoples of the area lived its own life and had its own history, upon which the colonial administration only thinly impinged.

For this reason the attempt to write Indonesian history from an Indonesian point of view at the level of the whole of modern Indonesia was bound to fail. It ignored the fact that the real history of the Indonesian peoples went on at the 'grass-roots' level. What was required, Sartono Kartodirdjo postulated, was more knowledge of the history of single localities and regions, for this was where the real life of the people occurred, whereas 'national' history only existed at the level of colonial society. A purely 'political' history left out too much. In order to penetrate to the 'grass-roots' level, it was necessary to abandon the conventional political approach, with its emphasis on political events and institutions and the leading political figures, and to turn instead to social history in its broadest connotation, to the social movements, the social changes and the social conflicts which

569. Cf. *International Encyclopedia of the Social Sciences*, Vol. VI (1968), p. 426 (Wang Gungwu).
570. Cf. the Indonesian report, pp. 64, 69.
571. Kartodirdjo's main work is *The Peasants' Revolt of Banten in 1888. A Case Study of Social Movements in Indonesia* (1966); cf. also *Kolonialisme dan nasionalisme dalam Sedjarah Indonesia, Abad XIX-XX* (= Colonialism and Nationalism in Indonesian History, XIXth-XXth Centuries) (1967), and *Beberapa fasal dari historiografi Indonesia* (= Some Points of Indonesian Historiography) (1968). Kartodordjo does not, of course, stand alone: other representatives of the new trend, including Teuku Iskandar, are referred to in the Indonesian report, p. 22.

involved the Indonesian peoples in their daily life. It was necessary, in other words, to focus attention on the micro-history of local developments rather than the macro-history which delineates 'grand events' on a national scale. But this vast and virtually unexplored field also required a new methodology and the extensive use of untapped source material. If Sartono Kartodirdjo's main contribution to Indonesian historiography is a new and infinitely more sophisticated conceptual framework, scarcely less important are the new techniques of research he has brought to bear. The conventional tools of textual analysis and documentary criticism may be adequate for historians dealing with political events; they are of more limited value when the object is to unravel the complex communal life of peasant societies. Hence the need for a new research mechanism, and this Sartono Kartodirdjo found in the convergence of approaches derived from anthropology and the other social sciences. In this way alone was it possible to encompass all the multi-dimensional aspects of the Indonesian people's history.[572]

What is significant about Sartono Kartodirdjo's work, and the reason for discussing it rather more fully, is that it points the way out of the apparent *impasse* into which the problem of finding an appropriate framework for Indonesian history had led. Merely to reject a Eurocentric and set up in its place an Indonesia-centric viewpoint was not enough; it merely substituted one set of presuppositions, or one subjective value-system, for another. Furthermore, its dependence on broad concepts too often resulted in 'inadequate formulae' which could not be converted into a productive programme of historical research.[573] Hence the failure, already remarked, of Indonesian historiography in the first ten or fifteen years after independence to produce significant new contributions to knowledge.[574] The great change which took place after 1960 was the switch from descriptive narrative, often cast in an anti-colonialist mould and singing the praises of the heroic Indonesian past, to the investigation of concrete problems or to exact, detailed and critical studies of particular events or episodes. The new generation of historians was as committed as the old to an 'Indonesia-centric' point of view, in the sense of writing history 'from within'; but they realized that mere reiteration of the nationalist theme was bound eventually to be sterile and unproductive. Instead of remaining content to revise and criticize the interpretation of Indonesian history put forward by colonial historians, they brought new critical insights and new critical methods to bear on nationalist history as well.

The result was the rise of a more sophisticated and more mature historiography, which went beyond the mere assertion of the autonomy and individuality of Indonesia's past. Four main characteristics distinguish the new 'Indonesia-centric' historiography from the old. First, it is concerned with problems, not with the mere narration of political events; it is, in

572. For the above, cf. the admirable summary of Kartodirdjo's work in tne Indonesian report, p. 30.
573. *Ibid.*, p. 69.
574. Cf. above, p. 98.

other words, analytical rather than descriptive. Secondly, it approaches the past not from a national but from a local level; it is, in short, 'micro-historical', not 'macro-historical'. In this way, it hopes to provide the groundwork, hitherto missing, upon which a real 'national' history can eventually be built. Thirdly, emphasis has shifted from political events on a 'national' scale to the internal dynamic of social forces; in other words, to the 'grass roots' of politics, and to the local communities in which the forces of social change and social continuity were generated. Fourthly, the new generation of historians has developed new methods and techniques, derived from the social sciences, to equip them for these tasks.[575]

Although these new trends are at an early stage, they mark a significant advance. They promise, first, a genuine accretion of new knowledge, instead of a series of interesting but often highly speculative theories and generalizations. And, secondly, they suggest that the preoccupation with national identity, which was so marked a feature of South-East Asian history after independence, is no longer so obsessive. Terms such as 'Eurocentric', 'Asia-centric', 'Indonesia-centric', it is now realized, represent a false antithesis, and if used without discrimination are more likely to obscure than to illuminate the actual course of historical development.[576] To overcome the problem of a Eurocentric perspective, it is not sufficient simply to give 'the other side of the story': it is necessary to tell a different story – a story centred on social and cultural rather than political change.[577] In so far as it is doing this, contemporary Indonesian historiography can be said to have embarked on a path which promises well for the future.

In **India** historians have already taken this decisive step forward. This is not simply because the development and organization of historical study in India, as already noted,[578] is something like a generation in advance of of that in South-East Asia. More significant is the fact that Indian historiography has for the most part transcended the intense preoccupation with the problems of cultural identity and national unity which exercise the minds of so many Asian historians today. Nationalism came early to India, hard on the heels of the founding of the Indian National Congress in 1885, and the nationalist and anti-imperialist phase of Indian historiography coincided roughly with the life of Jawaharlal Nehru, whose *Discovery of India*, written in prison during the Second World War and published in 1946, may be taken as its apogee. Since independence, the concern to assert the spiritual and cultural unity of India and combat the British view that India was never a nation but simply a conglomeration of races, religions and castes – a concern which underlies not only Nehru's book but the work of a whole generation of Indian historians – has ceased to be a matter of urgency, and since around 1955 Indian historians have felt free to turn from such broad,

575. Cf. the Indonesian report, pp. 70-71.
576. Cf. SMAIL, *op. cit.* (1961), p. 100.
577. Cf. LEGGE, *Indonesia* (1964), p. 65.
578. Cf. above, p. 125.

overriding questions to the concrete problems of Indian society and its growth.

When we turn to the actual products of Indian historiography today, we find as their main characteristic a pragmatic and practical approach which seeks above all else to deepen our knowledge of the realities of Indian history at all stages of the past. Like their colleagues elsewhere in Asia, Indian historians are concerned first and foremost to see Indian society from within, and it is significant that work on the British impact on India – for example, on the policies of different British Governors-General and Viceroys – is more actively pursued today in England than in India itself.[579] The same is true to a large extent of the study of the rise of the Indian national movement, with which American and Soviet as well as British historians are actively concerned, whereas in India itself the current trend is to place more emphasis on the social processes of Indian society before the advent of the British.[580] Behind this shift of emphasis is a desire to establish a periodization of Indian history based not on extrinsic events (e.g., the arrival of foreign invaders) or on concepts introduced from outside (e.g., the middle ages), or simply on the accidents of the race and religion of the ruling class, but on the evolution of Indian social forms.[581] Hence interest has shifted from the mechanics of political rule to the impact of empires, such as the Moghul empire, on Indian society and its growth, and to the problem of Indian 'feudalism', that is to say, the rise of a powerful class of territorial magnates (thakurs, zamindars) who disposed of the rural surplus and became the socially dominant class in India. In this way it is hoped to discover the underlying social changes which account for the decline of the classical age and the establishment of Turkish rule.[582]

A characteristic feature of the contemporary phase in Indian historiography is therefore the shift – which we have already observed in other Asian countries – from narrative history to problem-orientated studies, and from political to social and economic history. With it goes a new methodology and the use of new source materials, and a marked tendency to avoid broad generalizations and study limited segments and particular problems in depth. Among the problems which are engaging attention at present, the following have been singled out as particularly important:[583]

(i) Did Indian society, or more specifically the Moghul empire, have the potential for, or was it on the verge of a capitalist revolution, which was aborted by the British?

579. As pointed out (p. 25) in the valuable Indian report referred to above, p. 323, n. 404. For example, S. GOPAL's monographs on *The Viceroyalty of Lord Ripon* (1953) and *The Viceroyalty of Lord Irwin* (1957); cf. also GOPAL, *British Policy in India, 1858-1905* (1965), were all produced in England, at the time when he was Reader in South Asian History in Oxford University, although Gopal, of course, is himself an Indian.

580. Cf. the Indian report, p. 27.

581. Cf. THAPAR, 'Interpretations of ancient Indian history' (1968), p. 335 in *History and Theory*, Vol. VII.

582. Cf. Indian report, p. 19.

583. *Ibid.*, pp. 23-27.

(ii) What was the role in Indian society before the advent of the British of 'minority groups', e.g., minority religions such as Buddhism or Jainism and other heterodox religious movements, and of oppositional movements such as those of the Jats, Sikhs, Marathas or Afghans? How did they interact with Hindu caste society, and with what results?

(iii) Were there specific social factors (i.e., not merely conflicts of personality and discord between Moslems and Hindus) accounting for the disintegration of the Moghul empire, e.g., contradictions within the ruling class (between zamindars and nobility) or a clash of interests between the ruling class and the peasantry?

(iv) Did the British rulers deliberately set out (as nationalist historians argue) to thwart India's economic development, or alternatively did British policy result (whether deliberately or not) in a growing social and economic imbalance in Indian society? Did India, in other words, develop economically, or stagnate, or even suffer a decline under British rule, or alternatively is it possible to establish different phases of growth, stagnation and/or decline?

(v) To what extent were élitist conflicts a factor in the growth of Indian nationalism? Did the nationalist movement, in other words, represent a struggle between élites, foreign and indigenous, or did it involve the interests of the broad masses of the Indian population?

(vi) Was the partition of India the result of conscious British policy, or did it have historical roots in Indian society and culture?

The most conspicuous gap, at least to the outside observer, in the available surveys of contemporary Indian historiography is any reference to specific detailed research on the history of the Indian peasantry: on peasant movements, peasant unrest, and the rôle of the peasant masses in the evolution of Indian society.[584] When we turn to **China**, it is at once evident that this is the most striking difference between current trends in Indian and in Chinese historical work today. In other respects there are significant parallels. Just as Indian historians, for example, are investigating the evidence of early capitalist developments in the Moghul empire, so Chinese historians since 1949 have devoted much time and effort to the incipient capitalism of late Ming and early Ching times. Like Indian historians, but to an even greater extent, they have turned their attention to the minority peoples in the Han empire, the Muslims, the Miao and the Mongols. And the Indian preoccupation with the economic consequences of British rule is paralleled in China by intensive study of the impact of foreign imperialism on the

584. Among the few works I have noted are NATARAYAN, *Peasant Uprisings in India, 1850-1900* (1953), CHAUDHURI, *Civil Disturbances during the British Rule in India, 1765-1857* (1955), and HABIB, *The Agrarian System of Mughal India, 1556-1707* (1963); but none, it will be noted, is particularly recent. For the contemporary (post-1947) period there is a certain amount of literature, but sociological or political rather than historical; cf. ALAVI, 'Peasants and revolution' (1965).

Chinese economy after 1840. These common trends evidently reflect basic similarities in the position of colonial and semi-colonial peoples in the era of European dominance. But the distinctive feature of Chinese historical writing and research, at least since around 1955, is its concern with peasant revolts and peasant wars. According to Mao Tse-tung, 'these class struggles of the peasants' ,were 'the real motive force' which brought about the changes in China's long feudal history;[585] and one of the main aims of the new historiography has been, in Chien Po-tsan's words, to 'reveal the great revolutionary tradition of the oppressed peoples of China'.[586] Between 1949 and 1961, and mainly in the latter half of the period, more than 400 articles were published on the peasant wars of the feudal period, as well as a comparable amount of material on nineteenth-century peasant uprisings, and the debate still continues. The evaluation of the part played by peasant movements in Chinese history, it is no exaggeration to say, is a central preoccupation of Chinese communist historiography today.

The development of Chinese historiography since 1949 has received a great deal of attention in the western world and in the Soviet Union, where it has largely been assessed in ideological and political terms.[587] No one is likely to deny that there are strong political overtones both in the choice of subject-matter and in its handling; but we are concerned here with the positive results, and even unsympathetic critics are impressed with both the quantity of new work and its positive achievements. In economic history, in particular, 'many new fields are being opened and the foundation laid for writing the economic history of modern China at a higher level of theoretical sophistication and with a more comprehensive control of the empirical data than was the case in the past.'[588] There is general agreement that much valuable new documentary material has been made available, but it is recognized also that there have been significant advances in methodology and that a real effort is being made to create a new view of the Chinese past to take the place of the discarded Confucian version.[589]

585. *Selected Works*, Vol. II, p. 629, Vol. III, p. 76.
586. Cf. HARRISON, *The Communists and Chinese Peasant Rebellions* (1969), p. 6.
587. In addition to the general works cited above p. 349, n. 522, cf. FEUERWERKER & CHENG, *Chinese Communist Studies of Modern Chinese History* (1961); WIET-HOFF, *Grundzüge der älteren chinesischen Geschichte* (1971), pp. 9-38; FEUER-WERKER, 'Rewriting Chinese history' (1961); FEUERWERKER (ed.), *History in Communist China* (1968), a re-issue, with other material, of eleven articles from *The China Quarterly*, Nos. 22-24 (1965); LIU Chung-jo, *Controversies in Modern Chinese Intellectual History* (1964); HARRISON, *The Communists and Chinese Peasant Rebellions* (1969); MARCHISIO, 'Les études historiques en Chine populaire' (1963); CHESNEAUX, 'Histoire moderne et contemporaine de Chine' (1970); VYATKIN & TIKHVINSKY, 'Some questions of historical science in the Chinese People's Republic' (1963, reproduced in English translation in FEUERWERKER (ed.), *History in Communist China*, 1968).
588. Cf. FEUERWERKER & CHENG, *op. cit.* (1961), p. 169.
589. Cf. KAHN & FEUERWERKER, pp. 6, 10 in FEUERWERKER (ed.), *History in Communist China, op. cit.* (1968).

It must be remembered that the collapse of the traditional framework ot Chinese historiography reaches back to 1919, if not to 1905, and that the Chinese communists, when they came to power in 1949, inherited the search for a new, more realistic conception of Chinese history. As might be expected, their interpretations are largely shaped by Marxist-Maoist concepts, and particularly by the Marxist periodization of history.

The overriding problem for Chinese historians today is to relate the historical development of China to the categories of the Marxist periodization of history, without doing violence to the unique features and special qualities of China's past. All the main controversies among Chinese historians today centre round this basic question, and there is no doubt that their preoccupation with periodization has to a large extent determined the choice of topics upon which they are currently engaged. Broadly speaking, the problem areas of current Chinese historiography are the 'nodal points' – in other words, the periods of transition from one social structure to another (from slave society to feudal society, for example, or from feudalism to capitalism) – in China's history. This has led to concentration on a relatively small number of key topics: the formation of the Han nation, the nature of landholding in feudal China, the interpretation of peasant rebellions, the transition from feudalism to capitalism and the origins of capitalism in China, and the periodization of modern Chinese history (1840-1949) with special reference to the impact and consequences of western imperialism.[590]

This is not the place to discuss in detail the work done on these different topics, nor the controversies and different interpretations to which they have given rise. Chinese historians have pointed out the 'blanks' and 'weak spots', particularly the lack of 'analytic research'.[591] Nevertheless the intensity of the discussion remains impressive. It can be gauged from the fact

590. Cf. MARCHISIO, *op. cit.* (1963), p. 160 in *Revue historique*, Vol. CCXXIX; FEUERWERKER, 'Rewriting Chinese history', *op. cit.* (1961), pp. 275-276 in *The Far East: China and Japan* (*University of Toronto Quarterly*, Supp. No. 5).

591. The observations of YEN Chung-p'ing, cited by FEUERWERKER in FEUER-WERKER (ed.), *History in Communist China* (1968), p. 239, are worth quoting at length for the light they throw upon the current situation. After stating that the achievements in modern economic history since 1949 are 'extremely rich, far surpassing those accumulated in the Old China over many years', he observes that development is nevertheless 'very uneven'. Geographically, attention was concentrated on the 'coastal provinces and the few large cities' to the detriment of 'the interior provinces and their many large villages and densely populated townships.... And no attention has been paid to the various national minority areas...' 'With respect to the several sectors of the economy, the emphasis has been on modern industry and commerce, and rather less on agriculture and handicrafts, although the latter accounted for 90 per cent of the total value of production in the old China...' 'As for periodisation, more works have been produced on the Ming and Ch'ing dynasties prior to the Opium War because of the extensive discussions of the birth of capitalism. Inadequate attention has been given to the post-Opium War period...' Turning to the forms of research, Yen said that 'data collection' had predominated over 'finished research work' and that there was a 'lack of carefully processed statistical data. Among the written works produced, there are many short

that over 150 articles were published in less than seven years on the periodization of ancient history alone.[592] But the central problem for Chinese historians is the interpretation of the feudal period, which in China stretches (according to current calculations) from 475 B.C. to A.D. 1840, and thus covers the greater span of Chinese history. How was the history of this long and critical period to be approached? Marxist doctrine is relatively uninterested in the feudal epoch, except as the seedbed of capitalism; but to write it off as static not only suggested that Chinese history was peculiarly stagnant and backward, but also did less than justice to the known facts. In reality, the so-called 'feudal' epoch was a dynamic period of Chinese history with radical changes in class relationships, land tenure and agricultural techniques. The problem for Chinese historians is to account for this dynamism within the Marxist framework. The answer has been found by the new emphasis on the peasantry as, in Mao's words, the 'motive force' in China's feudal society. Historians may dispute – and a number of western historians have rejected – the central importance attached by contemporary Chinese historians to peasant movements, peasant wars and peasant uprisings. What is indisputable is that they have added a new dimension to Chinese history.

Mao's statement that the Chinese peasant wars are 'without parallel in the world', both in scale and frequency, has often been noted.[593] It is important that historians should take note of this fact and assess its role in Chinese history. Traditional Chinese historiography avoided the issue, as we have seen,[594] painting instead a harmonious view of Chinese society, and writing off the peasant leaders as 'bandits' and disturbers of order; hence, for all practical purposes, the history of the peasant wars was unwritten before 1949. The new Chinese historiography has at the very least restored the balance. It has sometimes been objected that this change of emphasis, from kings and battles to the ordinary man, was only possible by tampering with the evidence; but this is certainly an exaggeration. As Lattimore says, 'the evidence is all there', and 'it is only a question of selecting evidence that was not emphasized by the traditional historians.'[595]

In 1958 Chinese historians were exhorted to 'emphasize the present and de-emphasize the past.'[596] As Yen Chung-ping pointed out, more was being written on Ming and Ching history prior to the Opium War than on the

---

articles, but few completed books. There are a great number of subjects and a great diversity of levels of synthetic generalisation, but there has been little analytic research.'

592. Cf. HULSEWÉ, p. 101 in FEUERWERKER (ed.), *History in Communist China* (1968).

593. Cf. HARRISON, *ibid.*, p. 213.

594. Cf. above, p. 96.

595. Cf. LATTIMORE, *From China, Looking Outwards* (1964), p. 15.

596. '*Hou-chin Po-ku*': cf. KUO Mo-jo, 'Kuan-yü *Hou-chin Po-ku* Wen-t'i' (= On the question of 'emphasizing the present and de-emphasizing the past') (1958); cf. FEUERWERKER & CHENG, *Chinese Communist Studies . . ., op. cit.* (1961), p. xi.

post-Opium War period.[597] But at the same time Mao insisted that it was as important to know the history of the day before yesterday as it was to know the history of today and yesterday,[598] and at present it would seem that writing and research is spread fairly evenly over all periods of Chinese history from the very ancient to the very modern. On the one hand, efforts are being made to bring together first-hand reports from participants in recent events beginning with the revolution of 1911.[599] On the other hand, as Marchisio has pointed out, no less than 24 out of a total of 39 articles in the first six numbers of the new historical review *Li-shih yen-chiu* were devoted to ancient history and the feudal period.[600] This may be attributed in part to the emphasis in Marxist historiography on the importance of studying human society at all stages of its development. It also reflects the long-standing interest of Chinese historians in Chinese antiquity, a tradition as strong in China as the interest of Indian historians in the age of the Vedas. The traditional Chinese preoccupation with textual interpretation and emendation is far from dead, and excellent punctuated editions of basic texts such as the *Han Shu* have been published in large numbers.

Nevertheless, the characteristic feature of the new historiography is the priority given to social and economic aspects. This, of course, had begun – like so many other innovations in Chinese historiography – long before the communist take-over in 1949, and a work such as Kuo Mo-jo's *Studies in the Society of Ancient China*, originally published in 1930, showed the profusion of new insights that could be obtained by intelligent Marxist analysis and a socio-economic approach.[601] Since 1949 a Marxist and socio-economic approach has become almost obligatory. The results may not always have come up to expectations, for it is clear that ideas which at one stage provided stimulus and inspiration might at another stage degenerate into dogma. Nevertheless the overall progress of Chinese historiography since 1949 is very impressive. There is widespread agreement that the study of history in China today is more 'fluid' and less 'petrified' than at any time in the past, its basic approach more dynamic, its grasp of the operative factors more comprehensive.[602] Through its stress on the revolutionary qualities of the Chinese peasantry and their rôle as the agents of social change, the new historiography has 'changed the very language of Chinese history' and set up new criteria for the evaluation and reconstruction of China's past.

597. Cf. above, p. 138, n. 591.

598. *Selected Works*, Vol. III, p. 821.

599. Cf. BERGÈRE, 'La révolution de 1911 jugée par les historiens de la République populaire de Chine' (1963), pp. 405-406 in *Revue historique*, Vol. CCXXX.

600. Cf. MARCHISIO, *op. cit.* (1963), p. 160 in *Revue historique*, Vol. CCXXIX.

601. Cf. KUO Mo-jo, *Chung-kuo Ku-tai She-huei Yen-chiu* (= Studies of Ancient Chinese Society) (1930); revised editions were published in 1954 and 1960.

602. Cf. FEUERWERKER (ed.), *History in Communist China* (1968), pp. 5 (KAHN & FEUERWERKER) and 123 (HULSEWÉ). A. F. WRIGHT, on the other hand, holds that 'dogmatic concerns have made sterile the historical studies since 1949': cf. *International Encyclopedia of the Social Sciences*, Vol. VI (1968), p. 406.

The Present Situation of Historical Studies in the Third World

If, at the conclusion of this rapid survey of recent developments in the Third World, an attempt is made to take stock, there are fairly obvious reasons for concentrating on the situation in Asia and Africa. It is, of course, true that there have been important and far-reaching changes in Latin America also. But they have taken place, as we have seen,[603] in the framework of an active tradition of historical writing and research reaching back to the early years of the nineteenth century, without any real break in continuity. The change has largely been one of approach and orientation, and as such requires little further comment. In Asia and Africa, on the other hand, it would hardly be an exaggeration to speak of a new beginning. Not only has there in many cases been a deliberate break with traditional historiography,[604] but also a shift of viewpoint and a change of personnel. Apart from Japan, where historians have long been engaged in fundamental research on the history of East Asia, and to a lesser extent from India,[605] the modern study of Asian and African history down to the middle of the twentieth century was largely in the hands of Europeans. With the passing of the colonial era in Asia after the winning of Indian independence in 1947 and the emergence of the new China in 1949, and with the emancipation of most of Africa following the independence of Ghana in 1957, this situation has changed, and one of the most striking features of historical study in the past two decades has been its rapid growth in the newly emancipated countries of Asia and Africa. It is important to evaluate its results and prospects.

The first result, without doubt, is the appearance of a growing body of trained and experienced historians in the Asian and African countries (in Latin America, of course, such a body had long been in existence). As their number increases, we must expect them to take over an increasingly large and ultimately preponderant share in the writing of their own history. That does not mean, of course, that the participation of European and American historians in Asian and African studies is likely to decline. On the contrary, their scholarly interest in the historic past of Asia and Africa has been reinforced by the political changes in the world since 1945, and the need to take account of these changes and replace the old Eurocentric view of history by a global perspective is certainly as fully appreciated in Europe as it is elsewhere. In some ways, indeed, it might be held that the need for European historians, both in eastern and in western Europe, to participate in Asian and African studies, is greater than before. If, as we have more than once observed,[606] Asian and African historians have a strong tendency to confine their work almost exclusively to their own country, there is a real need for the wider range of vision which other historians

603. Cf. above, p. 115.
604. Cf. above, pp. 96-98, 123.
605. Cf. above, p. 125.
606. Cf. above, pp. 103, 125, 130, etc.

can bring to bear. As Hulsewé has pointed out,[607] it is one thing 'to stress the uniqueness of China's attainment and the Chinese way of development against the wide background of developments elsewhere', but quite another to stress China's uniqueness 'in ignorance of all other historical phenomena'. In so far as European historians can rectify the balance, there is no reason to doubt that European scholarship, which has contributed so much in the past, will continue to perform a valuable function in Asian and African studies. In the end Asian and African history, like European history, must be placed in a global setting, if it is to bear fruit; and this is a task in which European and American historians, just as much as Asian and African historians, have a part to play.

This having been said, it nevertheless remains true that fundamental research is bound to gravitate more and more into the hands of local scholars. Practical considerations – the availability of source material, written, oral, and archaeological, and the language barrier – alone make this inevitable. Even for native historians linguistic difficulties, in some areas at least, are a formidable problem: in Malaya, for example, it is almost impossible to embark on serious research until at least the four main languages of the country have been mastered.[608] During the colonial period this problem was mitigated for European historians by the establishment of institutes and training centres such as the École française d'Extrême-Orient, founded in 1900, which not only provided language teaching but also built up specialist libraries and afforded facilities for historians and archaeologists to carry out research and field work.[609] Today these responsibilities have devolved on to the national governments. The number of Europeans working in African universities is still relatively large, but in Asia the type of scholar who spent his life in colonial service – in Java, for example, or in Vietnam – and who was thoroughly acquainted with the historical monuments and versed in the native languages, is virtually extinct. His place has been taken by local historians, and it is to the latter that we must now look for the accretion of new knowledge upon which further progress depends. In China today it is in practice almost impossible for foreign historians, even those with a thorough grasp of classical and colloquial Chinese, to gain access to the vast untapped historical sources spread far and wide through the Chinese provinces. Increasingly, therefore, European students are coming to depend for their primary knowledge upon the work of native scholars. In East Asian history, as Twitchett pointed out a few years ago, 'there can be no question that in the foreseeable future it will be our Chinese and Japanese colleagues who will set the pace';[610] and though it is probably true that China and Japan, like India, are somewhat in advance,

607. Cf. p. 123 in Feuerwerker (ed.), *History in Communist China, op. cit.* (1968).

608. Cf. Wahid (ed.), *History Teaching. Its Problems in Malaya, op. cit.* (1964), p. 119.

609. Cf. *Historical Writing on the Peoples of Asia, op. cit.*, Vol. II (1961), p. 99.

610. Cf. Twitchett, *Land Tenure and the Social Order in T'ang and Sung China* (1962), p. 34.

it is clear that we may expect the same to apply to Asian and African history in general, as other countries, such as Indonesia, make up the leeway.

All the present evidence, therefore, indicates that historical study in Asia and Africa is at the beginning of a period of rapid advance. In most areas the middle of the 1950's and the 1960's saw the opening of a new phase, in which the inspired amateur was largely displaced by the trained professional historian.[611] In spite of a certain resistance, particularly in the Islamic countries of the Middle East and in Pakistan, the adoption and assimilation of western concepts and methods is now generally accepted, and if, as Wang Gungwu observed,[612] there was to begin with a 'time lag in methodological change', the gap has been rapidly closed during the past decade. The result is a marked increase in methodological sophistication, and a significant readiness to experiment with new techniques. In Africa the inadequacy at most periods of the written sources has forced historians to devise new methods to cope with the special problems of oral tradition.[613] Elsewhere it seems likely that Marxism, which is a powerful influence in most Asian countries, has played an important part in stimulating the search for methods with greater explanatory and heuristic potency. In any case, there is no doubt that the younger generation of Asian and African historians is no longer satisfied with narrative history of a descriptive and literary kind, but is moving into the field of social and economic analysis, using modern social science techniques as well as the more conventional tools of historical criticism. The same, we have seen, is true of the new generation of Latin American historians.[614]

This methodological advance, which for the most part falls within the last ten years, is of fundamental importance because it opens up new prospects for Asian and African history. The first generation of nationalist historians, while they rejected Eurocentric and colonialist interpretations and perceived that European influence was only one factor in the transformation of societies which had long been subject to abrupt upheavals and more gradual change, lacked the analytical tools with which to study the internal development of Asian and African society. Today this is no longer true. The importance of the new techniques is that they make it possible, in a way that was not possible earlier, to study Asian and African society 'from within', and in a sense simply 'stood colonialist history on its head'. This is a great advance by comparison not only with colonialist history but also with the earlier forms of nationalist history, which worked largely within the same framework as the European historians whose views it attacked, and in a sense simply 'stood colonialist history on its head'. The new generation of Asian and African historians, on the other hand, has shifted the focus from external factors, particularly colonialism and the relations between indigenous societies and the colonial powers, to the dynamics of social develop-

611. Cf. above, pp. 124, 125, 133.
612. Cf. *International Encyclopedia of the Social Sciences,* Vol. VI (1968), p. 424.
613. Cf. above, p. 113.
614. Cf. above, p. 116.

ment. They are concerned not merely with Asian and African reactions to foreign influence but also with the forces at work in Asian and African society before the advent of the Europeans, and more fundamentally still with the question how new the new Asia or the new Africa is. Compared with the earlier generation of nationalist historians they view national history from a different point of view: not as the antithesis of colonial history, but as the study of an evolving society in which, for good or for ill, the colonial presence is one factor among many which have to be taken into account.

The consequences of this change of attitude are far-reaching, and there is every reason to believe that it marks the opening of a new and more productive period of historical study in Asia and Africa. The priority now being given to the internal evolution of Asian and African societies, to their development 'from within', not only means a substantial extension of the range of historical writing and research, but also marks a very significant departure from what was long the conventionally accepted approach to Asian and African history. With few exceptions this concentrated on either the colonial period or the remote past, which were regarded as the only periods of general significance. Prior to independence, as we have seen, African history was written almost exclusively from the standpoint of the colonizing powers, and little if any attempt was made to view it from within, from the point of view of the African peoples.[615] In the case of Asia, this preoccupation with the European impact – though by no means absent – was counterbalanced by the deep and genuine interest of Orientalists in the Asian past for its own sake. But Sinologists and Indologists and other Orientalists accepted almost without qualification the assumptions of the traditional historiography of the countries in which they were interested; they adopted the view that the golden age of Asian civilization lay far back in the past and devoted themselves for preference to the great classical texts, which they located, edited and commented upon. They also took over the stereotyped divisions of dynastic history, a superficial, short-term scheme of periodization which, as Twitchett has said, by concentrating attention on court politics, obscured 'the pattern of far-reaching long-term historical changes which were taking place in society.'[616] And since, from a dynastic point of view, great patches of history seemed barren and insignificant, many periods were virtually ignored. Islamic scholars jumped from the great age of the Omayyad and Abbasid dynasties to the Arab awakening, while in India and China the huge gulf between the classical period and the end of the eighteenth century – in the case of China some two millennia, in the case of India more than a thousand years of history – was until recently undeservedly neglected.[617]

It is only when we are aware of the limitations of the earlier historiography of Asia and Africa, when we perceive the narrow framework in which it was conceived and written, that the extent and significance of the

615. Cf. above, pp. 111-112.
616. *Op. cit.* (1962), p. 15.
617. Cf. above, pp. 123-124, 125-126, 139-141.

recent advance becomes fully apparent. If we wish to sum it up, we may say that since 1960 the study of history in Asia and Africa has come of age. In some countries such as India, significant changes had occurred earlier; but in general it is the great innovations in orientation and method during the last ten or fifteen years that have raised historical study in Asia and Africa to a new level of maturity and sophistication. No doubt, it is true that nationalist impulses provided the essential motivation for intensive study of the past; but it was only when nationalism was matched by an appropriate methodology and a firm conceptual grasp, that the decisive step forward became possible. In so far as it diverted attention from internal development to external factors, the preoccupation of the earlier nationalist historians with colonialism tended to be self-defeating; and one of the distinctive features of the new historiography is the way it has transcended the earlier nationalist preoccupations by shifting the emphasis to the study of Asian and African history from within. This is a necessary corrective. In the state of knowledge at the time the early attempts to pass judgement on colonialism were premature. Only when we have more detailed and more concrete knowledge of the structure and actual working of Asian and African societies, only when the complex, multi-dimensional aspects of their social life have been unravelled, shall we be in a position to turn to the question of colonialism with any real prospect of assessing its impact objectively and scientifically.

The study of Asian and African society from within is only at its beginning, and is likely to be the dominant trend in the years to come. What is most apparent at the moment is the extent of our ignorance. Without in any way under-estimating the progress achieved to date by Indian, Japanese and Chinese historians, it is hardly too much to say that for many areas of Asia and Africa practically everything remains to be done. Even in India and China we still know far too little about the centuries stretching from classical times to the beginning of the nineteenth century. For the Tang and Sung periods of Chinese history, as Twitchett has emphasized, 'we are still at a very primitive stage of our studies', roughly comparable in his estimation with the stage English medieval history had reached a century ago in the time of Seebohm.[618] Elsewhere the position is less satisfactory still. As late as 1961 it was possible to write that history in South-East Asia was still primarily concerned with the correct reconstruction of royal genealogies, the life of courts and palaces, and the tenure of office and policies of important ministers of state; that 'deplorably little' was known about the actual conditions of life in the past; and that the groundwork for serious analysis of the structure of society – that is to say, the structure of the many different societies of South-East Asia – was still entirely lacking.[619] The fact is that the attempt to understand Asian and African society from within means in most respects starting again from the beginning on different foundations and with basically different presupposi-

618. *Op. cit.* (1962), p. 32.
619. Cf. *Historical Writing . . ., op. cit.*, Vol. II (1961), p. 327.

tions from those of the older historiography. It presupposes, on a scale far in excess of anything which has yet been attempted, the study in depth of particular situations and strictly limited areas; in short, 'micro-history' rather than 'macro-history'.[620] This is a formidable challenge which is likely to occupy the energies of Asian and African historians for many years to come; but it is probably the only way in which a random and haphazard assemblage of fragments of knowledge about the past can be transformed into a systematic and meaningful investigation of the historical development of Asian and African societies in all their different forms and stages through the centuries.

The new generation of Asian and African historians is well aware that the necessary condition of progress at the present stage is meticulous, detailed study in depth of specific problems. As in Latin America, where the endeavour to approach history 'from within' is equally characteristic of the younger generation, this realization determines the direction of current research. It is important, therefore, to add that study in depth may easily be stultifying if it is not matched by study in breadth. Specialization carries with it its own particular dangers, and there is no doubt that the history of Asia and Africa has suffered in the past from being set aside from the mainstream and treated as the special preserve of a small band of highly specialized Oriental and African scholars. There is some risk that this attitude, which has also to some degree affected the writing of Latin American history in the past, may be perpetuated today by the currently fashionable concept of 'regional studies'. It is therefore important to insist, as R. F. Wall has done, that 'the time when specialists on Asia were only required to communicate with others in the same field is past', and that the real challenge facing Asian and African historians today is 'how to make their material manageable and meaningful for people conditioned by other environments.'[621]

Looking back over developments in Asian and African history during the past fifteen or twenty years, nothing is more striking than the way they have emerged from isolation. No one today would regard them, as they were regarded until comparatively recently, as esoteric fields of study which can safely be left in the hands of specialists. This fundamental change of attitude is, without doubt, a response to world events as they have developed since 1945, but today it extends far beyond the original impulse which called it forth. If in the first place the object was to explain the immediate origins of the Asian and African revolutions, today it is realized not only that this is impossible without much fuller knowledge of their Asian and African antecedents than we yet possess, but also that this pragmatic and contemporary approach leaves too much out of account. What has happened in the last ten or fifteen years is a shift from short-term objectives − on the part of Asian and African historians the refutation of 'colonialist' interpretations, on the part of European and American historians the explana-

620. Cf. above, pp. 124, 133, 134, etc.
621. Cf. 'New openings: Asia', *op. cit.*, p. 302 in *New Ways in History* (*Times Literary Supplement*, 1966).

tion of the rise and triumph of nationalist movements in Asia and Africa – to a genuine interest in Asian and African history not merely for their own sake, but still more as an integral part of world history. It is not merely that the view from Asia is the view of the majority of the world's population; far more important is the need to understand Asia in Asian terms and Africa in African terms – to see them from within and not from outside – if their historical experience is to become meaningful in a universal context. When we say that the rapid growth of interest in Asian and African history in the last twenty years has added a new dimension to historical studies, what we mean is not that they were neglected before that – that is obviously not true – but that the history of the Asian and African peoples, instead of being considered in isolation, has been integrated into the pattern of world history, and has profoundly altered the parameters of world history in the process. This is a further major change, which requires separate consideration.

5. The Search for Meaning in History: National History, Comparative History, and 'Meta-History'

The enlargement of the field of history which has occurred in the last two or three decades poses fundamental questions for the historian. With the rapid progress of Asian, African, and Latin American history, with the establishment of new branches of study, such as the history of science and technology,[622] and with the extension of the historian's time-span through the work of pre-historians and archaeologists, history has broken through its old frontiers. The accretion of new knowledge, particularly in areas which had previously received less than their due share of attention, is a precondition of further progress; but it is also evident that it cannot be regarded as an end in itself. In what framework is it to be placed, if it is to be made meaningful and manageable?

In answering this question most historians today would agree that the framework commonly adopted in the nineteenth and the earlier part of the twentieth centuries is no longer adequate, if it ever was. Between 1945 and 1955 doubt about the validity of the old patterns became widespread.[623] In a world in which the peoples of Asia and Africa were evidently destined to play a much larger role than in the immediate past, there was growing impatience with the type of history which took as its standard of measurement the European national state and as its culmination the expansion of Europe. As William McNeill has recently stated,[624] 'new patterns for the

622. Briefly surveyed by R. J. FORBES, 'The history of science and technology', in Vol. I of the *Rapports* of the *XIth International Congress* (1960), and A. R. HALL, 'The history of science', in FINBERG (ed.), *Approaches to History* (1962).
623. Cf. BARRACLOUGH, *History in a Changing World* (1955), where I tried to survey some of the misgivings expressed at that time.
624. Page 21 in BALLARD (ed.), *New Movements in the Study and Teaching of History* (1970).

comprehension of the past are urgently in demand'; but what should they be?

This is a question which many practising historians find it unnecessary to consider, devoting themselves instead to detailed empirical research, in the belief that, in J. B. Bury's words, 'a complete assemblage of the smallest facts [...] will tell in the end.'[625] But it is nevertheless a question which goes to the heart of the historian's work. As Philip Guedella once observed, though 'brick-makers are well enough, [...] the edifice of history calls for an architect as well.'[626] Since history is concerned not merely with establishing as accurately as possible what happened in the past, but also with the meaning and mechanism of what happened – with the significance and explanation of particular events – detailed research must be related to a larger scheme and placed in a wider context, if it is to have any general relevance. The danger that specialization and the proliferation of new branches of history, each going its own way without reference to the rest, will result in fragmentation, requires no emphasis. The further specialization goes, the greater is the need for integration, and integration itself is only possible within the context of a larger pattern.

Not, of course, that the search for a pattern in history is in any way new. The attempt to perceive, behind the transient incidents, the underlying trends and movements, and the motive forces and relationships which give them significance and meaning, preoccupied philosophers and historians from Voltaire and Condorcet in the eighteenth century to Hegel, Comte and Marx.[627] What has changed is that the vast accumulation of new historical knowledge is compelling historians to reconsider and re-assess the patterns which they took over from their predecessors. It has become evident, for example, that the pattern set out by Ranke in his lectures *On the Epochs of Modern History* – an interpretation which influenced generations of historians in western Europe – reflected circumstances and attitudes which have ceased to be valid.[628] On the other hand, new knowledge of Asian history has raised the question, among communist as well as non-communist historians, how far Marx's conception of a specific Asian mode of production is tenable.[629] More generally, the question has arisen – at least among non-Marxist historians – whether at the present stage it is possible to construct a satisfactory overall view of the course of human history, and, if not, what should be put in its place. Writers such as Popper have maintained that there is no history of mankind, only an indefinite number of histories of different aspects of human life, and that

625. BURY, *Selected Essays* (1930), p. 17.
626. Cited in WILLIAMS, C. H., *The Modern Historian* (1938), p. 77.
627. Cf. MAZLISH, *The Riddle of History. The Great Speculators from Vico to Freud* (1966).
628. For criticism of Ranke's interpretation of modern history, cf. BARRACLOUGH, *History in a Changing World* (1955), pp. 168-184.
629. According to FEUERWERKER, *History in Communist China*, p. 227, it is no longer explicitly adhered to either in China or in the Soviet Union. Cf. LICHTHEIM, 'Marx and "the Asiatic mode of production"' (1963).

the search for permanent or recurrent patterns of historical development is therefore doomed to failure.[630] Even so, the historian is still left with the question how best to organize these different histories of different aspects of human life. Is, for example, the national framework adequate, and, if not, what are we to put in its place? The denial of an overall 'meta-historical' view of the past does not avoid the question of integration; it only transfers it to another level.

Apart from the wider question of the meaning of history, and the interpretation of the total historical process, a good deal of attention is therefore being paid today to more limited problems, such as the possibility and methods of writing world history and the validity as an organizing principle of the conventional 'linear' pattern, i.e., the familiar framework of chronological sequence. In this section we shall review the current attitudes of historians to these and similar questions without any pretence of comprehensiveness or finality. We shall be dealing often with implicit assumptions, which many historians simply take on trust, rather than with explicit postulates; but one of the significant contemporary trends is the increasing readiness of historians to analyse and criticize their assumptions in the light of a wider knowledge and their own deepening experience. In this respect the closer affiliation between history and the social sciences – particularly anthropology and sociology – has made many of the older explanations of the historical process seem jejune and simplistic, and has encouraged historians to think more deeply about the framework of their studies.

National History and Regional History

One of the characteristic features of historical study since 1945 has been a revulsion against the type of nationalist history so prevalent before 1939. In Europe at least – in Hungary and Poland as well as in Germany and France – it was felt that history which exalted the nation was one of the factors responsible for the catastrophe which had engulfed the continent; it also seemed manifestly unsuitable for a world increasingly integrated by science and technology and the revolutionary advance of mass communications. In short, the intellectual adequacy of national history seemed to be contradicted by events. But it is also true that by far the greater part of history today – probably at least 90 per cent – is still written in a national framework; indeed, paradoxically, as belief in the adequacy of national history has declined in the west, the resurgence of historical study in Asia has given it new life. Asian historians, as we have had many occasions to observe, still concentrate almost exclusively on their own society and its growth, and appear to accept a national framework almost without question. In Africa, on the other hand, where the current political boundaries are largely the almost accidental by-product of European intervention

---

630. Cf. POPPER, *The Open Society and its Enemies*, Vol. II (1945), p. 257.

after 1880, the tendency to think in terms of African history as a whole, or as grouped in a few main regions, is stronger.

The resilience of nationalist history is partly due to inertia, to the fact that it is easier to continue in old and well-tried paths, to familiarity and the greater ease of dealing with material immediately available in one's own country in one's own language. It is also due in some instances to patriotic pressures and to the survival of the belief, so strong in the nineteenth century, that one of the main purposes of history is to foster national consciousness. But other, less pragmatic arguments also continue to be advanced in its favour. In the first place, it is hard to deny the pervasive reality of the nation-state, the fact that the apparatus of the state is the focus perhaps not of all but certainly of the greater part of human activity, the embodiment of the lives of its citizens. Even if we wish to transcend the national state and write world history, it is arguable that the basic units of world history are the nation-states, in the sense that it is in the national communities, in the hearts of the peoples and the minds of their leaders, that the driving forces originate. For this reason many historians, even to-day, would reject the view that 'world history is best written without limitations of frontiers' on the grounds that 'national character, national development, and national power' are the ultimate facts in history.[631]

It would be out of place in a survey such as this, even were the present writer competent to do so, to discuss the validity of such arguments. It is sufficient to note that they have not quelled doubts about the intellectual adequacy of national history. There is, first of all, the doubt, to which A. J. Toynbee gave classic expression, whether national history is an 'intelligible field of historical study', whether any single nation or national state can boast of a history which is self-contained and self-explanatory.[632] When we examine the history of any particular country in detail, we find that it depends, in Lord Acton's words, 'on the action of forces which are not national but proceed from wider causes'.[633] Thus, we may doubt whether the histories of France, Germany, the Low Countries and Great Britain are intelligible except within a wider European, or west European framework, and in the same way one may wonder whether Indonesia is an intelligible unit of historical study and whether it might not be better to treat it as part of a larger unit called 'south-east Asia'.[634]

It is also obvious that the national state is an inappropriate unit at many periods – perhaps at most periods – of the past, and if we make it our standard of measurement – if we speak, for example, of French history at a time when, in fact, profound differences separated Languedoc, Brittany,

---

631. This view is explicitly maintained, for example, in the Editorial Foreword to *The Pelican History of the World*, which precedes each of the volumes in the series.
632. Cf. TOYNBEE, *A Study of History*, Vol. I (1934), p. 45.
633. *Lectures on Modern History* (1906), p. 180.
634. Cf. above, pp. 131-132.

Lorraine and Gascony[635] – we are simultaneously imposing an anachronistic pattern and a teleological interpretation. And, finally, the deficiencies of the national criterion become strikingly apparent, once we shift our attention from political events and political history, for which the national state or even the nascent national state may plausibly be said to provide a point of concentration, to such areas as the history of science. It may be argued that in many fields – art and literature, for example, or political ideas and institutions – while we are certainly confronted by activities which are 'supra-national' in essence (feudalism, for example, and impressionism, or baroque architecture, transcend national frontiers), nevertheless they are caught up in national life and marked by a distinctive national imprint. But no one (or certainly no one but a rabid nationalist) would suppose that the history of mathematics or astronomy, or even of the steam engine or electric power, can be made intelligible in a national framework. Newton, no doubt, was an Englishman and has a place in English history; but if we want to know the place of Newtonian physics in the history of science, it makes no difference that Newton was born in Woolsthorpe, any more than it does that Copernicus was born in Toruń or Kepler in Weil. At this level a national framework is not so much inadequate as irrelevant.

For these reasons and others there is a growing tendency among historians today to turn from a national to a regional framework. Examples which have already been noted are Braudel's history of 'the Mediterranean world' in the time of Philip II and Stoianovich's study of 'Balkan civilisation' as an intelligible unit in place of the separate histories of the Greeks, Rumanians, Bulgarians, Serbs and Croats. Similar in many respects is the attempt to write the history of South-East Asia as a single area 'worthy of consideration in its own right.'[636] But the reasons for the present emphasis on regional studies, or 'area studies', are for the most part practical rather than theoretical. The growth of regional studies in the past twenty years and the setting up of institutes or centres for 'area studies', often with a liberal endowment of public money, has usually taken place in response to a particular political situation, e.g., the ferment in the Middle East around 1956 or the Cuban revolution of 1959, with the scarcely veiled object of compiling 'background material' for coping with immediate problems. More than one historian has criticized the shortsightedness of this preoccupation with short-term expedients.[637] On the other hand, many historians welcomed the development of area studies as a means of encompassing new fields on an inter-disciplinary basis. An institute for African or Middle East studies provides a centre for bringing together historians, linguists, anthropologists, economists, students of religion, and other specialists, and this inter-

635. Cf. above, p. 55.
636. Cf. HALL, D. G. E., *A History of South-East Asia* (1955), p. vii.
637. Cf., for example, TWITCHETT's strictures (*Land Tenure and the Social Order in T'ang and Sung China* (1962), pp. 32-35) on the policies imposed in Great Britain by the Hayter Sub-Committee of the University Grants Committee 'for reasons of the purest political contingency'.

disciplinary approach corresponds closely to recent developments in historical practice. As an example of the sort of results which may be obtained one may cite G. H. T. Kimble's *Tropical Africa,* based upon the co-operative work of forty-six experts.[638]

There is every reason to think that regional and area studies will continue to develop during the coming decade. The necessary institutional bases have been established, and they correspond to an immediate practical need. It would nevertheless be a mistake to suppose that they provide the historian with more than a temporary and partial answer to the need for an organizing principle. Apart from the strongly pragmatic (and often outspokenly political) motivation of such studies, there must always be a doubt whether geographical divisions provide an entirely satisfactory framework. It is by no means self-evident, for example, that South-East Asia forms a single, intelligible historical unit,[639] and Thomas Hodgkin has pointed out that the concept of 'African history', while it has 'a certain practical value', may also easily become 'a limiting concept'.[640] The result of treating particular areas as separate regions is a tendency to cut them off from general history and to create new specialisms in a subject which already suffers from fragmentation, and in which, it is often complained, the specialists do not even read, let alone understand, each other.[641] Moreover, it is noticeable that regional history tends to be confined to areas, such as western Europe, Africa or South-East Asia, where the national states are small and precariously balanced, whereas elsewhere – e.g., China, the Soviet Union, the United States of America – the political unit is regarded as sufficient. No one, it has often been pointed out, would think of treating Asia as a single region, and 'western Europe' is an hypothesis, not an historical or even a geographical fact.[642] Paradoxical though it may seem, the only reason why 'regional studies' have been established at all is because the world is no longer, if it ever was, a regional world.[643] In the final analysis, therefore 'regional' or 'area' studies are best regarded as a stage on the way to a larger conception of world history, as a practical means, useful in certain instances but less useful in others, of organizing historical knowledge in manageable, interrelatable units. They supplement and to some degree correct the faults of national history; but they are no substitute for a history which is universal in spirit and concept and looks beyond regional history to humanity in all lands and ages.

638. KIMBLE, *Tropical Africa* (2 vols., 1960).

639. Cf. above, pp. 130-131.

640. 'New openings: Africa', p. 305 in *New Ways in History* (*Times Literary Supplement*, 1966).

641. Cf. FINBERG, p. vii in FINBERG (ed.), *Approaches to History* (1962).

642. 'It has become almost anathema to speak of Asia as a unity', writes Wm. Th. DE BARY (p. vii in DE BARY & EMBREE (eds.), *Approaches to Asian Civilizations,* 1961); as to the concept of western Europe, or 'the west', I have myself polemicized against it at length in *History in a Changing World* (1955) (particularly pp. 49-51).

643. As R. F. WALL has pertinently remarked ('New openings: Asia', p. 302 in *New Ways in History, op. cit.,* 1966).

The Prospects of World History

Awareness of the need for a universal view of history – for a history which transcends national and regional boundaries and comprehends the entire globe – is one of the marks of the present.[644] As early as 1936, the great Dutch historian, Huizinga, pointed out that 'our civilization is the first to have for its past the past of the world, our history is the first to be world-history',[645] and subsequent events have only confirmed his verdict. As since 1945 the world has moved into a new phase of global integration, the demand for a history which reflects this new situation has become more insistent.[646] It is, particularly at a pedagogical level, a practical demand. How can we, in the world as constituted today, safely teach a history nine-tenths of which is devoted to a quarter of the world's inhabitants? As E. H. Dance has pertinently pointed out, so long as every people remains ignorant of the basic ideals and cultures of other peoples, disaster will always be just round the corner; and 'yet there are no world histories in any language which give one-fifth, let alone the just four-fifths, of their space to the great "coloured" civilisations, living and dead.'[647]

The case for world history is undoubtedly very powerful. The world history of mankind, as Schieder has said, is no longer a speculative goal to-wards which the history of past events is directed, but is a living experience calling for corroboration in and through history.[648] The very forces which have transformed our view of the present – above all, the emergence of the greater part of mankind from political subjection to political independence and political influence – have compelled us to widen our view of the past. As recently as 1955 it was still necessary to plead that China should not 'be regarded as outside the mainstream of human history'.[649] It is a measure of the progress achieved in a short space of time that no one today would question this proposition. But the more the conviction of the need for an overall vision of world history has grown, the more historians have become aware of the problems and practical difficulties involved in writing it. There

---

644. Cf. GOTTSCHALK, 'Projects and concepts of world history in the twentieth century', in Vol. IV of the *Reports* of the *XIIth International Congress of Historical Sciences* (1965); ZHUKOV, 'The periodization of world history', in Vol. I of the *Rapports* of the *XIth International Congress* (1960); ONABE, *Sekaishi no kanosei* (= The Possibility of a World History) (1950); WAGNER, *Der Historiker und die Weltgeschichte*; WITTRAM, 'Die Möglichkeit einer Weltgeschichte', in WITTRAM, *Das Interesse an der Geschichte* (1958); BARRACLOUGH, 'Universal history', in FINBERG (ed.), *Approaches to History* (1962).

645. 'A definition of the concept of history', p. 8 in KLIBANSKY & PATON (eds.), *Philosophy and History* (1936).

646. Cf. STAVRIANOS, 'The teaching of world history' (1959), p. 111 in *Journal of Modern History*, Vol. XXXI.

647. Cf. DANCE, *History the Betrayer. A Study of Bias* (1960), pp. 26, 48, 125.

648. Cf. SCHIEDER, Th., *Staat und Gesellschaft im Wandel unserer Zeit* (1958), p. 197.

649. PULLEYBLANK, *Chinese History and World History* (1955), p. 36.

appears to be general agreement that few attempts to write universal history so far have been really successful,[650] but there is still no consensus about aims and methods.

The prevalent view of universal or world history conceives of it as a continuous narrative, in one or more volumes, linking together as an intelligible whole the story of mankind from its earliest beginnings, two million years before civilization, to the present day. The practical difficulties of encompassing such a task, given the complexity of the subject-matter and the rapid accumulation of new knowledge – particularly knowledge of the history of the extra-European world – need no emphasis. No single historian can hope to write with authority on every area and every phase of human endeavour. The current tendency is therefore to have recourse to collective histories, written by teams of specialists; and since the appearance in 1963 of the first volume of the six-volume Unesco *History of Mankind,* there has been a steady output of such composite or co-operative histories, mainly but not exclusively in the European languages.[651] It is generally conceded that they serve a useful purpose; but their reception by professional historians has for the most part been cool and sceptical. They 'cull out', in William McNeill's words, 'much interesting data'; but on an intellectual level they 'have conspicuously failed to provide any clear, intelligible pattern.'[652] Precisely because they are written by teams of specialists, they tend to fall apart into a series of loosely linked chapters or monographs, and this – even where, as in the ten-volume Soviet world history, the collaborators share a common *Weltanschauung* – is no substitute for the unitary vision of the individual historian.[653] Hence, in spite of the

650. Such, at least, is the impression left by the discussion at the *Twelfth International Congress of Historical Sciences* in 1965 (*Reports,* Vol. V: *Proceedings* (1968), pp. 525-540).

651. In addition to the Unesco *History of Mankind,* they include (without attempting to list more than a few of the more outstanding titles) *The New Cambridge Modern History,* ed. G. N. CLARK (12 vols., 1957-70); *Historia Mundi,* eds. F. KERN & F. VALJAVEC (10 vols., 1952-61); *Propyläen Weltgeschichte,* ed. G. MANN (10 vols., 1960-65); *Histoire générale des civilisations,* ed. M. CROUZET (7 vols., 1953-57); *Vsemirnaja istorija,* ed. E. M. ZHUKOV (10 vols., 1955-65), and the shorter world history, *Kratkaja vsemirnaja istorija* (2 vols., 1967). There are also a number of single-volume collective world histories (i.e., in which different chapters are entrusted to different authors), among which J. BOWLE (ed.), *The Concise Encyclopaedia of World History* (1958) seems to me to be outstanding; cf. also MURAKAWA, EGAMI & HAYASHI, *Sekai shi* (= History of the World) (5th edn., 1955), and ONABE & NAKAYA, *Gendai sekai no naritachi* (= The Making of the Contemporary World) (1955).

652. Page 23 in BALLARD (ed.), *New Movements in the Study and Teaching of History* (1970).

653. Cf. the pertinent comments of H. KATZ of the University of Lodz, pp. 539-540 in Vol. V (*Proceedings,* 1968) of the *Reports* of the *XIIth International Congress of Historical Sciences, 1965.* Katz expresses 'doubt as to the value and ability of efforts to construct world histories, embodied in many volumes and hundreds of consecutive chapters written by hundreds of authors. We get usually disconnected fragments of world history, mosaics, very rarely beautiful, very often boring. They serve sometimes students and teachers, who would yet profit more

contemporary propensity for more or less encyclopaedic collective histories, the individual work continues to hold its own; and some of the most stimulating attempts in recent years to re-write history on a global scale and in a global perspective have been the work of individual historians, among whom L. S. Stavrianos and W. H. McNeill are perhaps the best known.[654]

This is not the place for a detailed criticism of the various world histories which have appeared in the last decade.[655] Whatever their shortcomings, there is no doubt that they represent a distinct advance, in conceptualization and in breadth of vision, on similar works of an earlier date, and this without doubt reflects the global perspectives of the world in which we live. On the other hand, it is important to consider, however briefly, the criticisms – or at least the limitations – of the conception of world history which they all, in one degree or another, represent.[656] On a practical level, in the first place, they are open to a twofold criticism: either, because they are compilations, based on secondary knowledge, they lag behind the current level of research and, in order to encompass the whole world, reduce his-

---

by reading good monographs; they often serve as reference books, but in this respect they are successfully superseded by historical encyclopedias. [...] They quickly age, become out of date – mainly because of the rapid increase of historical knowledge, because of the quickly changing historical perspectives and the changes in the relative importance of different branches and subjects of history. I would rather welcome the promotion of several different one-volume world histories written by authors who obviously could not be experts on the totality of human history, but who would possess literary talent, a keen insight into human and social psychology, who would convey to the reading public the sense of drama of human history, the wonderful achievements and the extreme follies of the species "man". I would welcome e.g. a volume written by a Marxist, by an Existentialist and by a Christian Personalist. An enterprise of this sort would help to engineer a more sane and humane world order, and that is a very important task of history writing.'

654. Cf. STAVRIANOS, *The World to 1500. A Global History* (1970), and *The World since 1500. A Global History* (1966); MCNEILL, *A World History* (1967). The recent book by DANCE, *History for a United World* (1971), though fresh and stimulating, is different in character, in so far as it offers less a consistent narrative, than a series of points of view. There are, of course, also a number of works dealing with restricted periods of world history, particularly recent world history, e.g., THOMSON, *World History, 1914-1961* (1963), BRUCE, *The Shaping of the Modern World, 1870-1939* (1958), FRANZEL, *1870-1950. Geschichte unserer Zeit* (1952), WATT, SPENCER & BROWN, *A History of the World in the Twentieth Century* (1967), EASTON, *World History since 1945* (1968).

655. I have deliberately ignored, whatever their individual merits, the many collections of national (or, sometimes, regional) histories grouped together by publishers for their own purposes as 'histories of the world' – what have somewhat unsympathetically been called 'Buchbindersynthese'– of which *The Pelican History of the World*, referred to above, p. 378, n. 631, is one. Others include the *Fischer Weltgeschichte*, *The University of Michigan History of the Modern World*, eds. A. NEVINS & H. M. EHRMANN, *The History of Human Society*, ed. J. H. PLUMB, *Nouvelle Clio*, eds. R. BOUTRUCHE & P. LEMERLE. Commendable as some of these series may be, they do not seem to me to present, or seek to present, a coherent view of world history, and do not therefore require further consideration here.

656. Cf. the careful appraisal by J.-P. AGUET, 'De quelques "grands ensembles" historiques récents. Essai d'analyse historiographique' (1964).

tory to broad and vague generalizations, or, on the contrary, they simply present a mass of relatively undigested and unrelated factual knowledge.[657] Furthermore, with rare exceptions the existing world histories continue the old tradition of narrative history, simply transferring it from the national arena to the world stage. If, as I have suggested elsewhere, history is to be regarded not as a sequence of happenings but as a series of problems,[658] this is evidently unsatisfactory; it dulls rather than stimulates and creates the illusion of a body of generally accepted fact rather than encouraging the student to probe the great unresolved problems. The better historians, of course, are aware of these criticisms and have sought to meet them. Nevertheless, while it is generally agreed that world history is, or should be, at once something more and something less than an aggregate of national histories, and should be approached in a different spirit and manner, the problem of how to construct such a history has not yet been satisfactorily solved.

Perhaps more important than the practical difficulties are the theoretical problems involved in this type of world history. The former may conceivably be overcome with the passage of time and with increasing experience and knowledge; the latter are inherent. The first, and most insistent problem, as W. T. de Bary has pointed out, is that 'we have no convenient and accepted framework in which to present world civilization as a whole'.[659] There is, after all, no reason to assume that the view of world history from the Tarim basin and the view of world history from the Thames valley will ever be even broadly identical. Stavrianos claims that the standpoint he adopts is 'that of an observer perched on the moon, surveying our planet as a whole, rather than that of one who is ensconced in London or Paris, or for that matter, in Peking or Delhi.'[660] But in reality his approach, though more objective than that of most other writers, is distinctly western-centred. Nor is this implicit Eurocentrism exceptional. It is hard, for example, to believe that an Indian or African Marxist would wholeheartedly endorse a periodization of world history which hinges, like E. M. Zhukov's, on the 'British bourgeois revolution' of the seventeenth century, the French revolution of 1789, and the Russian revolution of 1917, as the decisive steps in 'the logical road of the advancement of mankind'.[661] If Zhukov's views are representative, it would seem that the Soviet conception of world history is no less Eurocentric than that of non-Marxist western historians, and it is not surprising that Asian historians, such as Naito Torajiro, Miy-

657. Either, as one writer has said, 'eclectic colourlessness' or 'monistic self-righteousness' (p. 540 in the *Proceedings* (*op. cit.*, 1968) of the *XIIth International Congress, 1965*).
658. *History in a Changing World* (1955), p. 159.
659. *Approaches to Asian Civilizations* (1961), p. x.
660. *The World to 1500* (1970), p. 3.
661. 'The periodization of world history', pp. 79-83 in *Rapports, XIe Congrès International* (1960), Vol. I. In fact, the application of western concepts of periodization, 'Marxist or non-Marxist', to Asia was explicitly repudiated by T. YAMAMOTO (and others); *ibid., Actes* (1962), p. 64.

azaki Ichisado, and Maeda Naonori, have sought to replace such views by a periodization of world history which does justice to eastern culture as a whole.[662] How successful these attempts have been, we do not need to consider. It is sufficient in the present context to recognize that world history looked at from Peking or Cairo may well be very different from world history looked at from Paris or Chicago or Moscow.

Stavrianos is not alone in postulating that the history of man 'to an overwhelming degree' is a history of the 'Eurasian civilisations' and that from 1500, as a participant in the Twelfth International Congress of Historical Sciences put it, 'the evolution of Europe' was the 'determining' event in the course of world history.[663] African and Asian historians who might have contradicted this view were conspicuously absent;[664] but E. H. Carr was surely right when he wrote that a view of history which treats the four hundred years between Vasco de Gama and Lenin 'as the centre-piece of universal history, and everything else as peripheral to it, is an unhappy distortion of perspective'.[665] On the other hand, it would be equally presumptuous to suppose, as traditional Chinese historiography did, that the whole of history is enshrined in the Middle Kingdom, and the rest is peripheral. It may be true that the history of Asia in modern times cannot be understood without reference to the western impact, but it is equally true that western history cannot be understood without reference to the impact of Asia on the west.[666] So far, however, the former has received far more attention than the latter.[667]

In addition to the problem of finding a more or less universal consensus as to the shape and proportions of world history, there is the almost equally elusive question of an organizing principle. Granted that world history is more than a loosely articulated sum or aggregate of national histories, the historian is immediately faced by the problem of establishing a criterion of what is, and what is not, of 'world-historical' importance. Here also there is no consensus of opinion. For many historians the distinctive feature of world history is that it deals not with nations, but with continents and civilizations.[668] One has only to recall the criticism of A. J. Toynbee's

662. NAITO, *Shina joko shi* (= Ancient History of China) (1944); MIYAZAKI, *Toyo-teki kinsei* (= The Modern Age in the Orient) (1950); cf. PULLEYBLANK, *Chinese History and World History* (1955), pp. 16-18, 23.

663. STAVRIANOS, *op. cit.* (1970), p. 5; cf. *Proceedings* (*op. cit.*, 1968) of the *XIIth International Congress, 1965*, p. 539.

664. It was, however, challenged by a number of contributors to IYER (ed.), *The Glass Curtain between Asia and Europe* (1965).

665. CARR, E. H., *What Is History?* (1961), p. 146.

666. Cf. LEWIS, M. D., 'Problems of approach to Asia's modern history', p. 14 in *Studies on Asia* (1963).

667. The outstanding exceptions are the distinguished book by D. F. LACH, *Asia in the Making of Europe* (Vol. I, 1965) and the pioneering works of Joseph NEEDHAM, *Science and Civilisation in China* (4 vols. to date, 1954-71), *The Grand Titration. Science and Society in East and West* (1969), and *Clerks and Craftsmen in China and the West* (1970).

668. Cf. *Proceedings* (*op. cit.*, 1968) of the *XIIth International Congress, 1965*, p. 526.

attempts to draw up a list of the world's civilizations to see that this hypothesis raises as many problems as it answers.[669] For J. L. Talmon, on the other hand, the criterion of world history is that it 'should be concerned with a meaningful totality',[670] but this leaves open the question of the criterion of meaningfulness.

If it is to offer a coherent, meaningful and comprehensive pattern, world history cannot, as Marx pointed out, be 'devoid of premises',[671] and these premises may be classified broadly as idealist or materialist. Among the former, we may instance Lord Acton's conception of liberty as 'the central thread of all history',[672] or the views of more recent Christian writers, such as Christopher Dawson or Herbert Butterfield, for whom the unifying factor in history is the working out of divine providence.[673] Such views, however, are more frequently found today among theologians and religious thinkers[674] than among professional historians, among whom the prevalent tendency is to adopt a broadly materialist position, in the sense that their central theme is man's conflict with his environment. This is the position of William McNeill, for whom (it would appear) technological advance (in agriculture, in warfare, etc.) is the key factor in human development, and J. H. Plumb has explicitly stated that 'the material progress of mankind' is 'the one aspect of the human story which both makes sense of it and also gives some slender grounds for the hopes of men.'[675]

The prevalence of a materialist interpretation of world history is, no doubt, due in part to the ubiquitous influence of Marxism; in addition, it probably owes something to the influence of archaeology and pre-history, with their insistence upon the importance of human artefacts as a main source of historical knowledge, and to the current emphasis on social and economic rather than political history.[676] But the main reason for its widespread acceptance is probably simply its evident heuristic potency. Not only

669. Cf. SOROKIN, p. 381 in *Journal of Modern History*, Vol. XII (1940), and JASPERS, *Vom Ursprung und Ziel der Geschichte* (1949), p. 321; for Toynbee more generally, cf. below, pp. 393-394.

670. *Proceedings* of the *XIIth International Congress, op. cit.*, p. 530.

671. Cf. MARX-ENGELS, *German Ideology*, p̂. 47.

672. Cf. GOOCH, *History and Historians in the Nineteenth Century* (2nd edn., 1959, p. 360).

673. Cf. DAWSON, *Progress and Religion* (1929), *Religion and Culture* (1948), and *The Dynamics of World History*, ed. J. J. Mulloy (1957); BUTTERFIELD, *Christianity and History* (1949).

674. E.g., MARITAIN, *On the Philosophy of History* (1959); BULTMANN, *History and Eschatology* (1957); NIEBUHR, *The Nature and Destiny of Man* (2 vols., 1941) and *Faith and History* (1949); LÖWITH, *Meaning in History* (1949); and the work of JASPERS referred to above, n. 669 (English translation, *Origin and Goal of History*, 1953).

675. Cf. PLUMB, 'The historian's dilemma', p. 32 in PLUMB (ed.), *Crisis in the Humanities* (1964), and the general preface at the beginning of each volume in the series *The History of Human Society*, which PLUMB edits.

676. The influence of archaeology (and of Marxism) was particularly evident in the writings of V. Gordon CHILDE, notably *What Happened in History* (1942).

does a materialist interpretation, as Marx pointed out,[677] substitute 'real premises' for 'arbitrary ones', but it also emphasizes the unifying features of human history. Whereas a synthesis of world history based on political events tends to be concerned, in Seizo Ohe's words, 'with the features which differentiate the respective subject-cultures',[678] an interpretation whose central theme is the growth of man's control over his environment not only postulates an organizing principle which is common to the whole of mankind, but also establishes a measurable criterion of progress and direction, without which – at least for the great majority of people – world history would be meaningless. It also provides the historian with a standard for deciding what is and what is not important from a global perspective, for selecting those particular facts and events which should and which should not be included. In particular, it shifts the emphasis from events on a national or local level, which affect only one people or ethnic group, to broad movements – for example, the Neolithic agricultural revolution – which involve the whole of mankind. Karl Jaspers, for example, has postulated an 'axial period' in which a decisive historical breakthrough in the basic conditions of life and thought occurred at the same time in all the major civilizations of the world.[679]

The assumptions upon which this structure of world history is based are nevertheless less self-evident than is sometimes assumed. No one is likely to question the fact that mankind as a species is everywhere basically the same; but the relevant question, as Bodo Wiethoff has pointed out, is whether this is true of man as a social and historical being.[680] Furthermore, the very idea that world history has purpose, direction and a goal, is a peculiarly western tradition, and it is well known that many of the world's great civilizations have taken a different view, seeing the meaning and goal of human existence outside history.[681] It is also at least questionable whether 'the story of man', in Stavrianos' words, 'from its very beginnings has a basic unity that must be recognized and respected.'[682] No doubt, all human groups everywhere are motivated from the start by the need to cope with the material facts of life, but this is a tenuous basis for assuming that their historical development is, or can plausibly be reconstructed as, a single unitary process. As Troeltsch pointed out many years ago, it is one thing to speak of points of contact between different civilizations and different cultural groups, and quite another to suppose that their histories are linked by a real causal connexion which makes them subordinate parts of a single his-

---

677. *German Ideology*, p. 42.

678. Cf. OHE, 'Toward a comparative and unified history of human culture, with special reference to Japan', p. 197 in *International Symposium on History of Eastern and Western Cultural Contacts* (1959).

679. Cf. JASPERS, *op. cit.* (1949), pp. 19-20.

680. Cf. WIETHOFF, *Grundzüge der älteren chinesischen Geschichte* (1971), p. 19.

681. Cf. WIDGERY, *Interpretations of History from Confucius to Toynbee* (1961).

682. *The World to 1500* (1970), p. 4.

torical process.[683] Marx himself took the view that the unity of world history only came into existence gradually, and apparently at a relatively late stage, as a result of 'intercourse and the division of labour between nations'; this was what transformed history – i.e., the history of separate peoples – into world history.[684]

But if it is granted that history only gradually becomes a single historical process, other difficulties arise. One is the familiar one, to which Zhukov among others draws attention, that even if there is a progression through economic stages in the mode of production, this progression does 'not necessarily' take place 'in a straightforward way'.[685] Partly for this reason Soviet historians, like most other European and American historians, have fallen back upon the conventional European division into 'ancient', 'medieval' and 'modern' history as a scheme for grouping and ordering events.[686] But the validity of this schematization, even for Europe, is highly controversial,[687] and its applicability to Asia and Africa is even more questionable; in fact, most competent historians of Asia have rejected it out of hand.[688]

Nor is it by any means as clear as its advocates sometimes imply that the weight of evidence supports a 'linear and unitary' view of world history, 'in the sense that interactions across relatively large distances even in very ancient times are sufficient to make mankind's history a single, if loosely articulated, whole.' The foremost proponent of this common assumption is W. H. McNeill,[689] but even McNeill is forced to concede, at the very beginning of his work, that the Neolithic agricultural revolution, which allegedly began in the Middle East and spread from there into Europe, India, China and parts of Africa, may have been less than universal, and that 'the Americas, monsoon Asia, and west Africa may have seen the independent inauguration of agriculture.'[690] On present evidence, in other

---

683. TROELTSCH, *Gesammelte Schriften*, Vol. III (1920), p. 609.

684. Cf. *German Ideology*, p. 58, where Marx adduces the famous example of a machine invented in England 'which deprives countless workers of bread in India and China and overturns the whole form of existence of these empires', and thus 'becomes a world-historical fact.'

685. 'The periodization of world history', p. 76 in *Rapports, XIe Congrès International* (1960), Vol. I.

686. *Ibid.*, p. 84.

687. I have questioned its validity on many occasions, e.g., *History in a Changing World* (1955), pp. 57-61.

688. Cf. PULLEYBLANK, *Chinese History and World History* (1955), pp. 16-17.

689. Cf. his contribution to BALLARD (ed.), *New Movements in the Study and Teaching of History* (1970), p. 24.

690. *A World History* (1967), p. 1. This, McNeill adds, is 'not certain.' McNeill's formulation betrays his prejudice, for evidently, on the basis of his own reasoning, it would be equally true to describe the 'migrations and borrowings' on which his whole account is based, but 'few of which' (he concedes) 'can be reconstructed by modern scholars', as 'not certain.' This having been said, it is perhaps worth adding that my sympathies are with McNeill. But it is also true, if the evidence, as McNeill admits, is less than conclusive, that any such judgment is no more than tentative and a weak foundation for a whole interpretation of world history.

words, what McNeill calls 'the segmented, pluralistic view of the human past' cannot be rejected out of hand.[691] No one would deny, for example, the existence from an early date of relations and interactions between the Chinese and the Mediterranean peoples, and Joseph Needham in particular has conclusively demonstrated their importance.[692] But these relations were the exception rather than the rule and the development of China and the Mediterranean lands over the course of centuries followed virtually independent paths. If we attempt to force them into a single mould, the resulting reconstruction is likely to do violence to the historical truth.

The other main objection to a 'diffusionist' interpretation of world history – i.e., to a conception which sees the unifying thread as the spread of culture and cultural innovation from one or more centres – is its teleological overtone. The danger of any such approach, as F. M. Powicke once wrote, is its inherent tendency to arrange the past 'as a process in which the most significant things are those which are most easily appropriated by the present', or which seem to have immediate present relevance.[693] In particular, it views history as a progressive movement leading by stages to the contemporary world, and since the contemporary world has largely been shaped by the west, it results in a marked, if subconscious, western ethnocentrism, centring on the belief that the social forms developed in Europe (including Russia) and North America during the present century are in some sense the 'goal' towards which history has been working. But the 'one world' of today, shaped and structured by the West, may, for all we know, be as impermanent and transitory as the Hellenistic *oikoumene*, or the Middle Kingdom which Confucian historians thought of as the culmination of history. In any case, a view of world history which makes 'the rise of the West' its central theme – as W. H. McNeill has done – is unlikely to be regarded as the last word by historians in other parts of the world.[694]

These critical observations are intended to indicate some of the reasons why a growing number of historians today have begun to question the intellectual assumptions upon which most recent attempts to write world history rest. In their view, world history is concerned with points of contact and inter-relationships; it does not call for a synthetic reconstruction of the whole of the past, but rather for the study of the processes of development of human society in different environments and different civilizations. Their argument is not merely that attempts to systematize the whole of known history and set it out in chronological sequence are premature, when

691. In fact, the current tendency among pre-historians is to question and reject the diffusionist theory of the origins of civilizatic , ... ᴅᴀɴɪᴇʟ, *The First Civilizations* (1968).

692. I refer, of course, to his great work, *Science and Civilisation in China*, 4 vols. to date (1954-71), one of the outstanding works of historical scholarship of the post-war era.

693. Cf. ᴘᴏᴡɪᴄᴋᴇ, *The Christian Life in the Middle Ages* (1935), p. v.

694. Cf. ᴍᴄɴᴇɪʟʟ, *The Rise of the West. A History of the Human Community* (1963). This is not to deny the stimulating quality of a remarkable book.

so little has been done to examine specific phases or problems in depth, but rather that the 'linear' conception of world history itself is stultifying and misconceived. Raghavan Iyer has called upon historians to 'discard the unitary view of civilisation' and 'accept the irreducible plurality of civilisations',[695] and Satish Chandra has urged the need to 'abandon the concept of centre and periphery' – whether the centre is identified with Washington, Moscow or Peking – and replace it by 'a concept of the multi-focal growth of human civilisation'.[696]

The implication is that the subject-matter of world history is not the sequence of civilizations –'according' (in Lord Acton's well known formulation) 'to the time and degree in which they contributed to the common fortunes of mankind'[697] – but rather the study of the differences between different countries, areas and civilizations, and of their interactions. When the past is viewed in a world-wide perspective, 'history becomes' – as R. F. Wail has written[698] – 'not a study of facts, but a study of inter-relationships: cultural, social and commercial, as well as diplomatic and religious.' And E. Hölzle has suggested that what is necessary for an understanding of world history is not 'grandiose conceptions' covering the whole of known history, but specific, concrete research 'concerned with establishing historical relationships, material and ideal, between the continents'.[699]

The study of world history in this sense is still in its beginnings. Because it cuts into the past at a different angle from other types of history, it cuts across the lines they have traced. The very fact that it asks new questions – questions, for example, about the processes by which ideas, inventions and products are transmitted between the various regions of the world – means that it requires not only a new approach but also the mobilization of a body of material and knowledge which, on the whole, historians concerned with one area or a single continent have neglected.[700] World history in its contemporary connotation is not a synthesis of known fact or a juxtaposition of the histories of different continents or cultures, arranged in some sort of order of relative importance; rather it is a search for the links and connexions across political and cultural frontiers. It is concerned not so much with development in time or with the goal and meaning of history –

695. Cf. IYER, p. 19 in IYER (ed.), *The Glass Curtain between Asia and Europe* (1965).

696. Cf. Satish Chandra, 'A note on the decentring of history', pp. 4, 12, 19 of typescript. This paper was specially prepared by Professor Chandra for the present undertaking, and I should like to express my gratitude to him for his valuable observations.

697. Cf. Lord ACTON, *Lectures on Modern History* (1906), p. 317.

698. Cf. 'New openings: Asia', p. 302 in *New Ways in History* (*Times Literary Supplement*, 1966).

699. Cf. HÖLZLE, *Idee und Ideologie* (1969), p. 81.

700. Naturally, there are exceptions. In particular, a good deal has been written about the rôle of Islam as an intermediary, particularly about the transmission of Greek thought and Greek science to the west by the Arabs. Cf. also HUDSON, *Europe and China. Their Relations to 1800* (1931).

western preoccupations which non-western cultures for the most part do not share – as with the perennial problems which have assailed mankind everywhere and with the different responses to them. This, for an increasing number of historians today, is the stuff of world history, and it has turned their attention, as we shall see,[701] away from linear development, from the thread allegedly running through history from its earliest beginnings to the present day, to the comparative study of the institutions, habits, ideas and assumptions of men in all times and places.

Philosophy of History and 'Meta-history'

The boundaries between world history, considered as the story of mankind from its earliest beginnings to the present day, and the 'philosophy of history', in the sense in which the phrase was used by Voltaire and Hegel, are narrow and fluctuating.[702] As we have seen, every attempt to interpret the course and meaning of world history implies some criterion of judgement, or philosophical view of the past, and Marx himself described communism as a solution to 'the riddle of history'.[703] Nevertheless it is only necessary to compare a work such as Arnold Toynbee's *A Study of History* with contemporary examples of the writing of world history (e.g., *The World to 1500* by L. S. Stavrianos) to see that there are far-reaching differences of attitude and method. Philosophers of history are more concerned with theory than with fact; they use the factual sub-structure, often non-sequentially, to adumbrate and illustrate a view of the meaning of man's nature and development. Writers of world history, on the other hand, use theoretical concepts (e.g., cultural diffusion, changing modes of production) as a means to an end: namely, as the links which seem to them most satisfactorily to account for and articulate the series of events they are seeking to relate.

701. Below, pp. 168 sqq.

702. It is perhaps hardly necessary to state that the following section is not concerned with the questions of epistemology, methodology and the nature of historical knowledge, which are sometimes described as the 'critical' by contrast with the 'speculative' philosophy of History. In practice, these questions are more the concern of philosophers than of historians, and are dealt with in *Main Trends in Philosophy* by Paul Ricoeur, especially paragraph A-3, 'Epistemology of the historical sciences', under III: 'Man and social reality'; cf. also the works referred to above, p. 43, n. 175. Most handbooks deal briefly (and inadequately) with the 'speculative' philosophy of history. Recent, more specialized work is not, so far as my knowledge extends, very abundant; but cf. MEYERHOFF (ed.), *The Philosophy of History in Our Time* (1959), Pt. IV (the preceding sections are largely methodological); BAGBY, *Culture and History* (1958); KAHLER, *The Meaning of History* (1964); ANDERLE (ed.), *Problems of Civilizations* (1964); DAWSON, *Dynamics of World History* (ed. J. J. Mulloy, 1957); MAZLISH, *The Riddle of History* (1966); and cf. also the literature on Toynbee's philosophy of history cited below, p. 166, n. 715.

703. MARX, *Economic and Philosophic Manuscripts of 1844* (London, 1970), p. 135.

The philosophy of history – or what is sometimes termed 'meta-history'[704] [–] is conspicuously out of favour among historians (though not among theologians) today. If there is one contemporary trend more marked than others, it is for historians to brush aside the philosophy of history as irrelevant to their work and preoccupations, and it is probably significant that the most influential forays in this direction in recent times have come not from historians, but from social scientists, such as Kroeber and Sorokin.[705] Since the completion in 1961 of Toynbee's *Study of History,* there have, to the best of my knowledge, been no comparable large-scale attempts by historians to distil the essence and meaning of the human story, and none, so far as present trends allow one to judge, is likely in the immediate future.[706] At the present time one 'philosophy of history' alone retains its vigour and heuristic potency, and that, of course, is Marxism. As we have seen,[707] Marxism is a powerful intellectual force not only in the Communist countries of the world, but throughout Asia, and its impact in the non-Communist west is scarcely less powerful. Few modern writers of stature, even among those who profoundly disagree with his analysis, have failed to pay tribute to the seminal influence of Marx's philosophy of history. Of all the 'great sociological theories of history,' writes Isaiah Berlin, 'Marxism is much the boldest and the most intelligent.'[708]

Though non-Marxists and anti-Marxists may be reluctant to accept the fact, it would be difficult to deny that Marxism is the only coherent theory of the evolution of man in society, and in that sense the only philosophy of history, which exercises a demonstrable influence over the minds of historians today. That does not mean that it is, or should be allowed to serve as, a dogma; in some respects Marx was the least dogmatic, the most flexible of writers.[709] He was well aware – perhaps more aware than some later

704. According to A. Bullock (cited in MEYERHOFF, *op. cit.* (1959), p. 292), the term 'metahistory' was coined by I. Berlin, but I have not been able to locate the source; it is discussed by DAWSON, *op. cit.* (1957), pp. 287-293, and by TOYNBEE, *A Study of History,* Vol. XII (1961), pp. 227-229.

705. Cf. KROEBER, *Configurations of Culture Growth* (1944) and *The Nature of Culture* (1952); SOROKIN, *Social and Cultural Dynamics* (rev. one-vol. edn., 1959). Cf. COWELL, *History, Civilization and Culture. An Introduction to the Historical and Social Philosophy of Pitirim A. Sorokin* (1952).

706. Perhaps the nearest approach is VOEGELIN's study of *Order and History,* of which three volumes appeared in 1956-57, and a fourth ('The Ecumenic Age') in 1975. On a smaller scale, cf. the works of DIEZ DEL CORRAL, *El rapto de Europa* (1954; *English translation,* 1959), and *Del Nuevo al Viejo Mundo* (1963).

707. Cf. above, pp. 98, 122, 127, 138-140, 143.

708. BERLIN, *Historical Inevitability* (1954), p. 71. Similarly H. BUTTERFIELD, *History and Human Relations* (1951), pp. 66-100, writes enthusiastically of Marxist history, while attacking, as communist historians do, the simplifications of 'vulgar Marxism'.

709. Needless to say, it is no part of my purpose to discuss Marxism or Marxist history in this place, and it would be out of place to refer to the general literature on the subject; all I wish to do is to describe as factually and briefly as possible its influence today as a philosophy of history. This can, I hope, be done without indulging in pro-Marxist or anti-Marxist polemics.

Marxists, from whom he dissociated himself – that the historical knowledge upon which he perforce had to rely, was still relatively primitive, and he never tired of repeating, often with great emphasis, from his early writings before 1848 to his correspondence at the close of his life, that the 'real problems' only began with the confrontation between his theorems and the historical evidence, by which he meant not that historians should seek evidence to support his theorems (historical evidence can be adduced to support any theorem), but to test and if necessary to adjust them.[710] The persistence of Marxism as an acceptable philosophy of history, even in non-communist countries, shows not only its intellectual potency, but also its success in withstanding this test; but it is also obvious that, if he had been writing today with all the evidence now available, Marx would have formulated his ideas in different terms. Not only has historical knowledge increased a hundredfold since Marx's day, but so also have sociological analysis and psychological insight, and it is evident, for Marxists and non-Marxists alike, that any Marxist philosophy of history must eventually take cognizance of these facts. Meanwhile, it is only necessary to repeat, with E. M. Zhukov, that Marx's philosophy of history only sets out – and, indeed, only claims to set out – 'a general trend', and that 'no scholar of history can be satisfied with this general pattern' alone.[711] This is no criticism of Marx – still less, a repudiation of his attempt to reveal the internal logic of historical events and to discover the true motives and rules of social development – but simply a recognition of the need to advance to a new stage of refinement and sophistication, which the progress of the social sciences (including history) – to which Marx himself gave so great an impetus – has necessitated.

These few words must suffice as an indication of the place and continuing strength of Marxism as a philosophy of history in the contemporary world. When we turn to the only original (or, considering his dependence on Spengler, it might be more correct to say semi-original) post-war attempt to formulate a philosophy of history, fewer words are necessary. Arnold Toynbee's great lifework, *A Study of History*, had an immense vogue between 1945 and 1955.[712] Today it is already clear that its impact is spent, and one critic has ventured the opinion that it 'will be only a curiosity in twenty or thirty years'.[713] In retrospect, it would seem that the popularity of Toynbee's work in the west was the reflection of the anxieties and discomfortures of one section of western society at a particularly critical moment in its history (it is scarcely accidental that the volume dealing with 'the prospects of western civilisation' appeared in 1954), and that its impact has passed with the situation which called it forth.[714]

710. Cf. above, pp. 19, 25.
711. 'The periodization of world history', p. 82 in *Rapports, XIe Congrès International des Sciences Historiques* (1960), Vol. I.
712. TOYNBEE, *A Study of History* (12 vols., 1934-61).
713. MAZLISH, *op. cit.* (1966), p. 363.
714. It is worth noting that the first six volumes of Toynbee's work, published

The reception of Toynbee's work by historians has been negative from the start.[715] In so far as it has hinged on empirical error and omission, their criticism is largely beside the point; nothing is easier for specialists, as Toynbee himself pointed out at the start of his enterprise, than to criticize the errors they discover where, during his long journey through time and space, he happens to 'traverse their tiny allotments.'[716] The real charge against Toynbee is rather a deep-seated lack of conceptual clarity, which robs his work of heuristic value. 'Never,' one critic has written, 'has such an imposing architectonic synthesis rested on such spindly theoretical foundations.'[717] Instead of rigorous scientific analysis his technique is that of literary metaphor. This is not, of course, to deny Toynbee's insights and intuitions, still less the liberating effect of his onslaught on 'the professional Scribes and Pharisees' of the historical world, which, together with his early and vigorous attack on Eurocentrism (though, paradoxically, his whole view of history is shot through with the Eurocentric 'heresy' he attacks), will probably remain as his chief claim to distinction.[718] Toynbee recalled historians, lost in a maze of specialization, to the need for a comprehensive vision of the totality of human history, and this is an achievement which deserves every recognition. But none of this adds up, if the term is used with any pretence of precision, to a philosophy of history. Instead Toynbee proffers 'a heroic though misguided attempt at universal history, covered over with a patchwork quilt of metaphysics.'[719] 'What emerges,' in M. M. Postan's words, 'is not a new philosophy of history but a multiplicity of old philosophies muffled and veiled.'[720] The contrast with Marx – if such a comparison can be made – could not be more glaring.

'Toynbee,' Bagby wrote,[721] 'has done a great disservice to the comparative study of civilizations and tended to bring discredit on the whole enterprise by undertaking his investigations in so ill-conceived and unscientific a manner.' Nevertheless, it may be suggested that if, for the present, historians have turned their faces against meta-history, it is not primarily for this reason nor on account of the theoretical doubts about its feasibility

---

between 1934 and 1939, received little attention outside scholarly circles. Their popularity after 1945 was due not only to the changed world situation but also to the appearance in 1946 of the first volume of D. C. SOMERVELL's brilliant *Abridgement* (2 vols., 1946 and 1957).

715. There is a vast literature (much of it listed by Toynbee himself, Vol. XII, pp. 680-690), among which it is sufficient to note the two collective volumes, *Toynbee and History*, ed. M. F. Ashley MONTAGU (1956) and *The Intent of Toynbee's History. A Co-operative Appraisal*, ed. E. T. GARGAN (1961), and the analysis by O. F. ANDERLE, 'Die Toynbee-Kritik' (1958).

716. Volume I, p. 4.

717. A. S. Hook, cited by TOYNBEE, Vol. XII, p. 645; cf. MAZLISH, *op. cit.* (1966), p. 372.

718. Cf. TOYNBEE, *The World and the West* (1953).

719. MAZLISH, *op. cit.* (1966), p. 375.

720. POSTAN, *Fact and Relevance. Essays on Historical Method* (1971), p. 149.

721. BAGBY, *op. cit.* (1958), p. 181.

expressed by writers such as K. R. Popper,[722] but because their current preoccupations lie elsewhere. In view of the vast increase in historical knowledge, which has still to be processed and digested, they do not believe – Toynbee's arguments to the contrary notwithstanding – that the time is ripe for a massed frontal attack on the riddle of man's past. Two preconditions are generally regarded as necessary at the present stage. The first is a closer pursuit of the *rapprochement* between history and the social sciences, which is the most striking contemporary trend in the historical world; the second is a much fuller and more profound knowledge of Asian and African history – indeed, of extra-European history as a whole – than we yet possess. The very fact that Toynbee's theories are built, as he freely concedes, on the model of Hellenic civilization is, in the eyes of most historians today, a damaging limitation, and it is evident that any future attempt to present a philosophy of history will necessarily have to be constructed on a far broader and more universal basis. But no less important is the clarification of the basic concepts – of terms such as civilization or class, or Toynbee's own peculiar concept of 'challenge and response' – and this is something which is only possible by means of scientific analysis of particular situations, that is to say, by more restricted studies. When these restricted studies reach a certain level, are better grounded in empirical data and more precise and sophisticated in their conceptual structure, we may expect that historians will once again turn to the task – whether in a Marxist or in a non-Marxist context is perhaps immaterial – of discovering and analysing the large-scale regularities and the pattern of social development running through human history.

The questions Toynbee asks, I have written elsewhere, 'will continue to stimulate and engross,' because they 'reflect preoccupations to which none of us can be oblivious.'[723] The argument frequently advanced, that the abundance of knowledge now at the disposal of historians makes any synthetic view of history, or any attempt to discover its ultimate meaning, 'a technical impossibility', is (as Toynbee rightly insists) a form of defeatism.[724] That the present indifference to the philosophy of history will persist, that historians will desist from the search for a constructive outlook over the past, or alternatively will rest content with a naive Marxism which Marx himself (it may be surmised) would at the present stage have repudiated, is not easily conceivable. The craving for a creative interpretation of history,

---

722. POPPER, *The Poverty of Historicism* (1944-45, 1957); almost equally virulent are the attacks of I. BERLIN, *Historical Inevitability* (1954), R. ARON, *Introduction à la philosophie de l'histoire* (rev. edn., 1948) (English translation, *Introduction to the Philosophy of History*, 1961), and M. OAKESHOTT, *Rationalism in Politics* (1962). None of these writers, it will be noticied, is an historian, and it is perhaps sufficient here to say that they overshoot the mark. Oakeshott's anti-rationalism was faithfully dealt with by POSTAN, *op. cit.* (1971), pp. 1-14.

723. Page 121 in MONTAGU (ed.), *Toynbee and History* (1956).

724. It implies, as he says, that 'the abundance in our larder condemns us to starve.' – *A Study of History*, Vol. XII, p. 648.

as F. M. Powicke once urged, is too deep-rooted for this to happen.[725] But it may also be surmised, on the basis of present indications, that future writers will be chary of grandiose, all-embracing constructions, and will prefer to work from the bottom upwards, starting with the analysis of specific concepts and problems.

The belief that the problems of civilization and society can be solved by a bold frontal attack appears to have had its day, and to have been replaced by a more patient approach within narrower and more manageable fields. It will involve defining and classifying social groups and institutions and counting and measuring the differences in social arrangements from place to place and from time to time; it will be concerned with the study in the widest possible range of different societies of the perennial problems that have assailed mankind everywhere – the basic biological urges of hunger and sex, the struggle with a grudging environment for the means of livelihood, the inadequacies of established social patterns to deal with newly emerging conditions, the problems of power and corruption, the oppression of the weak by the strong and the reaction of men driven by hunger and oppression to desperation. This is something in which both Marxists and non-Marxists can co-operate and to which both have a positive contribution to make. It is a process which depends essentially on the comparative method for its results; and to that we may now turn. Before we do so, it is only fair to add that it owes something to Toynbee, even if it parts company with his methods. Because, like Spengler, he repudiated the 'linear' view of history as a single progressive story and substituted instead a 'cyclical' view, in which a series of civilizations went through more or less equivalent phases of growth and decline, Toynbee opened historians' eyes to the potentialities of comparison. We do not need to share Toynbee's (or Spengler's) cyclical views to see that the comparative study of civilizations, or of particular institutions or concepts within civilizations, offers a road to understanding which it would be folly to reject out of hand. In fact, it represents at the present time the prevalent approach both to the problems of world history and to the search for meaning and regularities in history, and it is in this field that some of the most stimulating work is being done – even if, sometimes, the stimulus is to criticism and contradiction, rather than to endorsement and acceptance.

Comparative History

Comparative history may be defined[726] as the conceptualization and study of the past according to political, social, economic, cultural and psychological paradigms and categories, rather than according to national divisions or

---

725. Cf. POWICKE, *Modern Historians and the Study of History* (1955), p. 174.
726. I adopt here the formulation used in the prospectus of the graduate programme in comparative history at Brandeis University, in which it has been my privilege to teach.

artificial periods. Historians, as we have seen, are dissatisfied with both national history and the conventional chronological divisions, and still more with the causal-genetic presuppositions which underlie both schemes. It is, no doubt, true that any scheme for organizing the past is in the last resort only an intellectual construction; but, partly as a consequence of dissatisfaction with the results and heuristic potentialities of conventional narrative history, partly because of the influence of the social sciences, historians today are increasingly concerned with patterns of social and political behaviour which transcend or cut across national and chronological boundaries. England, France and Germany in the twelfth century, for example, have many problems in common, if we range their history under the category of feudal society. The forms of government in all west European countries from 1400 to 1750 were the result of varying relationships between royal autocracy, aristocracy and bureaucracy; the end result may have varied in each case − and the variations are of considerable historical importance − but the dimensions within which governments operated, whether in England or France, Spain or Germany, were everywhere the same. Or again, the common problem of all societies in the nineteenth and twentieth centuries was the degree of adaptation to the needs of an industrialized and urbanized society, the fundamental dividing point in history was that between underdeveloped, primarily agrarian societies, and industrial and urbanized societies, rather than between such constructs as France and Germany, or between modern times and the Middle Ages or the Renaissance.

These examples give some indication of the stuff of comparative history, the reasons for its rapid development in recent years, and the sort of question it sets out to answer.[727] Like 'philosophy of history', comparative history is concerned less with the question '*how* it happened', than with the question '*why* it happened'; the questions it asks of the past are designed to discover (e.g.) the nature of government, the forms of social organization, the causes of economic change, the roots of intellectual creativity. Where it differs from 'meta-history' is in asking precise, finite questions about a specific topic, pursued in depth. Its underlying assumption is that it is premature and self-defeating to make broad generalizations about family, property, legal custom, class divisions, until we have established against the broadest possible historical spectrum what each of these institutions actually meant and how it actually functioned in particular societies at particular times.[728] Looked at from this point of view, comparative his-

727. On comparative history in general, cf. SCHIEDER, Th., 'Möglichkeiten und Grenzen vergleichender Methoden in der Geschichtswissenschaft' (1965); WITTRAM, *Das Interesse an der Geschichte* (1958), pp. 46-58; GERHARD, *Alte und Neue Welt in vergleichender Geschichtsbetrachtung* (1962), pp. 89-107; HOSELITZ, 'On comparative history' (1957).

728. What, to take one concrete example, are we to say of a theory of international trade which bases important conclusions on the interregional movements of capital and labour, but which, as POSTAN points out (*Fact and Relevance, op. cit.* (1971), p. 28), leaves 'the social processes behind the migration of capital and labour [. . .] unexplored and unexplained'?

tory is the modern answer – the preferred method of approach of contemporary historians – to the question of the meaning of history. It seeks meaning not, like universal historians, in a continuous narrative of human development, nor, like meta-historians, in a comprehensive, overall pattern, but in elucidating the nature of the perennial problems which have assailed mankind throughout its history. That it does so by organizing the past in the paradigms and categories by which social and behavioural scientists seek to make sense out of the present is a consequence of developments in historical research which we have already dealt with at length.

The modern emphasis on comparative history owes much to the teaching and example of Marc Bloch, who wrote a programmatic essay on the comparative history of European societies in 1928, and whose famous book on feudalism set a pattern for the future.[729] Equally active at the same period, though less widely influential, was Otto Hintze, whose work on the typology of the representative systems of western Europe made a lasting impression on my own mind when I read it on its first appearance in 1930.[730] Two factors distinguish contemporary practice from these earlier forays into comparative history. The one is the far more conscious and deliberate recourse to social science concepts and methods, which in the meantime have been steadily refined and sharpened; the other is the extension of the comparative method from Europe to the extra-European world. The *rapprochement* between history and the social sciences almost of necessity forced historians in the direction of comparative history, because, as M. M. Postan has said, 'it is impossible to derive a sociological generalization from a single concrete event'; 'to be valid' it 'must be based on [. . .] the comparative method.'[731] But comparisons of universal validity must also look beyond single geographical areas or cultural groups. Marc Bloch, in his study of feudal society, was content to take one short glance outside western Europe (he scarcely even widened his view to take in the feudal societies of eastern Europe), and in this way left open the question – which is nevertheless fundamental – whether feudalism is a specifically western European or a universal form of social organization.[732] Hintze, on the other hand, insisted that the institution of representative estates (the *ständische Verfassung*), was specifically European, the product of an historical situation unique to Europe, but it may be questioned whether the comparative material upon which he based this view was (or, perhaps, at

729. Cf. BLOCH, 'Pour une histoire comparée des sociétés européennes' (1928), and *La société féodale* (2 vols., 1939-40) (English translation, *Feudal Society*, 1965).

730. Cf. HINTZE, 'Typologie der ständischen Verfassungen des Abendlandes' (1930); cf. also 'Weltgeschichtliche Bedingungen der Repräsentativverfassung' (1931); both reprinted in *Gesammelte Abhandlungen*, ed. G. Oestreich, Vol. I (2nd edn., 1962), pp. 120-185.

731. POSTAN, *op. cit.* (1971), p. 20.

732. Cf. *La société féodale*, Vol. II, pp. 249-252, for a few words on Japan, under the heading 'Une coupe à travers l'histoire comparée'. COULBORN (ed.), *Feudalism in History* (1956), attempted a wider view, but was criticized on cogent methodological grounds by HOSELITZ in the article 'On comparative history' (1957).

that time could have been) sufficiently wide and representative. In the longer term, the most significant result of the recent upsurge of Asian and African history, and of the far more widespread interest in non-European history generally, is the prospect it opens up of establishing for the first time a solid foundation for a truly universal comparative history, which may eventually provide a valid basis for the understanding of the recurrent patterns of social processes and of the great continuities and discontinuities of history.

It is also obvious that the comparative method carries with it its own problems and dangers. These have been much discussed, and it is only necessary to refer to two or three of the more obvious ones by way of illustration. The first, which M. M. Postan has emphasized, is that the purpose of comparative history is not to verify theoretical propositions (the propositions, for example, of economic theory) 'for the simple reason that most of the conclusions are so derived as to be incapable of empirical verification'.[733] Secondly, we must beware of loose analogies.[734] These, alas, are still in practice the commonest form of comparison among historians; they underpin the whole of Toynbee's work, but they are lacking in scientific or heuristic value, and have no place in serious comparative history.[735] Thirdly, as I recently observed, the ground rule in all such work is that meaningful comparison is only possible between comparables.[736] And, finally, individualization and generalization must go hand in hand, or as R. Wittram has put it, only when everything has been taken into account which makes for the individuality of a particular historical situation, can we safely proceed to the investigation of what it has in common with other apparently parallel situations.[737]

Historians have, broadly speaking, approached comparative history from two different angles. On the one hand, they have seen it in terms of historical structures and their components; on the other, they have used it as a means of establishing uniformities in events or recurrent series, or sequences, of events. The latter was until recently the more usual approach, but is under a cloud today. It underlies the work of both Spengler and Toynbee, who sought in this way to trace recurrent and typical stages in the rise and fall of civilizations, and it is probable that scepticism about

733. Postan, *op. cit.* (1971), p. 26; it is, of course, also true (as Postan adds) that 'some of them are so constructed as not to require it and to be illuminating and important even though unverifiable'.

734. Cf. Wittram, *op. cit.* (1958), pp. 50-53; Schieder, Th., *op. cit.* (1965), pp. 535-536 in *Historische Zeitschrift*, Vol. CC.

735. On the 'fallacy of the holistic analogy' and its place in Toynbee's thought, cf. Fischer, *Historian's Fallacies. Toward a Logic of Historical Thought* (1970), p. 255.

736. Cf. p. 154 in *Political Science Quarterly*, Vol. LXXXVI (1971).

737. 'Erst wenn man alles herausgeholt hat, was die Individualität der geschichtlichen Erscheinung ausmacht, wird man in die Hand nehmen dürfen, was eben doch noch gemeinsam ist.' – Wittram, *Das Interesse an der Geschichte* (1958), p. 50.

their methods – particularly the use of biological analogies – has contributed to the current disfavour into which it has fallen. It is, however, applicable to more limited problems. An example is Crane Brinton's well known book in which he seeks, by reference to four examples (the English, American, French and Russian revolutions) to set out paradigmatically the stages through which revolutions pass.[738] Another, more recent and even better known attempt to establish by comparative methods the stages of an historical process is W. W. Rostow's much discussed study of economic growth and the preconditions of 'take off' from a pre-industrial to an industrial society.[739]

This is not the place for a detailed criticism of these books, but one or two general points are relevant. In the first place, it will be noted that both Rostow's study (which draws essentially on the experience of Great Britain and the United States) and Crane Brinton's work are narrowly based, and that the latter (perhaps not surprisingly, considering its date) confines its examples to Europe and takes no account of revolutions in the Third World. It is evidently an open question whether the four instances upon which Brinton relies are a sufficiently wide and representative basis to establish (for example) the 'universality of the Thermidorean reaction',[740] though presumably the validity of such propositions could be tested by empirical research into the history of other revolutions elsewhere and at different times. In the case of Rostow, such research has in fact been done, and its result has been to discredit his arguments; that is to say, the theory built up from an examination of the experience of Great Britain and the United States has failed to stand up to criticism based upon the experience of other industrializing countries, e.g., Russia, Germany, Japan.[741] But the real objections to this type of comparative history are different. The fundamental question is whether they take sufficient account of the basic structural difference between the societies involved, e.g., between England in 1640 and France in 1789, or between France in 1789 and Russia in 1917. In the case of Rostow it has been objected that the pattern of growth, or the stages of take-off, in England or the United States are not applicable to a country as different in its whole social structure as India, and that his conclusions are vitiated by the fact that he simply postulates modern industrial society in its western form as his criterion, without seeking to isolate and analyse, by comparative methods, the structural

738. BRINTON, *The Anatomy of Revolution* (1939; rev. paperback edn., 1957).
739. Cf. ROSTOW, *The Process of Economic Growth* (1953); *The Stages of Economic Growth* (1960); 'The take-off into self-sustained growth' (1956).
740. BRINTON, *op. cit.*, p. 215.
741. Cf. MARCZEWSKI, *Introduction à l'histoire quantitative* (1965), p. 43. Rostow's arguments were examined at a conference of economists and economic historians in 1960, and the results were published in a volume edited by ROSTOW himself, *The Economics of Take-Off into Sustained Growth* (1963); cf. also the first section ('L'industrialisation comme facteur de la croissance économique depuis 1700') of the proceedings of the *Première Conférence internationale de l'Histoire économique* (1960).

features (and consequently what he calls the 'propensities') which make it unique.[742]

These are some of the reasons why historians today have moved away from this type of comparative history (sometimes called *Verlaufsvergleich*) in the direction of more broadly based structural comparisons (*Struktur-vergleich*). This does not mean that the type of comparative history which seeks to establish, e.g., a typology of revolutions must necessarily be re-garded as invalid, but rather that, at the present stage, more is to be gained by a comparison of social structures. Few topics in recent history have received more attention in the last few years than the nature and history of fascism, but it cannot be said that the results, in so far as they have attempted to define it as a general phenomenon and to set up a typology, have proved very satisfactory.[743] No one questions the importance of clarifying such concepts, but it is equally important to see them in the con-text of the different historical structures in which they occur. Only when we have seen what is unique in German and Italian fascism, and in the fascist (or crypto-fascist, or pseudo-fascist) régimes of other countries, and how each relates to the society in which it grew, can we begin to make meaningful comparisons. This does not imply a relapse into the old and discredited principle of the singularity of historical events – such a reaction, as Sigmund Neumann has written, 'would spell the end of any systematic discipline'[744] – but simply that structural factors play their part and cannot simply be ignored or brushed aside as chance 'variables'. How otherwise, as Barrington Moore pertinently asks,[745] are we to account for the fact that, though rural misery has certainly been as constant a factor in Indian as in Chinese history, in the latter it generated massive peasant revolts and revolutions, both in pre-modern and in modern times, while in the former it did not? Anyone who wishes to answer this question must begin by probing deep into the respective social structures.

One way in which historians' attitudes have changed in recent years may be seen by comparing Crane Brinton's approach to the question of revolu-

---

742. GERHARD, *Alte und Neue Welt . . ., op. cit.* (1962), pp. 94-95; cf. POSTAN, *Fact and Relevance, op. cit.* (1971), p. 88.

743. The literature on fascism is now immense and endlessly repetitive. The ball was set rolling, so far as comparative studies are concerned, by NOLTE, *Der Faschismus in seiner Epoche* (1963), generally agreed to be too much concerned with intellectual origins and the realm of ideas, and *Die faschistischen Bewegungen* (1966); cf. also WEBER, E., *Varieties of Fascism* (1964) and WEISS, *The Fascist Tradition* (1967). Of subsequent writing – including CARSTEN, *The Rise of Fascism* (1967), WOOLF (ed.), *European Fascism* (1968) and *The Nature of Fascism* (1968), ALLARDYCE (ed.), *The Place of Fascism in European History* (1971), and KEDWARD, *Fascism in Western Europe* (1971) – perhaps the most charitable thing to say is that it illustrates the law of diminishing returns. The unsatisfactory state of current research is well summed up in Wolfgang SCHIEDER's critique of Carsten's book in *Historische Zeitschrift*, Vol. CCIX (1969), p. 185.

744. Cf. NEUMANN, 'The comparative study of politics' (1965), p. 108 in *Comparative Studies in Society and History*, Vol. I.

745. MOORE, *Social Origins of Dictatorship and Democracy* (1966), p. xvi.

tion with the more recent works of R. R. Palmer and J. Godechot.[746] Whereas Brinton, as we have seen, was concerned to establish a recurrent sequence of events, Palmer and Godechot set out to examine the common factors underlying the revolutionary movements in western Europe and America in the last forty years of the eighteenth century – in Holland and Switzerland, for example, as well as in France and the British North American colonies – and in this way to trace a unitary pattern and a movement of ideas and social change which transcended frontiers. Whatever reservations may have been expressed about the general concept which Palmer and Godechot propound[747] – the most pertinent, perhaps, being the political terms in which it is formulated – it clearly represents a different and potentially valuable attitude to comparative history. Another example of a similar approach is Silvio Zavala's work on the colonial history of the New World: here again, developments which have usually been treated separately as aspects of the history of the colonizing powers – Spain, Holland, France, England – are brought into comparative perspective and treated as part of a general movement.[748]

Such work is important as a means of overcoming the fragmentation of specialized (and particularly of national) history. It directs our attention instead to the integrating factors and enables us to approach general history by an analysis of key movements at specified periods. Other historians have proceeded differently, directing their attention not to what Marc Bloch called 'sociétés synchrones',[749] but to specific problems, or institutions, in societies widely separated in space and time. An example is Ronald Syme's comparison of colonial élites in Rome, Spain and the Americas.[750] Another is the collection of nine studies on civil-military relations compiled and edited by Michael Howard.[751] The obvious drawback of such volumes, as of a similar collection of studies of the European nobility in the eighteenth century,[752] is their lack of coherence. Merely to set parallel developments in different countries side by side may provide a basis for comparative history, but it leaves the reader to synthetize or draw general conclusions. As a reviewer of Heinrich Mitteis' comparative constitutional history of feudal Europe observed, 'the juxtaposition of the course of development in individual states provides the necessary material for comparing them, but is in itself no comparison.'[753]

746. PALMER, *The Age of the Democratic Revolution* (2 vols., 1959-64); GODE-CHOT, *France and the Atlantic Revolution of the Eighteenth Century* (1965).

747. Cf. COBBAN, 'The age of democratic revolution' (1960), pp. 234-239 in *History*, Vol. XLV.

748. Cf. ZAVALA, 'A general view of the colonial history of the New World' (1961) and *The Colonial Period in the History of the New World* (1962).

749. 'Pour une histoire comparée des sociétés européennes' (1928), p. 20 in *Revue de synthèse historique*, Vol. XLVI.

750. SYME, *Colonial Élites. Rome, Spain and the Americas* (1958).

751. HOWARD (ed.), *Soldiers and Governments. Nine Studies in Civil-Military Relations* (1957).

752. GOODWIN (ed.), *The European Nobility in the Eighteenth Century* (1953).

753. Von SCHWERIN, p. 420 in *Zeitschrift der Savigny-Stiftung, Germanist. Abt.*,

The trend of recent work is at once more ambitious and more sophisticated: more ambitious not only in the sense that its span is wider and its 'case studies' cover Africa and Asia as well as the more familiar European terrain, but also because it specifically seeks meaningful comparisons, and more sophisticated because it uses the tools of social science, and thus constitutes a significant advance in method and viewpoint.[754] Two well-known examples are Barrington Moore's stimulating analysis, already referred to, of the 'main historical routes from the pre-industrial to the modern world', and Eric Wolf's more recent study – based on the examples of Mexico, Russia, China, Vietnam, Algeria and Cuba – of peasant wars of the twentieth century.[755] The hallmark of these books is that they approach a central problem of history not (in Wolf's words) 'in terms of abstract categories, [. . .] but in terms of a concrete historical experience which lives on in the present', and yet at the same time demonstrate (in Barrington Moore's words) 'that empirically based categories may transcend particular cases'.[756]

Comparative analysis is, of course, no substitute for detailed investigation of specific cases, and both Wolf's book and Moore's book are built up, as is Dunn's, on the basis of secondary material, of specialized articles and monographs. But it is also true that detailed investigation of specific cases is no substitute for comparative analysis, that no accumulation, for example, of special studies of Chinese peasant life in single villages or areas can by itself provide the wider perspectives we expect of history. They are indispensable in so far as they make it possible to break down the abstract concept of 'the peasantry' into finer categories, indicate regional differences, help us to distinguish between rich and poor and 'medium' peasants, between those who own or rent their land and wage labourers. But it is essential, at some point, that the ground they cover should be mapped out – even if the map may need subsequent correction – and that the facts they reveal should be compared with the situations disclosed in similar studies of peasant life and society in other areas – in Iran, for example, or in India, or Brazil.

Barrington Moore has modestly summarized the 'advantages' of a comparative perspective under three headings: (i) it 'can lead to asking very useful and sometimes new questions'; (ii) it provides 'a rough negative check on accepted historical explanations'; (iii) it 'may lead to new historical gen-

---

Vol. LXII (1942), reviewing MITTEIS, *Der Staat des hohen Mittelalters. Grundlinien einer vergleichenden Verfassungsgeschichte des Lehenszeitalters* (1st edn., 1940; 3rd rev. edn., 1958).

754. The difference is nowhere better seen than by a comparison of the studies of revolutoin by Brinton and Palmer (cf. above p. 400, n. 738, and p. 402, n. 746) and John DUNN, *Modern Revolutions* (Cambridge, 1972). The latter reflects a completely new conception of how the subject should be approached.

755. MOORE, *Social Origins* . . . (1966); cf. above, p. 401, n. 745; WOLF, *Peasant Wars of the Twentieth Century* (1969).

756. *Ibid.*, p. 276; MOORE, *op. cit.*, p. xvii.

eralizations'.[757] Others will go further. Heinrich Mitteis, for example, defended comparative history on the grounds that 'only comparison brings out the essential features of individual states with complete clarity' and 'makes it possible to distinguish the incidental from the essential, the singular from the typical'.[758] For T. J. G. Locher it offers the most fruitful approach to universal history. 'At the present time,' he writes, 'general history can only satisfy if it takes the form of a comparison of cultures.'[759] The evident advantage of studies such as those of Wolf or Palmer, and others which have been mentioned, over full-scale world histories or works such as Toynbee's is that their range is not too wide for effective coverage by one person nor too narrow to yield sound generalizations; they seem to represent approximately the level at which historical synthesis is possible without sacrificing scholarship or incurring the charge of superficiality or abstract systematization.

This, in the final analysis, is probably the reason why comparative history is the most widely practised form of general history today. The part it currently plays in historical study is evidenced by the appearance since 1950 of a number of periodicals specifically designed to provide a forum for comparative universal history, among which the west German *Saeculum* (sub-titled *Jahrbuch für Universalgeschichte*), founded in 1950, the *Cahiers d'Histoire mondiale/Journal of World History,* published under the auspices of Unesco since 1953, and the American periodical *Comparative Studies in Society and History*, launched in 1958, are the best known, though other periodicals such as the English *Past and Present* (1952) and the French *Annales* also devote much space to comparative questions.

The characteristic feature of these journals is their universality; they are not satisfied, in other words, with the older comparisons between different European countries and European institutions, but have set out to extend the range of comparative history to include Asia, Africa and Latin America.[760] Indeed, it is safe to say that the main factor stimulating the demand for a comparative and synthetic view of the past has been the rapid advance in recent years of knowledge of and interest in non-European societies, and the realization, stemming from it, of the need for a new and, this time, truly ecumenical interpretation of world history. For many historians today comparative history, pursued as the concrete study of specific problems and aspects across the whole spectrum of the world's societies, is the key to such an interpretation; and that is why it looms large among current preoccupations. We shall not, perhaps, be far wrong if we describe it as one of the most promising trends of the future, which is likely increasingly to engross the minds of the more progressive and intelligent historians of

757. *Op. cit.,* p. xiii.

758. *Der Staat des hohen Mittelalters ...,* op. cit. (1940, 1958), p. 4.

759. LOCHER, *Die Überwindung des europäozentrischen Geschichtsbildes* (1954), p. 17.

760. Cf. for example, PASTI, 'Comparative studies of East Asian and West European history: some topics and problems', published in *Comparative Studies in Society and History*, Vol. VII (1964).

the rising generation. Here, more than anywhere else, many historians believe, history has the opportunity to make a vital contribution to the study
of human society and add a new and indispensable dimension to social
science.

6. The Organization of Historical Work

The preceding chapter has carried us to the frontiers of history, to the
boundary-line between history and philosophy, and to the ultimate questions of the meaning of history. In the following section we return to the
practical questions of the organization of the historian's work. For these
questions, though in the end subordinate and secondary, play a considerable rôle – some historians may say, too large a rôle – in historical research
today. F. M. Powicke may have been right in protesting that 'an historian does not equip himself for his work by donning the vesture of erudition as a man in a laboratory puts on an overall';[761] but it is nevertheless
a fact that one of the distinctive contemporary trends is for historians to
become more like laboratory assistants. They work 'par équipes';[762] they
use elaborate and sophisticated apparatus, which requires a highly technical
training; they are organized in commissions and academies with – except
in England where older traditions still prevail – an extensive secretariat and
a task-force of qualified research assistants; and they spend – by comparison
with forty years ago, if not by comparison with nuclear physics – a formidable sum of public and private money. They have become, in short, an
industry, though one of the smaller and less profitable ones – a service
industry rather than a great manufacturing industry – and the familiar
picture of the historian ensconced in solitude in his ivory tower and submerged in *fiches*, like a character from Anatole France, is a thing of the
past – except, perhaps, in Oxford. The man who sat down next to a world-
famous historian, replete with brief-case and furled umbrella, reading
Time magazine, in a transatlantic airliner, and remarked with surprise:
'He might have been a business executive', was bearing witness unconsciously to one of the great revolutions in the contemporary historical world.
Many historians *are* business executives. It is not only at Harvard that a
successful historical career may lead from a full professorship to Chairman
of the Department, to Dean, perhaps even to President – and then to coro-
nary thrombosis and oblivion.

  The organization of historical research and writing varies greatly from
country to country. In some countries, notably in eastern Europe, the Academy of Sciences operates as an active organizing, directing and centralizing
body; in others, such as Great Britain, it appears to be more like a self-
electing club of notabilities close to the Establishment, with no specific or-

761. POWICKE, *Modern Historians and the Study of History* (1955), p. 173.
762. Cf. BRAUDEL, 'Positions de l'histoire en 1950' (Leçon inaugurale), p. 25 in
Ecrits sur l'histoire (1969).

ganizing function. In some countries, the link with the universities is close, the old belief still holds that teaching and research go hand in hand and fructify each other; in others, the object of historians is to escape as quickly as possible from the university and the 'burden' of teaching to a more exalted status and a more rarified atmosphere, and the university professor falls into the second rank, while teaching is handed over to a lesser breed. To attempt here to describe these and other differences from country to country would be as otiose and invidious as tedious. In any case there are adequate handbooks, and it is sufficient to refer anyone who is interested in the detail to the relevant literature.[763] In this section, as in the preceding ones, I shall try instead to pick out what seem to be the more significant general trends in historical research, referring where necessary to some of the salient national differences, but concentrating so

763. Apart from the well-known general works of reference – e.g., *Minerva. Jahrbuch der gelehrten Welt* (34th to 38th Years, Berlin, 6 vols. published between 1966 and 1972), *The World of Learning* (21st Year, London, 1970-71) – and similar works for individual countries (e.g., the *Répertoire des bibliothèques d'étude et organismes de documentation*, Paris, 1963), whose number is legion, and which of course deal with all the learned disciplines, reference may be made to the following: for France, Western Germany, Great Britain and the United States, a useful recent short survey by Shafer, François, Mommsen and Milne, *Historical Study in the West* (1968); for France, *La recherche historique en France de 1940 à 1965* (1965); for Great Britain, Barlow & Harrison, B. (eds.), *History at the Universities* (Historical Association, 1966; 3rd edn., 1971), and Kitson Clark & Elton, *Guide to Research Facilities in History in the Universities of Great Britain and Ireland* (2nd edn., 1965); for the Soviet Union, cf. the collective work, *Očerki istorii istoričeskoj nauki v SSSR* (= Essays on the History of Historical Science in the USSR) (Vol. IV, 1966), and the survey by Sidorov, 'Hauptprobleme und einige Entwicklungsergebnisse der sowjetischen Geschichtswissenschaft', in the *Relazioni* of the Tenth International Congress, Vol. VI (1955); for Poland, the report by Leśnodorski, 'Les sciences historiques en Pologne au cours des années 1945-1955', *ibid.*; for Hungary, cf. Andics in the volume *Etudes des délégués hongrois au Xe Congrès international* (1955), pp. 1-14; for Jugoslavia, *Ten Years of Yugoslav Historiography* (1955); for the German Federal Republic, cf. Heimpel, 'Über Organisationsformen historischer Forschung in Deutschland', in Schieder, Th. (ed.), *Hundert Jahre Historische Zeitschrift, 1859-1959* (special issue of *Historische Zeitschrift*, 1959); for Austria, cf. Lhotsky, *ibid.*; for Switzerland, cf. Fueter, *ibid.*; for the German Democratic Republic, cf. Castellan in *Revue historique*, Vol. CCXXVI (1961) and Vol. CCXXVIII (1962); for Czechoslovakia, cf. Tapié, *ibid.* (1962); for Latin America, cf. Chaunu, *ibid.*, Vol. CCXXXI (1964). I have also had the benefit of a number of excellent reports prepared by the National Commissions of Unesco, for which I am particularly grateful. They include reports on 'Achievements of Soviet historical science', 'The organization and financing of scientific research in the USSR', and 'Soviet archives', by F. Fedorova; 'The development of historical science in the Ukrainian SSR', by A. Sancevič & V. Sarbej, and a second report by V. A. Djadičenko, S. M. Parhomčuk & V. G. Sarbej; ' A view of historical research in Finland', by Vilho Niitemaa; 'Trends in historical research in Hungary', by P. Hanák; 'L'historiographie en Yougoslavie', by B. Grafenauer; 'Main trends in historical sciences in India', by S. Chandra; 'Main trends in Indonesian historiography', by Sartono Kartodirdjo, Nugroho Notosusanto, Buchari, & Abdurachman Surjomihardjo; 'Main trends of Australian research in the historical sciences', by J. J. Auchmuty. It is scarcely necessary to add that without these invaluable papers, which supplement and bring up to date the published information, it would have been impossible to write this survey.

far as possible on developments relevant to historical work in all lands and continents. Here, as elsewhere, we can perceive tendencies which – like the impact of the social sciences discussed in an earlier section – are common to historians everywhere, in Asia and Africa as well as in Europe and in America, and in Marxist and non-Marxist countries. They are, in short, developments which cut across geographical, ethnic and ideological boundaries; and it is as such that they demand consideration.

The main reasons for the changes in the organization of historical work, which are so evident a feature of the contemporary scene, are the vast increase both in the quantity and types of historical material and the rapid development of the historical profession itself. To discuss the latter in detail would require a survey of the changing attitudes towards education, particularly secondary and advanced education, in the modern world. It is sufficient here to note the explosion in the university population, and the extraordinarily rapid increase in the numbers of universities – particularly in newer countries, such as Canada and Australia, but also, for example, in the until recently less advanced republics of the Soviet Union, to say nothing of the emergent states of post-war Africa and Asia. It is important also to recall how relatively recent the development of history as an independent academic discipline is. In many countries of Asia, as we have already noted,[764] it scarcely ante-dates the Second World War; but in Australia also, as Dr. Auchmuty has pointed out,[765] 'the real organization of Australian history' only took place 'parallel with, but always somewhat behind, the great development in the Australian universities in the 1950's.'

Nor is the position in Europe so different as is sometimes supposed. Here, it is true, the organization of history as a separate discipline is visible from approximately the last decade of the nineteenth century, and France and Germany were perhaps somewhat ahead. But in England it was not until 1923 that T. F. Tout felt able to declare that 'the battle for the recognition of the subject is as good as won',[766] and even then the value of historical research was hotly contested from within the profession, though by then its opponents were clearly fighting a losing battle.[767] Down to the time of the Second World War the numbers of professionally trained and academically qualified historians were, by modern standards, extremely small. Comparative statistical figures are hard to obtain and perhaps do not exist on a world-wide scale; but it was certainly not in Australia alone that, prior to 1940, the staffs allocated to History Departments were 'very tiny – two or three at most.' According to A. F. Pollard, when he became professor in the University of London in 1903, only 'about one student every other year' graduated in history.[768] I have been unable to find accu-

---

764. Cf. above, pp. 98, 122, 125.
765. 'Main trends of Australian research', p. 3 of typescript.
766. Cf. *The Historical Association, 1906-1956* (1957), p. 38.
767. Cf. the controversy between E. BARKER and A. F. POLLARD in *History*, Vol. VII (1922), pp. 81-91 and pp. 161-177.
768. Cf. *The Historical Association*, p. 6.

rate figures, and such as are available are not always easily comparable, but it is certainly no exaggeration to say that, world-wide, the numbers engaged in the historical profession must have trebled – and almost certainly more than trebled – in the last twenty years. In England, where eight new universities were founded between 1946 and 1966, and many others upgraded, there were 1,160 university teachers of history (excluding research assistants and graduate students) in 1968.[769] In the Ukraine, according to a recent report, there were over 3,000 research historians ('some doing research, some teaching') but this figure apparently includes doctoral candidates.[770] In the U.S.S.R. as a whole there were by 1955 about 3,000 professors and other teachers and 296 chairs in the various historical disciplines (including archaeology and ethnography, which are not included in the British figures), and this figure has no doubt increased substantially in the interval.[771] In Indonesia, where in 1940 there was only one department of history, there are now forty institutions of higher learning which have 'either a separate department of history or one or more courses in history'.[772] In a few countries, e.g., Switzerland, the rate of growth appears to be considerably slower;[773] but the developing countries more than compensate and the overall increase is beyond doubt stupendous, even if, in some countries (e.g., Indonesia), it still leaves much to be desired.[774] In the United States, where already in 1952 official statistics enumerated 2,434 historians, the numbers have probably doubled in the meantime.[775] Whereas in 1941 there were in the United States 58 institutions offering a doctorate in history and 158 degrees were awarded, by 1966 the corresponding numbers had increased to 116 and 560 respectively; 'the annual production was now nearing the total number of Ph.D.'s in history who were living in 1925.'[776]

769. Cf. SHAFER, FRANÇOIS, MOMMSEN and MILNE, *Historical Study in the West* (1968), p. 146.

770. 'The development of historical science in the Ukrainian SSR', p. 12 of typescript. One suspects that it also includes teachers in secondary schools; of the total of 3,000, it is stated that 'about a hundred have doctorates'.

771. Cf. SIDOROV, *op. cit.* (1955), p. 404. F. Fedorova (cf. above, p. 406, n. 763) has supplied figures from the *Soviet Statistical Yearbook* for 1968 (p. 267) showing a total of 30,310 'scientific workers' in history and philosophy, of whom 1,019 held doctorates; but the category is difficult to break down and it is not clear what it includes.

772. 'Main trends in Indonesian historiography', p. 8 of typescript.

773. According to FUETER (*op. cit.* (1959), p. 504) those engaged in historical work, including archivists and museum staff, still comprised less than 3 per cent (i.e., around 120-140) of a total scientific work force of 4,000-5,000 in 1959.

774. Cf. 'Main trends in Indonesian historiography', p. 72 of typescript.

775. Cf. *Personnel Resources in the Social Sciences and Humanities* (Washington, 1959), p. 39. According to SHAFER (*Historical Study in the West*, p. 184), there were '12,000 or more historians in the United States of the early 1960's', but it is not easy to know what this figure comprises; it looks like the membership of the American Historical Association, which of course includes amateurs and non-active members and is relatively small by comparison with the Historical Association of Great Britain (over 11,500 members in 1966).

776. Cf. SHAFER, *op. cit.* (1968), p. 204.

These figures are, and under current circumstances can only be, random samples. They are nevertheless sufficient to give some indication of the problems of organization which swelling numbers have created. Clearly the somewhat haphazard attitudes towards and methods of organization which were still prevalent in 1940 have been overtaken by events. It is not only in the Soviet Union that 'the scale of historical research is creating new problems for the historiographer'.[777] One obvious fact is the growth of specialization, the appearance of an ever increasing number of new branches of historical study. Some of these – historical demography, for example, or industrial archaeology – have already been mentioned.[778] Others are the history of technology, the history of climate, business history, and of course the history of science.[779] Here it is only necessary to recall Joseph Needham's famous work, *Science and Civilisation in China*, which is universally acclaimed as one of the most distinguished historical undertakings of recent times.[780] But it has been observed that most of those engaged in such work (like Needham himself) are not professional historians in the ordinary sense, and that the links between them and the mainstream of the historical profession are extremely tenuous.[781] What is certain, in any case, is that new specialisms, often working (in Margaret Gowing's words) 'on a microscopic or even sub-microscopic scale', most of them with their own specialized periodicals, together with the increasing specialization among general historians, have created new problems. If history is not to break up into a disconnected series of specializations, reorganization of research structures is an unavoidable necessity.

The other factor affecting the organization of historical research is the immense increase in source material, both traditional and new, which modern techniques have made possible. Historical method, as devised in the nineteenth century, was predicated not only upon the primacy but also upon the paucity of written sources; its foundation was the meticulous, critical examination of single documents. Today historians are faced with the problem of the abundance – and, indeed, over-abundance – of records,

---

777. Cf. Fedorova, 'Achievements of Soviet historical science', p. 26 of typescript of English translation (Russian original, p. 25).

778. Cf. above, pp. 77 sqq., 107-108.

779. All of these sectors or branches have now an extensive and often technical literature of their own, best approached through the many specialized periodicals created to cater for them, e.g., *Revue d'histoire des sciences et de leurs applications* (founded 1947), *Isis. An International Review devoted to the History of Science* (founded by George Sarton in 1912), *History of Science. An Annual Review of Literature, Research and Teaching* (founded 1962). For business history cf. LARSON, *Guide to Business History* (1948); BARKER, T. C., *Business History* (1960). Recent works on technology include DAUMAS (ed.), *Histoire générale des techniques* (4 vols., 1962-68), and MUSSON & ROBINSON, E., *Science and Technology in the Industrial Revolution* (1969); on climate LAMB, *The Changing Climate* (1966), and LE ROY LADURIE, *Histoire du climat depuis l'an mil* (1967).

780. NEEDHAM, *Science and Civilisation in China*, Vols. I-IV.iii (1954-71); the work is planned to comprise seven volumes in all, when complete.

781. Cf. GOWING, 'Science and the modern historian' (1970).

creating a situation with which the traditional methodology is unfitted to cope and incapable of coping. No historian, not even a team of historians, or a series of teams, could conceivably sift even the written, documentary records in Europe alone for the first year of the Second World War in their totality, as they could for (let us say) the first year of the Hundred Years' War, nor is it evident, if they did so, that the result would be in any way commensurate with the effort and expenditure of time and effort involved. But, in addition, we have to take into account the great expansion of historical research in countries, particularly in Asia and Africa, in which in many cases the historical records have not, until very recently, been systematically assembled, sorted, listed, catalogued and published. As this work gets under way, we may expect a veritable flood of new source-material, which will require a high degree of organization and new organizational skills, if it is ever to be mastered. One has only to think of the immense labour, over a period of more than seventy years, which has gone into collecting and editing the sparse records of the papacy from the earliest times to 1198 – and which is still far from completion – to see that the methods and objectives of an earlier and more leisurely age are impracticable and inapposite today.[782] New tasks, new objectives, new source-materials, have enforced, and will continue to enforce, a far-reaching methodological reappraisal of a discipline which traditionally has been individualist and recalcitrant to all forms of collective organization.

If, as we have seen, history has become more scientific in the sense of forming links with (and in the case of many of) the younger generation of historians accepting the view that history is one of the social sciences, it is also clear that it has become, and will continue to become, more scientific in the sense of using the mechanical aids provided by modern technology. Simple examples of this are photography, microfilms, ultra-red and infra-violet rays, the former of which have displaced the old, slow, and often inaccurate hand-copying of documentary sources. Moreover, in certain fields – e.g., art history – by allowing the collection of photographic material from far scattered sources, photography has made possible the collation and comparative study of the work of individuals or schools in a way which was simply impracticable before.[783] Another well-known example of new, scientific techniques is the use, particularly in archaeology and pre-history, of radio-carbon readings (Carbon 14) and dendrochronology for purposes of dating.[784] Indeed, those who study the past by means other than the written record have been forced to elaborate techniques of far greater complexity than those necessary in dealing with documentary sources.[785] But,

---

782. The first volume of Paul KEHR's great undertaking, the *Regesta pontificum Romanorum* (*Italia pontificia*, Vol. I), appeared in Berlin in 1906.

783. In the words of Talbot RICE ('The history of art' (1962), p. 172 in FINBERG (ed.), *Approaches to History*), 'it is well-nigh impossible to attempt to work without them.'

784. Cf. ZEUNER, *Dating the Past* (4th rev. edn., 1958).

785. Cf. PIGGOTT, *Approach to Archaeology* (1959), p. 26.

once introduced, they have been taken over, where practicable, by historians in other fields. Thus aerial photography, originally developed by O. G. S. Crawford after the First World War as an aid to archaeology, has been applied successfully to medieval agrarian and urban history.[786]

The significant fact about these new techniques, from the point of view of the organization of research, is that, because they require a more or less elaborate apparatus, they are not in general available to the individual historian. Few individuals, after all, are likely to possess, or to be able to afford to hire, an aeroplane; and only those who have undergone a special training can hope to interpret aerial photographs successfully. The same is true, for obvious reasons, of the electronic computer and of computer science, which are playing an increasingly important rôle in historical research. Whether they like it or not – and some like it very much – these, and similar changes, are forcing a new degree of organization upon historians. Already as early as 1955 J. K. St. Joseph called for 'a central authority that would collect and maintain the air photographs already available from many lands',[787] and although this demand has not been met, it is symptomatic of the changing attitude of historians to their work. Heimpel has pointed out the significance of the railroad age in enabling historians to gather material from far and near.[788] The age of air travel has carried this tendency a stage further and made historical material available on a world-wide scale. It is against this background of an expanding, increasingly specialized profession confronted by a swelling mass of evidence and source-material and increasingly elaborate techniques for processing it, that we shall review, without too much attention to national and local differences, what seem to be the main trends in the organization of historical research today.

Accessibility of Material and Organization of Archives

Generally speaking, the historian relies upon the archivist for his source-materials, and there is no doubt that the immense increase in documentation in recent years poses problems for the archivist which were scarcely thought of before 1940. It is not merely that the archival repositories which were in existence in 1945 were simply too few in number, too small in physical size, too poorly equipped, and too under-staffed to house and process the sudden upsurge of historical records flowing in from many sides. In addition, the changing character of documentation involved a reconsideration of the traditional techniques and of many of the basic concepts of archives science. If any attempt were to be made to cope with the vast expansion

786. Cf. BERESFORD & St. JOSEPH, *Medieval England: An Aerial Survey* (1958).
787. Cf. *Xo Congresso internazionale di Scienze storiche, Relazioni*, Vol. VII, p. 103.
788. H. HEIMPEL, 'Über Organisationsformen ...', *op. cit.* (1959), p. 152 in SCHIEDER (ed.), *Hundert Jahre Historische Zeitschrift*.

of documentation, it was obvious that the whole archive organization – including, not least of all, the status and salaries of archivists – must be developed and up-graded and that this was only possible through a greatly increased outlay of public funds.

Four main factors underlay the post-war explosion of documentation. The first, universal in its effects, is the bureaucratic nature of modern government, the continuous surveys, enquiries, investigations, censuses, questionnaires, plans and projects, which emanate not only from governments but from businesses and other corporate bodies, all producing a weight of paper unparalleled in the past, though already growing to formidable proportions from the closing decades of the nineteenth century, as the typewriter, stenography, dictating-machines and similar devices passed into common currency. Secondly, there is the supplementation, to which reference has already been made, of written documentary material, the stock in trade of the archivist, by other forms of record: oral tradition (particularly, but not exclusively, important in Africa), photographs, films, tape-recordings, interviews. A third factor, less immediately obvious but equally important in its effects, is the shift of focus, as historian's interest has turned from political to social and economic history, away from the type of record which traditionally received priority in archives and manuscript repositories – exceptional documents (of which the English Magna Carta may be regarded as a classical example), chronicles, annals, the political records of governments – in favour of the more diffuse documentation of social history (leases, accounts, rentals, tax-returns, notarial protocols, commercial records, etc.), which exist in thousands in every locality, but which obviously cannot be analysed and calendared in detail. The result of this shift of focus, as Fernand Braudel has pointed out, is that the historian, when he goes to the archives, is frequently unable to find ready to hand the type of documentation he requires and is faced by the enormous task of compiling a documentation which throws light on the new questions he is asking.[789] Finally, there is the swelling growth of documentation in the newly emergent countries of the 'third world' as, from around 1950, the imperative need was recognized to organize and make available their historical records on a scale far in excess of anything undertaken, before independence, by the colonial governments.[790]

The building up of record offices and archive repositories, and with it the quantity of record material stored and sorted and classified, has gone ahead by leaps and bounds in the past twenty years. Naturally the need was greatest in areas where hitherto the preservation of historical records had been neglected. In Sub-Saharan Africa, according to a report prepared by T. W. Baxter for the Commission for Technical Co-operation in Sub-Saharan Africa, there were 27 record repositories in existence by 1957,

789. BRAUDEL, 'Positions de l'histoire en 1950' (Leçon inaugurale), p. 25 in *Ecrits sur l'histoire* (1969); cf. also GLÉNISSON, p. xlv in *La recherche historique en France* (1955).
790. Cf. above, pp. 124-125.

most of them new centres set up after 1945.⁷⁹¹ In the Gold Coast (later Ghana) there was no record office until after 1945. In Nigeria the initiative was taken by K. O. Diké who submitted a report advocating the establishment of a public record office in 1954.⁷⁹² Elsewhere effective action only occurred still later. In Nepal it was not until 1961 that the first steps towards systematic record preservation were taken, with Indian technical assistance. In New Zealand, though an archives division had been in existence since 1929, little was done until a disastrous fire in 1952 stimulated active interest, with the result that an effective national records centre was finally in operation by 1961-62.⁷⁹³ Even in Australia, though the state of New South Wales had been publishing its historical records ever since 1893, it was only in 1957 that it was decided that the Commonwealth archives, hitherto a department of the National Library at Canberra, should be reconstituted as an independent organization.⁷⁹⁴

It is, of course, not only in Asia and Africa and Australasia that the multiplication of record offices has gone ahead by leaps and bounds. In England after the Second World War (and partly during the war as a precaution against destruction by enemy action) local record offices were opened in practically every county and large city, and a vast quantity of hitherto unknown or scattered material, much of it from the middle ages and the sixteenth and seventeenth centuries, was brought together, sorted, listed and catalogued. Since this material was rich in local sources for social and economic developments, it may be said to have contributed in no small degree to the transformation of English history.⁷⁹⁵ Its sheer quantitative impact is sufficiently indicated by the single example of the county of Essex where, between the publication of the first *Guide to the Essex Record Office* in 1946 and the issue of a new revised and expanded edition in 1969, the collection of deeds grew from under five thousand to about half-a-million, of which 30,000 were fully calendared.⁷⁹⁶ This is one instance of a process which is world-wide, as everywhere the number of archives and record repositories increases. In Bulgaria, for example, where no central organization was in existence until 1952, during the next five years over 2,300 documentary collections were taken in and made accessible.⁷⁹⁷ G. A. Belov reported in 1963 on the large programme in the Soviet Union for setting up new archive repositories.⁷⁹⁸ During the five years between

791. Cf. Baxter, *Archival Facilities in Sub-Saharan Africa* (1959).

792. Cf. Dike, *Report on the Preservation and Administration of Historical Records and the Establishment of a Public Record Office in Nigeria* (1954); for East Africa, cf. Charman & Cook, 'The archive services of East Africa' (1967-68).

793. Cf. Cocks, 'The development of the National Archives of New Zealand' (1965-69).

794. Cf. Macmillan, 'Archival reform in Australia' (1955-59).

795. For some indications of its significance, cf. my articles in *The Listener*, 10 Mar. 1949, pp. 395-396, and in *Festschrift zum 200-jährigen Bestand des Haus-, Hof- und Staatsarchivs*, Vol. I (Vienna, 1949), pp. 392-395.

796. Cf. 'Short notice', p. 636 in *English Historical Review*, Vol. LXXXV (1970).

797. Cf. Mijatev, 'Organizing archives in Bulgaria' (1957-58).

798. 'The organization of the archive system in the USSR' (1963-64).

1956 and 1961 twenty-two new record offices were opened, in which nearly 30 million items were deposited, and a further twenty-one were under construction. In 1958, on the initiative of M. N. Tihomirov, a start was made on the examination of the archives of Siberia, since then the work has been steadily carried forward by the archivists of the Siberian branch of the Soviet Academy of Sciences. Meanwhile, in Africa an elaborate project was launched in 1957 to collect both oral and written records, comprising both material in Africa and sources in European and American archives and libraries, and in 1960 Unesco undertook the preparation of a large-scale series of guides, beginning with Latin America and following up, in 1963, with plans for a similar guide to the sources for African history.[799]

The mass of new material brought into circulation in this way poses problems – and opportunities – both for historians and archivists. For the former it is the old question, but now on a new scale, of finding the needle in the haystack. Guides, bibliographies, handlists, on every level appear constantly in every country, often obsolescent by the time of publication; their preparation has become a major industry.[800] But what individual, unless perchance his research is concentrated on a narrowly local theme, can hope to keep up with and digest them all? As early as 1929 F. M. Powicke wrote of the 'ever accumulating mass of intractable material' and expressed doubt whether 'any man, dealing with any period of European history or world history since the eleventh century, could write a really great book which covered more than fifty years.'[801] Today a sceptic might reduce his fifty years to five and add a geographical limitation of fifty kilometres as well. What is beyond doubt is that a disproportionate amount of the historian's time is necessarily spent on the preliminaries and the sheer mechanics of research and that even so – so great is the volume of material to be mastered – the resources accumulated by the individual historian working alone are almost certainly bound to be haphazard and incomplete. The old concept that the historian should proceed to collect and analyse *all* his sources before setting pen to paper (always, it must be said, more honoured in theory than in practice) has completely broken down under the accumulating weight of new material.[802]

For the archivist the problems are no less considerable but more tech-

---

799. There is a preliminary survey in *XIIth International Congress, Reports*, Vol. II (1965), pp. 182-198; for the Unesco initiative, *ibid.*, p. 191.

800. There can be no question here of listing even a sample of the multitude of bibliographical aids appearing regularly in every country and every language; the stage has now been reached where it has become necessary to compile bibliographies of bibliographies. Cf. BESTERMAN (ed.), *A World Bibliography of Bibliographies* (5 vols., 4th edn., 1965-66), and *The Bibliographic Index. A Cumulative Bibliography of Bibliographies* (11th volume, 1971), which, however, only includes works written in the Latin alphabet.

801. POWICKE, *Modern Historians and the Study of History* (1955), pp. 176-202.

802. Nevertheless, it is still maintained; thus CANTOR & SCHNEIDER, *How to Study History* (1967), p. 194, still exhort students to 'make sure that you can find and read all the sources for your subject.'

nical. Their result is a slow but inexorable transformation of the theory and practice of archive administration, which has only got under way since about 1950 but which – if only because of the sheer pressure of the accumulating documentation – is bound to gather momentum. Archive science,[803] because it grew up at a time when archivists were mainly involved with early records, was hypothecated upon scarcity. Its primary concern was preservation, and every scrap of evidence was treasured. In the older archives, particularly in Europe, this is still a major preoccupation, and much time and thought and ingenuity are given to modern processes of preservation, such as lamination.[804] But today, paradoxically, even in the older archives, destruction – technically termed 'disposal' or 'Kassation' – at least in the form of the elimination of duplication and the establishment of criteria for deciding what should, and what should not, be retained, is rapidly becoming as important a part of the archivist's work as preservation. The reason, of course, is the sheer bulk and unwieldiness of the mass documentation of modern times, and in many instances its ephemeral character. In archives where the bulk of the records – or, as (for example) in the case of the Commonwealth of Australia, which only came into existence in 1901, all the records – are modern, different qualifications and different attitudes are called for on the part of archivists from those traditionally provided by such institutions as the *École des Chartes* in Paris or the *Institut für österreichische Geschichtsforschung* in Vienna, which most subsequent centres for archive training, except in the United States, took as their model. As, with new accessions, the proportion of modern records increases, there is less call for palaeography, diplomatic, and the other traditional 'auxiliary sciences', and more for practical training in administrative techniques, and this shift of emphasis is certainly furthered by the growing concentration of historical research upon modern themes and the nineteenth and twentieth centuries. An analysis of recent historical publications shows that currently between one-third and two-fifths deal with the period 1789–1945 and that for the period 1933–56 the relative proportion has increased from one-

803. Among the basic works, it must suffice to mention BRENNEKE, *Archivkunde* (1953), with an excellent bibliography of older literature; MEISNER, *Urkunden- und Aktenlehre der Neuzeit* (2nd edn., 1952); and SCHELLENBERG, *Modern Archives: Principles and Techniques* (1955). These adequately indicate the starting-point of modern archive practice, which is now best followed in the international journal *Archivum. Revue internationale des Archives* (founded 1951), and in the many national periodicals which have appeared since (and, of course, in some cases, such as the *Archivalische Zeitschrift*, since long before) the war. They include *Archives* (Great Britain, 1949), *Arhivi Ukraini* (Ukrainian S.S.R.), *Archeion* (Poland, 1927, re-established 1948), *Archivmitteilungen* (German Democratic Republic, 1951), *The American Archivist* (1938), *Archivi* (Italy, 1956), and many others.

804. Cf. LANGWELL, *The Conservation of Books and Documents* (1957). It is, of course, true and important to note that conservation is not only concerned with ancient documents. Since the expectation of life of the cheap mechanically produced paper marketed for bulk use today is not more, in many cases, than 30 years, almost any modern documentation scheduled for permanent preservation requires treatment to preserve its mechanical strength. A similar problem is posed by changes in the chemical composition of ink.

tenth in 1955–56 to one-seventh today.[805] The importance of modern records has grown correspondingly.

The massive character of modern records creates other problems as well. Traditionally, as Heimpel has pointed out, the handling of historical material was predicated upon a simple sequence: edition, research, narrative exposition.[806] The assumption behind such undertakings as the *Monumenta Germaniae historica*, when it was launched in 1824, was that all the sources for a definitive history could be recovered, published and made available. Hence the innumerable societies, national and local, in all countries devoted to the edition and publication of historical texts, some undertaken officially (like the enrolments of the English medieval chancery prepared by the Public Record Office in London), more (for example, medieval cartularies or bishops' registers) the product of individual scholars working (usually) through societies. The task of the archivist was to reconstitute the *fonds*, to provide lists, indexes, inventories, manuscript catalogues, in favourable circumstances to make available at least a short *résumé* of the individual documents, where possible with dates or approximate dates, at which point the historian would take over and produce a fully edited text in a critical edition with a full analysis of the sources, a palaeographical survey of the texts, and a statement of the principles followed by the editor. There are many distinguished examples of such work, some of it still continuing, and no one would wish to minimize the devoted and often entirely disinterested labour that has gone into it.[807] History would be incomparably poorer – indeed, would be virtually impossible – without it. But what was desirable and seemed the most effective method of proceeding at one period is not necessarily the most satisfactory at another. Two observations may be made upon this ardent preoccupation with the collection and criticism of original texts. First, it has long been evident that it is a losing battle. Feasible, perhaps, with medieval documents (down, in the case of western Europe, to 1200 or perhaps to 1300), useful perhaps in recent times for a few particular areas, such as foreign policy, as soon as we reach the modern period the sheer quantity of material swells to such an extent that there can be no hope of ever catching up.[808] Secondly, it must also be asked whether publication *in extenso,* even if it were feasible (which it is not), is really the most appropriate method of dealing with historical sources,

805. Cf. Schochow, p. 375 in *Historische Zeitschrift*, Vol. CCXII (1971).

806. 'Edition, Forschung und Darstellung'; cf. Heimpel, *op. cit.* (1959), p. 152.

807. Among continuing series, for example, the *Registres des papes* (13th and 14th centuries) undertaken by the Ecole française de Rome, or the various series of publications of reports and correspondence of papal nuncios, on which cf. Fink, *Das Vatikanische Archiv* (1951), pp. 173-179. Others of more than local or national interest include *Acta Aragonensia*, ed. Finke (1908-22), and *Regesta Historico-Diplomatica Ordinis S. Mariae Theutonicorum*, eds. Joachim & Hubatsch (4 vols., 1948-65).

808. All the great collections of diplomatic documents dealing with the origins of the First and Second World Wars are (necessarily) highly selective and no one would think of publishing the diplomatic archives *in extenso.* This has led to serious

except in a few (not easily defined) special cases, and whether it does not rest upon assumptions about the nature of history and of historical research which have been overtaken by events. The new interest of historians in quantitative data calls for a new approach – perhaps for a number of new ways of approach – to historical records. Documentation which is invaluable in bulk for statistical purposes is not necessarily intrinsically significant or interesting enough for elaborate processing, still less for individual publication. So long as printing was the only method of making material generally available, the emphasis on the edition of texts was understandable; but today that is no longer the case.

Thus historians and archivists are faced by a twofold change. First, because of the new focus of historical interests, much of the erudition of the eighteenth and nineteenth centuries, impressive as it is, has gone stale, or at least does not correspond to modern preoccupations and modern requirements. Secondly, the methods used for mobilizing that erudition, though they have not been (and are unlikely to be) entirely displaced, are no longer adequate either for the purposes of modern historians – who are no longer primarily concerned with the particular, the unusual, the exceptional – or for coping with the vast documentation accumulating today and growing by leaps and bounds with every year that passes.

No one, of course, would suggest that the old type of multi-volume documentary series will not continue. The *Monumenta Germaniae* was quickly revived after 1945, and sought to bring itself more into line with current interests by adding, on the initiative of Herbert Grundmann, a new section on the sources for medieval spirituality ('Geistesgeschichte').[809] Under the direction of H. Heimpel the publication of the German *Reichstagsakten,* the records of the Diets of the fifteenth and sixteenth centuries, begun as long ago as 1867 but, neglected between 1933 and 1945, was taken up with new vigour. In the Soviet Union not only have old series been continued, but a considerable number of new series have been initiated, many of them (e.g., the ten-volume series of documents and materials on 'The Great October Socialist Revolution') dealing with recent times. Mention has already been made of the lively attention being given to the publication of source-materials in China,[810] and there is no doubt that a major desideratum in many of the newly constituted independent states of Asia and Africa is a comprehensive and critically edited collection of basic sources. But it is also evident that such publications do no more, and can do no more, than touch the fringe of the problem. The sheer expense of full-scale publication under present-day conditions is a major limiting factor, unless

---

misgivings about the principles of selection (cf. among others BUTTERFIELD, 'Official history. Its pitfalls and criteria', 1951), and means in any case that such collections, however extensive, can only serve as a guide and do not obviate recourse to the unpublished archives for the purposes of serious research.

809. Cf. GRUNDMANN, 'Geistesgeschichte in den *Monumenta Germaniae historica*' (1950), and 'Neue Aufgaben der *Monumenta Germaniae historica*' (1951).

810. Cf. above, p. 140.

the undertakings are subsidized either directly out of public funds or by wealthy foundations, and it is no secret that many of the old record publishing societies, which did stalwart work down to 1940, are in dire financial straits. One may also question, as F. Hartung did in the case of the German *Reichstagsakten*, whether such undertakings may not be fundamentally misconceived.[811]

Against this background it is understandable that the whole question of historical sources and their processing is in a state of flux. As the Deputy Keeper of the Records of Northern Ireland has recently pointed out, the archivist today is faced by new problems, and existing theory and practice offer little, if any, systematic guidance as to how to solve them.[812] The one thing that is evident is that the conventional solutions (e.g., calendaring) are at best a counsel of perfection and at worst a snare and a delusion. In these circumstances, it is not surprising that archivists have begun – still tentatively, but with growing interest – to explore the potentialities of mechanical aids. The first and simplest, the value of which was triumphantly demonstrated in coping with the mass of captured German documents transferred to Whaddon Hall (Buckinghamshire) in England and to Alexandria (Virginia) in the United States shortly after the war, was microfilming.[813] For more sophisticated techniques, using electronic data retrieval methods, pioneering work was done – because of its special genealogical requirements – by the Mormon Historical Society in Salt Lake City, Utah. A third initiative was taken, once again in the United States, by the Inter-University Consortium for Political Research, which decided in the early 1960's to build an historical data bank under the direction of Howard W. Allen.[814]

This is not the place to discuss or describe in detail the new techniques which are being introduced. The essential point, perhaps, is the replacement of manual by mechanical sorting and recording. Thus instead of summarizing or transcribing documentary information on handwritten slips, it may be recorded directly on Hollerith cards or punched on to tapes from which not only can the required data be extracted or retrieved by mechanical means but also a 'print-out' catalogue can be compiled. One important result of this method of handling is the avoidance of duplicated effort; indeed, one of the reasons for the setting up of the historical data archives by the Inter-University Consortium was the discovery by a number of historians that they were wasting their time in searching out and processing material

811. Cf. HARTUNG, *Deutsche Verfassungsgeschichte vom 15. Jahrhundert bis zur Gegenwart* (8th edn., 1950), pp. 3-4.

812. Cf. DARWIN, 'The use of the computer in indexing records' (1971).

813. Cf. EPSTEIN & WEINBERG, *Guide to Captured German Documents* (1952), and *Supplement to the Guide to Captured German Documents* (1959); *A Catalogue of Files and Microfilms of the German Foreign Ministry Archives* (1959), and, for documents which fell into Soviet hands and were turned over to the East German government, LÖTZKE & BRATHER, *Übersicht über die Bestände des deutschen Zentralarchivs Potsdam* (1957).

814. Cf. ROWNEY & GRAHAM (eds.), *Quantitative History* (1969), pp. 114-116.

which others had already recorded. No computerized retrieval system can dispense with individual searching in records, nor is it intended to do so; but depending upon its degree of sophistication (that is to say, upon the quantity of information recorded on tapes or cards) it can substantially reduce the amount of time spent upon it and also enable the individual to work more efficiently. A simple system might, for example, only pick out the names of parties and localities, the grantor and recipient of a lease or charter, and the name of the village concerned. Even this would be a great help to research. But it is also possible to construct a far more complicated code, covering up to 3,000 or more words or subjects (estate-map, plough, enclosure, ditch, highway, etc.). It is also important that a properly trained staff can punch such information directly on to cards or tapes from the original documents, cutting out intermediary stages and thus achieving a substantial saving in staff time.

It is perhaps true that mechanical processes of this sort are more useful for some classes of historical records than for others. At present they are used in the main for routine documents of second rank. Even so, the advantages should not be under-estimated. In the first place, it is precisely routine material of second quality which is piling up in record offices in forbidding quantities, and which, for purely practical reasons of time pressure and staff shortage, tends to be pushed aside or given summary treatment; and yet, as we have seen, it is this material which historians today, because they are concerned with quantitative problems, are anxious to have made available. Secondly, there is no doubt that, as archivists' practical experience of mechanical processes grows, they will find that there is an increasing number of archive classes which can be appropriately handled in this way. Merely from the point of view of physical retrieval, there is no doubt that computerization has a wide variety of archival uses; and quick, efficient, comprehensive and accurate data retrieval is the first prerequisite of all archive users, both administrators and historians. But this requires far-reaching changes in archive organization. One, already referred to, is a change in the attitude and training of the profession of archivist which, as a practising archivist has observed, is still too much dominated by tradition.[815] Another is finance. Mechanical aids of all sorts involve substantial capital outlay (not necessarily greater than the cumulative wage-bill of staff working on conventional lines, but more difficult to find in one lump sum), and it is hard to see how record offices can be brought up to the standard necessary to enable them to cope with the vast inflow of new material without a substantial increase in public funds. But the corollary of this, thirdly, is co-operation. Expensive machines are only a paying proposition if they are fully used. Whether a multiplicity of small local record offices is any longer justifiable is a debatable question; but it would seem that more centralization, at least into bigger regional centres, or more co-operation and 'team-work', is a probable development. As we shall see, the

815. DARWIN, *op. cit.* (1971), p. 222.

same considerations apply more generally to the organization of historical research.

The Impact of New Techniques

If new techniques affect the historian indirectly as a mean of making his sources more readily available, their direct effects both upon his work and his attitude to his work, and upon the organization of historical research, are potentially even more significant. Among them the most important is the electronic computer. 'History,' it has been said, 'is not the first academic discipline to have been changed by the presence of data-processing equipment',[816] indeed, it is one of the last. But it is already evident that the consequences are likely to be both far-reaching and irreversible. Of all the modern auxiliary sciences at the historian's command computer technology is the most revolutionary in its implications.

A considerable and rapidly growing literature is already available on the use of computers and computer science in historical research.[817] At the risk of stating the obvious it is desirable, without entering into the technical aspects, to indicate summarily its findings. First, it must be emphasized – as all the writers concerned take care to do – that computer science is an auxiliary science, in the same way as palaeography and diplomatic are auxiliary sciences, and that it does not eliminate (indeed, in some respects it increases) the human element and the importance of the historian's judgement. It is not merely that the historian has to use the same standards of critical scholarship to evaluate computerized data as he uses to evaluate any other sources, but also that the results of computerized research can never be better than the data originally 'fed in' by the historian. If, for example, inaccurate or faulty statistics are used, the computer will reproduce (and

816. ROWNEY & GRAHAM (eds.), *op. cit.* (1969), p. viii.

817. Cf. USTINOV, *Primenenie vyčisliteľnyh mašin v istoričeskoj nauke* (= The Use of Computing Machines in Historical Science) (1964) and 'O primenenii èlektronnyh matematičeskyh mašin v istoričeskoj nauke' (1962) (French translation, with an introduction by J.-Cl. GARDIN, 'Les calculateurs électroniques appliqués à la science historique', in *Annales*, Vol. XVIII, 1963); KAHK, 'Novaja vyčisliteľnaja tehnika na službu istoričeskoj nauke' (= The new computing tcehnique at the service of historical science) (1964); GEL'MAN-VINOGRADOV & HROMČENKO, *Kibernetika i istoričeskaja nauka* (= Cybernetics and Historical Science) (1967); SMELSER & DAVISSON, 'The historian and the computer' (in *Essex Institute Historical Collections*, Vol. CIV, 1968); DOLLAR, 'Innovation in historical research. A computer approach' (1969); LÜCKERATH, 'Prolegomena zur elektronischen Datenverarbeitung im Bereich der Geschichtswissenschaft' (in *Historische Zeitschrift*, Vol. CCVII, 1968); DEOPIK, DOBROV et al., *Quantitative and Machine Methods of Processing Historical Information* (XIIIth International Congress, Moscow, 1970); SCHNEIDER, *La machine et l'histoire* (ibid., Moscow, 1970); MURPHY & MUELLER, 'On making historical techniques more specific: "real types" constructed with a computer', in ROWNEY & GRAHAM (eds.), *Quantitative History* (1969). There is also much that is pertinent in AYDELOTTE, 'Quantification in history' (ibid.), to which reference has already been made in the sub-section on quantitative history.

may even compound) the inaccuracies.[818] Secondly the computer can deal with verbal as well as numerical problems; that is to say, though in practice most useful (or, at least, at the present stage, most commonly used) for processing quantitative or statistical material, there is no reason in principle why computers should not be used for qualitative material as well. In this case, however, the programming will almost certainly be more difficult and more hazardous, since the correct choice of indicators, as J. C. Gardin has pointed out,[819] is by no means self-evident in a complicated historical process in which there may be a considerable number of equally admissible classifications. The computer, in other words, can only usefully be employed for analysing problems which deal with multitudes of facts in recognizable categories. If the information is so ambiguous that it is impossible to summarize it in intelligible and generally acceptable categories – or if, of course, it is simply insufficient in quantity – it is useless and probably misleading to attempt to reduce it to a form suitable for computer analysis. The essential precondition of all computer operations is a reliable prior classification scheme, and it is only on the basis of preliminary qualitative analysis of the processes, phenomena or objects being studied that the objectives of quantitative analysis can be properly set out. That is the meaning of Ustinov's at first sight paradoxical statement that the work of constructing the algorism – that is to say, the transcription of the data into the language of the machine – 'constitutes, in effect, the solution of the problem.' Once the programme is set up, the computer's operations are purely mechanical.[820]

Once these fundamental limitations are understood, there is no doubting the immense benefits of the use of computers in historical research. Essentially they perform two functions without which research cannot proceed: data storage, or the setting up of a 'data-bank', and data retrieval. These are, of course, operations which historians have always performed, collecting their source-material and then sorting it and selecting it according to the programme upon which they are working, but the individual historian, using 'manual means' (i.e., pencil and paper and his own limited time) cannot perform them on the scale, or with anything like the speed, which the computer commands; indeed, the most obvious advantage of computer analysis is economy of scale. One example is the study by Kovalchenko and

818. The point is well put by P. MATHIAS (p. 80 in BALLARD (ed.), *New Movements in the Study and Teaching of History*, 1970): 'The search for quantification [. . .] will require much *more* critical evaluation of sources [. . .] not less. The greater the extent of mathematical processing being applied to data, the greater the premium upon knowing the reliability of sources, or the potential degree of error built into them.'

819. Cf. his introduction to the French translation of USTINOV's paper, *op. cit.* (1962), 'Les calculateurs électroniques appliqués à la science historique', pp. 261-262 in *Annales*, Vol. XVIII (1963).

820. Cf. the French translation of his article *op. cit.* (1962), p. 274 in *Annales*, Vol. XVIII (1963); SMELSER & DAVISSON, *op. cit.* (1968), p. 118; DEOPIK *et al., op. cit.* (1970), p. 13.

Milov of the formation of a single all-Russian market between the eighteenth and twentieth centuries, which required approximately 100,000 correlation co-efficients.[821] Another example given by Smelser and Davisson is the processing on some 26,000 data cards of all the inventories of estates in the records of Essex county, Massachusetts, from 1640 to 1682, which contain all that can now be known of the wealth of the county in those forty-two years. To process this material a manual worker would require at least 500 hours and some 125,000 calculations; the computer can present the essential information in systematic form in about ten minutes.[822] As such examples show, the sheer magnitude of information, the complexity of organizing it on the necessary scale, and the volume of calculations involved, effectively rule out conventional manual techniques. If history is to tackle problems of this type, the computer is indispensable.

The first conclusion to be drawn, therefore, is that the computer opens new vistas to the historian, makes it possible to undertake research which, however desirable, was previously totally impracticable. It can, of course, be used at a lower level simply as a convenient means of carrying out more expeditiously mechanical tasks, such as sorting, listing or compiling simple statistical tables. That, as we have seen, is essentially its use in the record office.[823] But such work, in so far as it involves mere counting, can often be done as effectively with ordinary mechanical calculators, and it is not always clear that in such cases the use of the computer's valuable time is really justified.[824] The real value of computer analysis is at a more advanced and sophisticated level, where it is a question of bringing together two or more collections of facts, correlating them and abstracting the results according to a particular set of instructions, or programme. In fact, if the prior classification scheme is exhaustive, the data-bank can be used repeatedly for a variety of different programmes; it becomes, in other words, a permanent acquisition, upon which later generations can build (unlike the notes and extracts of an individual scholar, which, as a general rule, only he can understand and use), and thus holds out the promise of history becoming – what it has so far failed to become – a cumulative science.

The use of computers has other important implications for the future of historical research. First, it forces the investigator to ask clear, precise and accurate questions, and to eliminate the loose vocabulary which has hitherto been the bane of historical writing. As Lückerath has pointed out, many of the ideas with which historians operate are so abstract or equivocal that they obscure rather than enlighten; before they can be computerized, they must be broken down into their precisely defined elements, and though there may be a residue, there is no doubt that far more than is commonly

821.   Cf. KOVAL'ČENKO & MILOV, 'O principah issledovanija processa formirovanija vserossijskogo agrarno rynka (XVIII–XX vv.)' (= On the principles of research on the process of the formation of an all-Russia agricultural market) (1969); see also DEOPIK *et al., op. cit.* (1970), p. 12.

822.   SMELSER & DAVISSON, *op. cit.* (1968), p. 113.

823.   Cf. above, pp. 190–191.

824.   As is pointed out by SCHNEIDER, *op. cit.* (1970), p. 9.

believed can be reduced to a series of value-free (and in this sense objective) statements, which can be manipulated by a computer.[825] At the stage of programming qualitative and therefore subjective criteria will always enter in, but the mere fact of programming them makes them more readily identifiable, and in any case the reduction of the scope for subjective interpretation is extremely significant. This is the case because, secondly, the computer obviates once and for all any justification for the traditional practice of generalizing from scraps of evidence haphazardly put together. The basic rule of research is that 'all the aspects of the processes under study, rather than merely several of their individual indicators, should be investigated.'[826] With the computer *all* the data can be assimilated and analysed, as the example adduced by Smelser and Davisson shows, and there is no excuse for the old and dubious device of sampling.[827] Finally, as Lückerath points out, the computer offers for the first time a real chance to break out of the notorious 'vicious circle', which so far has prevented history from being in any real sense a progressive science, which consists in setting up generalized 'ideal types' or crypto-types from a sample of individual cases and then knocking them down again (or confirming them) by reference to other individual cases.[828] Because it is able to assimilate and process all the facts simultaneously, the computer eliminates this basic methodological obstacle and makes it possible for the historian to establish the constants on the basis of which objective conclusions can be formulated.

There is, therefore, much justification for the view, advanced both by Lückerath and by Schneider, that the introduction of the computer and the use of computer techniques may lead to revolutionary changes in historical methodology, or at least point a way out of the methodological difficulties of which reflective historians have long been acutely aware. The obvious benefit of the computer is that, properly used, it should allow historical research to advance at a speed which was inconceivable so long as the historian had to rely on slow and laborious manual operations. Secondly, by taking over the preliminary technicalities, which under ordinary conditions often consume three-quarters or more of the research worker's time, it frees the historian for what is, after all, his essential function: interpretation and explanation.[829] For here, of course, however much preliminary work the computer performs, the historian reigns supreme. The machine can answer specific questions put to it more precisely and with a far lower margin of error than the human brain; but the essential creative work – namely, the evaluation of the mechanically processed data – remains. Thirdly, computerized analysis is probably in practice the only effective basis for the co-operative, inter-disciplinary work upon which, as many

825. Cf. LÜCKERATH, *op. cit.* (1968), pp. 274-275, 283.
826. Cf. DEOPIK *et al., op. cit.* (1970), p. 5.
827. For further discussion of this important point, cf. SMELSER & DAVISSON, *op. cit.* (1968), pp. 113, 119.
828. Cf. LÜCKERATH, *op. cit.* (1968), pp. 270-271.
829. This point is emphasized independently both by LÜCKERATH, *ibid.*, p. 293, and by USTINOV, *op. cit.* (1962), pp. 290, 291, 294 of French translation (1963).

people believe, the progress of the human sciences in general, and of history in particular, depends today. As an example Ustinov points out that any attempt to reconstruct the economic life of a community in the ancient world requires the analysis not merely of such literary sources as remain, but also the employment of three different historical disciplines: numismatics, epigraphy and archaeology. For an individual to undertake all these simultaneously is virtually impossible, but even if each aspect, or body of evidence, is investigated separately by qualified specialists, each approaching it from his own particular angle, the result will be not a synthesis but a composite picture. Only the computer, which can absorb and correlate all the materials, and establish their relations by objective criteria, can treat the problem as a whole.[830] And finally, the computer, by storing the information fed into it, can build a 'data-bank', which, in principle at least, should be available to historians at all times and places; indeed, it is already possible to envisage the creation of vast, co-ordinated, international 'data-banks', which will – at last – enable historians to build systematically on the work of their predecessors, instead of, as in the past (and present), constantly going back to the sources to check, supplement and 'revise' not, indeed, their predecessors' theories and conclusions – for these may always be in need of revision – but the factual substratum upon which their theories and conclusions are based. Perhaps, after all, Smelser and Davisson are not exaggerating when they claim that history, 'because it can now bring to bear all relevant data, can become a science at least as exact as astronomy or palaeontology, both of which concern themselves with the past, and both of which develop despite the knowledge that there are gaps in their sources which may never be filled'.[831] If so, we may say without fear of contradiction that history, with the aid of computer technology, has reached a stage at which it may, at last, make the transition from a pre-scientific to a scientific discipline.

All this, of course, presupposes fundamental changes in the traditional attitudes of historians, and, as Gardin says,[832] the surmounting of deep-seated psychological and institutional impediments. Nor, in any case, should rapid progress be expected at this stage. Though the first experimental phase has passed and the place of computer technology among the historian's auxiliary sciences is not seriously questioned, the accumulation of an adequate corpus of data processed for computer analysis is a formidable undertaking, and most of the basic work remains to be done. It would therefore be totally unrealistic to expect results on a grand scale – that is to say, on a scale permitting significant conclusions of a universal character – within the next decade. Moreover, computer time is extremely expensive

830. Cf. Ustinov, *ibid.*, p. 288.

831. Cf. Smelser & Davisson, *op. cit.* (1968), p. 126; they refer specifically to economic history, rather than to history in general; but it is hard to perceive any *a priori* ground for the limitation.

832. Cf. his introduction to Ustinov's paper, p. 263 in *Annales*, Vol. XVIII (1963).

and highly competitive, and it is quite certain, as Schneider points out, that historians will not get a high priority unless they can show that their work has a demonstrably useful social function to perform, first and foremost by casting new light upon and furthering understanding of the basic social processes of human communities.[833] This may, happily, bring to an end some of the abstruse and (to the outside observer at least) useless 'research' which clutters up the historical scene to an alarming extent at the present time. It will certainly involve fundamental changes in the historian's basic attitudes, particularly the end of the free-for-all, happy-go-lucky way in which historical work is organized – or, to be precise, not organized – in most parts of the world today.

If much, or most, or all, of the mechanical work is in future to be done by computer, this will necessitate not only collective work, but also planning on a scale never attained (and rarely contemplated) in the past. The computer can only work effectively if it works to a plan – not only the short-term plan of a particular programme, but also the long-term plan of a co-ordinated campaign. It would be foolish to deny that this development will bring losses, as well as gains. Some of the best and most original historical work in the past has been the result of individual inspiration, of leaving the spirit free to blow where it listeth. Co-ordinated research may easily impose restraints and damp down initiative. There is also the danger, too obvious to need elaboration, that it may undermine the historian's independence and make him a cog in a machine manipulated by non-historians for purposes which are alien to the best interests of history. These disadvantages of the newly developing situation should be squarely faced. We may nevertheless be sure that the new developments will continue and may even gather pace, because they are in the logic of the present situation. A concentration of the means of research in a few main centres, increased planning, a reorganization of the historical profession on lines more consonant with modern social actualities, are all developments which are in the air. Though they do not by any means stem solely from the introduction of computer science into historical research, and many were visibly taking shape before the computer was brought into use, there is no doubt that computer technology has given them added impetus; but they require to be considered separately, and to this aspect of the changing organization of historical work we may now turn.

Universities, Academies, Institutes

One of the earlier and more fundamental factors affecting the organization of historical research was the evolution of the universities and of university education, to which allusion has already been made.[834] Even before the

833. Cf. SCHNEIDER's judicious remarks, *op. cit.* (1970), p. 10, with which I entirely concur.
834. Cf. above, p. 179.

Second World War, the hallowed principle of the unity of teaching and research, which reached back to Schelling and Humboldt and was accepted wherever German educational influences were strong – particularly in the United States – was visibly fraying at the edges. The collapse of the old idea of the university population as a highly selective and restricted élite and the rise and proliferation of the new type of mass university – of which the University of California, with its array of campuses, most of them designed when fully developed to house a quota of 27,000 students, may be regarded as a prototype – dealt it a death-blow. As everywhere the numbers of graduate students grew, the seminar, which its originators had conceived of as a tool of research, a workshop where, under professorial direction, a dozen or half-a-dozen apprentices would manufacture 'new contributions to knowledge', expanded rapidly in size and became instead a centre of more advanced instruction; and research, formerly centred in the seminar, tended increasingly to shift from doctoral candidates, who now normally spent at least the first two years of their post-graduate careers in formal study, preparing for their 'qualifying examinations', to post-doctoral studies.

The results of these developments[835] were many, and they were not, of course, confined to history.[836] One was that the professorial staff, or at least its upper echelons, increasingly withdrew from undergraduate to graduate, and then to post-graduate, instruction, leaving the bulk of undergraduate teaching – in the circumstances, perhaps inevitably – to 'teaching assistants' (usually doctoral candidates). A second was a certain down-grading of the universities, which tended increasingly to take on the appearance of glorified high schools or colleges, and the withdrawal of the best brains into other institutions, centres of research or academies, where they could

835.   It may be said that the way I have formulated them unduly reflects American conditions (for which cf. SHAFER, pp. 196-206 in SHAFER *et al., Historical Study in the West*, 1968). This is a criticism I would not wish to challenge. But it is also true that they represent a situation endemic in all countries (and the exceptions are now few) where university education is thrown open to all technically qualified candidates and one which – naturally with local variations – is spreading to all parts of the world. The local variations seem to me less worth attention – particularly as we are concerned here not with higher education in general but with its effects on historical research – than the general trends.

836.   Since the development of history proceeds parallel with that of the other social (and to a smaller extent natural) sciences, and many of the organizational problems overlap, there is much that is relevant in the brilliant and informative chapter by E. TRIST, 'The organization and financing of research', in the First Part of this Unesco Study (*Main Trends of Research in the Social and Human Sciences,, Part I, Social Sciences*, 1970), though history is formally outside the scope of Trist's enquiry. Most of the literature specifically referring to history upon which I have relied, and which helps to fill out Trist's picture, has been listed above, p.178, n.763. In view of Trist's work and because of the very general nature of the questions of organization here discussed, I shall be sparing of more specific references; a detailed country-by-country survey, it seems to me, would carry us too far and would not do much to elucidate the general problems which confront the historical profession.

pursue scientific studies unimpeded by university teaching and administration. The link, in short, between the universities and research, though not severed, was weakened. Various devices – like the notorious American injunction: 'Publish or perish' – sought to keep it intact, though far more effective was the genuine desire of the individual scholar to fulfil his scholarly impulses; but the fact remains that the professor with sometimes as many as 200 dissertations to supervise (and such instances were not unknown in some of the world's most distinguished universities) has no real possibility, much as he may desire it, of engaging on full-scale, major research of his own.[837] Hence, among other reasons, the proliferation of short articles on special points, which are all, in the given circumstances, most senior professors can encompass; hence, also, the number of scholars who die before the *magnum opus*, to which their life's work has been devoted, has seen the light of day.

Another development affecting the position of the universities, particularly in the Soviet Union and the other socialist countries of Eastern Europe, but spreading from these to many of the newly emergent states of Asia and Africa, was the establishment of the Academy of Sciences as the chief central directing agency which both lays down policy and carries out the greater share of problem-orientated research.[838] In the U.S.S.R., which may be regarded in many ways as exemplary, a Socialist Academy of Social Sciences was set up as early as 1918 with the famous historian, M. M. Pokrovsky, as president. But it was not until after 1936, when the Communist Academy and the U.S.S.R. Academy of Sciences were fused, that an Institue of History was set up.[839] In the first place, it would seem, its primary concern was to sponsor and supervise the preparation of suitable text-books, which appeared in huge editions;[840] but though this still remains an important function, as is indicated by the ten-volume *World History* to which

837. The figure of 200 dissertations is based on information received personally in the early 1950's. Things appear to have improved in the meantime. According to *Historical Study in the West*, p. 45, in 1964 one professor at the Sorbonne was supervising 60 theses and two others had 30 each.

838. The position of the Academies in general is adequately dealt with by TRIST, *op. cit.* (1970), pp. 696, 746-748, and it is unnecessary to repeat what he has written. So far as history is concerned, I am particularly indebted for more detailed information to F. Fedorova for her paper on 'The organization and financing of scientific research in the U.S.S.R.' (cf. above, p. 406, n. 763) and to I. S. Kon, who has also provided an invaluable contribution; cf. also HVOSTOV, 'L'activité scientifique de l'Institut d'Histoire de l'Académie des Sciences d'U.R.S.S.' (1966); and in Vol. 2 (1970) of the English-language periodical *Social Sciences* (USSR Academy of Sciences, Moscow), the article by Mstislav KELDYSH, 'The USSR Academy of Sciences: center of Soviet scientific thought' and the series of notes placed under the general title: 'Scientific and research work in the Historical Institutes of the USSR Academy of Sciences, and historical journals'. For Poland, cf. *La Pologne au XIIe Congrès international*, pp. 371-399.

839. Cf. above, pp. 21-22, 24-25.

840. Cf. HVOSTOV, *op. cit.* (1966), p. 130 in *Revue historique*. Vol. CCXXXVI; some typical figures are provided by SIDOROV, *op. cit.* (1955), pp. 403-404 in the *Relazioni* of the Xth International Congress.

reference has previously been made,[841] the scope of activities was soon extended and the Institute of History quickly emerged as the country's leading research institute. In 1968, in view of the increasing scope, it was split up to form an Institute of General History and an Institute of the History of the U.S.S.R.; but in addition there is an Institute of Military History, and historians also participate in the many inter-disciplinary institutes, such as the Institute of the Asian Peoples and the Far Eastern Institute. It goes without saying that the constituent republics of the Soviet Union also have their Academies each with its own specialized institutes, but the co-ordination of their work and that of other higher educational establishments and research institutions is ultimately the responsibility of the Academy of Sciences of the U.S.S.R. Among its other functions the Academy approves draft plans for major research projects, acts as the intermediary (rather like the University Grants Commission in Great Britain, but on a far wider scale) for negotiations with the government for obtaining finance, equipment and development capital for its own and other research establishments, reviews the whole development of research throughout the Union and organizes councils, committees and conferences to, deal with major research problems and undertakings.[842]

It is evident that this form of centralized control – though it should be emphasized that the Academy is not a governmental organization – has important implications for the development of historical research. Although the academies do not exercise a research monopoly,[843] one result is certainly to favour and facilitate overall planning. Secondly, great emphasis is placed on collective work and overall surveys carried out by teams of historians working together in close co-operation with regular consultation between specialists. This trend figures prominently in all accounts of the organization of historical work in the socialist countries, though it also seems that there is growing realization that it may become stultifying and counterproductive unless it is supported and made fruitful by research in depth and specialized monographs by individual historians.[844] Thirdly, though the relationship between the academies and the universities is not closely defined so far as personnel is concerned, and prominent historians may both be members of the academy and hold university chairs on more than an hon-

841. Cf. above, p. 382, n.-154.
842. The above is based primarily on Fedorova's review of 'Organization and financing', p. 2 of typescript of English translation (Russian original, pp. 2-3).
843. This, and the fact that the academies are 'outside government', are both rightly emphasized by TRIST, *op. cit.* (1970), p. 746.
844. While Fedorova, 'Achievements of Soviet historical science', p. 25 of typescript of English translation (Russian original, p. 23), singles out 'the trend towards the compilation of general surveys' as still 'first and foremost' among the 'general trends' of contemporary Soviet historiography, she also leaves no doubt (p. 14) that there has been a great upsurge of specialized monographs since 1965. For Poland, cf. *La Pologne au XIIe Congrès*, p. 374; for the Ukraine, cf. Djadičenko, Parhomčuk & Sarbej, *op. cit.*, § 10; for the German Democratic Republic, cf. CASTELLAN, 'Remarques sur l'historiographie de la République Démocratique Allemande', p. 413 in *Revue historique*, Vol. CCXXVIII (1962).

orary basis, it is evident as a general trend that the rank of 'Academician' is emerging – or, indeed, has emerged – as superior to that of university professor. Generalization is not easy, because individual circumstances may vary considerably, as is the case in all countries, and while one professor may be engaged full-time in teaching, another may be relieved of two-thirds or three-quarters of his teaching duties to take part in collective research within an institute; but there is no doubt that this distincion of rank and status indicates a growing rift between teaching and research. Even more significant in the long run, however, is, fourthly, the setting up of specialized institutes to which university teachers may (and do) belong, but which are staffed on a more permanent basis by technical experts, who are not part of the university system. This means, in effect, that the research worker – rather like the archivist, librarian, or museum curator – is divorced from university and teaching functions, and research tends increasingly to become an independent profession.

The Soviet model has set a precedent not only in eastern Europe but also, as already noted, in many of the developing countries of Asia and Africa. In all these countries there is an urgent and overriding need to educate a trained cadre of administrators, and the inevitable result, as Indonesian historians have pointed out, is that 'the principal preoccupation of the academic body is teaching and not research'.[845] In western Europe and in America conditions are different. Here also there is in some countries – e.g., France[846] – a relatively high degree of centralized control; while in others – e.g., Great Britain – it is minimal and 'the long tradition of "amateurism" ' has 'tended to discourage anything like organized training of historians', particularly at Oxford and Cambridge.[847] With the exception of France, with its *Centre national de la Recherche scientifique*, research projects and institutes tend in these countries to be financed less by the state than by private foundations (e.g., the Rockefeller Foundation, the Guggenheim Foundation, the American Council of Learned Societies). But, in spite of differences in organization and the different social environment, the general course of development is not basically different from that elsewhere, at least to the extent that historical study is becoming more highly structured and less individualistic.

The most significant feature, without doubt, is the rise of independent research organizations and the concentration of research – except for the private undertakings of individual scholars – outside (but still more or less loosely connected with) the universities in separate, autonomous or semi-autonomous research institutions. Their number is now very considerable; indeed, in some cases, as a German historian has observed, there may at present 'be too many research institutes and commissions and too few

845. 'Main trends in Indonesian historiography', p. 72 of typescript.
846. Cf. SHAFER, FRANÇOIS, MOMMSEN and MILNE, *Historical Study in the West* (1968), pp. 33, 47.
847. *Ibid.*, p. 140.

scholars'.[848] One reason for their growth which we have already noted, is the costly nature of modern research apparatus – particularly the computer – and the desirability of housing it in an appropriate centre. A second is the changing character of modern research and the elaboration of techniques which demand, if only for reasons of convenience and finance, at least 'a minimum of collective organisation'.[849] As Jean Glénisson has pointed out, it was the foundation in 1947 of the Sixth Section of the *École pratique des hautes Études* that provided the essential 'assise institutionnelle' for the work of the historians associated with the *Annales,* and it is hard to think that it would have proceeded so energetically or made so decisive an impact without it.[850] The very character of modern historical research involves undertakings which can only be carried out effectively by teams of research assistants working together in institutes under a director of studies responsible for co-ordinating their labours.[851]

Other more general and long-term trends favouring the setting up of specialized research institutes have been admirably set out by H. Heimpel. As long ago as 1913, he reminds us, Paul Kehr complained that too much work was undertaken without any sort of co-ordination; like Sir Paul Vinogradoff in England at the same period, but with equal lack of success, he advocated the establishment of formal research centres.[852] Research, he perceived, should be a continuing task, not merely preparation for a particular book or article; only an institute with a permanent staff could make adequate provision for work the completion of which required more time, more effort and greater means than any individual could command. It should provide the opportunity for a group, or 'Arbeitsgemeinschaft', to work together day by day in one house.[853] But this, as Heimpel points out, requires a change of attitude, in which research is no longer treated as merely a stage in the preparation of a young historian for an academic career – for which he may or may not be otherwise fitted – but as an honourable and rewarding career in itself. So long as history was considered, in the spirit of the nineteenth

848. *Ibid.,* pp. 115-116. For research institutes in the German Federal Republic, cf. *ibid.,* pp. 111-115; for France, cf. the list in *La recherche historique en France de 1940 à 1965* (1965), pp. 67-132; for Jugoslavia, Grafenauer, 'L'historiographie en Yougoslavie', pp. 15-16 of typescript; for Poland, *La Pologne au XIIe Congrès international,* pp. 371-399; for the Soviet Union, Fedorova, 'The organization and financing of scientific research in the USSR', pp. 4-5 of typescript, and the series of notes on the various Institutes and their periodicals, published in *Social Sciences,* Vol. 2 (1970) – already mentioned above, in note 838 of page 427. There is also a useful series of articles on 'Les centres de recherches historiques' in most volumes of the *Revue historique* between 1960 and 1966.

849. Cf. *La Recherche historique en France* (1965), p. 49.

850. *Ibid.,* p. xxv.

851. Cf. BRAUDEL, LABROUSSE & RENOUVIN, 'Les orientations de la recherche historique. Les recherches d'histoire moderne et contemporaine', p. 46 in *Revue historique,* Vol. CCXXII (1959).

852. Cf. HEIMPEL, 'Über Organisationsformen . . .', *op. cit.* (1959), pp. 176, 179 in SCHIEDER (ed.), *Hundert Jahre Historische Zeitschrift;* for Vinogradoff, cf. *Historical Study in the West* (1968), p. 140.

853. Cf. HEIMPEL, *op. cit.,* pp. 150, 153, 220.

century, as primarily a question of training in source-criticism, the old attitude prevailed; but the more sophisticated training – in statistics, for example, or in economic theory – required for historical research today, has brought a change.[854] In France, for example, it is now possible through the *Centre national de la Recherche scientifique* to 'make an actual career of research without the burden of teaching'.[855]

The Institute, in Heimpel's words, is 'the symbol of a period' – a period which requires decisions and positive attitudes, which presses for results, for synthesis and for the tackling of major themes, and which therefore is unwilling to accept the old assumption that, sooner or later, all and any research, however abstruse and remote, will bear fruit.[856] It is the symbol of the determination of historians to adopt the forms of organization which have contributed to the successes of the natural and social sciences, their answer to the problem of adapting the methods of historical research to the conditions and requirements of the present. So far as can be judged, it will supplement rather than displace the older form of organization; but it fulfils a function they cannot perform and a function which is growing in importance all the time, as the conditions of teaching and research evolve and change. Organization and team-work are a precondition for the realization of the new objectives upon which the future of history depends; and there is no doubt that they are likely to occupy a more important place, as the prejudices and extreme individualism of an older generation are overcome.

The Place of the Individual Historian

It may well be asked, at this stage, what place current trends and developments are likely to leave for the individual historian. The answer, perhaps paradoxically, is a very important place. In the end, there is no real conflict between 'free' research and 'organized' research; rather they complement each other.[857] Even the most highly organized institute is dependent for its sense of purpose and the vitality of its programme upon the insight and inspiration of the individual historian who directs it, and many earlier projects of collective research have flagged and fallen down, as Heimpel points out, by remaining rooted in old ways and routines long after they had ceased to be useful.[858] The danger of collective research, precisely because it is 'institutionalized', is that it can too easily become an end in itself, the routine occupation of a self-perpetuating organization, unless the individuals in charge have a keen sense of historical values and the ability, which comes from close personal familiarity with the sources, to see the

854. *Ibid.*, pp. 218, 220-221.
855. Cf. SHAFER, FRANÇOIS et al., *Historical Study in the West* (1968), p. 51.
856. HEIMPEL, *op. cit.*, p. 219.
857. Cf. *La recherche historique en France* (1965), p. 23.
858. Cf., for example, his judgement (*op. cit.*, pp. 171-172) on the Historical Commission of the Bavarian Academy of Sciences.

implications and to turn the unprocessed results of research into real history. In the end there is no substitute for the vision, grasp of essentials and, above all, the intellectual calibre of the individual historian.

There is no doubt that collective organization, centres of research and new mechanical techniques have come to stay. It is therefore all the more important to emphasize that organization and technological innovation, though a useful supplement, are no substitute for individual judgement. The computer can avoid, and even detect, mechanical error; but it cannot think, nor can it improve the quality of the historian's own workmanship. There is no inherent virtue in statistics or statistical methods. As we have seen, every research project is as good – or as bad – as the individual who organizes it. The results, as Smelser and Davisson remind us, will always depend upon the quality of the mind which devises the programme. Only the trained historian, well versed in the specific subject under investigation and its problems – only the historian, for example, who knows 'which super-annuated generalizations rest on inadequate statistical support' – can formulate appropriate questions; and when they have been answered, and the data has been processed and made available, 'the merit' – or demerit – 'of the interpretation is his, not the computer's.'[859] It may by now be a platitude to say, with Aydelotte, that the main problems in research 'are not technical and mechanical but intellectual and analytical', and that the essential qualities called for are not proficiency in method but 'logic and imagination';[860] but in view of the current emphasis on technique and organization, it is well to make clear that, in the last resort, the progress of history depends upon the individual qualities of historians themselves. It is therefore very important to assure, so far as is humanly possible, that history is so orientated – which has not always been the case in the recent past – that it attracts its fair share of the best brains.

It is also an important question – though one which it would be fool-hardy to try to answer at this stage – how far current developments in historical research may be weakening the historian's direct confrontation with the surviving records of the past and putting a premium instead upon technical aptitudes and proficiency in handling a given body of data. 'The historian,' I once ventured to write, 'who fails to refresh himself periodically in the fresh stream of original records, soon ceases to be a historian.'[861] The farther he gets away from the original sources, the more likely he is to be beguiled by his own theories and reconstructions, in which recorded facts all too easily become counters to be juggled with or bricks which he arranges neatly in patterns of his own making. In the second place, it is hard to think that the type of institutionalized collective history in which each individual concentrates on one limited sector, may not have a narrowing effect upon the historian's intellectual horizon and impede those flashes of enlighten-

859. Cf. Smelser & Davisson, 'The historian and the computer', *op. cit.* (1968), pp. 110, 112, 116, 126.
860. Cf. p. 21 in Rowney & Graham (eds.), *Quantitative History* (1969).
861. 'The historian and his archives' (1954), p. 412 in *History Today*, Vol. IV.

ment, and that sudden awareness of unsuspected inter-relationships, which come from allowing the imagination to roam far and wide over the past.

None of this is intended to be, or should be taken to imply, a criticism of the current trend to closer organization of historical research. It is only meant to suggest that, when all that is possible has been done – and I, for one, believe that much is needed – to ensure that historical work benefits from the articulation and the rational allocation and distribution of man-power and resources upon which the progress of all scientific endeavour depends, the position of the individual historian will still be secure, the con-tribution he has to make will still be fundamental. It was, after all, an individual of genius who propounded the theory of relativity, and there is no reason to think that history – or any other scientific undertaking – can dispense with the flashes of insight which only individual genius can provide. It is perfectly true – and certainly more true of history than of most other social and human sciences – that progress is still held up by what Eric Trist has called a 'dysfunctional persistence of academic individualism.'[862] But it is also important, if we do not wish to see the well-springs of creative re-search dry up, to ensure that the necessary measures to counteract this state of affairs should not impair or discourage the freedom of the individual.

Because of the scope and complexity of the problems which mainly en-gage historians' attention today, the rôle of individual research is bound to decline; most major projects are on a scale which cannot be encompassed by a single mind. The age of team-work has arrived; but it may stultify rather than enlarge the historian's opportunities, unless it leaves room for the individual of genius. History, as Guedella said,[863] calls for architects as well as bricklayers and stone-masons, and no amount of organization and expertise can take their place. But the happy, care-free individualism of an earlier age is a thing of the past, and the individual historian, while maintaining his scholarly integrity and his inherited professional standards, must learn to adapt himself to new conditions. The alternative to organiza-tion is not to go forward by a different route; it is to stand still, or even to go back. And that, in view of the remarkable advances on all fronts which history has made since 1950 or 1955, would be as self-defeating as it is unthinkable.

7. Present-day Trends and Problems: Some Concluding Observations

For anyone looking back over the preceding survey, the most striking fact is the progress of historical science in the last fifteen or twenty years. Not only the speed of advance but also the breadth of the front on which it has proceeded are remarkable, particularly by contrast with the stagnation – not, indeed, in output which grew at a staggering pace, but in intellectual conceptualization – during the preceding fifty years. When, fifteen years

862. Cf. TRIST, *op. cit.* (1970), p. 786.
863. Cf. above, p. 148.

ago, I tentatively attempted to survey the historical scene, it was difficult to avoid the conclusion that historical science was sunk in a deep rut churned by the ponderous cart-wheels of nineteenth-century historiography.[864] It is true that my survey scarcely extended beyond a rather limited western European horizon, and Communist historians may claim that the situation of Marxist historiography was different and more promising. Without entering into polemics, it is sufficient to say that the progress in historiography in Communist countries since 1955, at least in technological and conceptual refinement, has been as striking as that in the West. Along the whole front, and not least of all in the previously relatively neglected fields of Asian and African history, the progress since 1955 can fairly be described as revolutionary.

The fundamental reason for this revolutionary progress, in a world much more consciously attuned to science than was ever the case before 1940, was the impact upon a new generation of historians of a scientific view of the universe, of which the species man – the subject (perhaps mistakenly?) of 99 per cent of historical writing – is only a part. The alleged dichotomy between the human and the physical universe, which was accepted wisdom from the days of Kant, appears to a modern generation – to those, let us say, born after 1940 – quaintly old-fashioned, and the reasons for treating the history of the species man as qualitatively different from the history of (say) the species fish are suspiciously anthropomorphic; indeed, it is arguable – if one casts aside for a moment one's human prejudices – that the rôle of man in world history has been less prominent over the centuries than that of a number of other animals, e.g., lice or rats.[865] From the point of view of the biologist, history and biology are parts of one continuum, historical time is simply the continuation or 'climax' of biological time; and much the same is necessarily true for the geologist, in the sense that the shape of the earth, its contents, its changing climates, all influence, and in the long-term control, the evolution of organisms and the development of civilizations.[866] Hence the importance now attached, for example, to the science of paleoclimatology,[867] the realization (to take a banal instance) that the voyages of the Vikings cannot be explained in terms of the 'historical evidence' alone (e.g., the saga of Leif Ericsson), but must be related to climatic change.[868] In fact, the connexions between human his-

864. Cf. my article in *The Times Literary Supplement*, 6 Jan. 1956, and *History in a Changing World* (1955), particularly pp. 1-30.

865. Cf. for example ZINSSER, *Rats, Lice and History* (1935). The historian flying at the now normal height of 30,000 feet and observing from the air the miserable human scratchings of the world's surface may sometimes even wonder whether man's effect on the physical environment is in any way comparable in durability and intensity with that of the Anthozoan polyp.

866. Cf. DARLINGTON, 'History and biology', in BALLARD (ed.), *New Movements in the Study and Teaching of History* (1970), pp. 147-160.

867. For a report of the conference of the Committee on Paleoclimatology of the National Academy of Science held at Aspen (Colorado) in 1962, cf. LE ROY LADURIE in *Annales*, Vol. XVIII (1963), pp. 764-766.

868. The same applies to the famous problem of Hannibal's crossing of the

tory and sciences such as biology open up a whole new dimension which as yet has hardly been explored.

On the other hand, there is no doubt that the attitude of historians to their work has been profoundly affected by the scientific frame of mind prevalent in the modern world. The new generation, equipped with a more thorough groundwork of fundamental science, is far more willing than its predecessors to think in scientific categories; and it is this change of attitude and approach, rather than the application of specific scientific knowledge and techniques, that has produced a new atmosphere. The change, basically, is that historians – or, it would be more true to say, a growing number of historians – are prepared to ask scientific questions about historical facts, that they have decided that historical data are as capable as (for example) the data of botany of scientific study. They have made the choice, as M. M. Postan points out in a telling analogy, which Newton made on the famous day when he rested under the fabulous apple tree.[869] He might have asked himself the obvious question, why that particular apple chose that unrepeatable instant to fall on his unique head – which is what historians have traditionally done – but instead he asked himself why apples fall and so produced the theory of gravitation. If history has not yet produced a Newton or a theory of gravitation, it seems that it has at last reached the stage where it is capable of making the great leap forward – which other inexact sciences, such as botany, palaeontology or zoology, made long ago – from the collection and description of data to generalization and the formulation of scientific propositions.

The reasons for thinking that history has reached a decisive turning-point have been set out at length in the preceding pages, and there is no need to recapitulate them. Certainly there is an exhilaration in the historical world today, a sense of beckoning potentialities, which contrasts markedly with the doubt and discomforture on which F. M. Powicke commented a quarter of a century ago.[870] But the fact that history has reached a turning-point does not necessarily mean that it will take the right road, or avoid the temptation to stray into by-ways and side-tracks. If the declared purpose of this review is to pick out and comment upon current trends, the time has now come to confess that the prevalent trend among historians – some critics might say their characteristic occupational malady – is conservatism. At the moment resistance to change is at least as strong as, in all probability stronger than, the forces making for change. An old proverb has it that you can take a horse to the water, but you cannot make him drink, and it has to be recorded that at least 90 per cent of historical work published today is resolutely traditional in method, subject-matter and conceptualization. It is content to draw upon inherited capital and, like

Alps; cf. de BEER, *Alps and Elephants* (1955), where the climatic evidence is discussed on pp. 104-107.

869. Cf. POSTAN, *Fact and Relevance. Essays on Historical Method* (1971), p. 13.

870. Cf. POWICKE, *Modern Historians and the Study of History* (1955), pp. 229, 235-236.

some other industries in the older developed countries, to go on using antiquated machinery, which, even if below the best modern standards, still enables the manufacturer to supply, with a minimal outlay of new capital, a regular flow of sound traditional products for which there is a ready market.

This is not intended to imply that history, even of the most traditional sort, is stagnant. On the contrary, there is a steady flow of 'gentle revision', which may almost be called the traditional historians' stock-in-trade.[871] No matter where one looks, in time or in space, there is scarcely one of the shibboleths of fifty years ago that has not in the meantime been modified, corrected, refined, or even reversed (the same, it is true, applies to most of the modifications, corrections, refinements, and revisions).[872] There has also been a remarkable expansion of subject-matter, some but by no means all of which has been referred to in the preceding pages. But revision and change or emphasis, unless I have misunderstood the purpose of the present survey, are not the essential point; and it would hardly carry matters further if, as evidence of current trends in historical research, I were to survey in brief outline the changes (for example) in the interpretation of the history of the English parliament or of the origins of the First World War. In the same way, while some new subject-matter may involve radical innovations in method and approach, that is certainly not true of all; and I have not thought it necessary to discuss (for example) the currently fashionable subject of Afro-American history, not because I do not think it is important – on the contrary, it seems to me that a large part of writing on the internal history of the United States in the nineteenh and twentieth centuries, including the not inconsiderable volume of work on 'the peculiar institution' of slavery, has been vitiated by neglect of the Afro-American point of view – but because I cannot, subject to correction, find that it involves new concepts or new methods, other than those (e.g., due regard to oral tradition) already discussed.[873]

Since the purpose of this survey is to single out those trends which distinguish historical research today from historical research yesterday and the day before yesterday, it has not seemed necessary to dwell on the large body of work which, however impressive in itself, makes no pretence at, and in some instances expressly repudiates, innovation in method and conceptualization. Thus I have said nothing of intellectual history, or the history of ideas, which had a great vogue in certain countries in the 1950's,

871. For some examples of 'gentle revisionism', cf. MARWICK, *The Nature of History* (1970), pp. 181-182.

872. Typical of this phase was the series of 'Historical revisions' published regularly in the journal *History* for many years; they petered out in 1955 after a career reaching back to 1917, not so much because of a conviction that nothing remained to be revised, as because of the absurdity of revising its own revisions, and then revising those.

873. Cf. above, pp. 112-113. For a very brief introduction to Afro-American history, on which the literature is now immense, cf. CONWAY, *The History of the Negro in the United States* (1968).

but which seems to me, again subject to correction, to have contributed little specifically new or invigorating in the last ten or fifteen years.[874] Once in existence, this type of historical writing naturally goes on under its own momentum, just as there is a steady output of old-fashioned political narrative and historical biography; but on the whole it is fair to say that the tide, in the last fIfteen years, has turned in the opposite direction and that the conception of history as (in Butterfield's words), 'a field for the activity of disembodied ideas' has been discarded by the majority of historians.[875] Nevertheless it is important to insist that traditional attitudes still dominate by far the larger proportion of all historical writing, and that there is no guarantee that the new trends surveyed in this review will necessarily prevail. Certainly, at present, they represent – as is perhaps only to be expected – the aspirations of a minority. Furthermore, among those who welcome the new trends and believe they have come to stay, the majority see them more as useful supplementary techniques, which can be combined with traditional history, rather than as an alternative to an exploded philosophy and an out-dated methodology.[876]

It is, therefore, important, before we conclude, to consider briefly some of the main obstacles to the 'breakthrough', which seems now within the realm of possibility, from pre-scientific to scientific history. First and foremost, there are the deep-seated psychological impediments to which reference has already been made, the reluctance of historians to jettison their ingrained habits and to re-think the basic postulates of their work.[877] It is certainly the most formidable obstacle of all, since the old suppositions and preoccupations have become embedded in teaching and – at least in some of the older universities – are handed down from generation to generation as inherited wisdom. Demands for change are swept aside as 'wishing history to become something which it is not'; though why, considering the unsatisfactory and unscientific nature of history as it is, this wish should

874. The problem with intellectual history is its extreme nebulousness. It is almost impossible to define the boundariès between intellectual history (*Ideengeschichte*), *Kulturgeschichte* and *Geistesgeschichte*, as H. J. SCHOEPS, *Was ist und Was will die Geistesgeschichte* (1959), pp. 10-12, concedes, and it is only necessary to look at the bibliography of such a book as STROMBERG, *European Intellectual History since 1789* (1966, 1968), to see that practically anything and everything can be brought within its compass; but the intellectual parentage evidently descends from Burckhardt, Huizinga and Meinecke. By far the most distinguisthed recent exponent, in my view, and certainly the most influential, is H. Stuart HUGHES, whose *Consciousness and Society. The Reorientation of European Social Thought, 1890-1930* (1958), may be regarded as an outstanding example of modern *Ideengeschichte* at its best.

875. 'There is', Butterfield writes, 'no form of history more fallacious than that which is obtained by the merely literary study of ideas', or (as he adds) the sort of history which at its worst talks 'as though the human mind just decided to arise and expand at the Renaissance' – BUTTERFIELD, *History and Human Relations* (1951), pp. 76, 84.

876. This is the attitude, for example, of MARWICK, *op. cit.* (1970), p. 198.

877. Cf. above, p. 196.

be dismissed as unreasonable, is not explained.[878] There is no doubt that the empathy preached by F. M. Powicke – 'why am I stirred so deeply because I can trace the very sheepwalks of the monks of Furness?' – is still a powerful influence, that many historians see history as an invocation of the past, 'a museum of held reverberations.'[879] And this conception of history, not as a rational exercise, but as the evocation of the past, is fortified and confirmed by popular demand. History which adorns a story and points a moral is still immensely popular, particularly if the moral is one which the majority in any society wishes to hear; and the temptation for historians to pander to this demand is great, particularly as the intellectual effort involved in this type of historical writing is not excessive. The phenomenal success not only of semi-popular works, such as Cecil Woodham-Smith's *The Reason Why* or Barbara Tuchman's *The Guns of August,* but also – to name but one outstanding example – of the narrative histories of so distinguished a professional historian as Sir Steven Runciman,[880] provides the best evidence that lively, colourful and intelligent historical writing still exercises an immense hold over the minds of the educated reading public. In these circumstances, it is perhaps not surprising that historians cling to essentially descriptive and literary techniques which other sciences, such as botany or zoology, have long outgrown.

The other factor which stands in the way of a new and more scientific attitude to history is the inability of historians to dissociate themselves from their own environment. Science, on the whole, advances on an international front; there are as many sorts of history as there are peoples and nations. History, as we have already observed, came into existence as a form of myth,[881] and the association between history and mythology, particularly national mythology, is still a powerful factor. 'It is generally accepted,' writes the (exiled) Chinese historian Cheng Te-k'un, 'that the writing of history is more or less a political act', and the English historian Butterfield has admitted, apparently without qualms, that 'we teach and write the kind of history which is appropriate to our organization' and 'can scarcely help it if this kind of history is at the same time the one most adapted to the preservation of the existing régime'.[882] Many will think, if these remarks are true, that the future of history is bleak. In fact, as we have had ample opportunity to see, historical research is concentrated in all countries upon national history, and, it need hardly be added, for the most part reflects,

878. Cf. Marwick, *op. cit.*, pp. 104, 129. The unsatisfactory state of traditional history is well described by one of its English adherents, Kitson Clark, when he admits (*The Making of Victorian England*, 1962, p. 17) that, by breaking up the picture 'so that nothing can be seen as a whole', it leads 'to a kind of historical nominalism with innumerable accidentals and no universals.'

879. Cf. Powicke, *Modern Historians . . ., op. cit.* (1955), pp. 182-183.

880. I am referring, of course, to his celebrated *History of the Crusades* (3 vols., 1951-54), a work for which I have the highest admiration.

881. Cf. above, p. 96.

882. Cf. p. 73 in *China Quarterly*, No. 23 (1965) or p. 51 in Feuerwerker (ed.), *History in Communist China* (1968); Butterfield, *The Englishman and His History* (1945), p. 1.

consciously or unconsciously, a national mythology. 'Consensus history' is not a peculiarly North American aberration, as anti-American propaganda sometimes suggests. Most historians are defenders, often no doubt without deliberate intent, of their own *status quo* – or, it might perhaps be fairer to say, the dupes or victims of their own environment – and history is still the favourite home of the *fable convenue*. For anyone concerned for the future of history, this situation can only be profoundly disturbing. Unless history can emancipate itself from mythology, in the way that sciences such as astronomy or chemistry have done, unless it can break once and for all time with its mythological roots, as astronomy has emancipated itself from astrology and chemistry from alchemy, the chances of history breaking out of the vicious circle in which its past has imprisoned it, are not great.

Nor, in this respect, can it truthfully be said that all recent developments are encouraging. As F. Bédarida has pointed out, they have 'brought to light as many *impasses* and deviations as fruitful ways forward.'[883] Perhaps the most important of these, not mentioned by Bédarida, but briefly referred to above, is the weight of official pressures, and the possibility that they may be used to ensure a socially and politically acceptable history.[884] These pressures, of course, have always existed in all countries; indeed, Harold Temperley, who, as co-editor of the official *British Documents on the Origin of the War* of 1914, may be presumed to have known what he was talking about, expressed grave misgivings in 1930 concerning the harm that history might suffer from government patronage.[885] But the new and more sophisticated techniques now in use, the closer integration and official sponsorship of research, and the consequent demand for funds to meet the growing expenditure on machines and man-power, have rendered historians far more susceptible than at any time in the past to governmental control. In the words of Trist, 'the social sciences' – among which he specifically includes history – 'have become politically accountable',[886] and it is hardly to be expected that a government (or, for that matter, a private foundation) will choose to fund a project which it considers to be at variance with, or perhaps even which does not demonstrably further, its national interests. Herbert Butterfield has written eloquently of the 'pitfalls' of 'official history';[887] but it is evident that there are opportunities for more insidious pressures today, particularly as (in Butterfield's words) 'a well-run state needs no heavy-handed censorship', but is perfectly capable of binding 'the historian with soft charms and with subtle, comfortable chains'.[888]

There are other dangers in the current situation, of a more mundane sort but not to be lightly dismissed. One is a preoccupation – despite the

883. BÉDARIDA, 'L'historien et l'ambition de totalité', p. 180 in *L'histoire et l'historien* (1964).

884. Cf. above, p. 197.

885. Cf. TEMPERLEY, *Research and Modern History* (1930), p. 4.

886. Cf. TRIST, *op. cit.*, p. 799 in *Main Trends . . ., Part I: Social Sciences* (1970); on the position of history, *ibid.*, p. 793.

887. Cf. BUTTERFIELD, *History and Human Relations* (1951), pp. 182-224.

888. *Ibid.*, p. 198.

warnings of distinguished quantitative historians, such as Aydelotte – with techniques for their own sake, and particularly with the fascinating potentialities of computer science. It would be absurd, and is certainly not my intention, to minimize the importance of technological innovation. The progress of most sciences has depended upon, and often had to wait for, technological advance (in the case of botany, for example, the development of the compound microscope), and there is no reason to think that history is an exception. On the contrary, properly used, the computer makes it possible, as has already been pointed out, for history to become a cumulative science and to break out of the vicious circle in which it has been imprisoned by a false philosophy and a defective methodology.[889] But it must always be remembered that 'quantitative analysis is not an objective but a means of cognition',[890] and that it must not be allowed – as at one stage the availability or non-availability of written sources was allowed – to dictate the course and character of historical research. It is not only that 'mastery of techniques' alone, as Christopher Dawson has written, 'will not produce great history, any more than a mastery of metrical technique will produce great poetry';[891] more serious is the danger that research may concentrate upon insignificant subjects, simply because they are easily manipulated by machine methods.[892] In that case, the employment of new techniques, instead of carrying history to a higher level, will only perpetuate a malady from which – as anyone who reads through the lists of dissertations in preparation in universities in all parts of the world cannot fail to observe – historical research is already acutely suffering: the 'pedantic chase after the insignificant'.[893] Already the complaint has been made that the 'new economic history', far from defining and clarifying, has simply 'permitted the endless discussion' of issues which 'should long since have been buried'.[894]

These are problems which it would be unrealistic to shirk. There is a real danger that history, precisely because of the accumulation of knowledge which modern techniques and the growth of communications have made possible, may be passing into an 'Alexandrian age', in which the best that can be hoped for is encyclopaedic systematization. As André Malraux has reminded us, this is the first time in the history of the world in which it has become possible to survey simultaneously all the records, artefacts, arts, archaeological evidences and documentary sources, of the past.[895] The possibilities opened up should be stimulating and exhilarating, but they may

889. Cf. above, pp. 194-196.

890. Cf. Deopik, Dobrov et al., *Quantitative and Machine Methods of Processing Historical Information* (1970), p. 13.

891. Cf. Dawson, *The Dynamics of World History* (1957), p. 293.

892. Cf. Price, 'Recent quantitative work in history' (1969), p. 13 in *History and Theory*, Beiheft IX.

893. A malady already bemoaned by Powicke, *Modern Historians . . ., op. cit.* (1955), p. 192.

894. Cf. North, 'The state of economic history', p. 91 in *American Economic Review*, Vol. LV (1965), Supplement.

895. Cf. Mazlish, *The Riddle of History* (1966), p. 450, where Malraux's remarks are cited.

also be daunting. How is the historian to encompass this vast, expanding universe of knowledge? If, as Bédarida points out, he follows his traditional course –the scrupulous, meticulous investigation of the unique and individual – he will produce at best monographs, scattered fragments from which it is not merely impossible to deduce 'laws' or valid generalizations, but even to obtain an overall view of the whole.[896] The almost total decline of interest in 'philosophy of history', which we have already noted,[897] is perhaps symptomatic of this situation. It is safer, and easier, to take refuge in 'micro-history', and it cannot be denied that there is a stage at which 'micro-history', conscientiously and intelligently pursued, has more to contribute than grandiose generalization built on weak foundations.[898] But even convinced upholders of the 'micro-historical' approach, such as M. M. Postan, are aware that it is not enough, and that without a 'macro-historical' framework the 'micro-historical' phenomena cannot 'be fitted into any significant universe of discourse'.[899] Nevertheless the problem of quantity remains to haunt the historian. The gap between an ever-increasing, by now virtually unmanageable accumulation of small-scale research and the pretension of history – a pretension upon which its whole claim to serious consideration depends – to present a totality, is glaringly apparent, and is likely to grow wider. This and the central problem of objectivity are the two horns of the dilemma facing the historian today.

It would be idle to deny that most historians confront them with a good deal of complacency. History is a flourishing profession providing a steady income; it attracts large numbers of students (though the quantity is not, perhaps, always matched by the quality); it has a large following among the reading public, which delights almost as much as the principals themselves in the hollow controversies – let us say, without mentioning names, about the character and policies of Hitler, the coronation of Charlemagne, or the rise of the gentry, – which have become the historian's most popular contribution to public entertainment. They regard the criticisms levelled against them by social scientists such as Robert Merton as ill-conceived and ill-mannered, and reply, if at all, with the familiar retort of *tu quoque*, rather than by examining and seeking to remedy their own defects. A few atavists apart, who confidently claim that Thucydides was the greatest historian of all time – rather like the political scientists who believe tĥat all political wisdom is enshrined in Aristotle – their attitude to history is benignly evolutionary, and any suggestion that history is in need of revolutionary change is dismissed not with anger but with derision. Perhaps they are right. God is notoriously on the side of the big battalions, and the conservatives – or those, at least, who believe that history is nicely progressing under its own steam – are a mighty phalanx with adherents in every ideological camp. It is sufficient

896. Cf. BÉDARIDA, *op. cit.* (1964), p. 182.
897. Cf. above, p. 164.
898. This has already been pointed out with specific reference to Indonesian history; cf. above, pp. 132, 134.
899. Cf. POSTAN, *An Economic History of Western Europe, 1945-1964* (1967), p. 5.

for them, as one of the recent defenders of 'continuity of purpose' recently wrote, that, 'despite many set-backs and much asininity, historical study has on the whole advanced towards more refined techniques and more sophisticated concepts'.[900] It does not apparently strike them as odd how surprising it would be if, after more than two thousand years, it had not done so; still less are they concerned that it may – without a radical change of direction – be advancing into a wilderness.

If one attempts to sum up, the conclusion one must draw – platitudinous as it is – is that history today is confronted at once by immense possibilities and great dangers. Since this survey has concentrated upon the potentialities, upon the new perspectives opened up by recent trends, it is only right, in conclusion, to give due weight to the dangers, of which no thoughtful historian is entirely unaware. Perhaps because of its subject-matter, no study suffers more than history from the dead weight of the past. Whether it will be pulled under and drown or whether it will triumphantly emerge, refreshed and renewed, on the other side of the river, is something no one can foretell. We can only weigh the conflicting forces and draw our own conclusions, optimistic or pessimistic according to our own particular temperaments. At the end of this long survey I personally incline to a tempered optimism, though I think the forces are nicely balanced – too nicely balanced, indeed, for comfort or complacency. It is certainly possible that what Matthew Arnold termed 'that huge Mississippi of falsehood called history' may continue to flow between its ample banks, providing life-giving irrigation for a luxurious undergrowth of myth and legend, as it has traditionally done throughout the centuries. This was its original purpose, as we have seen,[901] and it would be an error to think that it has finally emancipated itself from its mythological antecedents. But it is also true that historians have the means, as never before, to turn their study into a science. It may be that the search for a scientific history will prove as elusive in the twentieth century as it was to Buckle, Comte and Spencer in the nineteenth century; but until it has been tried we shall not know, and those who deny the possibility *a priori* are like the historians of whom Heimpel has written, who deduce from a false philosophy of history not that their philosophy of history should be improved but that there can be no philosophy of history.[902] All that can be said at this stage is that the possibilities of elevating history to the status of a science are far greater, the understanding of what scientific history signifies is far more sophisticated, and the techniques available far more advanced, than they were in the days of Buckle, Comte and Spencer, and if historians choose to turn their backs on them, the responsibility will rest upon their shoulders.

Unfortunately the loss will not only be theirs. The most conspicuous

---

900. MARWICK, *The Nature of History* (1970), p. 23.

901. Cf. above, p. 96.

902. Cf. HEIMPEL, 'Über Organisationsformen historischer Forschung in Deutschland' (1959), p. 178 in SCHIEDER, Th. (ed.), *Hundert Jahre Historische Zeitschrift*.

weakness of social science at the present moment is the lack of a time-dimension, of the depth which comes from studying society not as static but as a dynamic constellation of forces manifesting itself in continuous and constant change.[903] This, as Marc Bloch was quick to see, was the historian's opportunity and challenge.[904] Without history – that is to say, without taking into consideration man not simply as he is today (for today is, after all, a mere shadow cast by the past on the future) but as he has existed at different periods throughout the ages – social science will always remain a torso. Only history can provide the insight we need for a full understanding of the working of social processes and social institutions in time. But it must be a history approached in a scientific spirit and infused with a social purpose. Recent developments have brought such a history within our grasp: it is for the new generation to take it and put it to good use. We live today in a society which requires positive returns from its investment not only in capital equipment but in expensively trained manpower, which expects the social scientist to frame working hypotheses by which we can harness nature to our purposes and transform our environment. The historian is not exempt from this demand. In the short run he may perhaps continue comfortably enough in the old ways. But in the long run he will be judged – and history will be judged with him – by the contribution he makes, in co-operation with other related disciplines, in using his knowledge of the past for the shaping of the future.

Epilogue

History by Any Other Name

In the mid-1970s, when Geoffrey Barraclough launched his survey of historiographical trends, a new "New History" was in full vogue. More than a half century before, the call had gone out for scholars to shake off the stultifying habits of conventional history—the rarefied stories of kings and queens, politicians and intellectuals, wars and treaties—and to probe, from a new perspective, with modern tools, the life of the "common man." A glance at the long third chapter of Thomas Babington Macaulay's *History of England*, with its sweeping portrait of "common" men and women in the seventeenth century, confirms that the seeds of the "New History" were planted early; but the gradual shift of focus that occurred in the years following World War I signaled more than renewed interest in "history from below," or, as G. M. Trevelyan called it, "history . . . with the politics left out."[1] It involved the application of new methodologies. Barraclough introduces the principal players in that revolution (among them, Marc Bloch, Lucien Febvre, and other members of the *Annales* school in France), and he charts the pervasive influence of their interdisciplinary approach. "The main feature of current trends is the alignment of history with the social sciences," Barraclough tells us, and this, "in the broadest sense, is the central achievement of the Ecole des Annales."[2] Similar changes occurred *pari passu* in Germany and the United States, especially in the cross-fertilization of history and sociology; and by the 1960s and 70s significant numbers of historians had taken up the challenge, expressed by Febvre, to emancipate themselves from the limitations of traditional documentary evidence. Implementing the discoveries of sociologists, archeologists, geographers, economists, psychologists, and anthropologists, Clio's disciples, long at home in the humanities, continued their modern migration toward the social sciences.

As the cumbersome title suggests, the new "New History" was a variation on the old "New History"; it built on the foundations of the social sciences while introducing, among other novel techniques, quantitative methods made possible by the technological innovations of the postwar epoch. Barraclough noted the exciting possibilities offered by the computer and was not alone in believing that quantitative analysis had emerged as "the most powerful of the new trends in history, the factor above all others which distinguished historical attitudes in the 1970s from historical attitudes in the 1930s."[3] Some observers maintained that quantification loomed "larger in theory than in practice,"[4] but legions of demographers in search of greater precision turned to computers to study birth rates and mortality trends, while economic historians and other species of "cliometricians" counted, charted, listed, and collated everything from bread prices in early modern Europe to the relative height of men and women in nineteenth-century West Africa. Quantitative methods may have been at a "tentative and exploratory stage" when Barraclough presented his survey,[5] but all the signs pointed to an ongoing and global revolution. Emmanuel Le Roy Ladurie, yet another *Annaliste,* had predicted that "the historian of tomorrow will be a programmer, or he will no longer be";[6] and with new generations of computer hardware and software available to scholars it appeared that the prediction would hold true. Angels on the head of a pin, it seemed, would soon go down for the count.

But revolution sparks reaction, and an academic Thermidor quickly set in. Like Dickens' attack on the "digit worshippers" of Victorian England ("men who see figures and averages, and nothing else—the representatives of the wickedest and most enormous vice of this time"), many historians echoed an early skeptic who had warned against worshiping "at the shrine of that Bitch-goddess, Quantification."[7] The mechanistic techniques of "quanto-history," they insisted, could only lead to a mechanistic view of society. Humankind is more than its measurements. The critics had a point; in the heady days of the 1960s and 70s, some historians for whom the journey through the numerical maze mattered more than the arrival failed to remember that quantitative analysis should be a "means of cognition."[8] A highly vocal group of doomsayers, out to debunk new methods rather than construct broad new bridges into the past, concentrated on those early excesses, while more judicious critics presented a balanced view of the problems and benefits of computer technology. By the early 1980s, historian and sociologist Charles Tilly (who used computers to process data on labor strikes and other forms of collective protest in Europe) was gently reminding colleagues that their "self discipline" should expand "at the same rate as the expansion in computing facilities available to them"; if it did not, Tilly suggested, scholars might emerge from the computer room with nothing more than "spurious explanations."[9] And David Herlihy, a social historian of Renaissance Italy, exposed the inaccuracy of much of the vast literature on computers and quantification; above all, the new machine is a "manipulator of symbols," wrote Herlihy, a tool that may facilitate the study of linguistics, historical geography, cartography, and more. It should not be confined to crunching numbers.[10]

Barraclough anticipated the broad outlines of this debate and agreed that computers might free historians for their essential function ("interpretation and explanation"). But he raised his own caution flag. Worried that the individual scholar would be forced into a "new degree of organization," he warned that white-coated research teams of computer scientists might "undermine the historian's independence and make him like a cog in a machine."[11] On the heels of Barraclough's comments, Lawrence Stone, historian of early modern Europe and another chronicler of historiographical trends, expressed his own concern about the organizational consequences of the computer, that "immensely powerful but very obtuse machine." The historian, wrote Stone, "despite his largely humanistic training, is as liable to this insidiously corrupting mental deformation as are his colleagues in the social sciences."[12] But Stone, Barraclough, and others did not anticipate the dramatic proliferation of personal computers in the 1980s or the ways in which modern technology could both ease access to distant and diverse resources (with time-saving benefits) and secure the scholar's independence. After emerging as a frightening symbol of microwave history, the computer, it became clear, could hasten many of the historian's basic tasks and allow more time for rumination. The new tool could preserve old habits.

A review of publications over the past decade—including doctoral dissertations, those weighty signposts of scholarly trends—confirms that while statistical analysis remains an important feature of historical research, the apparatus of quantification (the labyrinthine tables and serpentine graphs) have been either integrated into more "traditional" texts or relegated to the deep background of appendices. Meanwhile, as one historian tells us, the great majority of scholars "have not tired of quantification" because "they never took it up" in the first place.[13] And the trend toward laboratory research teams of historians huddled around a central data -processing unit also seems to have been reversed, or at least moderated, by the decentralization of computer technology and by the ever-expanding use of word processors. Many historians have put aside their pencils and covered up their Smith-Coronas; but they continue to work in a solitary fashion, in offices and studies as quiet as the new keyboards on which they tap out their many and varied stories.[14]

Psychology and psychoanalysis, other key ingredients in the new social science history examined by Barraclough, have met with similar waves of praise and alarm. In 1958, Professor William L. Langer, president of the American Historical Association, described the urgent need "to deepen our historical understanding through exploitation of the concepts and findings of modern psychology." He called it our "Next Assignment," and he attracted a significant number of followers.[15] Not surprisingly, the concepts were applied, for the most part, to biographies. The first "psychobiography," Freud's short essay on Leonardo da Vinci (a provocative analysis, though flawed by a mistranslation of the evidence), helped set the model for later and longer studies; Erik Erikson's work on Luther and Gandhi emerged as leading examples of the new approach, and into the 1960s and 1970s biographers, some of them professionally trained in psychoanalysis, turned their attention to the likes of T. E. Lawrence, Heinrich Himmler, and Richard Nixon.[16] They also began to psychoanalyze groups as well as personalities, and as the subdiscipline attracted more practitioners it gave rise to professional publications, including *The Journal of Psychohistory* (formerly the *History of Childhood Quarterly*) and *Psychohistory Review*. In keeping with his promise to explore contemporary trends "without passing judgement," Barraclough suppressed his own deep skepticism regarding this modern subdiscipline (in another context he paraphrased Henry Ford and called much of the new psychohistory "bunk"); but he did recognize the practical problem of coming to terms with "the silent life," and he agreed that psychoanalysis might "widen the horizons of historical understanding" if "handled with great caution."[17]

As with quantification, however, the most extreme examples of rigid methodology leading to relentless reductionism (what one observer has called "the much canvassed disasters of psychohistory")[18] attracted the critics' attention—and their ire. By refusing to place historical patients in broad social, cultural, and political context, by tracing the sources of evil actions to uncaring mothers, absent fathers, or anal impulses, some psychohistorians, though by no means all, gave their practice a bad name. The "considerable vogue" had "passed its peak" by the 1980s (as Barraclough believed it would),[19] and for the most part it has remained in a valley of ill repute.

Still, those psychohistorians who probed their subject's unconscious with caution and common sense, with an eye to the social context as well as to the libido, scored a victory of sorts; they helped raise the methodological consciousness of many of their colleagues. Though still wary of implementing (or even learning) psychoanalytical concepts, historians have become more sensitive to unraveling the deep complexities of human emotion.[20] One advocate of the responsible integration of history and psychoanalysis, Peter Gay, has recently embarked on a multivolume study of the nineteenth-century "bourgeois experience" in the West—an investigation strongly influenced by Freudian models but bound to no single theory or methodology. Professor Gay insists that a "reliance on psychoanalysis . . . need not entail a naive, reductionist, monocausal theory of history," and he reminds us that there is a crucial difference between "psychohistory" and "history informed by psychoanalysis."[21] Like the early fireworks surrounding the perils of computers, the alarmism over psychoanalytical methods has given way to quieter, less bellicose debates. But serious questions persist, especially in the realm of group psychology, and for now the practice of these particular doctors remains limited.[22]

If the specialized areas of quantification and psychohistory have had a hard time of it in recent years, the broad subdiscipline of "social history," which often encompasses statistical or psychological studies, has grown like Topsy. One of its flagship periodicals in the United States, *The Journal of Social History,* launched in 1967, continues to attract a wide range of historians with diverse interests, as does its British counterpart, *Social History,* and other specialized and mainstream publications worldwide.[23] In a general sense, of course, all history is social history—the study of human society—but social historians embrace certain assumptions which set them apart from their more "traditional" colleagues. Still too heterodox to agree on a single systematic methodology, scholars have reached a general consensus on the types of topics to investigate and the range of problems to address.

And, again, as Barraclough shows us, the *Annalistes* helped prepare the way. In reaction to "event history"—the stories of great battles fought by great men, of pivotal moments in political and intellectual history—the founders of the *Annales* school and their many followers outside France turned from the specific actions of individual elites to the "total history" of broad social groups and vast geographical areas. Inspired by Bloch's study of feudalism and Braudel's portrait of the Mediterranean world, they explored the long-term structure of human societies—of nomadic tribes or agrarian civilizations over an expanse of time *(la longue durée)*—and they implemented, as Lucien Febvre had suggested, the findings of other disciplines. Through the 1980s social historians of many methodological stripes and many nationalities were still building on those discoveries in their quest to analyze the "everyday activities of ordinary people" over the long term.[24]

The elements of time, space, and ecology, so brilliantly represented in the early work of the *Annales* school, have emerged as significant factors in contemporary historiography. Community studies and regional histories pay close attention to the environment and to continuity and change across generations (always important dimensions of "total history"); and geography has reassumed a central role in historical inquiry, due largely to Barraclough's influential *Times Atlas of World History* and to other studies that investigate vast regions over time. Following the lead of scholars versed in geography, economics, and agriculture, social historians travel down waterways and back roads, across plowed fields and mountain pastures; they chart exterior and interior spaces (a market square, a peasant household) as reflections of a society's habits and hierarchies; and they study "oral histories" (a way of working as old as Herodotus but not developed as a subdiscipline until this century) to help break their "traditional reliance on written records." Documentary evidence is still plumbed in archives and libraries; but, in keeping with their goal to learn more about the silent actors of the past, social historians study Afro-American slave narratives, the fairy tales of rural Europe, and the rare diaries of struggling artisans with the same attention, the same close reading, they bring to census records, newspapers, and the journals of local notables.[25]

Barraclough acknowledged the many forms of "archaeological excavation" pursued by historians,[26] but he underestimated the number and types of sources available and the extent to which imaginative scholars would dig their way into the near and distant past. In the 1980s African historians, for example, did not find the search for metallic objects to be a "futile" undertaking (as Barraclough suggested) but a rich and revealing quest; a recent study of copperworking in sub-Saharan Africa has provided new perspectives on trade, currency, and the life and labor of village women and men.[27] And the focus is not fixed on "primitive" or "prehistorical" societies; the artifacts of material culture have become crucial ingredients in the social historian's general grab bag of evidence. Spinning wheels and steam engines, soaps and scrub brushes, knives and forks, necklaces and bracelets, hansom cabs and bicycles-built-for-two tell us much about the work routines, sanitary habits, table manners, fashion trends, and leisure patterns of the past. In a recent multivolume work on "places of memory" in modern France, a contingent of distinguished historians marshaled evidence from mortuaries, maps, statues, and popular engravings; and another scholar has analyzed the noxious and perfumed odors that emanated from Parisian gutters, fish shops, and elegant boutiques and wafted across the Seine in the eighteenth and nineteenth centuries.[28]

Historians more at home with constitutions, political tracts, and voting registers may consider their sources the only valuable antiques in a world of research increasingly overrun by collectibles. But social historians insist that their primary materials, far from being the trivial detritus of another age, are as telling as manifestos, political ledgers, and Parliamentary debates—especially when "read" systematically as "texts." Informed by the science of semiotics, historians are learning a new "vocabulary" and "grammar" of signs and symbols, not in the abstract but in their "natural habitat"; and they are translating history's "languages" in many and varied ways. It is fitting that a book of great interest to historians in the 1980s, Umberto Eco's novel *The Name of the Rose,* was the work of a semiologist; blending hard fact and fiction, it recaptured the essence of the late Middle Ages through its masterful study of symbols and numbers and what they signified to the monks and inquisitors of the Mediterranean world.[29]

As these and other examples confirm, the interdisciplinary approach outlined by Barraclough more than a decade ago continues to shape and reshape the historian's craft; the social sciences, each in its turn, have expanded the scholar's horizon. Coming in uneven waves rather than in a massive deluge, sociology, economics, psychology, semiotics, and other disciplines and subdisciplines have enabled historians to enter and analyze places and people previously closed to them—or, at best, accessible down only a single avenue of inquiry. In a 1980 essay on this fertile mingling (or, some would say, confused muddling) of disciplines, anthropologist Clifford Geertz described the recent "refiguration of social thought." Hot on the trail of new discoveries, social scientists armed with "intellectual poaching licenses" have crossed many boundaries. They have, as Geertz puts it, "blurred genres." While academic institutions throughout the world still place their faculties in the neatly arranged categories of the humanities and social sciences, and in their clearly identified fields, the work produced by those scholars is more eclectic than ever. "Genre mixing" has become "the natural condition of things," says Geertz, and "the lines grouping scholars together into intellectual communities, or (what is the same thing) sorting them out into different ones, are these days running at some highly eccentric angles."[30]

For historians, the angles had always veered to some degree toward anthropology, and they have stayed that course through the 1980s. Barraclough mentions the affinities of the two disciplines and cites Evans-Pritchard's remark that "history must choose between being social anthropology or being nothing."[31] (Given another scholar's insistence that "social history is anthropology or it is nothing," and Le Roy Ladurie's statement that historians would be computer programmers or they would be nothing, it appears that academic threats, however gentle, have also emerged as a "main trend" of the recent past.) Historians and anthropologists have shared common interests, if not common methodologies, for generations, but in recent years the union has strengthened and the boundaries have decomposed to a great and considerable degree. Anthropologists now show a heightened sensitivity to historical context and change over time: "ethnohistory" has flourished as scholars probe the structures of human societies in a systematic fashion, as they identify and analyze the customs of the inarticulate, the *mentalités* of "ordinary" men and women. For guidance, they turn in many directions—to Mauss, Malinowski, Douglas, Lévi-Strauss, Goody, and other celebrated ethnographers and symbolic anthropologists. Victor Turner's work, for example, has prompted historians to look at rituals and social dramas (carnivals, riots, funerals) from a new perspective; and Clifford Geertz, who summarized the shift, also gave it impetus through the brilliant example of his own case studies. Inspired by Geertz's intricate account of a Balinese cockfight, historians have attempted to apply his methods of "thick description" to a variety of past episodes, including a particularly messy (and telling) cat massacre in eighteenth-century France.[32]

But of all the modern exemplars of genre mixing, the late Michel Foucault may have had the greatest influence on the new generation of social historians in the 1970s and 1980s. Like the quintessential urban "stranger" described by sociologists, Foucault was at once everywhere and nowhere; an elusive intellectual of vast knowledge, he traveled with ease through the humanities and social sciences, lighting for a brief moment among historians and then migrating toward the world of anthropologists or philosophers. And through his audacious studies of discipline, punishment, madness, and sexuality, he informed and, at times, confused them all. Even his style—lyrical then ruptured, clear then opaque—contributed to the problem of taxonomizing his work. Foucault had something for everyone, and for many historians he had, above all, new insights into the "archaeology of knowledge" and into the "discourse" (a word now firmly entrenched in the modern scholar's lexicon) of authority, conflict, and power.[33]

Drawing on Foucault's highly idiosyncratic accounts of, for example, institutions and sexuality, social historians have reexamined prisons, schools, hospitals, and factories and marriage, divorce, eroticism, and prostitution with a "structuralist" approach. And the results have been wildly uneven; many applications of Foucault's notions have led to accounts as ahistorical and impenetrable as the essays that inspired them, while other studies, by scholars who could sense the theoretical limits and profit from the brilliant insights, were enriched by Foucault's example. Edward Said's important reassessment of "the Orient's special place in European Western experience" (a reminder of those of us who, like Barraclough, use the word "Orient" without recognizing its Eurocentric implications) relies heavily on Foucault's definitions of "discourse." And Peter Brown, in his detailed and erudite history of sexual renunciation in early Christianity, acknowledges his debt to Foucault's work on sexuality and to his "humbling serenity and unaffected craftsmanship."[34] Offering scholars a kit of ideas and topics overflowing with the tools of the social sciences and humanities, Foucault must be numbered among the most fecund contributors to the recent trend toward "genre mixing."

His case is both extreme and typical of the times. Diverse legions of "brickmakers," as Barraclough put it in another context, carrying the implements of many disciplines, have set out to reshape the contours of historical investigation. For some observers, those modern artisans with specialized skills have enriched our understanding of the past, while for others they have shown more interest in the individual "bricks" than in the complete architectural form. History writing in the 1970s and 1980s has been distinguished by its fickle and haphazard relationship with other disciplines, goes this argument, and by its drift away from a "larger pattern"—be it the bold, integrative vision of the early *Annales* school, the sweeping "universal" history so important to Barraclough, or the Marxist and Weberian models that attracted many historians until the day before yesterday. The "creative ferment" that marks the interdisciplinary approach of the historical profession today, says one observer, reflects a "deadness . . . to grand theory."[35]

Surveying the landscape of recent historiography, not a few critics have sighted an epidemic of fragmentation and a modern revival of what Maurice Powicke described as a "pedantic chase after the insignificant."[36] Nearly a century ago, Oscar Wilde, flushed with enthusiasm over the Rational Dress Movement in England, said that the reformation of dress was of greater importance than the Reformation of religion. The comment—only half serious, of course, and, as always with Wilde, designed to shock—foreshadowed the very sober concerns of those social historians who reckon that dress reform is, in fact, as important as religious reform, or that a peasant's view of Czar Nicholas is as significant as the founding of the Duma, or that the household budgets of industrial laborers in nineteenth-century England should be studied with the same attention as that given to Parliamentary debates over Poor Laws and Factory Acts. "When the history of menarche is widely recognized as equal in importance to the history of monarchy," a leading advocate of this approach has written, "we will have arrived."[37] The statement is a dozen years old, but the spirit still infuses much of the current work in social history; and, most recently, it has triggered severe reactions against the trivialization of historical inquiry from a wide cross-section of critics.

Traditional scholars argue that the minutiae of social history have supplanted the broad study of classic texts, and that generations of students well versed in the truffle-hunting details of quotidian life know next to nothing about the grand monuments of high and official culture, about the treatises of Thomas Aquinas or the declarations of Thomas Jefferson. Responding to this worrisome state of affairs, historian Gertrude Himmelfarb has recently warned that the "'total history' that some new historians pride themselves on might turn out to be a total dissolution of history," and she has called for "renewed excitement in the drama of events, the power of ideas, and the dignity of individuals—'not only in things that are trivial,'" she says, quoting Bertrand Russell, "'but in the things that really matter.'"[38] Contemporary social historians have abandoned the timeless moral lessons of the humanities, these critics point out, and they have strayed from the great discoveries of the social sciences, including (and especially) the study of politics. Meanwhile, approaching the same problem on its left flank, a growing contingent of "radical" scholars (the name is their own) have launched an attack on the social historians' perceived willful blindness to political theory and the dynamics of class conflict. "Social history is suffering a severe case of pollution," historian Tony Judt announced in 1979, and his remarks echoed in more moderated form across the 1980s. The study of the past has become a "play-pit for the unattended urchins of other disciplines," according to Judt, a forum for interlopers who have transformed social history into "a sort of retrospective cultural anthropology." Politics have been "reduced to events of marginal significance"; they are "mere footnotes to a serial description of 'long-term social change.'"[39] Unlike critics who champion a return to conventional topics and documents, and to a scholarship unfettered by theoretical models and partisan engagement, "radical" historians aim to "educate those for whom struggle is a determined necessity today with the historical experience of those for whom struggle was a determined necessity yesterday."[40] These scholars, and they range from loyal to agnostic Marxists, insist that the study of women and men responding to the politics and material conditions of the societies in which they live and work must be returned to the center stage of historical investigation. "Class is a relationship, not a thing," the British historian E. P. Thompson wrote twenty-five years ago; it "is defined by men as they live their own history."[41] Contemporary historians are revisiting Thompson's concerns and adding "women" to the equation.

The Radical Historians Organization, founded in the United States in the early 1970s, "grew out of a shared commitment among younger scholars, teachers and students to resist the narrowing of the boundaries of professional history and the separation of the academy from social and political concerns." Through its journal, *Radical History Review,* as well as through *History Workshop: A Journal of Socialist and Feminist Historians* and other publications, the organization and its supporters wish to "develop a critical history that contributes to an understanding of capitalism as a mode of production and as a complex of changing social relations."[42] Following the lead of Eric Hobsbawm, Natalie Zemon Davis, David Montgomery, the late Herbert Gutman, and other scholars, these newly engaged historians, many of them veterans of the social revolutions of the late 1960s, keep a close eye on the political dimensions of their studies while applying anthropological methods of "thick description" to accounts of village festivals, Victorian divorces, working-class sociability, and calypso dances in nineteenth-century Trinidad.[43] In other words, they embrace the trend toward interdisciplinary scholarship, while rejecting the early social historians' tendency to downplay politics and elevate the details of "everyday life" to a level that is often misleading and frequently absurd.

One of the most significant revolutions of the past two decades provides another striking example of the shift away from historiography with no sense of pattern or purpose. Barraclough did not address the subject of women's history, though the "trend" had been firmly set by the mid-1970s, nor did he anticipate the outpouring of scholarship on feminist and gender issues (scholarship written by women and men) that would mark the United Nations Decade for Women and the years beyond. Like radical historians, with whom they are often though not always in agreement, many women's historians share a commitment to effecting social and political change through their scholarly publications. The editors of *Signs,* for example, a leading "journal of women in culture and society" founded in 1975, set out to "question the social, political, economic, cultural and psychological arrangements that have governed relations between females and males." They describe how "many feminists looked lovingly and intensely for parallels between their lives and those of other women. White American feminists attempted to compare themselves with women of color in this country, with women in the past, with women now living in other parts of the world, eager to empathize, to understand and—alas—instruct."[44] And the editors of *Feminist Studies,* a periodical launched in 1980, agreed that their charge is "fundamentally to reshape the way we view the world . . . not just to interpret women's experiences but to change women's conditions." Feminist thought, they say, "represents a transformation of consciousness, social forms, and modes of action."[45]

From Herodotus until the very recent past, women were part of that immense cast of invisible players largely ignored in conventional history writing; half the world's population and the mothers of the other half, they were represented only in the occasional reference to a saint, queen, or odd suffragette. Recently, however, and along with the feminist revolution that inspired it, the field of women's history has been marked by unprecedented growth and by the quest for new methodologies. In 1986, the journal of the *Annales* school, long considered a bastion of male scholarship, devoted an issue to "The History of Women"; and it was not the only mainstream periodical to recognize the importance of feminist studies, albeit *en retard.*[46]

As with other recent trends, the approach is interdisciplinary and the tools and techniques of research are multifaceted. To a great extent, early scholarship focused on women's work and battles for women's suffrage in western Europe and the United States in the nineteenth and twentieth centuries. Louise Tilly, Joan Scott, Brian Harrison, Michelle Perrot, and other historians explored patterns of labor and leisure in, for example, English cottage industries, the patriarchal factory settings of early industrial France, and the workplaces of the two world wars.[47] But across the 1970s and 1980s the horizons of time and space have expanded to include studies of antiquity and the Middle Ages, and accounts of Asian, African, and Latin American women. A recent investigation of feasts, fasts, and the religious significance of food to medieval women offers an ideal example of the imaginative interdisciplinary blend of anthropology, semiotics, church history, and women's history.[48] Comparing and contrasting the separate "spheres" of women and men, historians have reexamined the institution of *purdah* in South Asia and the Middle East, the political involvement of peasant women in Chinese society, and the spaces of domestic work on the farmsteads of the American frontier and in the villages of west and central Africa. In addition to group studies informed by sociology, anthropology, or political theory, the number of scholarly biographies—of Isak Dinesen and Alice James, of the French revolutionary Louise Michel, the German artist Käthe Kollwitz and the Austrian psychoanalyst Anna Freud—has increased dramatically since the 1970s. And there is every indication that the trend will continue over coming decades.[49]

The debates surrounding women's history involve issues of general interest to the broad community of scholars. There are lively differences of opinion, for example, regarding questions of class, race, region, and gender, and the ways in which women in history—slaves and slave owners, factory women and social workers—were divided as well as unified.[50] Like their social history colleagues, women's historians face the challenge to uncover new and diverse "texts" in order to probe events and actors rarely recorded in traditional documentary evidence. They have also learned from the discoveries of social scientists and, most recently, structuralist and poststructuralist literary critics. Semiotics, Foucault's notions of "discourse," and other contemporary trends have attracted historians who now question the usefulness of "binary oppositions"—of male and female spheres—and call for a "new history" in which "gender," rather than "women," could be "developed as a category of analysis." Historian Joan Wallach Scott has emerged as a leading advocate of this new "new history," and if some scholars reject her highly abstract "theoretical formulations," it is significant that Scott's thoughts on the subject enjoyed a prominent place in a recent issue of that resolutely mainstream publication, the *American Historical Review*.[51] Women's history, a topic absent from Barraclough's pages, has joined the ornate and crowded gallery of "main trends" in contemporary historiography.

The gallery glitters with new topics, new methods, and new practitioners; but amidst all the experimentation, the gallery also echoes with the old debate over History as Art and History as Science.[52] Barraclough, always partial to the side of science, had thought that the question had "fallen into oblivion,"[53] but shortly after the publication of his survey, scholars disenchanted with the trend toward analytical, structuralist, and theoretical historiography began to condemn the apotheosis of social science history and lament the rapid demise of traditional storytelling. The most militant keepers of the conventional flame insist that the contemporary smorgasbord of topics and concepts introduces more anarchy than enlightenment, and that the eclecticism which had always been a key ingredient in "the craft notion of historical studies" has given way to a modern Babel of mutually unintelligible disciplines and subdisciplines. Historians who, in the past, had cared about the literary style of their work and about its accessibility to more than a half-dozen experts in arcane fields, have been eclipsed, say these critics, by a new generation which seems to believe that "since history is a science, it needs no art to help it along."[54] The American historian C. Vann Woodward approaches the problem more generously, but he agrees that history, "once called a habitation of many mansions," is now described as "scattered suburbs, trailer camps and a deteriorating central city."[55] While some scholars continue to perfect the specialized and highly analytical skills of the social sciences, others call for a reversal of that trend and a "revival of narrative."[56]

At best, narrative history had come under siege as a superficial way of explaining the past, a telling of tales devoid of theoretical assumptions and an analytical framework; at worst, it was perceived as a mode of historiography dominated either by scholars with a conservative political agenda (those who charted the chronological march of events as a relentless march toward progress) or with a rigidly Marxist approach (those chained to the dialectic of class conflict). The *Annalistes* helped fuel this criticism when they rejected the conventional topics and methods of "event history," especially the old obsession with high and official culture, and more recently, critics interested in poststructuralism and deconstruction have maintained that historical "narrativity" is not only ideologically bound but a way of writing that is itself "imaginary" and fundamentally no different than fiction. No mode of discourse is purely objective, goes this argument, and least of all narrative history, that artificial reconstruction of events connected only in the fertile imagination of the architect.[57]

But if the critics of "narration" are many, varied, and, in the contemporary world of academe, powerful, they have not gone unchallenged in recent years. And, to a great extent, their most eloquent critics have been those scholars who actually write history rather than write about it. The truth is in the telling, say these "narrators" who weave stories with plots, settings, and casts of characters, and who believe that by honoring the evidence and remaining on guard against subjectivity they can reconstruct the past in a way that is meaningful, informative, and intelligible. They do not reject theory or analysis but embed those elements within the description of their story. Prompting the reader's imagination and respecting the reader's intelligence, they insist that carefully fashioned chronological accounts can illuminate both particular and broad-gauged issues of historical inquiry. Jonathan Spence, a leading scholar of Chinese history, has taken the death of a peasant woman and the travels of a hapless Chinese translator, and, through clear, compelling narratives that read like fiction but remain true to fact, he has taught us much about rural customs, cultural stereotypes, and the eighteenth-century peregrinations of European missionaries and their Chinese attendants. In a break with the highly analytical studies which had dominated the historiography of the French Revolution, much of the vast literature which appeared in 1989 to commemorate the Revolution's bicentennial "chronicled" events and told the dramatic stories of victims and victimizers; Simon Schama's *Citizens,* with its revisionist view of the aristocracy, was one of the most controversial contributions and one of the most resolutely "narrative" in its approach. And historian Natalie Zemon Davis integrates in her work the discoveries of symbolic anthropologists and the techniques of traditional storytellers to unravel, with meticulous scholarship and brilliant insight, the many worlds of early modern France.[58]

Davis is a model of the contemporary scholar who remains open to the broad array of new social science techniques and committed to the art of narrative history. Her interest in the "literary construction of the way we write" has been influenced by the narrative qualities of anthropological case studies and by her work as consultant on the 1983 film *The Return of Martin Guerre,* a highly successful motion picture that led to a scholarly book by Davis. Based on sixteenth-century judicial records uncovered in French archives, that story of intrigue and duplicity in a Languedoc village prompted Davis to rethink not only notions of status and gender in a rural community (crucial elements in the drama of Martin Guerre) but the ways in which film may recreate a "true" story and serve as a new mode of historical narration.[59]

In a modern world dominated by visual media (a world some observers have already labelled "postliterate"), increasing numbers of scholars are asking if it is "possible to tell historical stories on film and not lose our professional or intellectual souls."[60] It is a topic thick with problems. An account of the past on film, be it a documentary or a dramatic representation, can evoke the "thoughts, images, textures, [and] styles" of history, says one critic, and it can inform and engage the viewer through its powerful narrative flow.[61] But for many historians, the seduction of film, like the seduction of the novel, is as much a weakness as a strength. The successful filmmaker, like the novelist, concentrates on aesthetic effect and creates a masterful illusion; and the audience, drawn into that process, suspends disbelief. For poststructuralist critics and others who acknowledge little difference between fiction and the "facts" of history, film is a legitimate mode of historical discourse. But for those scholars who reckon that accounts of the past should be scrutinized with care and critical skill, the medium presents more peril than potential. The debate is sure to continue, and it is fitting that an eminent historian of "narratology" and "metahistory" has already coined a new word for the "representation of history and our thought about it in visual images and filmic discourse." The professional practice of historiography has been joined by the postmodern, "postliterate" practice of "historiophoty."[62]

In 1988, the editors of *Annales,* that enormously influential journal launched by Bloch and Febvre more than a half century before, thought it wise to step back and assess the work of contemporary historians world-wide. They noted the rich diversity of recent history writing and the obvious triumph of their founders' belief in the interdisciplinary approach. But they came away from their preliminary survey with a sense of malaise, a belief that a "general crisis" had overtaken the social sciences. And the French were not the only ones to signal a "crisis of legitimacy" in the discipline of history. Marxism, structuralism, quantification, and other historiographical trends and methods no longer inspired scholars, said the editors of *Annales,* and, in a revelation particularly hard for the antagonists of "event history" to swallow, they acknowledged the shift toward more "orderly" narrative histories, toward the study, for example, of politics and biography. The time had come, they said, to chart some new lines of inquiry in this period of "uncertainty," at this "critical turning point" in the historical profession. And, in the spirit of good Gallic researchers, they called for a poll. Scholars responded with interesting ruminations on the methodological problems of interdisciplinary research, but the general lines of inquiry were hardly new and the question of uncertainty remained. In a statement that could have been cribbed from their inaugural volume more than a half-century before (or from the notebooks of Gibbon or Ranke), the editors of *Annales* announced that "History is engaged in a work of redefinition of its projects and its practices."[63]

Geoffrey Barraclough would have been surprised by none of this, and he would have agreed with an anecdote told by his contemporary and coun-tryman, the British prime minister Harold Macmillan. An avid and in-sightful historian throughout his long life, Macmillan was asked if the late twentieth century would be considered a special "time of change." He responded with a story from an old and familiar "narrative history" which applies to historiographical trends as much as to the human condition. In flight from the Garden of Eden and beside himself with anxiety over what the future would hold, Adam turned to Eve for solace, and she told him not to fret. "Relax my dear," she said, taking his hand and leading him into a field of thorns and thistles, "it is simply a time of transition."[64]

Notes

1. The call for a "new history" early in this century is most often associated with James Harvey Robinson; see *The New History: Essays in Illustrating the Modern*

Historical Outlook (New York: Macmillan, 1912). For a recent summary of the question by a distinguished historian with a predilection for traditional history writing, see Gertrude Himmelfarb, *The New History and the Old: Critical Essays and Reappraisals* (Cambridge, Mass.: Harvard University Press, 1987).

2. See above, p. 43.

3. Ibid., p. 89; see also, pp. 58, 84.

4. Peter N. Stearns, "Some Comments on Social History," *Journal of Social History,* vol. 1, 1, 1967, p. 4. Stearns updates his thoughts on the subject in "Toward a Wider Vision: Trends in Social History," in Michael Kammen, ed., *The Past Before Us: Contemporary Historical Writing in the United States* (Ithaca: Cornell University Press, 1980), pp. 205–30.

5. See above, p. 48.

6. Emmanuel Le Roy Ladurie, *Le Territoire de l'historien* (Paris: Gallimard, 1973), p. 14: ("l'historien de demain sera programmeur ou il ne sera plus").

7. Carl Bridenbaugh quoted in J. Morgan Kousser, "Quantitative Social-Scientific History," in Kammen, *Past Before Us,* p. 434. On Dickens and "digit-worshippers," see William W. Watt's introduction to *Hard Times* (New York: Holt, Rinehart and Winston, 1967), p. xviii.

8. See above, p. 212. Jacques Barzun also exposed the problem in *Clio and the Doctors: Psycho-History and Quanto-History* (Chicago: University of Chicago Press, 1974); and Himmelfarb addresses it again in *The New History,* p. 46.

9. Charles Tilly, *As Sociology Meets History* (New York: Academic Press, 1981), p. 55.

10. David Herlihy, "Numerical and Formal Analysis in European History," in *Journal of Interdisciplinary History,* vol. 12, 1, Summer 1981, pp. 115–35.

11. See above, pp. 195–97; see also pp. 84–89.

12. Lawrence Stone, *The Past and the Present* (Boston: Routledge and Kegan Paul, 1981), pp. 28–29 and passim.

13. Keith Thomas, "The Ferment of Fashion," *Times Literary Supplement,* April 30, 1982. For a recent example of the new integration of sophisticated quantitative methods, see Robert Schwartz, *Policing the Poor in Eighteenth-Century France* (Chapel Hill: University of North Carolina Press, 1988).

14. If the use of word processors is on the rise, the historian's use of computers for quantitative analysis seems to have passed its peak: "In general," Theodore Rabb wrote in 1981, "the acceptance of quantification is grudging and limited, and its practitioners remain assured but isolated. The great hopes of the early days of the computer have apparently been disappointed; now there is a more limited role for those who wish to count" (see "Toward the Future," in *Journal of Interdisciplinary History,* vol. 12, 2, Autumn 1981, p. 322). Rabb's essay and others in that issue also appear in Theodore Rabb and Robert I. Rotberg, eds., *The New History: The 1980s and Beyond* (Princeton: Princeton University Press, 1982).

15. William L. Langer, "The Next Assignment," *American Historical Review,* vol. 63, 2, 1958, pp. 283–304.

16. See, for example, John E. Mack, *The Prince of Our Disorder: The Life of T. E. Lawrence* (Boston: Little, Brown, 1976); Peter Loewenberg, "The Unsuccessful Adolescence of Heinrich Himmler," *American Historical Review,* vol. 76, 3, June 1971, pp. 612–41; and Bruce Mazlish, *In Search of Nixon: A Psychohistorical Inquiry* (New York: Basic Books, 1972).

17. Geoffrey Barraclough, "Psycho-history Is Bunk," *Guardian* (Manchester and London), March 3, 1973. See above, pp. 68–71.

18. Peter Gay, *Freud for Historians* (New York: Oxford University Press, 1985), p. x.

19. See above, p. 65.

20. For an example, see Theodore Zeldin, "Personal History and the History of Emotions," *Journal of Social History,* vol. 15, 3, Spring 1982, pp. 339–47.

21. Gay, *Freud for Historians,* p. x; and *The Bourgeois Experience: Victoria to Freud,* vol. 1 (New York: Oxford University Press, 1984), p. 8. See the same author's *Freud: A Life for Our Time* (New York: W.W. Norton, 1988).

22. For more on the subject, see Peter Loewenberg, *Decoding the Past: The Psychohistorical Approach* (New York: Knopf, 1983); Miles Shore, "Biography in the 1980s: A Psychoanalytic Perspective," *Journal of Interdisciplinary History,* vol. 12, 1, Summer 1981, pp. 89–113; and the "special feature" on psychoanalysis and history in *History Workshop,* 26, Autumn 1988, pp. 102–52.

23. Examples of social history, in the broadest sense of the term, appear in nearly every general history periodical; it is also the main fare in an important publication not cited by Barraclough, *Journal of Interdisciplinary History,* founded in 1970.

24. For an introduction to the methods and priorities of the *Annales* school, see Fernand Braudel, *On History,* trans. Sarah Matthews (Chicago: University of Chicago Press, 1980). On the social historian's concern for studies of "everyday activities," see Stearns, "Toward a Wider Vision," p. 205.

25. Examples of regional studies using the "total history" approach include William Cronon, *Changes in the Land: Indians, Colonists and the Ecology of New England* (New York: Hill and Wang, 1984); John Mack Faragher, *Sugar Creek: Life on the Illinois Prairie* (New Haven: Yale University Press, 1986); and the enormously popular and influential book by a member of the *Annales* school, Emmanuel Le Roy Ladurie's *Montaillou, village occitan de 1294 à 1324* (Paris: Gallimard, 1975). The history of European fascism—discussed by Barraclough, but with a focus on traditional political accounts (see above, p. 173)—is also attracting scholars interested in local studies. One of the earliest books, and still one of the most widely read, is William Sheridan Allen's *The Nazi Seizure of Power: The Experience of a Single German Town* (Chicago: Quadrangle Books, 1965); for a more recent example, dealing with Italy, see Alice Kelikian, *Town and Country Under Fascism: The Transformation of Brescia, 1915–1926* (New York: Oxford University Press, 1986). Community study as an "expanding field of inquiry" is discussed by Kathleen Neils Conzen in Kammen, *Past Before Us,* pp. 270–91; and "oral history" is surveyed by Herbert T. Hoover in the same volume, pp. 391–407. On the importance of geography to the historical project, see, for example, Barraclough's *Times Atlas of World History* (Maplewood: Hammond, 1984); and D.W. Meinig, *The Shaping of America: A Geographical Perspective on 500 Years of History, vol. 1: Atlantic America, 1492–1800* (New Haven: Yale University Press, 1986). The factors of time and space are central to the following studies, though in very different ways: Jacques Le Goff, *L'Imaginaire médiéval* (Paris: Gallimard, 1985) and the same author's *Time, Work and Culture in the Middle Ages,* trans. Arthur Goldhammer (Chicago: University of Chicago Press, 1978); Stephen Kern, *The Culture of Time and Space, 1880–1918* (Cambridge, Mass.: Harvard University Press, 1983); and Michelle Perrot, "La Femme dans l'espace parisien du XIXe siècle," *Nouvelles annales de la recherche urbaine* (December 1980). For the application of new and diverse source materials, see, for example, Ira Berlin and Ronald Hoffman, eds., *Slavery and Freedom in the Age of the American Revolution* (Charlottesville: University of Virginia Press, 1983); Barbara Fields, *Slavery and Freedom in the Middle Ground: Maryland in the Nineteenth Century* (New Haven: Yale University Press, 1985); and Eugen Weber, "Fairies and Hard Facts: The Reality of Folktales," *Journal of the History of Ideas,* vol. 42, 1, 1980, pp. 93–113.

26. See above, pp. 106–9.

27. Compare Barraclough's thoughts on African historiography with those of Philip D. Curtin in Kammen, *Past Before Us*, pp. 113–30. For an investigation of African copperworking, material culture, village life, and much more, see Eugenia Herbert, *Red Gold of Africa: Copper in Precolonial History and Culture* (Madison: University of Wisconsin Press, 1984). Barraclough also recognized that the "central problem with the new African historiography is sources" (see above, p. 112), but in the past decade new discoveries have multiplied; see, for example, David Robinson and Douglas Smith, eds., *Sources of the African Past: Case Studies of Five Nineteenth-Century African Societies* (New York: Africana, 1979); and Robert Harms, *Games Against Nature: An Eco-Cultural History of The Nunu of Equatorial Africa* (Cambridge: Cambridge University Press, 1987).

28. Pierre Nora, ed., *Les Lieux de mémoire*, 4 vols. (Paris: Gallimard, 1986); and Alain Corbin, *The Foul and the Fragrant: Odor and the French Social Imagination* (Cambridge, Mass.: Harvard University Press, 1986). Another work which shares these concerns is George Vigarello's *Concepts of Cleanliness: Changing Attitudes in France Since the Middle Ages*, trans. Jean Birrell (New York: Cambridge University Press, 1988). Barraclough describes how Lucien Febvre had insisted that historians must use "all the artifacts of man—language, signs, the evidence of the countryside, field-systems, necklets, bracelets" (see above p. 36), and contemporary scholars have met Febvre's challenge. One book, first published in German in 1939 and recently translated, has served as an important source and model for many social historians; see Norbert Elias, *The Civilizing Process: The History of Manners*, trans. Edmund Jephcott (New York: Urizen Books, 1978).

29. Umberto Eco, *The Name of the Rose*, trans. William Weaver (San Diego: Harcourt Brace Jovanovich, 1980). Eco explains his research and methodology in *Postscript to the Name of the Rose*, trans. William Weaver (San Diego: Harcourt Brace Jovanovich, 1984); and for more on the meeting of semiology and history, see Eco's *Travels in Hyperreality*, trans. William Weaver (San Diego: Harcourt Brace Jovanovich, 1986). Lois Banner discusses signs, symbols and recent history writing in a review essay, "Fashion in History," *Journal of Interdisciplinary History*, vol. 13, 2, Autumn 1982, pp. 311–15. Anthropologist Claude Lévi-Strauss and literary critic Roland Barthes also influenced historians interested in semiotics; for applications of their methods, see Jean Soler, "The Semiotics of Food in the Bible," and Roland Barthes, "Toward a Psychosociology of Contemporary Food Consumption," in Robert Forster and Orest Ranum, eds., *Food and Drink in History: Selections from the Annales: Economies, Sociétés, Civilisations* (Baltimore: Johns Hopkins University Press, 1979), pp. 126–38, 166–73. On historians and other social scientists placing signs in their "natural habitat," see Clifford Geertz, *Local Knowledge: Further Essays in Interpretive Anthropology* (New York: Basic Books, 1983), p. 119.

30. Clifford Geertz, "Blurred Genres: The Refiguration of Social Thought," in *Local Knowledge*, pp. 19–35. (The article was first published in *The American Scholar*, vol. 29, 2, Spring 1980.)

31. See above, p. 51. Barraclough adds, however, that Evans-Pritchard "also asserted the reverse" (see note 209).

32. Among the many anthropological works that have inspired recent historians, see Victor Turner, *From Ritual to Theatre: The Human Seriousness of Play* (New York: Performing Arts Journal Publications, 1982); and Clifford Geertz, *The Interpretation of Cultures* (New York: Basic Books, 1973). Robert Darnton's *The Great Cat Massacre and Other Episodes in French Cultural History* (New York: Basic Books, 1984) owes much to Geertz's notions of "thick description," and it has engendered a lively debate; see the review essays by Dominick La Capra and James Fernandez in *Journal of Modern History*, vol. 60, 1, March 1988, pp. 95–127, and

Darnton's response in his most recent book, *The Kiss of Lamourette: Reflections in Cultural History* (New York: W.W. Norton, 1990). Nor is this approach, in its broad outlines, limited to European topics; see Anand Yang, "A Conversation of Rumors: The Language of Popular *Mentalités* in Late Nineteenth Century Colonial India," *Journal of Social History,* vol. 20, 1986–87, pp. 484–505. On "ethnohistory" in America, for example, see Francis Jennings' influential *The Invasion of America: Indians, Colonialism, and the Cant of Conquest* (Chapel Hill: University of North Carolina Press, 1975); and James Axtell, *The European and the Indian: Essays in the Ethnohistory of Colonial North America* (New York: Oxford University Press, 1981).

33. Historians have been influenced by many of Foucault's works, including *The Archeology of Knowledge,* trans. A. Sheridan Smith (New York: Harper and Row, 1976); *Histoire de la sexualité,* 3 vols. (Paris: Gallimard, 1976–84); *Madness and Civilization: A History of Insanity in the Age of Reason,* trans. Richard Howard (New York: Pantheon, 1965); and *Discipline and Punish: The Birth of the Prison,* trans. Alan Sheridan (New York: Pantheon, 1977). For an intriguing analysis of Foucault's impact on history writing, see Hayden White, *The Content of Form: Narrative Discourse and Historical Representation* (Baltimore: Johns Hopkins University Press, 1987), pp. 105–41. See also Michel de Certéau, *The Writing of History,* trans. Tom Conley (New York: Columbia University Press, 1988).

34. Peter Brown, *The Body and Society: Men, Women and Sexual Renunciation in Early Christianity* (New York: Columbia University Press, 1988), see especially pp. xvii–xviii; and Edward W. Said, *Orientalism* (New York: Pantheon, 1978). For Barraclough on "Orientalism," see above, p. 96.

35. See John Higham's comments in the *American Historical Review,* vol. 86, 1981, p. 808. Barraclough also understood the importance of the "larger pattern" (see above, p. 148).

36. Powicke quoted above, p. 8.

37. Peter N. Stearns, "Coming of Age," *Journal of Social History,* vol. 10, 2, 1976, p. 250.

38. Himmelfarb, *The New History,* pp. 8–12. The debate over academe's abandonment of the classic texts of Western civilization became especially heated in the late 1980s with the publication of Allan Bloom's popular and provocative *The Closing of the American Mind: How Higher Education has Failed Democracy and Impoverished the Souls of Today's Students* (New York: Simon and Schuster, 1987).

39. Tony Judt, "A Clown in Regal Purple: Social History and the Historians," *History Workshop: A Journal of Socialist Historians,* 7, Spring 1979, pp. 66–94. Lawrence Stone had anticipated the conflict: "The 'new historians' of the 1950s and 1960s," Stone wrote in 1979, "will undoubtedly be severely criticized for their obsession with social, economic and demographic forces in history, and their failure to take sufficient account of political organization and decision-making" (*The Past and the Present,* p. 81). For another critique of social history, see Elizabeth Fox-Genovese and Eugene D. Genovese, "The Political Crisis of Social History: A Marxian Perspective," *Journal of Social History,* vol. 10, 2, Winter 1976, pp. 205–20.

40. Harvey J. Kaye, *The British Marxist Historians* (Cambridge. Polity Press, 1984), pp. 248–49. Himmelfarb also discusses these trends in *The New History,* pp. 70–93.

41. E. P. Thompson, *The Making of the English Working Class* (New York: Vintage, 1966 [first ed., 1963]), p. 11. For a work which calls on the recent discoveries of the social sciences without ignoring the centrality of politics and class

conflict, see Gareth Stedman Jones, *Languages of Class: Studies in English Working Class History* (Cambridge: Cambridge University Press, 1984).

42. MARHO (The Radical Historians Organization), *Visions of History* (New York: Pantheon, 1983, p. 324. This book contains a series of informative interviews with "the pioneering radical historians of our time."

43. For these and other examples of current work by "radical" historians, see issues of *Radical History Review* and *History Workshop*.

44. *Signs: Journal of Women in Culture and Society*, vol. 8, 2, Winter 1982, p. 193; see also vol. 1, 1, Autumn 1975, p. v. It is interesting to note that *History Workshop* expanded its subtitle in the 1980s, from "a journal of socialist historians" to "a journal of socialist and feminist historians."

45. *Feminist Studies*, founded in 1972, includes this statement at the beginning of each issue.

46. *Annales: Economies, Sociétés, Civilisations*, 431, 2, 1986, pp. 271–323.

47. On work, suffrage, and more, see, for example, Louise Tilly and Joan Scott, *Women, Work and Family* (New York: Holt, Rinehart and Winston, 1978); Brian Harrison, *Separate Spheres: The Opposition to Women's Suffrage* (New York: Holmes and Meier, 1978); and Michelle Perrot, *Une Histoire des femmes: Est-il possible?* (Paris: Rivages, 1984). See also Judith Bennet's review essay, "'History That Stands Still': Women's Work in the European Past," *Feminist Studies*, vol. 14, 2, Summer 1988, pp. 269–83; and Mary Drake McFeely, *Women's Work in Britain and America: From the Nineties to World War I* (Boston: G. K. Hall, 1982).

48. Caroline Walker Bynum, *Holy Feast and Holy Fast: The Religious Significance of Food to Medieval Women* (Berkeley: University of California Press, 1987).

49. See the review essays on "Recent Work in Women's History: East and West," in *Trends in History*, vol. 4, 1, Fall 1985. Examples of biographies and edited memoirs include Judith Thurman, *Isak Dinesen: The Life of a Storyteller* (New York: St. Martin's Press, 1982); Jean Strouse, *Alice James: A Biography* (Boston: Houghton Mifflin, 1980); Bullit Lowry and Elizabeth E. Gunter, eds., *The Red Virgin: Memoirs of Louise Michel* (University, Ala.: University of Alabama Press, 1981); Martha Kearns, *Käthe Kollwitz: Woman and Artist* (Old Westbury: Feminist Press, 1976); and Elizabeth Young-Bruehl, *Anna Freud: A Biography* (New York: Summit, 1988). See also Carolyn G. Heilbrun, "Discovering the Lost Lives of Women," *New York Times Book Review*, June 24, 1984.

50. Elizabeth Fox-Genovese explores many of these questions in *Within the Plantation Household: Black and White Women of the Old South* (Chapel Hill: University of North Carolina Press, 1988).

51. Joan Wallach Scott, "Deconstructing Equality-Versus-Difference: Or, the Uses of Poststructuralist Theory for Feminism," *Feminist Studies*, vol. 14, 1, Spring 1988, pp. 33–50; and the same author's "Gender: A Useful Category of Historical Analysis," *American Historical Review*, vol. 91, 5, December 1986, pp. 1053–75. Scott has continued this line of analysis in *Gender and The Politics of History* (New York: Columbia University Press, 1988). See also Natalie Zemon Davis, "Gender and Genre: Women as Historical Writers, 1400–1820," in Patricia H. Labalme, ed., *Beyond Their Sex: Learned Women of the European Past* (New York: New York University Press, 1980). For other examples of the history of gender, see Margaret R. Higonnet, et al., eds., *Behind the Lines: Gender and the Two World Wars* (New Haven: Yale University Press, 1987); Linda J. Nicholson, *Gender and History: The Limits of Social Theory in the Age of the Family* (New York: Columbia University Press, 1986): Irene Silverblatt, *Moon, Sun and Witches: Gender Ideologies and Class in Inca and Colonial Peru* (Princeton: Princeton University Press, 1987);

Renate Bridenthal, et al., eds., *Becoming Visible: Women in European History* (Boston: Houghton Mifflin, 1987; first ed., 1977); and for a study which blends women's history, ethnography, and other contemporary trends, see Sylvia Van Kirk, *Many Tender Ties: Women in Fur-Trade Society, 1670–1870* (Winnepeg. Watson and Dwyer, 1980).

52. H. Stuart Hughes explored this debate more than twenty-five years ago in *History as Art and as Science: Twin Vistas of the Past* (New York: Harper and Row, 1964); and Lytton Strachey had opinions about it long before: "That the question has ever been, not only asked, but seriously debated, whether History was an art, is certainly one of the curiosities of human inaptitude. What else can it possibly be?" (Strachey quoted in André Maurois, *Aspects of Biography*, trans. S. Roberts [New York: D. Appleton, 1929]).

53. See above, p. 41.

54. Stone, *The Past and the Present*, p. 75. On the "craft notion" of history, see White, *Content of Form*, p. 31.

55. C. Vann Woodward, "A Short History of American History," *New York Times Book Review*, August 8, 1982.

56. Lawrence Stone has been the standard bearer of this revival, but see also Philip Abrams, "History, Sociology, Historical Sociology," *Past and Present*, 87, May 1980, pp. 3–16; James West Davidson, "The New Narrative History: How New? How Narrative?," *Reviews in American History*, vol. 12, 3, September 1984, pp. 322–33; Rabb, "Toward the Future," pp. 315–32; and Himmelfarb's comments in *The New History*, pp. 95–97 and passim.

57. See White, *Content of Form*, pp. 1–57 and passim. For another summary of the debate, by an advocate of the narrative approach, see William S. McFeely, "A Voice for History," an address to the *American Historical Association* Annual Meeting, December 1983.

58. Jonathan Spence, *The Death of Woman Wang* (New York: Viking Press, 1978), and *The Question of Hu* (New York: Knopf, 1988); Simon Schama, *Citizens: A Chronicle of the French Revolution* (New York: Knopf, 1989); Natalie Zemon Davis, *Society and Culture in Early Modern France* (Stanford: Stanford University Press, 1975), and *The Return of Martin Guerre: Imposture and Identity in a Sixteenth-Century Village* (Cambridge, Mass.: Harvard University Press, 1983).

59. See the interview with Davis quoted in Frederika Randall, "Why Scholars Become Storytellers," *New York Times Book Review*, January 29, 1984; and Natalie Zemon Davis, "'Any Resemblance to Persons Living or Dead': Film and the Challenge of Authenticity," *Yale Review*, 76, 1987, pp. 457–82. On the impact of anthropology, Carlo Ginzberg, historian of early modern Italy, agrees that "the revival of narrative . . . has been deeply influenced by the practice of case studies among anthropologists" ("Anthropology and History in the 1980s," *Journal of Interdisciplinary History*, vol. 12, 2, Autumn 1981, pp. 277–78). See also Ginzburg's influential book *The Cheese and the Worms: The Cosmos of a Sixteenth-Century Miller*, trans. John and Anne Tedeschi (Baltimore: Johns Hopkins University Press, 1980).

60. Robert A. Rosenstone, "History in Images/History in Words: Reflections on the Possibility of Really Putting History onto Film," *American Historical Review*, vol. 93, 5, December 1988, p. 1175. This number of the *AHR* was devoted to a "forum" on history and film, and the quotes cited below are all from that issue.

61. David Herlihy, "Am I a Camera?: Other Reflections on Films and History," pp. 1186–92.

62. Hayden White, "Historiography and Historiophoty," pp. 1193–99. See also the essays by John E. O'Conner and Robert Brent Toplin in the same issue. For

more on film and history, see Pierre Sorlin, *The Film in History: Restaging the Past* (Totowa: Barnes and Noble Books, 1980); Barbara Abrash and Janet Sternberg, eds., *Historians and Filmmakers; Toward Collaboration* (New York: Institute for Research in History, 1983); Daniel J. Czitrom, *Media and the American Mind: From Morse to McLuhan* (Chapel Hill: University of North Carolina Press, 1982); and on the depiction of women, see Teresa de Lauretis, *Alice Doesn't: Feminism, Semiotics, Cinema* (Bloomington: Indiana University Press, 1984).

63. "Histoire et sciences sociales: Un tournant critique?," *Annales: Economies, Sociétés, Civilisations,* 43, 2, 1988, pp. 291–93; and 44, 6, 1989, pp. 1317–1323 and passim. Another critic puts it this way: "it can be clearly observed that Euro-American intellectuals—anthropologists and historians alike—live in a postmodern period in which there is a 'crisis of legitimacy' concerning their enterprises. In part this crisis is provoked simply by a felt inadequacy of method. But it is also provoked by the 'incredulity toward grand narratives'" (see James Fernandez in *Journal of Modern History,* vol. 60, 1, March 1988, p. 125).

64. Harold Macmillan lecture, Yale University, 1978. Barraclough began this study of history's main trends with a disclaimer that still applies at the dawn of the 1990s: "Much historical work—perhaps as much as nine-tenths of the total output—is entirely conventional in approach, and while often adding considerably to knowledge, does not (and is not intended to) suggest new directions or methods" (see above, p. 1, note 1). For all those historians concerned with the recent discoveries of symbolic anthropologists, semiologists, deconstructionists, and feminist critics, there remain vast numbers who research and write in ways that, for want of a better word, can only be called "conventional." National political surveys, biographies, religious histories, military and diplomatic studies, and other "traditional" accounts still dominate the discipline. The historian's vision has expanded into remote regions previously ignored (or misunderstood), and even the most resolutely conventional scholars feel obliged to recognize the roles played by, say, the colonized as well as the colonizers, and by women as well as by men. But the way in which historians go about their work has changed for only a few, and much of the doomsaying that surrounds contemporary historiography (its allegedly flagrant abandonment of the great events and great texts of the past) has not a little in common with that celebrated report of Mark Twain's death. Perhaps historian Theodore Rabb put it best (see "Toward the Future," p. 332): "Since the house has long had many mansions without ill effects," writes Rabb, "we can assert with Donne that history still 'makes a little room an everywhere.'"

List of Works Cited

ABRAMS, Philip. 'History, sociology, historical sociology.' *Past and Present,* Vol. LXXXVII, May 1980, pp. 3–16.

ABRASH, Barbara and STERNBERG, Janet (eds.). *Historians and Filmmakers: Toward Collaboration.* New York, Institute for Research in History, 1983.

ACKERMAN, Nathan W. & JAHODA, Marie. *Anti-Semitism and Emotional Disorder: A Psychoanalytic Interpretation.* American Jewish Committee Social Studies Ser. No. 5. New York, Harper, 1950.

ACTON, Lord. 'Inaugural lecture on the study of history.' Reprinted in ACTON, *Lectures on Modern History, op. cit.* (1906).

———. 'Letter to contributors to the Cambridge Modern History.' Reprinted in ACTON, *Lectures on Modern History, op. cit.* (1906).

———. *Lectures on Modern History,* London, 1906.

———. *The Cambridge Modern History: Its Origin, Authorship and Production.* Cambridge, 1907.

ACTON, Lord (ed.). *The Cambridge Modern History.* Cambridge, Cambridge University Press, 1902–12.

ADORNO, Theodor W. *et al. The Authoritarian Personality: Studies in Prejudice.* American Jewish Committee Social Studies Ser. No. 3. New York, Harper, 1950.

African Perspectives (1970): see ALLEN & JOHNSON (eds.).

AGUET, Jean-Pierre. 'De quelques "grands ensembles" historiques récents: essai d'analyse historiographique.' *Cahiers d'Histoire mondiale / Journal of World History / Cuadernos de Historia Mundial* VIII (3), 1964, pp. 395–425.

ALAVI, H. 'Peasants and revolution.' *The Socialist Register, 1965,* London, 1965, pp. 241–277.

ALBERTINI, Rudolf von. *Das Ende des Kolonialismus.* Cologne, 1970.

ALLARDYCE, Gilbert (ed.). *The Place of Fascism in European History.* Englewood Cliffs (N.J.), Prentice-Hall, 1971.

ALLCHIN, Bridget & ALLCHIN, Raymond. *The Birth of Indian Civilization: India and Pakistan before Five Hundred B.C.* Harmondsworth (Middx.), Penguin Books, 1968.

ALLEN, Christopher & JOHNSON, R. W. (eds.). *African Perspectives.* Cambridge, Cambridge University Press, 1970.

ALLEN, William Sheridan. *The Nazi Seizure of Power: The Experience of a Single German Town.* Chicago, Quadrangle Books, 1965.

AL'PEROVIČ, M. S. *Sovetskaja istoriografia stran latinskoj Ameriki* (= Soviet Historiography of the Countries of Latin America). Moscow, 1968.

The American Archivist (The Society of American Archivists), founded in 1938; quarterly; ed. Edward WELDON: Washington (D.C.), The Society of American Archivists, The National Archives.

American History and the Social Sciences (1964): see SAVETH (ed.).

American Historical Review

The American Scholar

ANDERLE, Othmar F. 'Theoretische Geschichte: Betrachtungen zur Grundlagenkrise der Geschichtswissenschaft.' *Historische Zeitschrift* CLX-XXV (1), Feb. 1958, pp. 1–54.

——. 'Die Toynbee-Kritik.' *Saeculum,* Vol. IX, 1958, pp. 189–259.

ANDERLE, Othmar F. (ed.). 'Problems of Civilization (Report of the Synopsis Conference of the S.I.E.C.C., Salzburg, 8–15 Oct. 1961), with a preface by Pitirim A. SOROKIN. Publications of the International Society for the Comparative Study of Civilizations, Colloques, No. 1. The Hague, Mouton, 1964.

ANDICS, E.: see *Etudes des délégués hongrois au Xe Congrès international des Sciences historiques,* Rome, 1965.

ANDREANO, Ralph L. (ed.). *The New Economic History: Recent Papers in Methodology.* New York, Wiley, 1970.

Annales: Economies, Sociétés, Civilisations, founded in 1929 by Lucien FEBVRE & Marc BLOCH: quarterly 1929–59; bi-monthly since 1960; Comité de Direction: Fernand BRAUDEL, Marc FERRO, Georges FRIEDMANN, Jacques LE GOFF, Emmanuel LE ROY LADURIE, Charles MORAZÉ; Secrétaire de la Rédaction: André BURGIÈRE; Paris, Armand Colin.

ANTONI, Carlo. *Dallo storicismo alla sociologia.* Florence, Sansoni, 1940; new edn., 1951.

Approaches to Asian Civilizations (1961): see DE BARY & EMBREE (eds.).

Approaches to History (1962): see FINBERG (ed.).

Archeion, founded in 1927; publication resumed in 1948; 2/3 issues a year (summaries in English and Russian), Warsaw, Main Direction of State Archives.

Archivalische Zeitschrift (Bayrisches Hauptstaatsarchiv), ed. Otto SCHOTTENLOHER; reached Vol. 66 in 1970, Cologne-Nippes Boehlau Verlag.

Archives (British Records Association), founded in 1949; ed. A. E. B. OWEN; London, British Records Association.

Archivi (Archivi d'Italia & Rassegna internazionale degli Archivi), founded in 1956; quarterly; Rome.

Archivmitteilungen: Zeitschrift für Theorie und Praxis des Archivwesens, founded in 1951; bi-monthly; ed. Staatliche Archivverwaltung der DDR; Berlin (East), Staatsverlag der DDR.

Archivum: Revue internationale des Archives (published under the auspices of Unesco and the International Council of Archives); yearly; ed. Pierre MAROT: Paris, Presses Universitaires de France.

ARCIHOVSKIJ, A. V. (ed.). *Očerki po istorii sovetskoj nauki i kul'tury* (= Essays on the History of Soviet Science and Culture). Moscow, 1968.

ARENDT, Hannah. *The Origins of Totalitarianism.* New York, Harcourt, Brace & World, 1951, 3 vols. (French translation of 3rd part by Jean-Loup Bourget, Robert Davreu & Patrick Lévy, *Le système totalitaire,* Paris, Seuil, 1972; French translation of 1st part by Micheline Pouteau, *Sur l'antisémitisme,* Paris, Calmann-Lévy, 1973).

Arhivi Ukraini, bi-monthly; devoted to archives historical research work; Kiev.

ARIÈS, Philippe. *L'enfant et la vie familiale sous l'Ancien Régime.* 'Civilisations d'hier et d'aujourd'hui' ser. Paris, Plon, 1960 (English translation by Robert Baldick, *Centuries of Childhood: A Social History of Family Life,* London, Jonathan Cape/New York, Knopf, 1962).

——. 'La mort inversée: Le changement des attitudes devant la mort dans les sociétés occidentales.' *Archives européennes de Sociologie/European Journal of Sociology,* Vol. VIII, 1967, pp. 169–195.

ARON, Raymond. *Introduction à la philosophie de l'histoire: essai sur les limites de l'objectivité historique.* 'Bibliothèque des Idées.' Paris, Gallimard, 1938; rev. edn., 1948 (English translation by G. J. Irwin, *Introduction to the Philosophy of History: An Essay on the Limits of Historical Objectivity,* London, Weidenfeld/Boston, Beacon Press, 1961).

ARUTJUNJAN, I. V. *Mehanizatory sel'skogo hozjaistva SSSR v 1929–1957 gg.* (= The Agents of the Mechanization of Agriculture in the USSR from 1929 to 1957). Moscow, 1960.

AYDELOTTE, William O. 'Geschichte und Sozialwissenschaften.' *Die Welt als Geschichte,* Vol. XIV, 1954, pp. 212 sqq.

———. 'Quantification in history.' *American Historical Review,* Vol. LXXI, 1966, pp. 803–825; reprinted in ROWNEY & GRAHAM (eds.), *Quantitative History, op. cit.* (1969), pp. 3–22.

BAGBY, Philip. *Culture and History: Prolegomena to the Comparative Study of Civilizations.* London, Longmans, 1958.

BALAZS, Étienne. 'L'histoire comme guide de la pratique bureaucratique.' In *Historical Writing on the Peoples of Asia, op. cit.,* Vol. III (1961), pp. 78–94.

BALLARD, Martin (ed.). *New Movements in the Study and Teaching of History.* London, Maurice Temple Smith/Bloomington, Indiana University Press, 1970.

BANNER, Lois. 'Fashion in history.' *Journal of Interdisciplinary History,* Vol. XII (2), Autumn 1982, pp. 311–315.

BARG, M. A. 'Strukturnyj analiz v istoričeskom issledovanii' (= Structural analysis in historical research). *Voprosy filosofii,* 1964, No. 4.

———. *O nekotoryh predposylkah formalizacii istoričeskogo issledovanija* (= Premises for the Formalizations of Historical Research). Kazan, 1967.

BARKER, Sir Ernest. 'History and philosophy' (the substance of an address delivered during the Annual Meeting of the Historical Association of Great Britain, January 1922, at King's College, London). *History* VII (2), July 1922, pp. 81–91.

BARKER, Theodore C. *Business History.* London, The Historical Association, 1960.

BARLOW, George & HARRISON, Brian (eds.). *History at the Universities: A Comparative and Analytical Guide to Historical Syllabuses at Universities in the United Kingdom.* London, The Historical Association, 1966; 3rd edn., 1971.

BARRACLOUGH, Geoffrey. *Papal Provisions: Aspects of Church History, Constitutional, Legal and Administrative in the Later Middle Ages.* Oxford, Basil Blackwell, 1935.

———. *The Origins of Modern Germany.* Oxford, Basil Blackwell, 1946.

———. 'Briefe aus dem Reiche und andere Mitteilungen aus englischen Landesarchiven.' In *Festschrift zum 200-jährigen Bestand des Haus-Hof- und Staatsarchives.* Vienna, 1949, Vol. I, pp. 392–405.

———. 'Village Hampdens.' *The Listener,* 10 Mar. 1949, pp. 395–396.

———. *The Medieval Empire: Idea and Reality.* London, Published for the Historical Association by G. Phillip, 1950.

———. 'The historian and his archives.' *History Today* IV (6), June 1954, pp. 412–420.

———. *History in a Changing World.* Oxford, Blackwell, 1955.

———. 'The larger view of history.' *Times Literary Supplement,* 6 Jan. 1956 (special issue devoted to *Historical Writing*).

———. 'The prospects of the western world.' In Ashley MONTAGU (ed.), *Toynbee and History, op. cit.* (1956), pp. 118–121.

———. 'Scientific method and the work of the historian.' In E. NAGEL, P. SUPPES &

A. TARSKI (eds.), *Logic, Methodology and Philosophy of Science, Proceedings of the 1960 International Congress*. Stanford (Calif.), Stanford University Press, 1962, pp. 584–594.

―――. 'Universal history.' In FINBERG (ed.), *Approaches to History, op. cit.* (1962), pp. 83–109.

―――. *An Introduction to Contemporary History*. London, Watts, 1964; 2nd edn., 1967 (French translation by Anne Laurens, *Une introduction à l'histoire contemporaine*, Paris, Seuil, 1967).

―――. *History and the Common Man* (Presidential Address, Diamond Jubilee Conference, London, 12–16 Apr. 1966). London, The Historical Association, 1967.

―――. Review of Robert A. KANN's *The Problem of Restoration: A Study in Comparative Political History* (Berkeley, University of California Press, 1968). *Political Science Quarterly* LXXXVI (1), Mar. 1971, pp. 154–155. [See also *sub* LANGWELL.]

―――. 'Psycho-history is bunk.' *Guardian* (London and Manchester), 3 March 1973.

―――. *From Agadir to Armageddon: Anatomy of a Crisis*. New York, Holmes and Meier, 1982.

―――. *The Times Atlas of World History*. Maplewood, Hammond, 1984.

BARY, William Theodore de: see DE BARY, William Theodore.

BARZUN, Jacques. *Clio and the Doctors: Psycho-History and Quanto-History*. Chicago, University of Chicago Press, 1974.

BASHAM, A. L. 'Modern historians of ancient India.' In *Historical Writing on the Peoples of Asia, op. cit.*, Vol. I (1961), pp. 260–293.

BASTIDE, Roger. 'Colloque sur le mot "structure."' *Annales: Economies, Sociétés, Civilisations* XIV (2), Apr.–June 1959, pp. 351–353.

BAXTER, T. W. *Archival Facilities in Sub-Saharan Africa*. Hertford, 1959.

BEASELY, William G. & PULLEYBLANK, E. G. (eds.). *Historians of China and Japan* = Vol. III of *Historical Writing on the Peoples of Asia, op. cit.* (1961).

BÉDARIDA, François. 'L'historien et l'ambition de totalité.' In *L'Histoire et l'historien, op. cit.* (1964), pp. 178–186.

BEER, Sir Gavin De. *Alps and Elephants: Hannibal's March*. London, Geoffrey Bles, 1955.

BEHRENS, Betty. '"Straight history" and "history in depth": the experience of writers on eighteenth-century France.' *Historical Journal* VIII (1), 1965, pp. 117–126.

BELOV, G. A. 'The organization of the archive system in the USSR.' *Archives* (1963–64), VI (32), Oct. 1964, pp. 211–222.

BENDA, H. J. 'The structure of Southeast Asian history.' *Journal of Southeast Asian History* III (1), 1962, pp. 106–138.

BENNET, Judith. '"History that stands still": women's work in the European past.' *Feminist Studies*, Vol. XIV (2), Summer 1988, pp. 269–283.

BENSON, Lee. 'Research problems in American political historiography.' In KOMAROVSKY (ed.), *Common Frontiers of the Social Sciences, op. cit.* (1957), pp. 113–183.

―――. *The Concept of Jacksonian Democracy: New York as a Test Case*. Princeton (N.J.), Princeton University Press, 1961.

―――. 'A tentative classification for American voting behavior' (an excerpt from BENSON's *The Concept of Jacksonian Democracy, op. cit.*, 1961), in CAHNMAN & BOSKOFF (eds.), *Sociology and History: Theory and Research, op. cit.* (1964), pp. 415–421.

————. 'An approach to the scientific study of past public opinion.' In ROWNEY & GRAHAM (eds.), *Quantitative History, op. cit.* (1969), pp. 23–63.

————. *Toward the Scientific Study of History* (selected essays). Philadelphia, Lippincott, 1971.

BERESFORD, Maurice W. & St. JOSEPH, J. K. S. *Medieval England: An Aerial Survey.* 'Cambridge Air Surveys,' Vol. 2. Cambridge, Cambridge University Press, 1958.

BERG, C. C. 'The Javanese picture of the past.' in SOEDJATMOKO (ed.), *An Introduction to Indonesian Historiography, op. cit.* (1965), pp. 87–117.

BERGÈRE, Marie-Claire. 'La Révolution de 1911 jugée par les historiens de la République populaire de Chine: thèmes et controverses.' *Revue historique* CCXXX/2 (468), Oct.–Dec. 1963, pp. 403–436.

BERGUES, Hélène *et al. La prévention des naissances dans la famille: Ses origines dans les temps modernes.* Institut National d'Etudes Démographiques, Travaux et documents, Cahier No. 35, Paris, Presses Universitaires de France, 1960.

BERLIN, Ira and HOFFMAN, Ronald (eds.). *Slavery and Freedom in the Age of the American Revolution.* Charlottesville, University of Virginia Press, 1983.

BERLIN, Sir Isaiah. *Historical Inevitability.* London, Oxford University Press, 1954.

BERNHEIM, E. *Lehrbuch der historischen Methode.* Leipzig, 1889.

BERR, Henri. 'Sur notre programme.' *Revue de synthèse historique,* No. 1, July to Dec. 1900, pp. 1–8 (English translation by Deborah H. Roberts, 'About our program,' in STERN [ed.], *The Varieties of History, op. cit.* [1956], pp. 250–255).

————. *La synthèse en histoire: Son rapport avec la synthèse générale.* Paris 1911; new edn., Paris, Albin Michel, 1953.

————. *L'histoire traditionnelle et la synthèse historique.* Paris, Alcan, 1935.

————. 'Les étapes de ma propre route depuis 1900.' *Revue de synthèse,* Vol. LXVII, 1950, pp. 5–68.

BERTALANFFY, Ludwig von. *General Systems.* Vol. VII. Ann Arbor (Mich.), Society for General System Research, 1962.

BESANÇON, Alain. 'Histoire et psychanalyse.' *Annales* XIX (2), Mar.–Apr. 1964, pp. 237–249.

————. 'Psychoanalysis: auxiliary science or historical method?' *Journal of Contemporary History* III (2), Apr. 1968 (special issue: *Reappraisals*), pp. 149–162.

————. 'Vers une histoire psychanalytique.' *Annales* (1969), XXIV (3), May–June, pp. 594–616 and (4), July–Aug., pp. 1011–1033.

BESTERMAN, Theodore (ed.). *A World Bibliography of Bibliographies,* 4th edn. Totowa (N.J.), Rowman & Littlefield, 1965–66, 5 vols.

The Bibliographic Index: A Cumulative Bibliography of Bibliographies, 11th vol., New York, H. W. Wilson, 1971.

BLACK, Cyrill E. (ed.). *Rewriting Russian History: Soviet Interpretations of Russia's Past.* New York, Praeger, 1956.

BLAKE, J. W. 'The study of African history.' *Transactions of the Royal Historical Society,* 4th ser., vol. XXXII, 1950, pp. 49–69.

BLOCH, Marc. *Les rois thaumaturges: Etude sur le caractère surnaturel attribué à la puissance royale, particulièrement en France et en Angleterre.* Bibliothèque de la Faculté des Lettres de l'Université de Strasbourg, No. XIX, Strasbourg, 1924.

————. 'Pour une histoire comparée des sociétés européennes.' *Revue de synthèse historique* XLVI (28–29), 1928, pp. 15–50.

————. *Les caractères originaux de l'histoire rurale française* (Oslo, 1931); new edn. with a 2nd volume *(Supplément établi d'après les travaux de l'auteur)* written by Robert Dauvergne, 'Economies, Sociétés, Civilisations' ser., Paris, Armand Colin, 1952 (English translation by Janet Sondheimer, *French Rural History: An Essay on Its Basic Characteristics.* Foreword by Bruce Lyon. London, Routledge/Berkeley, University of California, 1966).

——. *La société féodale.* 'L'évolution de l'humanité' ser. Vols. XXXIV–XXXIV bis. Paris, Albin Michel, 1939–40. 2 vols.: Vol. I: *La formation des liens de dépendance;* Vol. II: *Les classes et la gouvernement des hommes;* new edn. in 1 vol., *ibid.,* 1968 (English translations by L. A. Manyon, *Feudal Society.* London, Routledge, 1965).

——. *Apologie pour l'histoire, ou Métier d'historien* (posthumous publ.). Paris, Armand Colin, 1949 (English translation by Peter Putnam, with an Introduction by Joseph R. Strayer, *Historian's Craft.* New York, Knopf/Manchester, Manchester University Press, 1954).

——. *L'Etrange défaite: témoignage écrit en 1940.* Paris, A. Michel, 1957.

BLOOM, Allan. *The Closing of the American Mind: How Higher Education Has Failed Democracy and Impoverished the Souls of Today's Students.* New York, Simon and Schuster, 1987.

BOBRINSKA, C. *Historyk, Fakt, Metoda.* Warsaw, 1964.

BOGUE, A. G. 'United States: The new political history.' *Journal of Contemporary History* III (1), 1968, pp. 5–27.

BÖHME, Helmut. *Deutschlands Weg zur Grossmacht: Studien zum Verhältnis von Wirtschaft und Staat während der Reichsgründungzeit.* Cologne-Berlin, Kiepenheuer & Witsch, 1966.

BOOTH, Charles. *Life and Labour of the People in London.* 3rd edn. London, 1902–03.

BORAH, Woodrow W. & COOK, S. F. *The Population of Central Mexico in 1548.* Berkeley, University of California Press, 1960.

——. *The Aboriginal Population of Central Mexico on the Eve of the Spanish Conquest.* Berkeley, University of California Press, 1963.

——. *Essays in Population History.* Vol. I. Berkeley, University of California Press, 1971.

BORN, K. E. 'Neue Wege der Wirtschafts- und Sozialgeschichte in Frankreich.' *Saeculum,* Vol. XV, 1964, pp. 298–309.

BOSKOFF, Alvin. 'Recent theories of social change.' In CAHNMAN and BOSKOFF (eds.), *Sociology and History: Theory and Research, op. cit.* (1964), pp. 140–157.

BOSL, K. 'Geschichte und Soziologie.' In Kunigunde SENNINGER (ed.), *Der Mensch in Staat und Gesellschaft.* Munich, Bayer, 1956, pp. 25–46.

——. 'Der "soziologische Aspekt" in der Geschichte: Wertfreie Geschichtswissenschaft und Idealtyp.' *Historische Zeitschrift,* Vol. CCI, 1965, pp. 613–630.

BOUTRUCHE, Robert & LEMERLE, Paul (eds.). *La Nouvelle Clio.* Series. Paris, Presses Universitaires de France.

BOWLE, J. (ed.). *The Concise Encyclopaedia of World History.* London, Hutchinson, 1958.

BOWSER, F. P. 'The African in colonial Spanish America.' *Latin American Research Review,* Vol. VII, 1972, pp. 77–94.

BRANDS, M. C. *Historisme als Ideologie.* Assen, 1965.

BRAUDEL, Fernand. *La Méditerranée et le monde méditerranéen à l'époque de Philippe II.* Paris, Armand Colin, 1949; 2nd edn., rev. and augm., *ibid.,* 1966, 2 vols. (English translation by Sian Reynolds, *The Mediterranean and the Medi-*

terranean World in the Age of Philip II, Vol. I. New York, Harper & Row, 1972; Vol. II, 1974).

———. 'Pour une économie historique.' *Revue économique* 85, May 1950, pp. 37–44; reproduced in BRAUDEL, *Ecrits sur l'histoire, op. cit.* (1969), pp. 123–133.

———. 'Positions de l'histoire en 1950' (Leçon inaugurale, Collège de France, 1 Dec. 1950). In BRAUDEL, *Ecrits sur l'histoire, op. cit.* (1969), pp. 15–38.

———. 'Histoire et sociologie = Chap. IV of the Introduction to Georges GURVITCH (ed.), *Traité de sociologie*, Paris, Presses Universitaires de France, 1958–60, 2 vols.; reprinted in BRAUDEL, *Ecrits sur l'histoire, op. cit.* (1969), pp. 97–122.

———. 'La longue durée.' *Annales* XIII (4), Oct.–Dec. 1958, pp. 725–753; reprinted in BRAUDEL, *Ecrits sur l'histoire, op. cit.* (1969), pp. 41–83.

———. 'Stockholm 1960' (a report on the Stockholm Congress). *Annales* XVI (3), May–June 1961, pp. 497–500.

———. *Ecrits sur l'histoire*. Paris, Flammarion, 1969.

———. LABROUSSE, Ernest & RENOUVIN, Pierre. 'Les recherches d'histoire moderne et contemporaine' = 2nd part (pp. 34–50) of M. SCHNEIDER, F. BRAUDEL, E. LABROUSSE & P. RENOUVIN, 'Les orientations de la recherche historique (Enquête du C.N.R.S.),' *Revue historique* CCXXII/1 (451), July–Sept. 1959, pp. 19–50 (1st part being M. SCHNEIDER, 'Les recherches d'histoire médiévale,' pp. 19–34).

———. *On History*. Translated by Sarah Matthews. Chicago, University of Chicago Press, 1980.

BRAUN, Rudolf. *Industrialisierung und Volksleben: Die Veränderungen der Lebensformen in einem ländlichen Industriegebiet vor 1800 (Zürcher Oberland)*. Erlenbach-Zurich & Stuttgart, Rentsch, 1960.

BRENNEKE, Adolf. *Archivkunde: Ein Beitrag zur Theorie u. Geschichte des europäischen Archivwesens*. Leipzig, Koehler & Amelang, 1953.

BRIDENTHAL, Renate *et al.* (eds.). *Becoming Visible: Women in European History*. Boston, Houghton Mifflin, 1987; 1st edn., 1977.

BRINTON, Crane. *The Jacobins: An Essay in the New History*. New York, Macmillan, 1930.

———. *The Anatomy of Revolution* (1939). Rev. paperback edn. New York, Random House, 1957.

BROWN, Peter. *The Body and Society: Men, Women and Sexual Renunciation in Early Christianity*. New York, Columbia University Press, 1988.

BRUCE, Maurice. *The Shaping of the Modern World, 1870–1939*. London, Hutchinson/New York, Random House, 1958.

BRUNDAGE, B. C. 'The birth of Clio.' In HUGHES, H. Stuart (ed.), *Teachers of History, op. cit.* (1954), pp. 199–230.

BUCKLE, H. T. *History of Civilisation*. New Edn. London, 1857.

BULTMANN, Rudolf K. *History and Eschatology* (Gifted Lectures, 1955). Edinburgh, Edinburgh University Press, 1957; also published under the title *Presence of Eternity: History and Eschatology*, New York, Harper, 1957; German version, *Geschichte und Eschatologie*, Tübingen, J. C. B. Mohr, 1958.

BURSTON, W. H., & THOMSON, D. (eds.). *Studies in the Nature and Teaching of History*. London, Routledge/New York, Humanities Press, 1967.

BURY, J. (John) B. *Selected Essays*. Ed. Harold W. V. Temperley. Cambridge, Cambridge University Press/New York, Macmillan, 1930.

BUSHNELL, David (ed.). *The Liberator: Simón Bolívar, Man and Image*. New York, Knopf, 1970.

BUTTERFIELD, Herbert. *The Englishman and His History*. Cambridge, Cambridge University Press/New York, Macmillan, 1944.

——. *Christianity and History.* London, G. Bell, 1949.

——. *History and Human Relations.* London, Collins, 1951; New York, Macmillan, 1952.

——. 'Official history: Its pitfalls and criteria.' In BUTTERFIELD, *History and Human Relations, op. cit.* (1951), pp. 182–224.

——. *History and Man's Attitude to the Past* (Foundation Day Lectures). London, University of London, School of Oriental and African Studies, 1961.

BYNUM, Caroline Walker. *Holy Feast and Holy Fast: The Religious Significance of Food to Medieval Women.* Berkeley, University of California Press, 1987.

CABRÍA, Rómulo D. *Historia crítica de la historiografía argentina desde sus orígenes.* Buenos Aires, 1940.

Cahiers d'Histoire Mondiale / Journal of World History / Cuadernos de Historia Mundial, founded in 1953 under the auspices of Unesco to assist the work of the International Commission for a History of the Scientific and Cultural Development of Mankind; quarterly; articles in English, French, or Spanish; editors: Lucien Febvre (1953–56), François Crouzet & Guy S. Métraux under the authority of the Bureau of the International Commission (1956–68), Guy S. Métraux (1969–72); Editions des Méridiens, Paris, for Vols. I–II; La Baconnière, Neuchâtel, for Vols. III–XIV; as from 1973, replaced by the new international quarterly *Cultures,* published jointly by Unesco and La Baconnière in separate English and French editions.

CAHNMAN, Werner J. & BOSKOFF, Alvin. 'Sociology and history: reunion and rapprochement.' In CAHNMAN & BOSKOFF (eds.), *Sociology and History: Theory and Research, op. cit.* (1964), pp. 1–18.

CAHNMAN, Werner J. & BOSKOFF, Alvin (eds.). *Sociology and History: Theory and Research.* New York, The Free Press of Glencoe/London, Collier-Macmillan, 1964.

CALLOW, Alexander B. (ed.). *American Urban History: An Interpretive Reader with Commentaries.* New York, Oxford University Press, 1969.

The Cambridge Modern History (1902–12): see ACTON (ed.).

CANTOR, Norman F. & SCHNEIDER, R. I. *How to Study History.* New York, Crowell, 1967.

CANTOR, Norman F. & WERTHMAN, M. S. (eds.). *The History of Popular Culture.* New York, Macmillan, 1968.

CARLTON, Robert J. (ed.). *Soviet Image of Contemporary Latin America: A Documentary History, 1960–1968* (translations by J. Gregory Oswald). Austin, University of Texas Press, 1970.

CARNEY, T. F. 'Content analysis.' *Journal of the Manitoba History Teachers' Association,* Vol. I, 1969, pp. 3–17, and *Bulletin de l'Association canadienne de Humanités,* 1969, pp. 27–48.

CARR, Edward Hallet. *What Is History?* (The George Macaulay Trevelyan Lectures). London, Macmillan, 1961; New York, Knopf, 1962.

CARR, Raymond. 'New openings: Latin America.' In *New Ways in History, op. cit. (The Times Literary Supplement,* 1966), p. 299.

CARSTEN, Francis L. *The Rise of Fascism.* London, B. T. Batsford/Berkeley, University of California Press, 1967.

[For a review of this work, see SCHIEDER, W.]

CASTELLAN, Georges. 'L'histoire en République démocratique allemande.' *Revue historique* CCXXVI/1 (459), July–Sept. 1961, pp. 163–170 (*sub* 'L'orientation actuelle des études historiques').

————. 'Remarques sur l'historiographie de la République Démocratique Allemande.' *Revue historique* CCXXVIII/2 (464), Oct.–Dec. 1962, pp. 409–426.

A Catalogue of Files and Microfilms of the German Foreign Ministry Archives. Washington (D.C.), 1959.

'Les centres de recherches historiques.' Series of articles, *Revue historique,* between 1960 and 1966.

ČEREPNIN, L. V., '50 let sovetskoj istoričeskoj nauki i nekotorye itogi e'e razvitija' (= 50 years of Soviet historical science and some results of its development). *Istorija SSSR,* 1967, No. 6.

CÉSPEDES DEL CASTILLO, Guillermo: see VICENS VIVES, *Historia social y económica de España y América* (1957–59).

CHAMBERS, Jonathan David. *The Vale of Trent, 1670–1800: A Regional Study of Economic Change.* Cambridge, Cambridge University Press, 1957.

CHAMOUX, Antoinette & DAUPHIN, Cécile. 'La contraception avant la Révolution française: l'exemple de Châtillon-sur-Seine.' *Annales* XXIV (3), May–June 1969, pp. 662–684.

CHARMAN, D. & COOK, M. 'The archive services of East Africa.' *Archives,* Vol. VIII, 1967–68, pp. 70–80.

CHAUDHURI, S. B. *Civil Disturbances during the British Rule in India, 1765–1857.* Calcutta, 1955.

CHAUNU, Pierre. 'L'Amérique latine: les grandes lignes de la production historique (1950–1962).' *Revue historique* CCXXXI/1 (469), Jan.–Mar. 1964, pp. 153–186.

————. 'Histoire quantitative ou histoire sérielle.' *Cahiers Vilfredo Pareto,* Vol. 3, 1964, pp. 165–176.

————. 'L'histoire sérielle, Bilan et perspectives.' *Revue historique* CCXLIII/2 (494), Apr.–June 1970, pp. 297–320.

CHEJNE, A. G. 'The use of history by modern Arab writers.' *Middle East Journal,* Vol. XIV, 1960, pp. 382–396.

CHENG TE-K'UN. 'Archaeology in communist China.' *China Quarterly,* No. 23, July–Sept. 1965, pp. 67–77; reprinted in FEUERWERKER (ed.), *History in Communist China, op. cit.* (1968), pp. 45–55.

CHESNEAUX, Jean. 'Histoire moderne et contemporaine de Chine (depuis 1840)' (review of work in western languages of the period 1964–68). *Revue historique* CCXLIII/1 (493), Jan.–Mar. 1970, pp. 135–166.

CHILDE, V. Gordon. 'A prehistorian's interpretation of diffusion.' In *Independence, Convergence, and Borrowing,* Harvard Tercentenary Conference of Arts and Sciences. Cambridge (Mass.), 1937; reprinted in STAVRIANOS (ed.), *The Epic of Man to 1500, op. cit.* (1970).

————. *What Happened in History.* Harmondsworth (Middx.), Penguin Books, 1942 (French translation by André Mansat & Jean Barthalan, *De la préhistoire à l'histoire,* with a preface by Raymond Furon, Paris, B. Arthaud, 1961; new edn., 'Idees' ser., Paris, Gallimard, 1963.

CIPOLLA, Carlo Maria. *Literacy and Development in the West.* Harmondsworth (Middx.), Penguin Books, 1969.

CLAPHAM, John H. (Sir John). *An Economic History of Modern Britain.* London-Cambridge, 1926–38, 3 vols.; new edn., Cambridge, Cambridge University Press, 1950–52.

CLARK, George KITSON: see KITSON CLARK, G.

CLARK, G. N. (Sir George). General Introduction to *The New Cambridge Modern History, op cit.,* Vol. I (1957).

CLARK, G. N. (Sir George) (ed.). *The New Cambridge Modern History.* Cambridge, Cambridge University Press, 1957–70.

CLINE, Howard F. (ed.). *Latin American History: Essays on Its Study and Teaching, 1898–1965* (published for the Conference on Latin American History). 2 vols. Austin, University of Texas Press, 1967.

COBBAN, Alfred B. 'The age of democratic revolution.' *History* XLV (155), Oct. 1960, pp. 234–239.

————. 'History and sociology.' *Historical Studies*, Vol. III, 1961, pp. 1–8.

————. *The Social Interpretation of the French Revolution* (Belfast, Queen's University, The Wiles Lectures, 1962). Cambridge, Cambridge University Press, 1964.

COCHRAN, Thomas C. 'The "presidential synthesis" in American history.' *American Historical Review* LIII (4), July 1948, pp. 748–759; reproduced in the following collections: Social Science Research Committee, *The Social Sciences in Historical Study, op. cit.* (1954), pp. 157–171; COCHRAN, *The Inner Revolution, op. cit.* (1964); LIPSET & HOFSTADTER (eds.), *Sociology and History: Methods, op. cit.* (1968), pp. 371–385; and (in a slightly different version) as 'The social sciences and the problem of historical synthesis,' in STERN (ed.), *The Varieties of History, op. cit.* (1956), pp. 348–359; also issued separately, Bobbs-Merrill Reprints.

————. *Railroad Leaders, 1845–1890: The Business Mind in Action.* Harvard University Research Center in Entrepreneurial History, Cambridge (Mass.), Harvard University Press/London, Oxford University Press, 1953.

————. 'History and the social sciences.' In *Xo* [Decimo] *Congresso internazionale di Scienze storiche: Relazioni, op. cit.* (1955), Vol. I, pp. 479–504; reprinted in EISENSTADT, A. S. (ed.), *The Craft of American History, op. cit.* (1966), Vol. II, pp. 90–109.

————. *The Inner Revolution: Essays on the Social Sciences in History.* New York, Harper & Row, 1964.

COCKS, P. S. 'The development of the National Archives of New Zealand." *Journal of the Society of Archivists*, Vol. III, 1965–69, pp. 121–126.

COLE, William Alan. *Economic History as a Social Science.* Swansea, University College of Swansea, 1967.

COLLINGWOOD, Robin G. *The Idea of History.* London, Oxford University Press, 1946; paperback edn., 1956.

Comité français des Sciences historiques: see *La Recherche historique en France de 1940 à 1965.*

Common Frontiers of the Social Sciences (1957): see KOMAROVSKY (ed.).

Comparative Studies in Society and History, an international quarterly; founded in 1958; eds. Sylvia L. THRUPP & Eric R. WOLF; New York-London, Cambridge University Press.

The Concise Encyclopaedia of World History (1958): see BOWLE (ed.).

CONFINO, Michael. 'Histoire et psychologie: A propos de la noblesse russe au XVIIIe siècle.' *Annales* XXII (6), Nov.–Dec. 1967, pp. 1163–1205.

Contemporary History in the Soviet Mirror (1964): see KEEP & BRISBY (eds.).

CONWAY, Alan. *The History of the Negro in the United States.* London, The Historical Association, 1968.

CONZE, Werner. 'Die Stellung der Sozialgeschichte in Forschung und Unterricht.' *Geschichte in Wissenschaft und Unterricht (Zeitschrift des Verbandes der Geschichtslehrer Deutschlands)*, Vol. III, 1952, pp. 648–657.

COOK, Sherburne F. & SIMPSON, L. B. *The Population of Central Mexico in the Sixteenth Century.* Ibero-Americana, No. 31. Berkeley. University of California Press, 1948.
[See also BORAH & COOK.]

CORBIN, Alain. *The Foul and the Fragrant: Odor and the French Social Imagination.* Cambridge, Mass., Harvard University Press, 1986.

CORNEVIN, Robert. *Histoire des peuples de l'Afrique noire.* Paris, Berger-Levrault, 1960.

COSÍO VILLEGAS, Daniel. *Nueva historiografía política del México moderno.* Mexico-City, 1965.

COULBORN, Rushton. *Feudalism in History.* With contributions by Joseph R. STRAYER *et al.* Foreword by A. L. KROEBER. Princeton (N.J.), Princeton University Press/London, Oxford University Press, 1956.

COURT, W. H. B. 'Economic history.' In FINBERG (ed.), *Approaches to History, op. cit.* (1963), pp. 17–50.

COWAN, Charles Donald. *South East Asian History in London.* Inaugural Lecture. London, University of London, School of Oriental and African Studies, 1963.

COWELL, Frank R. *History, Civilization and Culture: An Introduction to the Historical and Social Philosophy of Pitirim A. Sorokin.* London, A. & C. Black/ Boston, Beacon Press, 1952.

CRAEYBECKX, Jan. 'La notion d' "importance" à lumière de l'histoire moderne.' In PERLMAN (ed.), *Raisonnement et démarches de l'historien, op. cit.* (1963), pp. 65–81.

The Craft of American History: see EISENSTADT, A. S. (ed.).

CRANE, R. I. 'Indian history for the undergraduate.' In DE BARY & EMBREE (eds.), *Approaches to Asian Civilizations, op. cit.* (1961), pp. 21–51.

CROCE, Benedetto. *La storia come pensiero e come azione.* Bari, Laterza, 1938 (English translation by Sylvia Sprigge, *History as the Story of Liberty,* New York, Norton/London, Allen & Unwin, 1941).

CRONON, William. *Changes in the Land: Indians, Colonists and the Ecology of New England.* New York, Hill and Wang, 1983.

CROUZET, Maurice (ed.). *Histoire générale des civilisations.* 7 vols. Paris, Presses Universitaires de France, 1953–57.

CROWLEY, James B. (ed.). *Modern East Asia: Essays in Interpretation.* New York, Harcourt Brace Jovanovich, 1970.

ČUBAR'JAN, A. 'Itogi meždunarodnogo soveščanija kommunističskih i raboćih partij i zadaći istorićeskoj nauki' (= Conclusions of the International Congress of Communist and Workers' Parties and the aims of historical science). *Voprosy istorii,* 1969, No. 9.

The Current Digest of the Soviet Press, founded in 1949; published each week by the American Association for the Advancement of Slavic Studies; quarterly indexes; Columbus, Ohio State University.

CZITROM, Daniel. *Media and the American Mind: From Morse to McLuhan.* Chapel Hill, University of North Carolina Press, 1982.

DABAGJAN, È. S. '50 let sovestkoj latinoamerikanistiki. Bibliografićeskij oćerk' (= Fifty years of Soviet Latin American studies. Bibliographical essay). In *SSSR i Latinskaja Amerika, 1917–1967.* Moscow, 1967.

DAHRENDORF, Ralf. *Society and Democracy in Germany.* New York, Doubleday, 1967; London, Weidenfeld, 1968.

DANCE, Edward H. *History the Betrayer: A Study of Bias.* London, Hutchinson, 1960.

———. *History for a United World.* London, Harrap, 1971.

DANIEL, Glyn E. *The First Civilizations: The Archaeology of Their Origins.* London, Thames and Hudson/New York, Thomas Y. Crowell, 1968.

DANTO, Arthur Coleman. *Analytical Philosophy of History*. Cambridge, Cambridge University Press, 1965.

——. *The Kiss of Lamourette: Reflections in Cultural History*. New York, W.W. Norton, 1990.

DARLINGTON, Cyril Dean. 'History and biology.' In BALLARD (ed.), *New Movements in the Study and Teaching of History, op. cit.* (1970), pp. 147–160.

DARNTON, Robert. *The Great Cat Massacre and Other Episodes in French Cultural History*. New York, Basic Books, 1984.

DARWIN, K. 'The use of the computer in indexing records.' *Journal of the Society of Archivists*, Vol. IV, 1971, pp. 218–229.

DAUMAS, Maurice (ed.). *Histoire générale des techniques*. 4 vols. Paris, Presses Universitaires de France, 1962–68.

DAVID, Henry. 'Opinion research in the service of the historian.' In KOMAROVSKY (ed.), *Common Frontiers of the Social Sciences, op. cit.* (1957), pp. 269–278 (part of 'History and public opinion research: A debate').

DAVIDSON, James West. 'The new narrative history: how new? how narrative?' *Reviews in American History*, Vol. XII (3), September 1984, pp. 322–333.

DAVIES, R. R., 'Marc Bloch.' *History* LII (176), Oct. 1967, pp. 265–282.

DAVIS, Lance Edwin. 'The New Economic History: A Critique.' *Explorations in Entrepreneurial History*, 2nd ser., Vol. VI, 1968, pp. 75–92.

——. HUGHES, J. R. T. & McDOUGALL, D. M. *American Economic History: The Development of a National Economy*. Homewood (Ill.), Irwin, 1961.

DAVIS, Natalie Zemon. *Society and Culture in Early Modern France*. Stanford: Stanford University Press, 1975.

——. *The Return of Martin Guerre: Imposture and Identity in a Sixteenth Century Village*. Cambridge, Mass., Harvard University Press, 1983.

——. ' "Any resemblance to persons living or dead": film and the challenge of authenticity.' *Yale Review*, Vol. LXXVI, 1987, pp. 457–482.

DAVIS, Ralph. *History and the Social Sciences*. Leicester, 1965.

DAWSON, Christopher. *Progress and Religion: An Historical Enquiry*. London, Sheed, 1929.

——. *The Dynamics of World History*. Ed. by John J. Mulloy. London, Sheed, 1957.

DE BARY, William Theodore & EMBREE, Ainslie T. (eds.). *Approaches to Asian Civilizations*. New York, Columbia University Press, 1961.

DE BEER, Gavin: see BEER, Sir Gavin De.

Xo [Decimo] *Congresso internazionale di Scienze storiche, Roma, 4–11 settembre 1955: Relazioni*, A cura della Giunta centrale per gli studi storici, Florence, Sansoni, 1955, 7 vols.: Vol. I: *Metodologia. Problemi generali. Scienze ausiliarie della storia;* Vol. II: *Relazioni generali e supplementi;* Vol. VII: *Riassunti delle communicazioni.*

DE CERTEAU, Michel. *The Writing of History*. Translated by Tom Conley. New York, Columbia University Press, 1988.

DE JONGE, J. A.: see JONGE, J. A. de.

DE LAURETIS, Teresa. *Alice Doesn't: Feminism, Semiotics, Cinema*. Bloomington: Indiana University Press, 1984.

DELUZ-CHIVA, Ariane. 'Anthropologie, histoire et historiographie.' In *Histoire et Sciences sociales, op. cit. (Rev. int. d. Sciences soc., 1965)*, pp. 582–593; parallel publication in English translation, 'Anthropology, history and historiography," in *History and Social Science, op. cit. (Int. Soc. Sc. J., 1965)*, pp. 571–581.

DEMOS, John. 'Families in colonial Bristol," *William and Mary Quarterly,* Vol. XXV, 1968; reprinted in ROWNEY and GRAHAM, *Quantitative History, op. cit.* (1969), pp. 293–307.

DEOPIK, D. V., DOBROV, G. M., KAHK, Ju. Ju., KOVALCHENKO (= KOVAL'ČENKO), I. D. (head of the group), PALLI, H. E. & USTINOV, V. A. *Quantitative and Machine Methods of Processing Historical Information* (XIIIth International Congress of Historical Sciences, Moscow, 16–23 Aug., 1970). Moscow, Nauka, 1970.

DEVEREUX, Georges. 'La psychanalyse et l'histoire: une application à l'histoire de Sparte,' *Annales* XX (1), Jan.–Feb. 1965, pp. 18–44.

DIAMOND, Sigmund O. *The Reputation of the American Businessman.* 'Studies in Entrepreneurial History.' Cambridge (Mass.), Harvard University Press/ London, Oxford University Press, 1955.

DIEZ DEL CORRAL, Luis. *El rapto de Europa.* Madrid, Revista de Occidente, 1954 (English translation by H. V. Livermore, *The Rape of Europe,* New York, Macmillan/London, Allen & Unwin, 1959).

——. *Del Nuevo al Viejo Mundo.* Madrid, Revista de Occidente, 1963.

DIKE, Kenneth O. 'African history and self-government.' *West Africa,* Vol. XXXVII, 1953.

——. *Report on the Preservation and Administration of Historical Records and the Establishment of a Public Record Office in Nigeria.* Ibadan, 1954.

——. *Trade and Politics in the Niger Delta, 1830–1885: An Introduction to the Economic and Political History of Nigeria.* Oxford, Clarendon, 1956.

——. & AJAYI, J. F. A. 'African historiography.' In *International Encyclopedia of the Social Sciences, op. cit* (1968), Vol. VI, pp. 394–400 (*sub* 'Historiography').

DOLLAR, C. M. 'Innovation in historical research: A computer approach.' *Computers and the Humanities,* No. 3, 1969, pp. 139–151.

DONALD, D. 'Radical historians on the move.' *New York Times Book Review* LXXV (29), 1970 and *New York Times,* 17 Feb. 1970.

DOVRING, Folke. *History as a Social Science: An Essay on the Nature and Purpose of Historical Studies.* The Hague, M. Nijhoff, 1960.

DRAY, William H. *Laws and Explanations in History.* London, Oxford University Press, 1957.

DRUŽYNIN, N. M. (ed.). *Sovetskaja istoričeskaja nauka ot XX k XXII s'ezdu KPSS* (= Soviet Historical Science between the XXth and the XXIInd Congresses of the Communist Party of the Soviet Union), Moscow, 1962–63, 2 vols.

DUBUC, Alfred. *L'histoire au carrefour des sciences humaines* (XIIIth International Congress of Historical Sciences, Moscow, 16–23 Aug. 1970). Moscow, Nauka, 1970.

DUPÂQUIER, Jacques. 'Sur la population française au XVIIe au XVIIIe siècle.' *Revue historique,* CCXXXIX/1 (485), Jan.–Mar. 1968, pp. 43–79.

—— & LACHIVER, M. 'Sur les débuts de la contraception en France.' *Annales* XXIV (6), Nov.–Dec. 1969, pp. 1391–1406.

DUPRONT, Alphonse. 'Problèmes et méthodes d'une histoire de la psychologie collective' (Communication to the Stockholm Congress, 1960). *Annales* XVI (1), Jan.–Feb. 1961, pp. 3–11.

——. 'L'histoire après Freud.' *Revue de l'Enseignement supérieur* (Paris), Nos. 44–45, 1969, pp. 27–63.

——. *Langage et histoire* (XIIIth International Congress of Historical Sciences, Moscow, 16–23 Aug. 1970). Moscow, Nauka, 1970.

XX [Dvadcatyj] *S'ezd KPSS, Stenografičeskij otčet* (= XXth Congress of the Communist Party of the USSR. Stenographic Record), Vol. I, Moscow, 1956 (statements by Mme. PANKRATOVA on the guiding principles of historical research).

DYOS, Harold J. (ed.). *The Study of Urban History* (the proceedings of an international round-table conference of the Urban History Group at Gilbert Murray Hall, University of Leicester, on 23–26 Sept. 1966). London, E. Arnold/New York, St. Martin's Press, 1968.

EASTON, Stewart C. *World History since 1945.* San Francisco, Chandler Publ. Co., 1968.

ECO, Umberto. *The Name of the Rose.* Translated by William Weaver. San Diego, Harcourt Brace Jovanovich, 1983.

———. *Postscript to The Name of the Rose.* Translated by William Weaver. San Diego, Harcourt Brace Jovanovich, 1984.

———. *Travels in Hyperreality.* Translated by William Weaver. San Diego, Harcourt Brace Jovanovich, 1986.

EISENSTADT, Abraham S. 'American history and social science.' *Centennial Review,* Vol. VII, 1963, pp. 255–272; reprinted in EISENSTADT, A. S. (ed.), *The Craft of American History, op. cit.* (1966), Vol. II, pp. 110–125.

EISENSTADT, Abraham S. (ed.). *The Craft of American History: Selected Essays.* 2 vols. New York, Harper & Row, 1966.

EISENSTADT, Shmuel N. *The Political Systems of Empires.* New York, Free Press/London, Macmillan, 1963.

———. *The Decline of Empires.* Englewood Cliffs (N.J.), Prentice-Hall, 1967.

ELEKEC, L. *Connaissances historiques—Conscience sociale (Quelques aspects de recherche sur le rôle des connaissances historiques dans la formation de la pensée et des mentalités contemporaines)* (XIIIth International Congress of Historical Sciences, Moscow, 16–23 Aug. 1970). Moscow, Nauka, 1970.

XIth International Congress of Historical Sciences (1960): see *Xlème* [Onzième] *Congrès international des Sciences historiques.*

ELIAS, Norbert. *The Civilising Process: The History of Manners.* Translated by Edmund Jephcott. New York, Urizen Books, 1978.

ELKINS, Stanley M. *Slavery: A Problem in American Institutional and Intellectual Life.* Chicago, University of Chicago Press/Cambridge, Cambridge University Press, 1959.

ELTON, Geoffrey R. *The Practice of History.* Sydney, Sydney University Press/ New York, Crowell/London, Methuen, 1967. [See also KITSON CLARK & ELTON.]

Emerging Themes in African History: see RANGER (ed.).

ENDRES, F. C. 'Soziologische Struktur und ihr entsprechende Ideologien des deutschen Offizierkorps vor dem Weltkriege,' *Archiv für Sozialwissenschaft und Sozialpolitik,* LVIII, 1927, pp. 282–319.

ENGELBERG,. Ernst. 'Über Gegenstand und Ziel der marxistisch-leninistischen Geschichtswissenschaft.' *Zeitschrift für Geschichtswissenschaft,* Vol. XVI, 1968, pp. 1117–1145.

ENGELS, Friedrich. Letter to J. Bloch, Sept. 21–22, 1890. In MARX-ENGELS, *Werke,* Vol. 37, Berlin, Dietz, 1967, p. 462 (English translation in MARX-ENGELS, *Selected Works,* London, Lawrence & Wishart, Vol. II, p. 443).

———. Letter to Conrad Schmidt, Mar. 12, 1895. In MARX-ENGELS, *Werke,* Vol. 39, Berlin, Dietz, 1968, p. 431.

[See also MARX, Karl & ENGELS, Friedrich.]

ENGERMAN, S. L. 'The economic impact of the Civil War.' *Explorations in Entrepreneurial History,* 2nd ser., Vol. III, 1966, pp. 176–199.

Enquête sur les mouvements paysans dans le monde contemporain (de la fin du XVIIIe siècle à nos jours): Rapport général, presented by the Commission internationale d'Histoire des Mouvements sociaux et des Structures sociales (XIIIth International Congress of Historical Sciences, Moscow, 16–23 Aug. 1970). Moscow, Nauka, 1970.

EPSTEIN, F. T. & WEINBERG, G. L. *Guide to Captured German Documents.* Washington (D.C.), 1952.

———. *Supplement to the Guide to Captured German Documents.* Washington (D.C.), 1959.

ERIKSON, Erik H. *Young Man Luther: A Study in Psychoanalysis and History,* Austin Riggs Monograph No. 4, New York, Norton, 1958 (French translation by Nina Godneff, *Luther avant Luther: Psychanalyse et histoire,* Paris, Flammarion, 1968).

———. *Gandhi's Truth, or the Origins of Militant Nonviolence.* New York, Norton, 1969 (French translation by Vilma Fritsch, *La vérité de Gandhi: Les origines de la non-violence,* Paris, Flammarion, 1974).
[For reviews of this work, see: GEERTZ, Clifford; POMPER, Philip.]

ESQUENAZI-MAYO, Roberto & MEYER, C. (eds.). *Latin American Scholarship since World War II. Trends in History, Political Science, Literature, Geography, and Economics,* Lincoln, University of Nebraska Press, 1971.

Etudes des delégués hongrois au Xe Congrès international des Sciences historiques, Rome, 1965. Budapest, Akad. Kiadó, 1965.

EVANS-PRITCHARD, E. E., *The Divine Kingship of the Shilluk of the Nilotic Sudan.* Cambridge, Cambridge University Press, 1948; reprinted in EVANS-PRITCHARD, *Essays in Social Anthropology, op. cit.* (1962), pp. 66–86.

———. *Anthropology and History* (a lecture delivered at the University of Manchester in 1961). Manchester, Manchester University Press, 1961; reprinted in EVANS-PRITCHARD, *Essays in Social Anthropology, op. cit.* (1962), pp. 46–65.

———. *Essays in Social Anthropology.* London, Faber & Faber, 1962; New York, Free Press of Glencoe, 1963.

———. 'Social anthropology: Past and present.' In EVANS-PRITCHARD, *Essays in Social Anthropology, op. cit.* (1962), pp. 13–28.

EVERSLEY, D. E. C.: see GLASS & EVERSLEY (eds.); WRIGLEY, EVERSLEY & LASLETT (eds.).

FARAGHER, John Mack. *Sugar Creek: Life on the Illinois Prairie.* New Haven: Yale University Press, 1986.

FEBVRE, Lucien. *Le problème de l'incroyance au XVIe siècle: La religion de Rabelais.* 'L'évolution de l'humanité' ser., No. 53, Paris, Albin Michel 1942; new edn., rev., 1963, etc.

———. 'Avant-propos' to MORAZÉ, *Trois essais sur Histoire et Culture, op. cit.* (1948), pp. v–viii.

———. 'Vers une autre histoire.' In FEBVRE, *Combats pour l'histoire, op. cit.* (1953), pp. 491–438 (1st publication, *Revue de Métaphysique et de Morale,* 1949).

———. *Combats pour l'Histoire* (collected essays). Paris, Armand Colin, 1953.

FEDOSEEV, P. N. & FRANCEV, Ju. P. 'O razrabotke metodologičeskih voprosov istorii' (= On the working-out of the methodological questions of history). *Voprosy istorii,* 1964, No. 3, pp. 4–23; reproduced in *Istorija i sociologija, op. cit.* (1964).
[See also *sub* 'O metodologičeskih voprosah istoričeskoj nauki.']

FELIÚ CRUZ, Guillermo. *Historiografía colonial de Chile.* Santiago de Chile, 1968.

Feminist Studies.

FEUERWERKER, Albert. 'Rewriting Chinese history.' In *The Far East: China and Japan = University of Toronto Quarterly,* Suppl. No. 5, 1961, pp. 273–285.

————. 'China's modern economic history.' *The China Quarterly,* No. 22, Apr.–June 1965; reprinted in FEUERWERKER (ed.), *History in Communist China, op. cit.* (1968), pp. 216–246.

————. & CHENG, Sally. *Chinese Communist Studies of Modern Chinese History* (annotated bibliography), East Asian Monograph Ser., No. 11. Cambridge (Mass.), Harvard University Press, 1961.

FEUERWERKER, Albert (ed.). *History in Communist China.* Cambridge (Mass.), The M.I.T. Press, 1968; paperback edn., 1969. [See also KAHN & FEUERWERKER.]

FIELDS, Barbara. *Slavery and Freedom in the Middle Ground: Maryland in the Nineteenth Century.* New Haven, Yale University Press, 1985.

Filosofskie problemy istoričeskoj nauki (= Philosophical Problems of Historical Science), collective work. Moscow, Academy of Sciences of the USSR, Institute of Philosophy, 1969.

FINBERG, H. P. R. (ed.). *Approaches to History: A Symposium.* London, Routledge, 1962.

FINK, K. A. *Das vatikanische Archiv.* Rome, 1951.

FINKE, H. (ed.). *Acta Aragonensia.* 3 vols. Berlin-Leipzig, 1908–22.

FISCHER, David H. *Historians' Fallacies: Toward a Logic of Historical Thought.* New York, Harper, 1970.

Die Fischer Weltgeschichte, series. Frankfurt on the Main, Fischer Verlag.

FISHER, H. A. L. *A History of Europe.* Vol. I, London. Eyre & Spottiswoode/ Boston, Houghton Mifflin, 1935.

FLEURY, Michel & HENRY, Louis. *Des registres paroissiaux à l'histoire de la population.* Paris, Institut National d'Etudes Démographiques, 1956.

————. *Nouveau manuel de dépouillement et d'exploitation de l'état civil ancien* (being a revised and extended edition of the preceding work). Paris, Institut National d'Etudes Démographiques, 1965.

FOGEL, Robert Wm. 'Discussion' (of papers presented under 'Reappraisals in American economic history'). *American Economic Review* LIV (3), May 1964, Suppl. *(Papers and Proceedings of the Seventy-Sixth Annual Meeting of the American Economic Association, Boston, Massachusetts, December 27–29, 1963),* pp. 377–389.

————. *Railroads and American Economic Growth: Essays in Econometric History.* Baltimore (Md.), Johns Hopkins Press, 1964. [For a review and discussion of this work, see: HAWKE, G. R.; HUNT, E. H.]

————. 'The reunification of economic history with economic theory.' *American Economic Review,* Vol. LV, 1965, Supp., pp. 92-98.

————. 'The New Economic History, its findings and methods.' *Economic History Review,* 2nd ser., Vol. XIX, 1966, pp. 642–656; reprinted in ROWNEY and GRAHAM (eds.), *Quantitative History, op. cit.* (1969), pp. 320–335.

————. 'The specification problem in economic history.' *Journal of Economic History,* Vol. XXVII, 1967.

FORBES, R. J. 'The history of science and technology.' In *XIème Congrès international des Sciences historiques, Stockholm, 1960, Rapports, op. cit.* (1960), Vol. I, pp. 59–73.

FORSTER, Robert and OREST, Ranum (eds.). *Food and Drink in History: Selections from the Annales: Economies, Sociétés, Civilisations.* Baltimore, Johns Hopkins University Press, 1979.

FOUCAULT, Michel. *Madness and Civilization: A History of Insanity.* Translated by Richard Howard. New York, Pantheon Books, 1965.

———. *The Archeology of Language.* Translated by A. Sheridan Smith. New York, Harper and Row, 1972.

———. *Discipline and Punish: The Birth of the Prison.* Translated by Alan Sheridan. New York, Pantheon Books, 1977.

———. *Histoire de la sexualité.* 3 vols. Paris, Gallimard, 1976–1984.

FOX-GENOVESE, Elizabeth and GENOVESE, Eugene D. 'The political crisis of social history: a Marxian perspective.' *Journal of Social History,* Vol. X (2), Winter 1976, pp. 205–220.

FOX-GENOVESE, Elizabeth. *Within the Plantation Household: Black and White Women of the Old South.* Chapel Hill, University of North Carolina Press, 1988.

FRANK, Andre G. *Capitalism and Underdevelopment in Latin America: Historical Studies of Chile and Brazil.* New York, Monthly Review, 1969.

FRANZEL, Emil. *1870–1950: Geschichte unserer Zeit.* Munich, Oldenbourg, 1952.

FRYE, R. N. 'Soviet historiography on the Islamic Orient.' In *Historical Writing on the Peoples of Asia.* Vol. IV: *Historians of the Middle-East, op. cit.* (1962), pp. 367–374.

FUETER, Eduard K. 'Geschichte der gesamtschweizerischen historischen Organisation.' In SCHIEDER (ed.), *Hundert Jahre Historische Zeitschrift 1859–1959, op. cit.* (1959), pp. 449–505.

FURTADO, Celso. *The Economic Growth of Brazil: A Survey from Colonial to Modern Times.* Translated from the Portuguese by Ricardo W. de Aguiar & Eric Charles Drysdale. Berkeley, University of California Press, 1963.

———. *The Economic Development of Latin America: A Survey from Colonial Times to the Cuban Revolution.* Translated from the Portuguese by Suzette Macedo. Cambridge, Cambridge University Press, 1970.

GALLAGHER, John & ROBINSON, Ronald. 'The imperialism of free trade,' *Economic History Review,* 2nd ser., VI (1), Aug. 1953, pp. 1–15.
[See also ROBINSON, R. & GALLAGHER].

GALLIE, Walter B. *Philosophy and the Historical Understanding.* London, Chatto & Windus, 1964.

GARDIN, Jean-Claude. Introduction to USTINOV, 'Les calculateurs électroniques appliqués à la science historique' (French translation, *op. cit.*). *Annales* XVIII (2), Mar.–Apr. 1963, pp. 259–263.

———. 'Une approache linguistique,' *Le Monde* (Paris), No. 7476, 25 Jan. 1969, Supp., p. v.

GARDINER, Patrick L. (ed.). *The Nature of Historical Explanation.* London, Oxford University Press, 1952.

———. *Theories of History: Readings from Classical and Contemporary Sources.* Glencoe, The Free Press, 1959; London, Allen & Unwin, 1960.

GARGAN, Edward T. (ed.) *The Intent of Toynbee's History: A Co-operative Appraisal.* With a preface by Arnold J. TOYNBEE. Chicago, Loyola University Press, 1961.

GAUTIER, Etienne & HENRY, Louis. *La population de Crulai, paroisse normande: Etude historique.* Publications de l'Institut National d'Etudes Démographiques, Travaux et Documents, Cahier No. 33. Paris, Presses Universitaires de France, 1959.

GAY, Peter. *The Bourgeois Experience: Victoria to Freud.* Vol. I. New York, Oxford University Press, 1984.

———. *Freud for Historians.* New York, Oxford University Press, 1985.

————. *Freud: A Life for Our Time.* New York, Norton, 1988.

GEERTZ, Clifford. 'Gandhi: non-violence as therapy' (being a review of Erik H. ERIKSON, *Gandhi's Truth, op. cit.,* 1969). *The New York Review of Books* XIII (9), 20 Nov. 1969, pp. 3–4.

————. *The Interpretation of Cultures.* New York, Basic Books, 1973.

————. 'Blurred genres: the refiguration of social thought.' *The American Scholar,* Vol. XXIX (2), Spring 1980; reproduced in GEERTZ, *Local Knowledge: Further Essays in Interpretive Anthropology,* New York, Basic Books, 1983.

GEFTER, M. Ja. & MAL'KOV, V. L. 'Otvet amerikanskomu učenomu' (= Reply to an American scholar). *Voprosy istorii,* 1966, No. 10, pp. 29–50; English version, GEFTER, M. J. & MALKOV, V. L. 'Reply to a questionnaire on Soviet historiography,' *History and Theory* VI (2), 1967, pp. 180–207.

GEISS, I., *Das Entstehen der modernen Eliten in Afrika seit der Mitte des 18. Jahrhunderts* (XIIIth International Congress of Historical Sciences, Moscow, 16–23 Aug. 1970). Moscow, Nauka, 1970.

GEL'MAN-VINOGRADOV, K. B. & HROMČENKO, L. G. *Kibernetika i istoričeskaja nauka* (= Cybernetics and Historical Science), Trudy moskovskogo gosudarstvennogo istoriko-arhivnogo Instituta, t. 25. Moscow, 1967.

Generalization in the Writing of History (ed. L. GOTTSCHALK, 1963): see Social Science Research Council (Committee on Historiography).

Generalizations in Historical Writing (1963): see RIASANOVSKY & RIZNIK (eds.).

GERHARD, D. *Alte und neue Welt in vergleichender Geschichtsbetrachtung.* Göttingen, Vandenhoeck & Ruprecht, 1962.

————. 'Neusiedlung und institutionelle Erbe.' In GERHARD, *Alte und neue Welt in vergleichender Geschichtsbetrachtung, op. cit.* (1962), pp. 108–140.

GERSCHENKRON, Alexander. *Economic Backwardness in Historical Perspective: A Book of Essays.* Cambridge (Mass.), Harvard University Press, 1962.

GIBSON, Charles. 'Colonial institutions and contemporary Latin America: social and cultural life.' *The Hispanic American Historical Review* XLIII (3), Aug. 1963, pp. 380–389.

————. *The Aztecs under Spanish Rule: A History of the Indians of the Valley of Mexico, 1519–1810.* Stanford (Calif.), Stanford University Press, 1964.

————. *Spain in America.* New York, Harper, 1966.

GIEYSZTOROWA, J. 'Research into demographic history in Poland,' *Acta Poloniae Historica,* Vol. XVIII, 1968.

GINZBURG, Carlo. *The Cheese and the Worms: The Cosmos of a Sixteenth Century Miller.* Translated by Anne and John Tedeschi. Baltimore, Johns Hopkins University Press, 1980.

————. 'Anthropology and history in the 1980s.' *Journal of Interdisciplinary History,* Vol. XII (2), Autumn 1981, pp. 277–278.

GLASS, David V. & EVERSLEY, D. E. C. (eds.). *Population in History. Essays in Historical Demography.* Chicago, Aldine/London, E. Arnold, 1965.

GLÉNISSON, Jean. 'L'historiographie française contemporaine: tendances et réalisations.' In *La recherche historique en France de 1940 à 1965, op. cit.* (1965), pp. IX–LXIV.

[See also *sub* 'Les Problèmes des sources de l'histoire de l'Afrique noire. . .']

GODECHOT, Jacques. *France and the Atlantic Revolution of the Eighteenth Century.* Translated from the French by H. Rowen. New York, The Free Press/London, Macmillan, 1965.

GOOCH, George P. *History and Historians in the Nineteenth Century* (London, 1913); 2nd edn., with a new Introduction by the author. Boston, Beacon Press, 1959.

GOODWIN, Albert (ed.). *The European Nobility in the Eighteenth Century: Studies of the Nobilities of the Major European States in the Pre-Reform Era.* London, A. & C. Black, 1953.

GOPAL, Sarvepalli. *The Viceroyalty of Lord Ripon, 1880–1884.* London, Oxford University Press, 1953.

———. *The Viceroyalty of Lord Irwin, 1926–1931.* London, Oxford University Press, 1957.

———. *British Policy in India, 1858–1905.* Cambridge, Cambridge University Press, 1965.

GOTT, Richard. *Guerrilla Movements in Latin America.* London, Nelson, 1970; New York, Doubleday, 1971.

GOTTSCHALK, Louis R. 'Projects and concepts of world history in the twentieth century,' in *XIIth* [Twelfth] *International Congress of Historical Sciences / XIIème Congrès international des Sciences historiques: Reports / Rapports, op. cit.* (1965), Vol. IV, pp. 5–19; discussion, *ibid.,* Vol. V: *Proceedings / Actes* (1958), pp. 525–540.

GOTTSCHALK, Louis R. (ed.). *Generalization in the Writing of History* (1963): see Social Science Research Council (Committee on Historiography).

GOUBERT, Pierre. *Beauvais et le Beauvaisis de 1600 à 1730. Contribution à l'histoire sociale de la France du XVIIe siècle,* Paris, S.E.V.P.E.N., 1960 (see also republication as *Cent mille provinciaux au XVIIe siècle,* 1968).

———. *Louis XIV et vingt millions de Français.* 'L'histoire sans frontières' ser. Paris, Fayard, 1966.

———. *Cent mille provinciaux au XVIIe siècle: Beauvais et la Beauvaisis de 1600 à 1730* (new edition). 'Science' ser. Paris, Flammarion, 1968.

———. 'Historical demography and the reinterpretation of early modern French history.' *Journal of Interdisciplinary History* I (1), Autumn 1970, pp. 37–48.

GOWING, Margaret. 'Science and the modern historian.' *Times Literary Supplement,* 7 May 1970, pp. 315–316.

GRAHAM, Richard. 'Brazil: The national period.' In ESQUENAZI-MAYO & MEYER (eds.), *Latin American Scholarship since World War II, op. cit.* (1971).

GRAY, J. 'Historical writing in twentieth century China.' In *Historical Writing on the Peoples of Asia, op. cit.,* Vol. III (1961), pp. 186–212.

GREVEN, P. J. 'Historical demography and colonial America.' *William and Mary Quarterly,* Vol. XXIV, 1967, pp. 438–454.

GRIFFIN, Charles C. 'An essay on regionalism and nationalism in Latin America.' *Cahiers d'Histoire Mondiale / Journal of World History / Cuadernos de Historia Mundial* VIII (2), 1964, pp. 371–378.

GRIFFIN, Charles C. (ed., with the collaboration of J. Benedict WARREN). *Latin America: A Guide to the Historical Literature.* Austin, University of Texas Press, 1971.

GRUHLE, H. W. *Geschichtsschreibung und Psychologie.* Bonn, Bouvier Verlag, 1953.

GRUNDMANN, Herbert. 'Geistesgeschichte in den *Monumenta Germaniae historica.' Die Welt als Geschichte,* Vol. X, 1950, pp. 98–116.

———. 'Neue Aufgaben der *Monumenta Germaniae historica,' Geschichte in Wissenschaft und Unterricht,* Vol. II, 1951, pp. 530–547.

GRUNEBAUM, Gustav E. von. 'Self-image and approach to history.' In *Historical Writing on the Peoples of Asia,* Vol. IV: *Historians of the Middle-East, op. cit.* (1962), pp. 457–483.

GRUŠIN, B. A. *Očerki logiki istoričeskogo issledovanija: process razvitija i problemy ego naučnogo vosproizvedenija* (= Essays on the Logic of Historical

Research: the Process of Development and the Problems of Its Scientific Reconstruction). Moscow, Gosudarstvennoe Izd. 'Vysšaja Škola,' 1961.

GUNTER, Elizabeth E. and LOWRY, Bullit (eds.). *The Red Virgin: Memoirs of Louise Michel*. University, Ala., University of Alabama Press, 1981.

GUREVIČ, A. Ja. 'Obščij zakon i konkretnaja zakonomernost' v istorii' (= General law and concrete regularity in history). *Voprosy istorii*, 1965, No. 8.

HABIB, Irfan. *The Agrarian System of Mughal India, 1556–1707* (published for the Department of History, Aligarh Muslim University). Bombay-London, Asia Publishing House, 1963.

HACKER, L. M. 'The new revolution in economic history.' *Explorations in Entrepreneurial History*, 2nd ser., Vol. III, 1966, pp. 159–175.

HADDAD, G. M. 'Modern Arab historians and world history.' *The Muslim World*, Vol. LI, 1961, pp. 37–43.

HAGEN, Everett E. *On the Theory of Social Change: How Economic Growth Begins*. Homewood (Ill.), Dorsey Press, 1962; 2nd edn., London, Tavistock, 1964.

HALKIN, Léon E. *Initiation à la critique historique*. 'Cahiers des Annales' ser. Paris, Armand Colin, 1951.

HALL, A. R. 'The history of science.' In FINBERG (ed.), *Approaches to History, op. cit.* (1962), pp. 175–196.

HALL, D. G. E. *A History of South-East Asia*. London, Macmillan, 1955.

——. *East Asian History Today*. Hong Kong, Oxford University Press (East Asia), 1959.

HALL, D. G. E. (ed.). *Historians of South-East Asia* = Vol. II of *Historical Writing on the Peoples of Asia, op. cit.* (1961).

HALL, John W. 'Japanese historiography.' In *International Encyclopedia of the Social Sciences, op. cit.* (1968), Vol. VI, pp. 413–420 (*sub* 'Historiography').

HALPERN, Ben. 'History, sociology, and contemporary area studies.' *American Journal of Sociology* LXIII (1), July 1957, pp. 1–10.

HALPHEN, Louis. *Introduction à l'histoire*. Paris, Presses Universitaires de France, 1948.

HAMILTON, R. A. (ed.). *History and Archaeology in Africa* (proceedings of a conference on African history organized by the School of Oriental and African Studies, London, in 1953). Foreword by C. A. PHILIPS. London, The School, 1955.

HANDLIN, O. & BURCHARD, J. (eds.). *The Historian and the City*. Cambridge (Mass.), The M.I.T. Press, 1963.

HANKE, Lewis. 'A modest proposal for a moratorium on grand generalizations: some thoughts on the black legend.' *Hispanic American Historical Review*, Vol. LI, 1971, pp. 112–127.

HARRISON, Brian. *Separate Spheres: The Opposition to Women's Suffrage*. New York, Holmes and Meier, 1978.

HARRISON, James P. 'Chinese communist interpretations of the Chinese peasant wars.' *The China Quarterly*, No. 24, Oct.–Dec. 1965; reprinted in FEUERWERKER (ed.), *History in Communist China, op. cit.* (1968), pp. 189–215.

——. *The Communists and Chinese Peasant Rebellions: A Study in Rewriting of Chinese History*. Columbia University East Asian Institute Study, New York, Atheneum, 1969.

HARTUNG, Fritz. *Deutsche Verfassungsgeschichte vom 15. Jahrhundert bis zur Gegenwart*. 8th edn. Stuttgart, K. F. Koehler, 1950.

HAWKE, G. R. 'Mr. Hunt's study of the Fogel thesis: A comment.' *History* LIII

(177), Feb. 1968, pp. 18–23 (follows article by E. H. HUNT, 'The New Economic History: Professor Fogel's study of American railways,' *op. cit.*).

HAYS, Samuel P. 'History as human behavior.' In EISENSTADT, A. S. (ed.), *The Craft of American History, op. cit.* (1966), Vol. II, pp. 126–140.

HEBERLE, Rudolf. 'A regional background for Nazism.' In CAHNMAN & BOSKOFF (eds.), *Sociology and History: Theory and Research, op. cit.* (1964), pp. 407–414.

HEILBRUN, Carolyn G. 'Discovering the lost lives of women.' *New York Times Book Review,* 24 June 1988.

HEIMPEL, Hermann. 'Über Organisationsformen historischer Forschung in Deutschland.' In SCHIEDER, Th. (ed.), *Hundert Jahre Historische Zeitschrift 1859–1959, op. cit.* (1959), pp. 139–222.

HENRY, Louis. 'Une richesse démographique en friche: les registres paroissiaux.' *Population,* Vol. VIII, 1953, pp. 281–290.

———. *Anciennes familles genevoises.* Paris, Presses Universitaires de France, 1956.

———. *Manuel de démographie historique.* Geneva, Droz, 1967.

———. 'Historical demography.' In REVELLE (ed.), *Historical Population Studies, op. cit. (Daedalus,* 1968), pp. 385–396.

[See also: FLEURY & HENRY; GAUTIER & HENRY.]

HERBERT, Eugenia. *Red Gold of Africa: Copper in Precolonial History and Culture.* Madison, University of Wisconsin Press, 1984.

HERBERT, Jean. *Introduction à l'Asie.* Paris, Albin Michel, 1960 (English translation by Manu Banerji, *Introduction to Asia,* New York, Oxford University Press, 1968).

HERBST, Jurgen. *The German Historical School in American Scholarship: A Study in the Transfer of Culture.* Ithaca (N.Y.), Cornell University Press, 1965.

HERLIHY, David. 'Numerical and formal analysis in European history.' *Journal of Interdisciplinary History,* Vol. XII (1), Summer 1981, pp. 115–135.

———. 'Am I a Camera?: other reflections on films and history.' *American Historical Review,* Vol. XCIII (5), December 1988, p. 1186–1192.

HERZFELD, Hans. Introduction to MEINECKE, *Werke,* Vol. V, *Weltbürgertum und Nationalstaat, op. cit.* (2nd edn., 1969).

HEUSSI, Karl. *Die Krisis des Historismus.* Tübingen, J. C. B. Mohr, 1932.

HEXTER, J. H. *History, the Social Sciences, and Quantification* (XIIIth International Congress of Historical Sciences, Moscow, 16–23 Aug., 1970). Moscow, Nauka, 1970.

HIGGONET, Margaret *et al.* (eds.). *Behind the Lines: Gender and the Two World Wars.* New Haven, Yale University Press, 1987.

HIMMELFARB, Gertrude. *The New History and the Old: Critical Essays and Reappraisals.* Cambridge, Mass., Belknap Press of the Harvard University Press, 1987.

HINTZE, Otto. 'Typologie der ständischen Verfassungen des Abendlandes.' *Historische Zeitschrift,* Vol. CXLI, 1930, pp. 229–248; reprinted, with the following work, in HINTZE, *Gesammelte Abhandlungen,* ed. by Gerhard OESTREICH, Vol. I, 2nd edn., Göttingen, Vandenhoeck & Ruprecht, 1962, pp. 120–185.

———. 'Weltgeschichtliche Bedingungen der Repräsentativverfassung.' *Historische Zeitschrift,* Vol. CXLIII, 1931, pp. 1–47; reprinted in HINTZE, *Gesammelte Abhandlungen* (see preceding work).

L'Histoire et l'historien = Recherches et débats du Centre catholique des Intellectuels français, cahier No. 147, Paris, Librairie Arthème Fayard, 1964.

'Histoire et sciences sociales: un tournant critique?' *Annales: Economies, Sociétés, Civilisations,* Vol. XLIII (2), 1988, pp. 291–293.

Histoire générale des civilisations (1953–57): see CROUZET (ed.).

HISTORIA MUNDI (1952–61): see KERN & VALJAVEC (eds.).

The Historian in Tropical Africa / L'historien en Afrique tropicale (1964): see VANSINA, MAUNY & THOMAS, L. V. (eds.).

The Historical Association, 1906–1956. London, The Association, 1957.

Historical Population Studies: see REVELLE, Roger (ed.).

'Historical Revisions,' series of articles, *History,* between 1917 and 1955.

Historical Study in the West (1968): see SHAFER, FRANÇOIS, MOMMSEN and MILNE.

Historical Writing on the Peoples of Asia. London University, School of Oriental and African Studies. London, Oxford University Press, 1961–62. 4 vols.: Vol. I: C. H. PHILIPS (ed.), *Historians of India, Pakistan and Ceylon,* 1961; Vol. II: D. G. E. HALL (ed.), *Historians of South-East Asia,* 1961; Vol. III: W. G. BEASLEY & E. G. PULLEYBLANK (eds.), *Historians of China and Japan,* 1961; Vol. IV: B. LEWIS & P. M. HOLT (eds.), *Historians of the Middle-East,* 1962.

'Historiography.' In *International Encyclopedia of the Social Sciences, op. cit.* (1968), Vol. VI, pp. 368-428 (for individual contributions, see: DIKE & AJAYI; HALL, J. W.; ROSENTHAL; WANG Gungwu; WRIGHT, A. F.).

History and Archaeology in Africa (proceedings of the conferences on African history organized by the School of Oriental and African Studies, London, in 1953 and 1957): see HAMILTON, R. A. (ed.); JONES, D. H. (ed.).

'History and public opinion research: A debate' (discussion between LAZARSFELD, STRAYER and DAVID, *q.v.*). In KOMAROVSKY (ed.), *Common Frontiers of the Social Sciences, op. cit.* (1957), pp. 242–278.

History and Social Anthropology (1968): see LEWIS, I. M. (ed.).

History and Social Science = International Social Science Journal XVII (4), 1965 (parallel publication in French, *Histoire et sciences sociales = Revue internationale des Sciences sociales,* same ref.).

History as Social Science, The Behavioral and Social Sciences Survey (1971): see LANDES & TILLY (eds.).

History in Communist China (1968): see FEUERWERKER (ed.).

The History of Human Society, series: see PLUMB (ed.).

History of Mankind: Scientific and Cultural Development, under the auspices of Unesco, 6 vols. planned, London, Allen & Unwin/New York, Harper & Row, 4 vols.: Vol. I, 1963; Vol. II, 1965; Vol. IV, 1969; Vol. VI, 1966; Vols. III and V, forthcoming (parallel publication in French, *Histoire du développement scientifique et culturel de l'humanité,* 6 vols. (Vol. VI in two parts), Paris, Robert Laffont, 1967–68).

History of Science: An Annual Review of Literature, Research and Teaching, founded in 1962. Cambridge, W. Heffer & Sons.

'History, sociology and social anthropology' (report on the discussion at the Sixth *Past and Present* Conference, held in Birkbeck College, London, on 11 July 1963), *Past and Present,* No. 27, Apr. 1964, pp. 102–108.

History Workshop: A Journal of Socialist and Feminist Historians.

History Workshop XXVI, special feature on psychoanalysis and history, Autumn 1988, pp. 102–152.

HOBSBAWM, Eric J., *Primitive Rebels: Studies in Archaic Forms of Social Movements in the XIXth and XXth Centuries.* Manchester, Manchester University Press, 1959; another edn. entitled *Social Bandits and Primitive Rebels,* (New York, Free Press, 1960; 2nd edn. (under original title), Manchester, Manchester

University Press, 1962; New York, Praeger, 1963 (French translation by Reginald Laars, *Les primitifs de la révolte dans l'Europe moderne,* 'Présentation' by Jacques Le Goff, 'L'histoire sans frontières' ser., Paris, Fayard, 1966).

———. *Labouring Men: Studies in the History of Labour,* London, Weidenfeld, 1964.

HODGKIN, Thomas L. *Nationalism in Colonial Africa.* London, Muller, 1956.

———. 'New openings: Africa.' In *New Ways in History, op. cit.* (*Times Literary Supplement,* 1966), pp. 305–306.

HOFSTADTER, R. 'History and the social sciences.' In STERN (ed.), *The Varieties of History, op. cit.* (1956), pp. 359–370.

HOLLOWAY, S. W. F. 'Sociology and history.' *History* XLVIII (163), June 1963, pp. 154–180.

———. 'History and sociology.' In BURSTON & THOMSON (eds.), *Studies in the Nature and Teaching of History, op. cit.* (1967), pp. 1–8.

HÖLZLE, Edwin. *Idee und Ideologie.* Munich, A. Francke, 1969.

HONEY, P. J. 'Modern Vietnamese historiography.' In *Historical Writing on the Peoples of Asia,* Vol. II: *Historians of South-East Asia, op. cit.* (1961), pp. 94–104.

HOSELITZ, Bert. 'On comparative history.' *World Politics,* Vol. IX, 1957, pp. 267–279.

HOWARD, Michael (ed.). *Soldiers and Governments: Nine Studies in Civil-Military Relations.* London, Eyre & Spottiswoode, 1957.

HRBEK, I. Remarks made in the discussion on the theme 'Les Problèmes des sources de l'histoire de l'Afrique . . .,' *op. cit.* (*XIIth International Congress of Historical Sciences / XIIème Congrès international des Sciences historiques,* 1956), Vol. V (*Proceedings / Actes,* 1968), pp. 311–316.

HUDSON, Geoffrey F. *Europe and China: A Survey of Their Relations from the Earliest Times to 1800.* London, Arnold, 1931.

HUGHES, Henry Stuart. *Consciousness and Society: The Reorientation of European Social Thought, 1890–1930.* New York, Knopf, 1958.

———. 'The historian and the social scientist.' *American Historical Review,* Vol. LXVI, 1960, pp. 20–46; reprinted in RIASANOVSKY & RIZNIK (eds.), *Generalizations in Historical Writing, op. cit.* (1963), pp. 18–59.

———. *History as Art and as Science: Twin Vistas on the Past.* New York, Harper, 1964.

———. *The Obstructed Path: French Social Thought in the Years of Desperation, 1930–1960.* New York, Harper, 1966.

HUGHES, Henry Stuart (ed.). *Teachers of History: Essays in Honor of L. B. Packard.* Ithaca (N.Y.), Cornell University Press/London, Oxford University Press. 1954.

HUGHES, J. R. T. 'Fact and theory in economic history.' *Explorations in Entrepreneurial History,* 2nd ser., Vol. III, 1966, pp. 75–100; reprinted in ANDREANO (ed.), *The New Economic History: Recent Papers in Methodology, op. cit.* (1970).

[See also DAVIS, L. E., HUGHES, J. R. T. & McDOUGALL, D. M.]

HUIZINGA, Johan. 'De historische idee' (1934). In *Huizinga, Verzamelde werken,* Vol. VII, Haarlem, H. D. Tjeenk Willink & Zoon, 1951, pp. 134–150 (English translation by Rosalie Colie, 'The idea of history.' in STERN [ed.], *The Varieties of History, op. cit.* [1956], pp. 289–303).

———. 'A definition of the concept of history.' In KLIBANSKY & PATON (eds.), *Philosophy and History, op. cit.* (1936).

HULSEWÉ, A. F. P. 'Chinese communist treatment of the origins and the foundation of the Chinese empire.' *The China Quarterly,* No. 23, July–Sept. 1965; reprinted in FEUERWERKER (ed.), *History in Communist China, op. cit.* (1968), pp. 96–123.

Hundert Jahre Historische Zeitschrift (special centenary issue, *Historische Zeitschrift,* Vol. CLXXXIX, 1959): see SCHIEDER, Th. (ed.).

HUNT, E. H. 'The New Economic History: professor Fogel's study of American railways.' *History* LIII (177), Feb. 1968, pp. 3–18 (followed by a 'Comment' by G. R. HAWKE, *op cit.*).

HVOSTOV, V. 'L'activité scientifique de l'Institute d'Histoire de l'Académie des Sciences d'U.R.S.S.' *Revue historique,* CCXXXVI/1 (479), July–Sept. 1966, pp. 130–134 (*sub* 'Les centres d'études historiques').

IBN KHALDÛN. *Discours sur l'histoire universelle (al-Muqaddima).* French translation, preface and notes by Vincent Monteil. 'Collection Unesco d'Œuvres représentatives.' Beirut, Commission Internationale pour la Traduction des Chefs-d'Œuvre, 1967–68, 3 vols.

IGGERS, Georg G. *The German Conception of History: The National Tradition of Historical Thought from Herder to the Present.* Middletown (Conn.), Wesleyan University Press, 1968.

ILLERICKIJ, V. E. 'Problemy otečestvennoj istoriografii v sovetskoj istoričeskoj nauke (1917–1967)' (= Problems of national historiography in Soviet historical science—1917–1967). *Istorija SSSR,* 1968, No. 1.

————— & KUDRJAVCEV, I. A. *Istoriografija istorii SSSR s drevnejših vremen de Velikoj Oktjabr'skoj socialističeskoj revoljucii* (= Historiography of the History of the USSR from Ancient Times to the Great October Socialist Revolution) (handbook for higher schools). Moscow, 1961.

INALCIK, Halil. 'Some remarks on the study of history in Islamic countries.' *Middle East Journal,* Vol. VII, 1953, pp. 451–455.

'L'Industrialisation comme facteur de la croissance économique depuis 1700' = Section I in *Première Conférence internationale de l'Histoire économique,* The Hague, Mouton, 1960.

International Congresses of Historical Sciences: see *Xo* [Decimo] *Congresso internazionale di Scienze storiche, Roma, 4–11 settembre 1955: Relazioni; XIème* [Onzième] *Congrès international des Sciences historiques, Stockholm, 21–28 août 1960: Actes and Rapports; XIIth International Congress of Historical Sciences, Vienna, August 29–September 2, 1965: Reports;* XIIIth International Congress of Historical Sciences (Moscow, 16–23 Aug. 1970), publication of contributions in the form of separate brochures.

International Encyclopedia of the Social Sciences. Ed. David L. SILLS. 17 vols. New York, Macmillan Co. / Free Press, 1968.

IRIYE, A. 'Japanese imperialism and aggression.' *Journal of Asian Studies,* Vol. XXIII, 1963–64, pp. 103–113.

—————. 'Japan's foreign policies between the World Wars.' *Journal of Asian Studies,* Vol. XXVI, 1966–67, pp. 677–682.

Isis: An International Review devoted to the History of Science (official journal of the History of Science Society, U.S.A.), founded in 1912 by George SARTON; ed. Robert P. MULTHAUF; published in March, May, June, September and December (the May issue is the annual Critical Bibliography). Washington (D.C.), Smithsonian Institution.

ISSAWI, Charles. 'Reflections on the study of oriental civilizations.' In DE BARY & EMBREE (eds.) *Approaches to Asian Civilizations, op. cit.* (1961), pp. 59–68.

Istoričeskaja nauka i nekotorye problemy sovremennosti (= Historical Science and Some Contemporary Problems), collective work. Moscow, 1969.

Istorija i sociologija (= History and Sociology), collective volume. Moscow, Nauka, 1964.

IVANOVA, L. V. *U istokov sovetskoj istoričeskoj nauki, 1917–1927* (= On the Sources of Soviet Historical Sciences, 1917–1929). Moscow, 1968.

IYER, Raghavan. 'The glass curtain between Asia and Europe.' In IYER (ed.), *The Glass Curtain between Asia and Europe, op. cit.* (1965), pp. 3–27.

IYER, Raghavan (ed.). *The Glass Curtain between Asia and Europe: A Symposium on the Historical Encounters and the Changing Attitudes of the Peoples of the East and the West.* With a Foreword by the Dalai Lama. London, Oxford University Press, 1965.

Le Japon au XIe Congrès international des Sciences historiques à Stockholm: L'état actuel et les tendances des études historiques au Japon. Tokyo, 1960.

JASPERS, Karl. *Vom Ursprung und Ziel der Geschichte.* Munich, Piper/Zurich, Artemis, 1949 (English translation by Michael Bullock, *Origin and Goal of History*, New Haven (Conn.), Yale University Press, 1953).

JOACHIM, E. & HUBATSCH, W. (eds.). *Regesta Historico-Diplomatica Ordinis S. Mariae Theutonicorum.* 4 vols. Göttingen, Vandenhoeck & Ruprecht, 1948–65.

JOHNSON, Chalmers A. *Revolution and the Social System.* Stanford (Calif.). Stanford University Hoover Institute on War, Revolution and Peace, 1964.

JONES, D. H. (ed.). *History and Archaeology in Africa* (proceedings of a conference on African history organized by the School of Oriental and African Studies, London, in 1957). London, The School, 1959.

JONES, Gareth Stedman. *Languages of Class: Studies in English Working Class History.* Cambridge, Cambridge University Press, 1983.

JONGE, J. A. de. 'Geschiedenisbeoefening in Frankrijk' (= The practice of history in France). *Tijdschrift voor Geschiedenis*, Vol. LXXXII, 1969, pp. 158–183.

Journal of Contemporary History (London), III (2), Apr. 1968, pp. 1–252, special issue entitled *Reappraisals: A New Look at History; The Social Sciences and History* (includes, *inter alia,* articles by BESANÇON, MARCZEWSKI, MAZLISH, MORAZÉ, WOODWARD, all *op. cit.*).

Journal of the History of Ideas.

Journal of Interdisciplinary History.

Journal of Social History.

Journal of World History: see *Cahiers d'Histoire Mondiale / Journal of World History / Cuadernos de Historia Mundial.*

'Jubilejnoe obščee sobranie Otdelenija Istorii AN SSSR' (= Jubilee General Assembly of the Department of History of the USSR Academy of Sciences), *Voprosy istorii,* 1968, No. 1.

JUDT, Tony. 'A clown in regal purple: social history and the historians.' *History Workshop,* Vol. VII, Spring 1979, pp. 66–94.

KAHK, Ju. Ju. 'Novaja vyčislitel'naja tehnika na službu istoričeskoj nauke' (= The new technique of calculation at the service of historical science). *Istorija SSSR.* 1964, No. 1.

———. 'Nužna li novaja istoričeskaja nauka?' (= Do we need a new historical science?). *Voprosy istorii,* 1969, No. 3, pp. 41–54.

[See also DEOPIK, DOBROV, KAHK *et al.*]

KAHLER, Erich. *The Meaning of History.* New York, Braziller, 1964; London, Chapman, 1965.

KAHN, Harold & FEUERWERKER, Albert. 'The ideology of scholarship: China's new historiography.' *The China Quarterly,* No. 22, Apr.–June 1965; reprinted in FEUERWERKER (ed.), *History in Communist China, op. cit.* (1968), pp. 1–13.

KAKAR, S. 'The logic of psychohistory.' *Journal of Interdisciplinary History,* Vol. I, 1970, pp. 187–194.

KAMMEN, Michael (ed.). *The Past Before Us: Contemporary Historical Writing in the United States.* Ithaca, Cornell University Press, 1980.

KARTODIRDJO, Sartono. 'Historical study and historians in Indonesia today.' *Journal of Southeast Asian History* IV (1), 1963, pp. 22–29.

———. *The Peasants' Revolt of Banten in 1888: Its Conditions, Course and Sequel—A Case Study of Social Movements in Indonesia.* Koninklijk Inst. voor Taal-, Land- en Volkenkunde, Verhandelingen, deel 50. The Hague, M. Nijhoff, 1966.

———. *Kolonialisme dan Nasionalisme dalam Sedjarah Indonesia, Abad XIX–XX* (= Colonialism and Nationalism in Indonesian History, XIX–XX Centuries). Jogjakarta, 1967.

———. *Baberapa fasal dari historiografi Indonesia* (= Some Points of Indonesian Historiography). Jogjakarta, 1968.

KATZ, H. Remarks made in the discussion of the report by GOTTSCHALK, L. R., 'Projects and concepts of world history in the twentieth century,' *op. cit.* (*XIIth International Congress of Historical Sciences / XIIème Congrès international des Sciences historiques,* 1965, Vol. V: *Proceeding / Actes,* 1968), pp. 539–540.

KAYE, Harvey J. *The British Marxist Historians.* Cambridge, Polity Press, 1984.

KAZEMZADEH, Firuz. 'Iranian historiography.' In *Historical Writing on the Peoples of Asia,* Vol. IV: *Historians of the Middle-East, op. cit.* (1962), pp. 430–434.

KEARNS, Martha. *Käthe Kollwitz: Woman and Artist.* Old Westbury, Feminist Press, 1976.

KEDWARD, Harry Roderick. *Fascism in Western Europe, 1900–1945.* New York, New York University Press, 1971.

KEEN, B. 'The black legend revisited.' *Hispanic American Historical Review,* Vol. XLIX, 1969, pp. 708–719.

———. 'The white legend revisited.' *Hispanic American Historical Review,* Vol. LI, 1971, pp. 336–355.

KEEP, John L. H. & BRISBY, Liliana (eds.). *Contemporary History in the Soviet Mirror.* London, Allen & Unwin/New York, Praeger, 1964.

KEHR, Eckart. *Der Primat der Innenpolitik: Gesammelte Aufsätze zur preussischdeutschen Sozialgeschichte im 19. und 20. Jahrhundert.* Ed. by Hans-U. WEHLER with an Introduction *(op. cit.).* Berlin, W. de Gruyter, 1965.

KEHR, Paul. *Regesta pontificum Romanorum (Italia pontificia,* Vol. I). Berlin, 1906.

KELDYSH, Mstislav. 'The USSR Academy of Sciences: centre of Soviet scientific thought.' *Social Sciences (USSR Academy of Sciences),* Vol. 2, 1970.

KELIKIAN, Alice. *Town and Country Under Fascism: The Transformation of Brescia, 1915–1926.* New York, Oxford University Press, 1986.

KELLY, John B. *Eastern Arabian Frontiers.* London, Faber & Faber/New York, Praeger, 1964.

KERN, Fritz & VALJAVEC, Fritz (eds.). *Historia Mundi. Ein Handbuch der Weltgeschichte.* Bern, Francke, 1952–61, 10 vols.

KERN, Stephen. *The Culture of Time and Space, 1880–1918.* Cambridge, Mass., Harvard University Press, 1983.

KIM, G. F. & NIKIFOROV, V. N. *Researches in the History of the Countries of the East (1965–1969)* (XIIIth International Congress of Historical Sciences, Moscow, 16–23 Aug. 1970). Moscow, Nauka, 1970.

KIMBLE, George H. T. *Tropical Africa.* New York, Twentieth Century Fund, 1960, 2 vols.

KING, J. F. 'Negro history in continental Spanish America.' *Journal of Negro History,* Vol. XXIX, 1944, pp. 7–23.

KITSON CLARK, George. *The Making of Victorian England.* The Ford Lectures delivered before the University of Oxford. London, Methuen/Cambridge (Mass.), Harvard University Press, 1962.

———. *The Critical Historian.* London, Heinemann/New York, Basic Books, 1967.

——— & ELTON, G. R., *Guide to Research Facilities in History in the Universities of Great Britain and Ireland.* 2nd edn. Cambridge, Cambridge University Press, 1965.

KLIBANSKY, Raymond & PATON, H. J. (eds.). *Philosophy and History,* essays presented to Ernst Cassirer. Oxford, Oxford University Press, 1936.

'K novomu pod'emu istoriko-partijnoj nauki' (= For a new upsurge in the science of the history of the Party). *Voprosy istorii KPSS,* 1960, No. 5, pp. 3–20.

KOCHAN, Lionel. *Acton on History.* London, Deutsch, 1954.

KOMAROVSKY, Mirra. 'Introduction.' In KOMAROVSKY (ed.), *Common Frontiers of the Social Sciences, op. cit.* (1957), pp. 1–30 ('A guide to the contents,' pp. 1–12; 'Some recurrent issues of interdisciplinary polemics,' pp. 12–22; 'Interdisciplinary convergencies,' pp. 22–30).

KOMAROVSKY, Mirra (ed.). *Common Frontiers of the Social Sciences.* Glencoe (Ill.), Free Press, 1957.

KON, Igor A. *Filosofskij idealizm i krisis buržuaznoj istoričeskoj mysli* (= Philosophical Idealism and the Crisis of Bourgeois Historical Thought), Moscow, 1959; revised and supplemented German version, *Die Geschichtsphilosophie des 20. Jahrhunderts. Kritischer Abriss,* authorized translation by Willi Hoepp. Berlin, Akademie-Verlag, 1964, 2 vols.; 2nd German edn., 1966.

———. *Der Positivismus in der Soziologie: Geschichtlicher Abriss,* authorized translation from the Russian original by Willi Hoepp, Berlin, Akademie-Verlag, 1968.

———. 'Istorija i sociologija,' *Voprosy filosofii,* 1970, No. 8 (French translation, 'Histoire et sociologie,' *Social Science Information / Information sur les Sciences sociales* X (4), Aug. 1971, pp. 87–102).

KOSAMBI, Damodar Dharmanand. *An Introduction to the Study of Indian History.* New York, William S. Heinman, 1956; London, Arthur Probsthain, 1957.

———. *Culture and Civilization of Ancient India in Historical Outline.* London, Routledge, 1965; another edn. entitled *Ancient India: A History of Its Culture and Civilization.* New York, Pantheon Books, 1966.

KOSELLECK, Reinhart. 'Wozu noch Historie?' *Historische Zeitschrift* CCXII (1), Feb. 1971, pp. 1–18.

KOSMINSKIJ, Evgenij A. *Anglijskaja derevnja v XIII veke.* Moscow, 1935 (English translation by Ruth Kisch, ed. by R. H. Hilton, KOSMINSKY, E. A., *Studies in the Agrarian History of England in the Thirteenth Century,* 'Studies in Mediaeval History,' ed. by G. Barraclough, Vol. 8, Oxford, Blackwell, 1956.

KOVAL'ČENKO, I. D. & MILOV, L. V. 'O principah issledovanija processa formirovanija vserossijskogo agrarnogo rynka' (= On the principles of research on the process of formation of an all-Russia agricultural market), *Istorija SSSR,* 1969, No. 1.

[See also DEOPIK, DOBROV, KAHK, KOVALCHENKO *et al.*]

Kratkaja vsemirnaja istorija (= A Short History of the World). Ed. A. Z. MANFRED. Moscow, Nauka, 1967, 2 vols.

KROEBER, Alfred Louis. *Configurations of Culture Growth.* Berkeley-Los Angeles, University of California Press, 1944.

———. *The Nature of Culture.* Chicago, University of Chicago Press, 1952.

KROEF, J. M. van der: see VAN DER KROEF, J. M.

Kruithof, J. 'Qu'est-ce qui est important dans l'histoire? une approche sociologique.' In PERELMAN (ed.), *Raisonnement et démarches de l'historien, op. cit.* (1963), pp. 107–120.

KU Chieh-kang. *The Autobiography of a Chinese Historian* (the preface to a symposium on ancient Chinese history: *Ku shih pien*). Annotated English translation by Arthur W. Hummel. Leiden, Brill, 1931.

KUO Mo-jo. *Chung-kuo Ku-tai She-huei Yen-chiu* (= Studies in Ancient Chinese Society). Shanghai, Chung-ya Shu-chü, 1930; rev. edns., 1954 and 1960.

———. 'Kuan-yü *Hou-chin Po-ku* Wen-t'i' (= On the question of 'emphasizing the present and de-emphasizing the past'), *Pei-ching Ta-hsueh Pao, Jen-wen K'o-hsueh* (= Peking University Journal, Humanistic Sciences), No. 3, 1958, pp. 111–114; also *Jen-min Jih-pao* (= People's Daily), 11 June 1958, p. 7.

LABALME, Patricia H. (ed.). *Beyond Their Sex: Learned Women of the European Past.* New York, New York University Press, 1980.

LACH, Donald F., *Asia in the Making of Europe.* Vol. I: *The Century of Discovery.* Chicago, University of Chicago Press, 1965.

LAMB, Hubert H. *The Changing Climate* (selected papers). London, Methuen/New York, Barnes & Noble, 1966.

LANDES, Davis S. & TILLY, Charles H. (eds.). *History as Social Science.* The Behavioral and Social Sciences Survey. Englewood Cliffs (N.J.), Prentice-Hall, 1971.

LANGER, William L. 'The next assignment.' *American Historical Review,* Vol. LXIII, 1958, pp. 283–304; reprinted in LANGER, *Explorations in Crisis, op. cit.* (1969), pp. 408–432.

———. *Explorations in Crisis: Papers on International History.* ed. by Carl & Elizabeth Schorske. Cambridge (Mass.), Harvard University Press, 1969.

I ᴀɴɢLOIS, Charles V. & SEIGNOBOS, Charles. *Introduction aux études historiques,* Paris, 1898 (English translation, *Introduction to the Study of History,* London, Duckworth, 1925).

LANGWELL, William H. *The Conservation of Books and Documents.* With a Foreword by Geoffrey BARRACLOUGH. London, Pitman, 1957.

LARSON, Henrietta M. *Guide to Business History: Materials for the Study of American Business History and Suggestions for Their Use.* Cambridge (Mass.), Harvard University Press/London, Oxford University Press, 1948.

LASLETT, Peter. 'The history of population and social structure.' In *History and Social Science, op. cit.* (*Int. Soc. Sc. J.,* 1965), pp. 582–593 (parallel publication in French translation, 'L'histoire de la population et de la structure sociale,' in *Histoire et sciences sociales* (*Rev. int. des Sciences soc.,* 1965), pp. 626–639).

———. *The World We Have Lost.* London, Methuen, 1965.

———. 'History and the social sciences.' In *International Encyclopedia of the Social Sciences, op. cit.* (1968), Vol. VI, pp. 434–440 (*sub.* 'History').

[See also WRIGLEY, EVERSLEY & LASLETT (eds.).]

Latin America: A Guide to the Historical Literature (1971): see GRIFFIN (ed.).

Latin American Scholarship since World War II (1971): see ESQUENAZI-MAYO & MEYER (eds.).

LATTIMORE, Owen. 'The frontier in history.' In *Xo* [Decimo] *Congresso inter-*

nazionale di Scienze storiche: Relazioni, op. cit. (1955), Vol. I, pp. 103–138.

――――. *Inner Asian Frontiers of China.* 3rd edn. Boston, Beacon Press, 1962.

――――. *From China, Looking Outwards.* Leeds, Leeds University Press, 1964.

LAZARSFELD, Paul F. 'The historian and the pollster.' In KOMAROVSKY (ed.), *Common Frontiers of the Social Sciences, op. cit.* (1957), pp. 242–262 (part of 'History and public opinion research. A debate'); reproduced in LIPSET & HOFSTADTER (eds.), *Sociology and History: Methods, op. cit.* (1968), pp. 386–407.

LE BON, Gustave. *La psychologie des foules.* Paris, 1895; new edn., with an 'Avant-propos' by Otto KLINEBERG, Paris, Presses Universitaires de France, 1963.

LEBRUN, P. 'Structure et quantification: réflexions sur la science historique.' In PERELMAN, *Raisonnement et démarches de l'historien, op. cit.* (1963), pp. 29–51.

――――. 'Développement et histoire quantitative: vers une historiométrie?' *Revue de l'Institut de Sociologie* (Brussels), 1967, No. 4, pp. 569–605.

LEEDS, Edward T. *The Archaeology of the Anglo-Saxon Settlements.* Oxford, Oxford University Press, 1913.

LEFEBVRE, Georges. *La grande peur de 1789.* Paris, Armand Colin, 1932.

LEFF, Gordon. *History and Social Theory.* London, Merlin Press/University of Alabama Press, 1969; paperback edn., New York, Doubleday, 1971.

LEGGE, John D. *Indonesia.* Englewood Cliffs (N.J.), Prentice-Hall, 1964.

LE GOFF, Jacques. *Time, Work and Culture in the Middle Ages.* Translated by Arthur Goldhammer. Chicago, University of Chicago Press, 1980.

――――. *L'Imaginaire médiéval.* Paris, Gallimard, 1985.

LENSEN, G. A. 'Soviet approaches to oriental civilization.' In DE BARY & EMBREE (eds.), *Approaches to Asian Civilizations, op. cit.* (1961), pp. 262–265.

LEON, P. 'The terror of history.' *The Listener,* Vol. LIV, 1955.

LE ROY LADURIE, Emmanuel. 'La Conférence d'Aspen sur le climat des XIe et XVIe siècles.' *Annales* XVIII (4), July–Aug. 1963, pp. 764–766.

――――. *Les paysans de Languedoc.* Paris, S.E.V.P.E.N., 1966; new edn., Paris, Flammarion, 1969.

――――. *Histoire du climat depuis l'an mil.* 'Nouvelle Bibliothèque Scientifique.' Paris, Flamarion, 1967.

――――. *Le Territoire de l'historien.* Paris, Gallimard, 1973.

――――. *Montaillou, village occitan de 1294 à 1324.* Paris, Gallimard, 1975.

LEŚNODORSKI, Boguslaw. 'Les sciences historiques en Pologne au cours des années 1945–1955.' In *Xo* [Decimo] *Congresso internazionale di Scienze storiche, Relazioni, op. cit.* (1955), Vol. VI, pp. 457–515.

LEUR, Jacob C. van. 'The study of Indonesian history.' In van LEUR, *Indonesian Trade and Society, op. cit.* (1955), pp. 147–156.

――――. *Indonesian Trade and Society: Essays in Asian Social and Economic History.* English version by James S. Holmes & A. van Marle; published for the Royal Tropical Institute. Amsterdam, The Hague, Hoeve/New York, Institute of Pacific Relations, 1955.

LEVINE, Robert M. *The Vargas Regime: The Crucial Years, 1934–1938.* New York, Columbia University Press, 1970.

LÉVY-LEBOYER, Maurice. 'La "New Economic History."' *Annales* XXIV (5), Sept.–Oct. 1969, pp. 1035–1069.

LEWIS, Archibald R. & McGANN, Thomas F. (eds.). *The New World Looks at its History* (International Congress of Historians of the United States and Mexico, Austin, Tex., 1958); published for the Institute of Latin American Studies. Austin, University of Texas Press, 1963.

LEWIS, Bernard. 'History writing and the national revival in Turkey.' *Middle Eastern Affairs*, Vol. IV, 1953, pp. 218–227.

———. *The Middle East and the West*. Bloomington, Indiana University Press/ London, Weidenfeld, 1964.

LEWIS, Bernard & HOLT, P. M. (eds.). *Historians of the Middle East* = Vol. IV of *Historical Writing on the Peoples of Asia*, op. cit. (1962).

LEWIS, Ioan M. (ed.). *History and Social Anthropology*. London, Tavistock, 1968.

LEWIS, M. D. 'How many histories should we teach? Asia and Africa in a liberal arts education.' *Liberal Education*, Vol. XLVIII, 1962, pp. 1–9.

———. 'Problems of approach to Asia's modern history.' In *Studies on Asia, 1963*, ed. Robert K. SAKAI, Lincoln, University of Nebraska Press, 1963.

LHOTSKY, Alphons. 'Geschichtsforschung und Geschichtsschreibung in Österreich.' In SCHIEDER (ed.), *Hundert Jahre Historische Zeitschrift 1859–1959, op. cit.* (1959), pp. 379–448.

LICHTHEIM, George. 'Marx and "The Asiatic mode of production."' *St. Antony's Papers*, vol. XIV, 1963, pp. 86–112.

LIFTON, Robert J. 'On psychology and history.' *Comparative Studies in Society and History*, Vol. VII, 1964, pp. 127–132.

———. *Revolutionary Immortality: Mao Tse-tung and the Chinese Cultural Revolution*. New York, Random House/London, Weidenfeld, 1968.

———. *History and Human Survival: Essays on the Young and Old, Survivors and the Dead, Peace and War, and on Contemporary Psychohistory*. New York, Random House, 1969.

LIPSET, Seymour Martin, Review of Barrington MOORE, Jr. *Political Power and Social Theory* (Cambridge, Mass., Harvard University Press, 1958), *American Sociological Review* XXV (2), Apr. 1960, pp. 283–285.

LIPSET, Seymour Martin & HOFSTADTER, Richard (eds.). *Sociology and History: Methods*. New York, Basic Books, 1968.

LIPSON, Ephraim. *Economic History of England*. London, A. & G. Black/New York, Macmillan, 1915–31.

LIU, Chung-jo. *Controversies in Modern Chinese History: An Analytic Bibliography of Periodical Articles, mainly of the May 4th and post-May 4th Era*. Cambridge (Mass.), Harvard University Press, 1964.

LIU, J. T. C. 'An orientation course on Asian civilisations.' *Journal of General Education*, Vol. X, 1957, pp. 228–235.

LOCHER, Th. J. G. *Die Überwindung des europäozentrischen Geschichtsbildes*. Wiesbaden, Steiner, 1954.

LOEWENBERG, Peter. 'The unsuccessful adolescence of Heinrich Himmler.' *American Historical Review*, Vol. LXXVI (3), June 1971, pp. 612–641.

———. *Decoding the Past: The Psychohistorical Approach*. New York, Knopf, 1983.

LORENZ, Konrad. *Das sogenannte Böse: Zur Naturgeschichte der Aggression*. Vienna, Verlag Dr. G. Borotha-Schoeler, 1963 (English translation by Marjorie K. Wilson, *On Aggression*, New York, Harcourt, Brace & World/London, Methuen, 1966).

LÖTZKE, Helmut & BRATHER, Hans-Stephan. *Übersicht über die Bestände des Deutschen Zentralarchivs Potsdam*. Berlin, Rütten & Loening, 1957.

LÖWITH, Karl. *Meaning in History: The Theological Implications of the Philosophy of History*. Chicago, University of Chicago Press, 1949; Cambridge, Cambridge University Press, 1950.

LÜCKERATH, C. A. 'Prolegomena zur elektronischen Datenverarbeitung im Bereich der Geschichtswissenschaft.' *Historische Zeitschrift,* Vol. CCVII, 1968, pp. 265–296.

LYND, Robert S. & LYND, M. *Middletown: A Study in Contemporary American Culture.* New York, Harcourt, Brace & World/London, Constable, 1929.

——. *Middletown in Transition: A Study in Cultural Conflicts.* New York, Harcourt, Brace & World/London, Constable, 1937.

MCALISTER, L. N. 'Social structure and social change in New Spain.' *Hispanic American Historical Review,* Vol. XLIII, 1963, pp. 349–370; reproduced in CLINE (ed.), *Latin American History, op. cit.* (1967), pp. 750–764.

MCCALL, Daniel F. *Africa in Time-Perspective: A Discussion on Historical Reconstruction from Unwritten Sources.* Boston, Boston University Press/London, Oxford University Press, 1964.

MCCLELLAND, David C. *The Achieving Society.* 1st edn. Princeton (N.J.), Van Nostrand, 1961; paperback edn., New York, Free Press, 1967.

MCCORMICK, R. P. 'New perspectives on Jacksonian politics.' In ROWNEY & GRAHAM (eds.), *Quantitative History, op. cit.* (1969), pp. 372–384.

MACDONALD, A. W. 'The application of a South East Asia-centric conception of history to mainland South East Asia.' In *Historical Writing on the Peoples of Asia, op. cit.,* Vol. II (1961), pp. 326–335.

MCDOUGALL, William. *An Introduction to Social Psychology.* London, 1908; rev. and enl. edn., Boston, Luce, 1926.

MCFEELY, Mary Drake. *Women's Work in Britain and America: From the Nineties to World War I.* Berkeley, University of California Press, 1987.

MCFEELY, William S. 'A voice for History.' Address to the *American Historical Association* Annual Meeting, December 1983.

MACHLUP, F. 'Structure and structural change: weaselwords and jargon.' *Zeitschrift für Nationalökonomie,* 1958, pp. 280–298.

MACK, John E. *The Prince of Our Disorder: The Life of T. E. Lawrence.* Boston, Little, Brown, 1976.

MACMILLAN, D. S. 'Archival reform in Australia.' *Journal of the Society of Archivists,* Vol. I, 1955–59, pp. 210–213.

MCNEILL, William H. *The Rise of the West: A History of the Human Community.* Chicago, University of Chicago Press, 1963.

——. *A World History.* New York, Watts, 1967; London, Oxford University Press, 1967.

——. 'World history in the schools.' In BALLARD, *New Movements in the Study and Teaching of History, op. cit.* (1970), pp. 16–25.

MACRAE, Donald G. 'The crisis of sociology.' In PLUMB (ed.), *Crisis in the Humanities, op. cit.* (1964), pp. 124–138.

MAJUMDAR, Ramesh Chandra. 'Ideas of history in Sanskrit literature.' In *Historical Writing on the Peoples of Asia, op. cit.,* Vol. I (1961), pp. 13–28.

——. 'Nationalist historians.' In *Historical Writing on the Peoples of Asia, op. cit.,* Vol. I (1961), pp. 416–428.

——. *Historiography in Modern India* (Heras Memorial Lectures, 1967), issued under the auspices of the Heras Institute of Indian History and Culture. Bombay-London, Asia Publishing House, 1970.

MALIN, James C. *On the Nature of History: Essays about History and Dissidence.* Ann Arbor, 1954.

MANDROU, Robert. *Introduction à la France moderne, 1500–1640: Essai de psychologie historique,* 'L'évolution de l'humanité' ser. Paris, Albin Michel, 1961.

——. *De la culture populaire aux XVIIe et XVIIIe siècles.* Paris, Stock, 1964.

————. *Magistrats et sorciers en France au XVIIe siècle: Une analyse de psychologie historique.* 'Civilisations et mentalités' ser. Paris, Plon, 1968.

MANN, Golo *et al.* (eds.). *Propyläen Weltgeschichte,* series. Berlin, Propyläen Verlag, 1960–65, 10 vols.

MANNONI, Dominique Oliver. *Psychologie de la colonisation.* Paris, Seuil, 1950 (English translation by Pamela Powesland, *Prospero and Caliban: The Psychology of Colonization,* with a Foreword by Philip Mason, New York, Praeger/London, Methuen, 1956).

MAO Tse-tung Hsuan-chi. *Selected Works.* Peking, 1961, 4 vols.

MARAVALL, José Antonio. *Teoría del saber histórico.* Madrid, Revista de Occidente, 1958.

MARCHISIO, Joseph. 'Les études historiques en Chine populaire.' *Revue historique,* Vol. CCXXIX/1 (465), Jan.–Mar. 1963, pp. 159–168 (*sub* 'L'orientation actuelle des études historiques').

MARCZEWSKI, Jean. *Introduction à l'histoire quantitative.* Geneva, Droz, 1965.

————. 'Quantitative history.' *Journal of Contemporary History* III (2), Apr. 1968 (special issue: *Reappraisals*), pp. 179–191.

MARHO (The Radical Historians Organization). *Visions of History.* New York, Pantheon Books, 1983.

MARITAIN, Jacques. *On the Philosophy of History.* Ed. by Joseph W. Evans. New York, Charles Scribner's Sons, 1959; London, Geoffrey Bles, 1959 (French translation by Mgr. Charles Journet, *Pour une philosophie de l'histoire,* Paris, Seuil, 1960).

MARKOV, W. *Wege und Formen der Staatsbildung in Asien und Afrika seit dem zweiten Weltkrieg* (XIIIth International Congress of Historical Sciences. Moscow, 16–23 Aug. 1970). Moscow, Nauka, 1970.

MARROU, Henri-Irénée. *De la connaissance historique.* Paris, Seuil, 1954; 4th edn., rev. and augm., *ibid.,* 1962.

MARWICK, Arthur. *The Nature of History.* London, Macmillan/New York, Knopf, 1970.

MARX, Karl, *Economic and Philosophic Manuscripts of 1844.* English translation by Martin Milligan, ed. by Dirk J. Struik. London, Lawrence & Wishart/New York, International Publ. Co., 1970.

————. *Zur Kritik der politischen Ökonomie* (1859): English translations: *Contribution to the Critique of Political Economy,* in MARX-ENGELS, *Selected Works, op. cit.* (1950), Vol. I; same title, New York, International Publ. Co., 1970.

————. & ENGELS, Friedrich. *Selected Works.* London, Lawrence & Wishart, 1950, 2 vols.

————. *Die heilige Familie: Kritik der kritischen Kritik. Gegen Bruno Bauer und Consorten* (1945), in MARX-ENGELS, *Werke,* Vol. II, Berlin, 1959 (English translation by R. Dixon, *The Holy Family; or Critique of the Critical Critique,* London, Lawrence & Wishart, 1957).

————. *Manifest der Kommunistischen Partei* (1848), in MARX-ENGELS, *Gesamtausgabe,* Abt. I, Bd. 6, Moscow-Leningrad, 1933 (English translation by Samuel Moore, edited and with a study by Harold J. Laski, *Communist Manifesto,* London, Allen & Unwin, 1948).

————. *Die deutsche Ideologie.* English translation, ed. C. J. Arthur, *The German Ideology.* London, Lawrence & Wishart/New York, International Publ. Co., 1970.

MATHIAS, Peter. 'Economic history, direct and oblique.' In BALLARD (ed.), *New Movements in the Study and Teaching of History, op. cit.* (1970), pp. 76–92.

MAUNY, Raymond. 'Troisième section: l'archèologie.' In 'Les Problèmes des sources de l'histoire de l'Afrique noire jusqu'à la colonisation européenne', *op. cit. (XIIth International Congress of Historical Sciences/XIIème Congrès international des Sciences historiques: Reports/Rapports,* Vol. II: *History of the Continents/Histoire des continents,* 1965), pp. 208–213. [See also VANSINA, Mauny & THOMAS, L. V. (eds.).]

MAUROIS, André. *Aspects of Biography.* Translated by S. Roberts. New York, D. Appleton, 1929.

MAZLISH, Bruce (ed.). *Psychoanalysis and History.* Englewood Cliffs, Prentice-Hall, 1963.

———. *The Riddle of History: The Great Speculators from Vico to Freud.* New York, Harper, 1966.

———. 'Group psychology and problems of contemporary history.' *Journal of Contemporary History* III (2), Apr. 1968 (special issue: *Reappraisals*), pp. 163–177.

———. *In Search of Nixon: A Psychohistorical Inquiry.* New York, Basic Books, 1972.

MAZOUR, Anatol G. *Modern Russian Historiography.* 2nd edn. Princeton (N.J.), Van Nostrand, 1958.

MEINECKE, Friedrich. *Weltbürgertum und Nationalstaat.* 6th edn. Munich/Berlin 1922; reprinted in MEINECKE, *Werke,* Vol. V, ed. Hans Herzfeld, Munich, Oldenbourg/Stuttgart, K. F. Koehler/Darmstadt, Toeche-Mittler, 1969.

———. *Aphorismen und Skizzen zur Geschichte.* Leipzig, Koehler & Amelang, 1942.

———. *Ranke und Burckhardt: Ein Vortrag.* Berlin, Akademie-Verlag, 1948.

MEISNER, Heinrich Otto. *Urkunden-und Aktenlehre der Neuzeit.* 2nd edn. Leipzig, Koehler & Amelang, 1952.

Metodologičeskie i istoriografičeskie voprosy istoričeskoj nauki (= Methodological and Historiographical Questions of Historical Science), collective work. Tomsk, Tomsk University Publications, 1964.

MEYER, John R. & CONRAD, Alfred H. 'Economic theory, statistical inference and economic history.' *Journal of Economic History,* Vol. XVII, 1957, pp. 524–544; reprinted in A. H. CONRAD & J. R. MEYER, *The Economics of Slavery and other Studies in Econometric History,* Chicago, Aldine, 1964, pp. 3–30.

MEYERHOFF, Hans (ed.). *The philosophy of History in Our Time: An Anthology.* Garden City (N.Y.), Doubleday, 1959.

MIJATEV, Peter. 'Organizing archives in Bulgaria.' *Archives* (1957–58), III (20), Michaelmas 1958, pp. 235–237.

Minerva: Jahrbuch der gelehrten Welt. Berlin-New York, W. de Gruyter, 6 volumes published 1966–72; *Universitäten und Fachhochschulen,* Part I: *Europa,* 1966; Part II: *Aussereuropa,* 1969–70, 2 vols. and 1 vol. of Tables; *Internationales Verzeichnis Wissenschaftlicher Institutionen,* Part I: *Wissenschaftliche Gesellschaften,* 1972; Part II: *Forschungsinstitute,* 1972.

MITTEIS, Heinrich. *Der Staat des hohen Mittelalters: Grundlinien einer vergleichenden Verfassungsgeschichte des Lehenszeitalters.* Weimar, Böhlau, 1940; 3rd rev. edn., Darmstadt, Wissenschaftliche Buchgesellschaft, 1958.

MIYAZAKI, Ichisado. *Toyo-teki kinsei* (= The Modern Age in the Orient). Tokyo, 1950.

MOMIGLIANO, Arnaldo D. 'Lo storicismo nel pensiero contemporaneo: Discussione,' *Rivista Storica Italiana* LXXIII (1), Mar. 1961, pp. 104–119 (English version, 'Historicism in contemporary thought,' in MOMIGLIANO, *Studies in Historiography, op. cit.* (1966), pp. 221–238) [original Italian text followed in periodical by Pietro ROSSI's reply, pp. 119–132].

————. *Studies in Historiography*. London, Weidenfeld, 1966.

MOMMSEN, Wolfgang, J. *Die Geschichtswissenschaft jenseits des Historismus.* Düsseldorf, Droste Verlag, 1971.

[See also SHAFER, FRANÇOIS, MOMMSEN and MILNE.]

MONIOT, Henri. 'Pour une histoire de l'Afrique noire.' *Annales* XVII (1), Jan.–Feb. 1962, pp. 46–64.

[See also *sub* 'Les Problèmes des sources de l'histoire de l'Afrique noire jusqu'à la colonisation européenne.']

MONTAGU, M. F. Ashley (ed.). *Toynbee and History: Critical Essays and Reviews.* Boston, Sargent, 1956.

MONTEIL, Vincent. 'La décolonisation de l'histoire.' *Preuves*, No. 142, Dec. 1962, pp. 3–12 (English translation in WALLERSTEIN, *Social Change: The Colonial Situation, op. cit.*, 1966).

[See also *sub* IBN KHALDÛN, *Discours sur l'histoire universelle.*]

MOORE, Barrington. *Social Origins of Dictatorship and Democracy: Lord and Peasant in the Making of the Modern World.* Boston, Beacon Press, 1966.

MORAZÉ, Charles. *Trois essais sur Histoire et Culture* (with a Foreword by Lucien FEBVRE, *op. cit.*). 'Cahiers des *Annales*,' No. 2. Paris, Armand Colin, 1948.

————. *La logique de l'histoire.* 'Les Essais' series, No. CXXIX. Paris, Gallimard, 1967.

————. 'The application of the social sciences to history.' *Journal of Contemporary History* III (2), Apr. 1968 (special issue: *Reappraisals*), pp. 207–215.

MÖRNER, Magnus. 'The history of race relations in Latin America.' *Latin American Research Review*, Vol. I, 1966, pp. 17–44.

MORRISON, Karl F. *Europe's Middle Ages.* Glenview (Ill.), Scott Foresman, 1970.

MORSE, Richard M. 'Some characteristics of Latin American urban history.' *American Historical Review*, Vol. LXVII, 1962, pp. 317–338.

————. 'Trends and issues in Latin American urban research, 1965–1970.' *Latin American Research Review* (1970), VI (1), Spring, pp. 3–52 and (2), Summer, pp. 19–75.

MURAKAWA, Kentaro, EGAMI, Namio and HAYASHI, Kentaro. *Sekai shi* (= History of the World). 5th edn. Tokyo, 1955.

MURPHY, George G. S. 'The "new" history.' *Explorations in Entrepreneurial History*, 2nd ser., Vol. II, 1965, pp. 132–146.

————. 'On counterfactual propositions.' In *Studies in Quantitative History, op. cit.* (*History and Theory*, Beiheft 9, 1969), pp. 14–38.

————. & MUELLER, M. G. 'On making historical techniques more specific: "real types" constructed with a computer.' In ROWNEY & GRAHAM (eds.), *Quantitative History, op. cit.* (1969), pp. 81–98.

MUSSON, Albert E. ROBINSON, Eric. *Science and Technology in the Industrial Revolution.* Manchester, Manchester University Press, 1969.

NABHOLZ, Hans. *Einführung in das Studium der mittelalterlichen und der neueren Geschichte.* Zurich, Schulthess, 1948.

NAITO, Torajiro. *Shina joko shi* (= Ancient History of China). Tokyo, 1944.

NAMIER, Lewis B. *The Structure of Politics at the Accession of George III.* 2 vols. London, Macmillan, 1929.

————. *England in the Age of the American Revolution.* London, Macmillan, 1930.

NATARAJAN, L. *Peasant Uprisings in India, 1850–1900.* Bombay, 1953.

NEEDHAM, Joseph. *Science and Civilisation in China* (7 vols. projected). Vols. I–VI. Cambridge, Cambridge University Press, 1954–86.

————. *The Grand Titration: Science and Society in East and West.* London, Allen

& Unwin, 1969 (French translation by Eugène Jacob, *La science chinoise et l'Occident* [Le grand titrage], Paris, Seuil, 1973).

———. *Clerks and Craftsmen in China and the West: Lectures and Addresses on the History of Science and Technology.* Cambridge, Cambridge University Press, 1970.

'Nekotorye itogi raboty Instituta Istorii Akademii Nauk SSSR za 1959' (= Some results of the work of the Historical Institute of the USSR Academy of Science since 1959). *Voprosy istorii,* 1960, No. 5.

NERSESOV, G. A. *Soviet Literature on the History of the African Countries for the Period 1965–69* (XIIIth Intern. Congress of Historical Sciences, Moscow, 16–23 Aug. 1970). Moscow, Nauka, 1970.

NEUMANN, S. 'The comparative study of politics.' *Comparative Studies in Society and History,* vol. I, 1959.

NEVINS, Allan & EHRMANN, H. M. (eds.). *The University of Michigan History of the Modern World.* Series. Ann Arbor, University of Michigan Press.

The New Cambridge Modern History (1957–70): see CLARK, G. N. (Sir George) (ed.).

The New Economic History. Recent Papers in Methodology (1970): see ANDREANO (ed.).

New Movements in the Study and Teaching of History (1970): see BALLARD (ed.).

New Ways in History = The Times Literary Supplement, No. 3345 (special issue), 7 Apr. 1966.

NICHOLSON, Linda J. *Gender and History: The Limits of Social Theory in the Age of the Family.* New York, Columbia University Press, 1986.

NIEBUHR, Reinhold. *The Nature and Destiny of Man: A Christian Interpretation.* New York, Scribner's/London, Nisbet, 1941.

———. *Faith and History: A Comparison of Christian and Modern Views of History.* New York, Scribner's/London, Nisbet, 1949.

NOLTE, Ernst. *Der Faschismus in seiner Epoche.* Munich, Piper, 1963.

———. *Die faschistischen Bewegungen: Die Krise des liberalen Systems und die Entwicklung der Faschismen.* Munich, Piper, 1966.

NORA, Pierre (ed.). *Les Lieux de mémoire.* 4 vols. Paris, Gallimard, 1986.

NORTH, Douglass C. 'The state of economic history.' *American Economic Review,* Vol. LV, 1965, Suppl., pp. 86–98.

Nouvelle Clio, series: see BOUTRUCHE & LEMERLE (eds.).

'Novye rubeži sovetskih istorikov' (= New frontiers for Soviet historians), *Voprosy istorii,* 1969, No. 8.

OAKESHOTT, Michael J. *Rationalism in Politics, and Other Essays.* London, Methuen, 1962.

Očerki istorii istoričeskoj nauki v SSSR (= Essays on the History of Historical Science in the USSR). 4 vols. Moscow 1955–66.

O'CONNER, John E. 'History in images/images in history: reflections on the importance of film and television study for an understanding of the past.' *American Historical Review,* Vol. XCIII (5), December 1988, pp. 1200–1209.

OETOMO, Bambang. 'Some remarks on modern Indonesian historiography.' In *Historical Writing on the Peoples of Asia, op. cit.,* Vol. III (1961), pp. 73–84.

OGG, David. *Herbert Fisher, 1865–1940: A Short Biography.* London, Arnold, 1947.

O'GORMAN, Edmundo. *Crisis y porvenir de la ciencia histórica.* Mexico City, 1947.

OHE, Seizo. 'Toward a comparative and unified history of human culture, with special reference to Japan.' In *International Symposium on History of Eastern and Western Cultural Contacts.* Tokyo, 1959.

OLIVER, Roland & FAGE, John D. *A Short History of Africa.* Harmondsworth (Middx.), Penguin Books, 1962.

'O metodologičeskih voprosah istoričeskoj nauki' (report on the discussions of the methodology of history in the Social Science Section of the USSR Academy of Science on January 3–6, 1964, based on a paper by P. N. FEDOSEEV & Ju. P. FRANCEV, 'O razrabotke metodologičeskih voprosov istorii,' *op. cit.*), *Voprosy istorii*, 1964, No. 3, pp. 3–68; reproduced in *Istorija i sociologiya, op. cit.* (1964).

ONABE, Teruhiko. *Sekaishi no kanosei* (= The Possibility of a World History). Tokyo, 1950.

—— & NAKAYA, Kenichi. *Gendai sekai no naritachi* (= The Making of the Contemporary World). Tokyo, 1955.

XIème [Onzième] *Congrès international des Sciences historiques, Stockholm, 21– 28 août 1960: Rapports.* Göteborg-Stockholm-Uppsala, Almqvist & Wiksell, 1960, 5 vols.: Vol. I: *Méthodologie. Histoire des Universités. Histoire des prix avant 1750.*

XIème [Onzième] *Congrès international des Sciences historiques, Stockholm, 21– 28 août 1960: Actes.* Göteborg-Stockholm-Uppsala, Almqvist & Wiksell, 1962.

Orientalism and History (1954): see SINOR (ed.).

ORTEGA Y GASSET, José. *Guillermo Dilthey y la idea de la vida.* In *Obras completas,* Vol. VI. Madrid, Revista de Occidente, 4th edn., 1958.

——. *Historia como sistema.* In *Obras completas,* vol. VI, Madrid, Revista de Occidente, 4th edn., 1958.

'Osnovnye tečenija sovremennoj istoriografii na X Kongrese istoričeskih nauk' (= Main trends of contemporary historiography at the Xth Congress of Historical Sciences). *Voprosy istorii*, 1956, No. 2.

PALLAT, A. *Qualitative Change in the Development of Asian Countries after World War II*(XIIIth International Congress of Historical Sciences, Moscow, 16–23 Aug. 1970). Moscow, Nauka, 1970.

PALMER, Robert R. *The Age of the Democratic Revolution: A Political History of Europe and America, 1760–1800.* 2 vols. Princeton (N.J.), Princeton University Press, 1959–1964.

PANIKKAR, K. M. A Survey of Indian History. Bombay, Asia Publishing House, 1947.

——. *Asia and Western Dominance.* London, Allen & Unwin, 1953.

PAPADOPOULLOS, Théodore. *La Méthode des sciences sociales dans la recherche historique* (XIIIth International Congress of Historical Sciences, Moscow, 16– 23 Aug. 1970). Moscow, Nauka, 1970.

Past and Present, a Journal of Historical Studies; founded in 1952; ed. T. H. ASTON; Oxford, Corpus Christi College.

PASTI, G. 'Comparative studies of East Asian and West European history: Some topics and problems.' *Comparative Studies in Society and History,* Vol. VII, 1964, pp. 102–113.

The Pelican History of the World. Series. Harmondsworth (Middx.), Penguin Books.

PERELMAN, Chaïm (ed.). *Raisonnement et démarches de l'historien,* 'Travaux du Centre National de Recherches de Logique,' Brussels, Editions de l'Institut de Sociologie, Université libre de Bruxelles, 1963 (extract from *Revue de l'Institute de Sociologie,* 1963, No. 4).

PÉREZ CABRERA, J. M. *Fundamentos de una historia de la historiografía cubana.* Havana, 1959.

PERHAM, Margery. 'The British problem in Africa.' *Foreign Affairs* XXIX (4), July 1951, pp. 637–650.

PERKIN, Harold J. 'Social history.' In FINBERG (ed.), *Approaches to History, op. cit.* (1962), pp. 51–82.

PERROT, Michelle. 'La Femme dans l'espace parisien du XIXe siècle.' *Nouvelles annales de la recherche urbaine,* December 1980.

———. *Une Histoire des femmes: est-il possible?* Paris, Rivages, 1984.

PERSON, Yves. 'Tradition orale et chronologie.' *Cahiers d'études africaines,* Vol. II, 1962, pp. 462–476.

Personnel Resources in the Social Sciences and Humanities. Washington (D.C.), 1959.

PETRUŠEVSKIJ, D. M. *Očerki iz èconomičeskoj istorii srednevekovoj Evropi* (= Essays on the Economic History of Mediaeval Europe). Moscow, 1928.

PHILIPS, Cyril H. (ed.). *Historians of India, Pakistan and Ceylon* = Vol. I of *Historical Writing on the Peoples of Asia, op. cit.* (1961).

Philosophy and History (1936): see KLIBANSKY & PATON (eds.).

The Philosophy of History in Our Time (1959): see MEYERHOFF (ed.).

PIAGET, Jean. *Le structuralisme,* 'Que sais-je?' series, No. 1311, Paris, Presses Universitaires de France, 1968 (English translation by Chaninah Maschler, *Structuralism,* London, Routledge & Kegan Paul, 1971).

PIGGOTT, Stuart. *Approach to Archaeology.* London, A. & C. Black/ Cambridge (Mass.), Harvard University Press, 1959.

———. *Prehistoric India.* London, Cassell, 1961.

PINTO SANTA CRUZ, A. *Chile: un caso de desarrollo frustrado.* Santiago de Chile, 1959.

PIROSCHKOW, Vera. 'Sowjetische Geschichtswissenschaft im inneren Widerstreit (1956–1959),' *Saeculum* XI (1–2), 1960, pp. 180–198.

PITZ, E. 'Strukturen: Betrachtungen zur angeblichen Grundlagenkrise in der Geschichtswissenschaft.' *Historische Zeitschrift,* Vol. CXCVIII, 1964, pp. 265–305.

PLUMB, J. H. 'Introduction' and 'The historian's dilemma.' In PLUMB (ed.), *Crisis in the Humanities, op. cit.* (1964), pp. 7–10, 24–44.

PLUMB, J. H. (ed.). *Crisis in the Humanities.* Harmondsworth (Middx.), Penguin Books, 1964.

———. *The History of Human Society.* Series. London, Hutchinson, 1965.

POKROVSKIJ, Mihail N. *Russkaja istorija v samom sžatom očerke.* Leningrad, 1920 (English translation by D. S. Mirsky, *Brief History of Russia,* London, Lawrence & Wishart, 1933).

———. (POKROWSKI). *Historische Aufsätze.* Vienna, 1928.

POLLARD, A. F. 'An apology for historical research.' *History* VII (3), Oct. 1922, pp. 161–177.

POLLARD, Sidney. 'Economic history—A science of society?' *Past and Present,* No. 30, Apr. 1965, pp. 3–22.

La Pologne au Xe Congrès international des Sciences historiques à Rome. Warsaw, Polish Academy of Sciences, Institute of History, 1955.

La Pologne au XIIe Congrès international des Sciences historiques à Vienne (by Juliusz BARDACH *et al.*). Warsaw, Panstw. Wydawn. Nauk, 1965.

POMPER, Philip. Review essay on Erik H. ERIKSON's *Gandhi's Truth, op. cit.* (1969), *History and Theory,* Vol. IX, 1970, pp. 202-208.

PONOMAREV, B. N. 'Zadači istoričeskoj nauki i podgotovka naučno-pedagogičeskih kadrov v oblasti istorii' (report delivered to the All-Union Conference on Measures to Improve the Training of Historians and History Teachers, Moscow, 18 Dec. 1962), *Voprosy istorii,* 1963, No. 1, pp. 3–35; extensive summary in English, PONOMARYOV, B. N., 'The tasks confronting historical science and the training of historians and history teachers', *ibid.*, pp. 209–219.

POPPER, Karl R. *The Poverty of Historicism* (first publication, *Economica*, XI, 1944, pp. 86–103, 119–137, and XII, 1945, pp. 69–89). London, Routledge & Kegan Paul/Boston, Beacon Press, 1957 (French translation by Hervé Rousseau, *Misère de l'historicisme*, 'Recherches en Sciences humaines' ser. No. 8, Paris, Plon, 1956).

———. *The Open Society and its Enemies.* Vol. II. London, Routledge, 1945.

Population in History (1965): see GLASS & EVERSLEY (eds.).

PORŠNEV, Boris F., *Social'naja psihologija i istorija* (= Social Psychology and History), Moscow, 1966.

PORŠNEV, Boris F. & ANCIFEROVA, L. I. (eds.). *Istorija i psihologija* (= History and Psychology). Moscow, joint publication of the Institute of World History and Institute of Philosophy of the USSR Academy of Sciences, 1970.

POSTAN, M. M. 'The chronology of labour services.' *Transactions of the Royal Historical Society,* 4th ser., Vol. XX, 1937, pp. 169–193.

———. *Historical Method in Social Science: An Inaugural Lecture.* Cambridge, Cambridge University Press/New York, Macmillan, 1939; reprinted in POSTAN, *Fact and Relevance. Essays on Historical Method, op. cit.* (1971).

———. *An Economic History of Western Europe, 1945–1964.* London, Methuen/New York, Barnes & Noble, 1967.

———. *Fact and Relevance: Essays on Historical Method.* Cambridge, Cambridge University Press, 1971.

POTEHIN, I. I., *Formirovanie nacional'noj abščnosti južnoafrikanskih Bantu* (= Formation of the National Community of South-African Bantu). Moscow, 1956.

POWICKE, Sir (Frederick) Maurice. *The Christian Life in the Middle Ages, and Other Essays.* Oxford, Oxford University Press, 1935.

———. 'After fifty years.' *History,* Vol. XXIX, 1944; reprinted in POWICKE, *Modern Historians and the Study of History, op. cit.* (1955), pp. 225–239.

———. *Modern Historians and the Study of History: Essays and Papers.* London, Odhams, 1955.

Pravda (Moscow), 22 Feb. 1956 (statements by Mme. PANKRATOVA on the guiding principles of historical research).

PREBISCH, Raul. *The Economic Development of Latin America and Its Principal Problems* (United Nations, Dept. of Economic Affairs, Document E/CN.12/89/rev. 1), U.N. Publications, Sales No. 1950.II.G.2. Lake Success (N.Y.), United Nations, 1950.

Première Conférence internationale de l'Histoire économique: see 'L'Industrialisation comme facteur de la croissance . . .' (1960).

PRICE, Jacob M. 'Recent quantitative work in history: A survey of the main trends.' In *Studies in Quantitative History, op. cit.* (*History and Theory,* Beiheft 9, 1969), pp. 1–13.

'Les Problèmes des sources de l'histoire de l'Afrique noire jusqu'à la colonisation européenne' (a report prepared under the general editorship of Raymond MAUNY, Jean GLÉNISSON and Walter MARKOV by Henri MONIOT *et al.*). In *XIIth International Congress of Historical Sciences, Vienna, 1965 / XIIème Congrès international des Sciences historiques, Vienne, 1965: Reports / Rapports, op. cit.* (1965–68), Vol. II: *History of the Continents / Histoire des continents,* pp. 177–232; discussion, *ibid.,* Vol. V; *Proceedings / Actes,* pp. 311–326.

Proceedings of the XIth International Congress of Historical Sciences: see *XIème* [Onzième] *Congrès international des Sciences historiques, Stockholm, 21–28 août 1960: Actes (1962).*
[See also *XIème Congrès . . . : Rapports* (1960).]
Proceedings of the XII International Congress of Historical Sciences: see *XIIth International Congress of Historical Sciences, Vienna, August 29–September 2 1965: Reports,* Vol. V (1968).
Propyläen Weltgeschichte (1960–65): see MANN (ed.).
Psychoanalysis and History (1963): see MAZLISH (ed.).
PULLEYBLANK, E. G. 'China.' In SINOR (ed.), *Orientalism and History, op. cit.* (1954), pp. 68–92.
———. *Chinese History and World History: An Inaugural Lecture.* Cambridge, Cambridge University Press, 1955.
[See also BEASLEY & PULLEYBLANK (eds.).]
PUNDEFF, Marin. Review essay on B. A. GRUŠIN. *Očerki logiki istoričeskogo issledovanija* (*op. cit.,* 1961). *History and Theory* IV (1), 1964, pp. 72–78.
———. Review essay on the volume *Istorija i sociologija* (*op. cit.,* 1964). *History and Theory* VI (3), 1967, pp. 450–456.

Quantitative History (1969): see ROWNEY & GRAHAM (eds.).

RABB, Theodore. 'Toward the Future.' *Journal of Interdisciplinary History,* Vol. XII (2), Autumn 1981, p. 322.
RABB, Theodore and ROTBERG, Robert (eds.). *The New History: The 1980s and Beyond.* Princeton, Princeton University Press, 1982.
Radical History Review.
Raisonnement et démarches de l'historien (1963): see PERELMAN (ed.).
RAMOS, J. A. *Revolución y contrarevolución en la Argentina: las masas en nuestra historia.* 2nd edn., Buenos Aires, 1961.
RANDALL, Frederika. 'Why Scholars Become Storytellers.' *New York Times Book Review,* 29 January 1984.
RANGER, T. O. (ed.). *Emerging Themes in African History.* Nairobi, 1968.
RANKE, Leopold von. *Über die Epochen der neueren Geschichte.* Centenary edn., Darmstadt, Wissenschaftliche Buchgesellschaft, 1970.
RAYCHAUDHURI, Tapan. *Bengal under Akbar and Jahangir: An Introductory Study in Social History.* Delhi, Munshiram, 1966; 2nd edn., 1969.
Reappraisals: see *Journal of Contemporary History,* special issue (1968).
'Recent work in women's history: east and west.' *Trends in history,* vol. IV (1), Fall 1985.
La Recherche historique en France de 1940 à 1965 (Comité français des Sciences historiques), with an introductory study by Jean GLÉNISSON (*op. cit.*). Paris, Editions du C.N.R.S. (Centre de la Recherche Scientifique), 1965.
REDLICH, Fritz. 'New and traditional approaches to economic history and their interdependence.' *Journal of Economic History,* Vol. XXV, 1965, pp. 480–495.
———. 'Potentialities and pitfalls in economic history.' *Explorations in Entrepreneurial History,* 2nd ser., Vol. VI, 1968, pp. 93–108.
Registres des papes (13th and 14th centuries). Series undertaken by the Ecole française de Rome. Paris, De Boccard.
Relazioni, Xo Congresso internazionale di Scienze storiche: see *Xo* [Decimo] *Congresso internazionale di Scienze storiche, Roma, 4–11 settembre 1955: Relazioni.*

RENIER, Gustaaf J. *History: Its Purpose and Method*. London, Allen & Unwin/ Boston, Beacon Press, 1950.

Répertoire des bibliothèques d'étude et organismes de documentation. Ed. by Paul Poindron. 3 vols. Paris, Bibliothèque Nationale, 1963.

Reports of the Xth International Congress of Historical Sciences: see *Xo* [Decimo] *Congresso internazionale di Scienze storiche, Roma, 4–11 settembre 1955: Relazioni*.

Reports of the XIth International Congress of Historical Sciences: see *XIème* [Onzième] *Congrès international des Sciences historiques, Stockholm, 21–28 août 1960: Rapports* (1960).

[See also *XIème Congrès* . . . : *Actes* (1962).]

Reports of the XIIth International Congress of Historical Sciences: see *XIIth International Congress of Historical Sciences, Vienna, August 29–September 2 1965: Reports* (1965–68).

RESINK, Gertrudes Johan. *Indonesia's History between the Myths. Essays in Legal History and Historical Theory*. The Hague, Hoeve, 1967.

REVELLE, Roger (ed.). *Historical Population Studies = Daedalus*, Spring 1968, issued as Vol. XCVII, No. 2 of the *Proceedings of the American Academy of Arts and Sciences* (pp. 353–635).

Reviews in American History.

Revue d'Histoire des Sciences et de leurs applications (Centre international de Synthèse, Paris), founded in 1947 by Pierre BRUNET; quarterly; eds. Suzanne DELORME & René TATON; Paris, Presses Universitaires de France.

REYES HEROLES, J. 'La historia y la acción.' *Cuadernos Americanos*, Vol. CLXI, 1968, pp. 68–85.

RIASANOVSKY, Alexander V. & RIZNIK, Barnes (eds.). *Generalizations in Historical Writing*. Philadelphia (Pa.), University of Philadelphia Press, 1963.

RICE, D. Talbot. 'The history of art.' In FINBERG (ed.), *Approaches to History, op. cit.* (1962).

RITTER, Gerhard. 'Gegenwärtige Lage und Zukunftsaufgaben deutscher Geschichtswissenschaft.' *Historische Zeitschrift*, Vol. CLXX, 1950, pp. 1–22.

———. 'Betrachtungen über einige Gesamtergebnisse und Grundfragen moderner Historiographie (= Part B of G. RITTER, 'Leistungen, Probleme und Aufgaben der internationalen Geschichtsschreibung zur neueren Geschichte—16–18. Jahrhundert'). In *Xo* [Decimo] *Congresso internazionale di Scienze storiche: Relazioni, op. cit.* (1955), Vol. VI, pp. 280–330.

———. 'Zur Problematik gegenwärtige Geschichtsschreibung.' In G. RITTER, *Lebendige Vergangenheit: Beiträge zur historisch-politischen Selbstbesinnung*, Munich, Oldenbourg, 1958, pp. 255–283.

———. 'Scientific history, contemporary history and political science.' *History and Theory* I (3), 1961, pp. 261–279.

RIX, Michael. *Industrial Archaeology*. London, The Historical Association, 1967.

ROBINSON, DAVID AND SMITH, Douglas (eds.). *Sources of the African Past: Case Studies of Five Nineteenth Century African Societies*. New York, Africana Publishing Company, 1979.

ROBINSON, James Harvey. *The New History: Essays Illustrating the Modern Historical Outlook*. New York, Macmillan, 1912.

ROBINSON, Joan M. *Economic Philosophy*. London, Watts/Chicago, Aldine, 1962. (French translation by B. Stora, *Philosophie économique*, 'Les Essais' ser., No. CXXVII, Paris, Gallimard, 1967.)

ROBINSON, Ronald & GALLAGHER, John. *Africa and the Victorians: The Official*

Mind of Imperialism. London, Macmillan, 1961; another edn. with subtitle: *The Climax of Imperialism in the Dark Continent,* New York, St. Martin's Press, 1961.
[See also GALLAGHER & ROBINSON, R.]

RODRIGUES, José Honório. *Teoria da história do Brasil.* 2nd edn. São Paulo, 1957.

———. *Brasil e Africa.* 2nd edn. Rio de Janeiro, 1964 (English translation by Richard A. Mazzara & Sam Hileman, *Brazil and Africa,* Berkeley, University of California Press/Cambridge, Cambridge University Press, 1965).

———. *História e historiadores do Brasil.* São Paulo, 1965.

ROGAČEVSKAJA, L. S., *Iz istorii rab. klassa SSSR v pervye gody industrializacii, 1926–1927* (= History of the Labouring Class of the USSR in the First Years of Industrialization, 1926–1927). Moscow, 1959.

ROSENBLAT, Angel. *La población de América en 1492: Viejos y nuevos cálculos.* Mexico City, Colegio de México, 1967.

ROSENSTONE, Robert A. 'History in images/history in words: reflections on the possibility of really putting history onto film.' *American Historical Review,* Vol. XCIII (5), December 1988, pp. 1173–1185.

ROSENTHAL, Franz. 'Islamic historiography.' In *International Encyclopedia of the Social Sciences, op. cit.* (1968), Vol. VI, pp. 407–413 (*sub* 'Historiography').

ROSSI, Pietro. *Storia e storicismo nella filosofia contemporanea.* Milan, Lerici, 1960.

ROSTOW, Walt Whitman. *The Process of Economic Growth.* New York, Norton/London, Oxford University Press, 1953.

———. 'The take-off into self-sustained growth.' *Economic Journal,* Vol. LXVI, 1956, pp. 25–48.

———. *The Stages of Economic Growth.* 2nd edn., enl. Cambridge, Cambridge University Press, 1960 (French translation by M.-J. du Rouret, *Les étapes de la croissance économique,* Paris, Seuil, 1963).

ROSTOW, Walt Whitman (ed.). *The Economics of Take-Off into Sustained Growth.* proceedings of a conference held by the International Economic Association, London, Macmillan, 1963; New York, St. Martin's Press, 1964.

ROTBERG, R. I. 'Resistance and rebellion in British Nyasaland and German East-Africa, 1885–1915.' In Prosser, GIFFORD & W. R. LOUIS (eds.), *Britain and Germany in Africa: Imperial Rivalry and Colonial Rule,* New Haven (Conn.), Yale University Press, 1967, pp. 667–690.

ROWNEY, Don K. & GRAHAM, James Q., Jr. (eds.). *Quantitative History: Selected Readings in Quantitative Analysis of Historical Data.* Homewood (Ill.), Dorsey Press, 1969.

RUDÉ, George F. E. *The Crowd in the French Revolution.* London, Oxford University Press, 1959.

———. *The Crowd in History: A Study of Popular Disturbances in France and England, 1730–1848.* New York-London, John Wiley & Sons, 1965.

RUIZ GARCÍA, Enrique. *América Latina: anatomía de una revolución.* Madrid, Guadarrama, 1966.

RUMJANCEV, A. N. 'Obščestvennye nauki v SSSR i sovremennost' (= The social sciences in the USSR and the present time). *Voprosy istorii,* 1968, No. 9.

RUNCIMAN, Sir Steven. *History of the Crusades. 3 vols.* Cambridge, Cambridge University Press, 1951, 1952, 1954.

Saeculum. Jahrbuch für Universalgeschichte, founded in 1950; ed. Oskar KOEHLER; Freiburg i Br., Verlag Karl Alber.

SAHAROV, A. M. *Izučenie otečestvennoj istorii za 50 sovetskoj vlasti* (= The Study of National History during 50 Years of Soviet Rule). Moscow, 1968.

SAID, Edward W. *Orientalism.* New York, Pantheon Books, 1978.

SALIN, Édouard, *La civilisation mérovingienne d'après les sépultures, les textes et le laboratoire.* 2 vols. Paris, A. & J. Picard, 1950–52.

SÁNCHEZ-ALBORNOZ, N. 'Perfil y proyecciones de la demografía histórica en la Argentina.' *Anuario del Instituto de Investigaciónes Históricas,* Vol. VIII, 1965, pp. 31–56.

SÁNCHEZ-BARBA. Hernández: see VICENS VIVES, *Historia social y económica de España y América* (1957–59).

SAVELLE, Max. 'Historian's progress.' *Pacific Historical Review,* Vol. XXVII, 1958; reprinted in M. SAVELLE, *Is Liberalism Dead? and Other Essays,* Seattle, University of Washington Press, 1967.

[See also *sub* ZAVALA, *The Colonial Period in the History of the New World.*]

SAVETH, Edward Norman (ed.). *American History and the Social Sciences.* New York, The Free Press of Glencoe, 1964.

SCHAMA, Simon. *Citizens: A Chronicle of the French Revolution.* New York, Knopf, 1989.

SCHELLENBERG, Theodore R. *Modern Archives: Principles and Techniques.* Melbourne, F. B. Cheshire/London, Angus/Chicago, University of Chicago Press, 1955.

SCHIEDER, Theodor. 'Zum gegenwärtigen Verhältnis von Geschichte und Soziologie.' *Geschichte in Wissenschaft und Unterricht (Zeitschrift des Verbandes der Geschichtslehrer Deutschlands),* Vol. III, 1952, pp. 27–32.

———. *Staat und Gesellschaft im Wandel unserer Zeit: Studien zur Geschichte des 19. und 20. Jahrhunderts.* Munich, Oldenbourg, 1958; 2nd edn., 1970 (English translation by C. A. M. Sym, *The State and Society in Our Times: Studies in the History of the 19th and 20th Centuries,* London, Nelson, 1962).

———. 'Die deutsche Geschichtswissenschaft im Spiegel der *Historischen Zeitschrift.*' in SCHIEDER (ed.), *Hundert Jahre Historische Zeitschrift 1859– 1959, op. cit.* (1959), pp. 1–104.

———. 'Strukturen und Persönlichkeiten in der Geschichte,' *Historische Zeitschrift,* Vol. CXCV, 1962, pp. 265–296.

———. 'Möglichkeiten und Grenzen vergleichender Methoden in der Geschichtswissenschaft.' *Historische Zeitschrift,* Vol. CC, 1965, pp. 529–551.

———. *Unterschiede zwischen historischer und sozialwissenschaftlicher Methode* (XIIIth International Congress of Historical Sciences, Moscow, 16–23 Aug., 1970). Moscow, Nauka, 1970.

SCHIEDER, Theodor (ed.). *Hundert Jahre Historische Zeitschrift 1859–1959: Beiträge zur Geschichte der Historiographie in den deutschsprachigen Ländern = Historische Zeitschrift,* Vol. CLXXXIX, 1959 (special issue).

SCHIEDER, Wolfgang. Review of F. L. CARSTEN, *The Rise of Fascism, op. cit.* (1967), *Historische Zeitschrift* CCIX (1), Aug. 1969, p. 185.

SCHNEIDER, Jean. *La machine et l'histoire: De l'emploi des moyens mécaniques et électroniques dans la recherche historique* (XIIIth International Congress of Historical Sciences, Moscow, 16–23 Aug. 1970). Moscow, Nauka, 1970.

SCHOCHOW, Werner. Analysis of *International Bibliography of Historical Sciences,* Vol. 27 (1958) and of *Jahresberichte für deutsche Geschichte, Historische Zeitschrift* CCXII (2), Apr. 1971, pp. 367–375.

SCHOEPS, H. J. *Was ist und was will die Geistesgeschichte? Über die Theorie und Praxis der Zeitgeistforschung.* Göttingen, Musterschmidt, 1959.

SCHOFIELD, R. S. 'Population in the past: Computer linking of vital records.' *Bulletin of the Institute of Mathematics*, 1970.

SCHORER PETRONE, M. T. *A lavoura canavieira em São Paulo: Expansão e declinio, 1765–1871*. São Paulo, 1968.

Schulin, E. *Die weltgeschichtliche Erfassung des Orients bei Hegel und Ranke*. Göttingen, Vandenhoeck & Ruprecht, 1958.

SCHUMPETER, Joseph A. *The Theory of Economic Growth: An Enquiry into Profits, Capital, Credit, Interest, and the Business Cycle*. Translated from the German by Redvers Opie. Cambridge (Mass.), Harvard University Press/London, Oxford University Press, 1934 (French translation, *Théorie de l'évolution économique. Recherche sur le profit, le crédit, l'intérêt et le cycle de la conjoncture*, Paris, Dalloz, 1935).

———. *Capitalism, Socialism and Democracy*. New York, Harper & Row/London, Allen & Unwin, 1942; 2nd edn., 1946 (French translation by Gaël Fain, *Capitalisme, socialisme et démocratie*, Paris, Payot, 'Bibliothèque économique' 1951; new edn., 'Petite Bibliothèque Payot', 1969).

SCHWARTZ, Robert. *Policing the Poor in Eighteenth Century France*. Chapel Hill, University of North Carolina Press, 1988.

SCHWERIN, C. von. Review of MITTEIS, *Der Staat des hohen Mittelalters, op. cit.* (1940, 1958), *Zeitschrift der Savigny-Stiftung für Rechtsgeschichte, Germanist. Abt.*, Vol. LXII, 1942, p. 420.

'Scientific and research work in the Historical Institutes of the USSR Academy of Sciences, and historical journals.' *Social Sciences (USSR Academy of Sciences)*, Vol. 2, 1970.

SCOTT, Joan and TILLY, Louise. *Women, Work and Family*. New York, Holt, Rinehart and Winston, 1978.

SCOTT, Joan Wallach. 'Gender: a useful category of historical analysis.' *American Historical Review*, Vol. XCI (5), December 1986, pp. 1053–1075.

———. 'Deconstructing equality-versus-difference: or, the uses for poststructuralist theory of feminism.' *Feminist Studies*, Vol. XIV (1), Spring 1988, pp. 33–50.

———. *Gender and the Politics of History*. New York, Columbia University Press, 1988.

SELIGMAN, Charles G. *Races of Africa*. 3rd edn., ed. by I. Schapera *et al.* London, Oxford University Press, 1957.

SESTAN, Ernesto. *Storia degli avvenimenti e storia delle strutture* (XIIIth International Congress of Historical Sciences, Moscow, 16–23 Aug. 1970). Moscow, Nauka, 1970.

SHAFER, Boyd C., FRANÇOIS, Michel, MOMMSEN, W. J., and MILNE, A. T. *Historical Study in the West* (comprises: 'Introduction,' by B. C. SHAFER; 'France,' by M. FRANÇOIS; 'Great Britain,' by A. T. MILNE; 'Germany,' by W. J. MOMMSEN; and 'The United States,' by B. C. SHAFER. New York, Appleton-Century-Crofts, 1968.

SHEPPERSON, George & PRICE, Thomas. *Independent African: John Chilembwe and the Origins, Setting and Significance of the Nyasaland Native Rising of 1915*. Edinburgh, Edinburgh University Press, 1958.

SHORE, Miles. 'Biography in the 1980s: a psychoanalytic perspective.' *Journal of Interdisciplinary History*, Vol. XII (1), Summer 1981, pp. 89–113.

'Short Notice' about the new *Guide to the Essex Record Office* (1969) by Susan REYNOLDS. *English Historical Review* LXXXV (336), July 1970, pp. 636–637.

SIDOROV, Aleksandr L. 'Hauptprobleme und einige Entwicklungsergebnisse der sowjetischen Geschichtswissenschaft.' In *Xo* [Decimo] *Congresso internazionale di Scienze storiche: Relazioni, op. cit.* (1955), Vol. VI, pp. 389–456.

SIEGEL, Bernard J. (ed.). *Biennial Review of Anthropology, 1965*. Stanford (Calif.), Stanford University Press, 1965.

Signs: Journal of Women in Culture and Society.

SILVERBLATT, Irene. *Moon, Sun and Witches: Gender Ideologies and Class in Inca and Colonial Peru.* Princeton, Princeton University Press, 1987.

SIMMEL, Ernst (ed.). *Anti-Semitism: A Social Disease* (symposium, by Max HORKHEIMER *et al.*). Preface by Gordon W. ALLPORT. New York, International Universities Press, 1946.

SINOR, Denis (ed.). *Orientalism and History.* Cambridge, Heffer & Sons, 1954.

SKIDMORE, T. E. 'Gilberto Freyre and the early Brazilian republic,' *Comparative Studies in Society and History,* Vol. VI, 1964, pp. 490–505.

SLICHER VAN BATH, B. H. 'Nieuwe wegen in de amerikaanse economische en sociale geschiedenis' (= New ways in American economic and social history). *Tijdschrift voor geschiedenis,* Vol. LXXXXII, 1969, pp. 206–225.

SMAIL, J. R. W. 'On the possibility of an autonomous history of modern Southeast Asia.' *Journal of Southeast Asian History* II (2), 1961, pp. 72–102.

SMELSER, M. & DAVISSON, W. I. 'The historian and the computer.' *Essex Institute Historical Collections,* Vol. CIV, 1968, pp. 109–126.

SMITH, R. J. 'Aspects of mobility in pre-industrial Japanese cities.' In ROWNEY & GRAHAM (eds.), *Quantitative History, op. cit.* (1969), pp. 209–216.

SOBOUL, Albert. *Les sans-culottes parisiens en l'an II: Mouvement populaire et gouvernement révolutionnaire* (thesis, Paris). La Roche-sur-Yon (France), Imprimerie Pottier, 1958.

Social History (United Kingdom).

Social Science Research Council (Committee on Historiography). *Theory and Practice in Historical Study.* Social Science Research Council, Bulletin No. 54. New York, The Council, 1946.

——. *The Social Sciences in Historical Study: A Report.* Social Science Research Council, Bulletin No. 64. New York, The Council, 1954.

——. *Generalization in the Writing of History.* Ed. by Louis R. GOTTSCHALK. Chicago, University of Chicago Press, 1963.

The Social Sciences in Historical Study (1954): see Social Science Research Council (Committee on Historiography).

Sociology and History: Methods (1968): see LIPSET & HOFSTADTER (eds.).

Sociology and History: Theory and Research (1964): see CAHNMAN & BOSKOFF (eds.).

SOEDJATMOKO (ed.). *An Introduction to Indonesian Historiography.* Ithaca (N.Y.), Cornell University Press, 1965.

SOMERVELL, D. C. *Abridgement* of Arnold J. TOYNBEE's *A Study of History* (1946–1957): see TOYNBEE, *A Study of History: Abridgement* by D. C. SOMERVELL.

SORLIN, Pierre, *The Film in History: Restaging the Past.* Totowa, Barnes and Noble Books, 1980.

SOROKIN, Pitirim A. 'Arnold J. Toynbee's philosophy of history' (review article). *Journal of Modern History* XII (3), Sept. 1940, pp. 374–387.

——. *Social and Cultural Dynamics: A Study of Change in Major Systems of Art, Truth, Ethics, Law, and Social Relationships.* Rev. and abr. in 1 vol. by the author. Boston, Porter-Sargent/London, Peter Owen, 1957.

'Sovetskaja istoričeskaja nauka na novom ètape razvitija' (= Soviet historical science at a new stage of development), 'Peredovaja' (= Editorial). *Voprosy istorii,* 1960, No. 8, pp. 3–18.

Soviet Culture (Paris), Nos. 4–5, May–June 1956.

Soviet Studies in History, a Journal of Translations, founded in 1962, quarterly; ed. Paul ARON; White Plains (N.Y.), International Arts and Sciences Press.

SPAULDING, Kenneth. 'The Colonial Indian: past and future research perspectives.' *Latin American Research Review* VII (I), 1971, pp. 47–76.

SPENCE, Jonathan. *The Death of Woman Wang.* New York, Viking Press, 1978.

———. *The Question of Hu.* New York, Knopf, 1988.

SRBIK, Heinrich von. *Geist und Geschichte vom deutschen Humanismus.* Vol. II. Munich, F. Bruckmann, 1951.

STADTMÜLLER, Georg. *Die neue sowjetische Weltgeschichte = Saeculum. Jahrbuch für Universalgeschichte* XI (4), 1960, pp. 295–384; includes a bibliography of literature on Soviet historical writing, pp. 380–384.

STAERMAN, E. M. 'K probleme strukturnogo analiza v istorii' (= On the problem of structural analysis in history). *Voprosy istorii,* 1968, No. 6.

STAVRIANOS, Leften S. 'The teaching of world history.' *Journal of Modern History,* Vol. XXXI, 1959, pp. 110–117.

———. *The World since 1500: A Global History.* Englewood Cliffs (N.J.), Prentice-Hall, 1966.

———. *The World to 1500: A Global History.* Englewood Cliffs (N.J.), Prentice-Hall, 1970.

STAVRIANOS, Leften S. (ed.). *The Epic of Man to 1500: A Collection of Readings.* 2nd ed. Englewood Cliffs (N.J.), Prentice-Hall, 1970.

Stearns, Peter N. 'Some comments on social history.' *Journal of Social History,* Vol. I (1), 1967, p. 4.

———. 'Coming of age.' *Journal of Social History,* Vol. X (2), 1976, p. 250.

STEFANOV, N. K. *Vaprosi na metodologijata na istoričeskata nauka* (= Methodological Questions in Historical Science). Sofia, 1962.

STEIN, Stanley. *The Brazilian Cotton Manufacture: Textile Enterprise in an Underdeveloped Area, 1850–1950.* Cambridge (Mass.), Harvard University Press/ London, Oxford University Press, 1957.

———. 'The tasks ahead for Latin American historians' and 'Latin American historiography: Status and research opportunities.' Reproduced in CLINE (ed.), *Latin American History: Essays of Its Study and Teaching, 1898–1965, op. cit.* (1967), pp. 543–549, 574–597.

———. & STEIN, B. H. *The Colonial Heritage of Latin America: Essays on Economic Dependence in Perspective.* New York, Oxford University Press, 1970.

STERN, Fritz R. (ed.). *The Varieties of History, from Voltaire to the Present.* Cleveland-New York, Meridian Books, The World Publishing Company, 1956.

ST. JOSEPH, J. K. 'Air photography for archaeological and historical research.' In *Xo* [Decimo] *Congresso internazionale di Scienze storiche, Roma, 4–11 settembre 1955: Relazioni,* Vol. VII: *Riassunti delle comunicazioni, op. cit.* (1955), pp. 102–103. [See also BERESFORD & St. JOSEPH.]

STOIANOVICH, Traian. *A Study in Balkan Civilisation.* New York, Knopf, 1967.

STONE, Lawrence. *The Past and the Present.* Boston, Routledge and Kegan Paul, 1981.

STONE, L. 'Social mobility in England, 1500–1700.' In ROWNEY & GRAHAM (eds.). *Quantitative History, op. cit.* (1969), pp. 238–271.

STRAYER, Joseph R. 'The historian's concept of public opinion.' In KOMAROVSKY (ed.), *Common Frontiers of the Social Sciences, op. cit.* (1957), pp. 263–268 (part of 'History and public opinion research. A debate').

STROMBERG, Roland N. *An Intellectual History of Modern Europe*. New York, Appleton-Century-Crofts, 1966; republished as *European Intellectual History since 1789, ibid.*, 1968.

STROUSE, Jean. *Alice James: A Biography*. Boston, Houghton Mifflin, 1980.

STROUT, CUSHING. *The Pragmatic Revolt in American History: Carl Becker and Charles Beard*. New Haven (Conn.), Yale University Press, 1958.

STUART HUGHES, Henry: see HUGHES, Henry Stuart.

Studies in Quantitative History = *History and Theory* (Middletown (Conn.), Wesleyan University Press), VIII (Beiheft 9), 1969.

Studies in the Nature and Teaching of History (1967): see BURSTON & THOMSON (eds.).

SUDJATMOKO: see SOEDJATMOKO.

SYME, Sir Ronald. *Colonial Elites: Rome, Spain and the Americas* (Whidden Lectures, 1958). London, Oxford University Press, 1958.

TAPIÉ, Victor-L. 'Les études historiques en Tchécoslovaquie.' *Revue historique* CCXXVII/1 (463), July–Sept. 1962, pp. 119–128 (*sub* 'L'orientation actuelle des études historiques').

TAYLOR, Arthur J. *History in an Age of Growth* (Inaugural Lecture). Leeds. Leeds University Press, 1964.

TEMPERLEY, Harold W. V. *Research and Modern History: An Inaugural Lecture given in the Examination Hall, Cambridge, on Nov. 19th, 1930*. London, Macmillan, 1930.

Xth International Congress of Historical Sciences (1955): see *Xo* [Decimo] *Congresso internazionale di Scienze storiche*.

Ten Years of Yugoslav Historiography, 1945–1955, Belgrade, 1955.

THAPAR, Romila. 'Interpretations of ancient Indian history.' *History and Theory*, Vol. VII, 1968, pp. 318–335.

Theory and Practice in Historical Study (1946): see Social Science Research Council (Committee on Historiography).

THERNSTROM, Stephan. 'Notes on the historical study of social mobility.' In ROWNEY & GRAHAM (eds.), *Quantitative History, op. cit.* (1969), pp. 99–108.

XIIIth International Congress of Historical Sciences (Moscow, 16–23 Aug. 1970), publication of contributions in the form of separate brochures): see DEOPIK, DOBROV, KAHK, KOVALCHENKO, PALLI & USTINOV; DUBUC; DUPRONT; ELEKEC; *Enquête sur les mouvements paysans dans le monde contemporain;* GEISS; HEXTER; KIM & NIKIFOROV; MARKOV; NERSESOV; PALLAT; PAPADOPOULLOS; SCHIEDER, Th.; SCHNEIDER; SESTAN.

THOMAS, Keith. 'History and anthropology.' *Past and Present*, No. XXIV, 1963, pp. 3–24.

———. 'The tools and the job.' In *New Ways in History, op. cit.* (*The Times Literary Supplement*, 1966), pp. 275–276.

THOMAS, Keith. 'The ferment of fashion.' *Times Literary Supplement*, 30 April 1982.

THOMPSON, Edward P. *The Making of the English Working Class*. London, Gollancz, 1963; New York, Pantheon Books, 1964.

THOMSON, DAVID. *World History from 1914 to 1961*. 2nd edn. London, Oxford University Press, 1963.

[See also BURSTON & THOMSON (eds.).]

THORNTON, Archibald P. *Doctrines of Imperialism*. New York, Wiley, 1965.

THRUPP, Sylvia L. 'History and sociology: New opportunities for co-operation.' *American Journal of Sociology* LXIII (1), July 1957, pp. 11–16.

THURMAN, Judith. *Isak Dinesen: The Life of a Storyteller.* New York, St. Martin's Press, 1982.

TIHOMIROV, M. N. 'O značenii istoričeskoj nauki' (= On the significance of historical science), *Vestnik moskovskogo universiteta, Istorija,* 1969, No. 1.

TILLY, Charles H. 'The analysis of a counter-revolution.' In ROWNEY & GRAHAM (eds.), *Quantitative History, op. cit.* (1969), pp. 181–208.
[See also LANDES & TILLY (eds.).]

TOUT, T. F. *Chapters in the Administrative History of Medieval England: The Wardrobe, the Chamber and the Small Seals.* Vol. I, Manchester, Manchester University Press, 1920; new edn., *ibid.,* 1967.
———. 'The place of the Middle Ages in the teaching of history.' *History* VIII (29), Apr. 1923, pp. 1–18.

TOYNBEE, Arnold J. *A Study of History.* 12 vols. London, Oxford University Press, 1934–61.
———. *A Study of History: Abridgement* by D. C. SOMERVELL, London, Oxford University Press, 2 vols.: Vol. I: *Abridgement of Volumes I–VI,* 1946; Vol. II; *Abridgement of Volumes VII–X,* 1957 (French translation of Vol. I by Elisabeth Julia, *L'histoire: Un essai d'interprétation,* 'Bibliothèque des Idées,' Paris, Gallimard, 1951).
———. *The World and the West* (Reith Lectures, 1952). London, Oxford University Press, 1953 (French translation, *Le monde et l'Occident,* 'Bibliothèque Médiations.' No. 15, Paris, Gonthier, 1964).
[See also *sub* GARGAN (ed).]

The Treatment of Asia in Western Textbooks and Teaching Materials. Paris, Unesco publication ED/147, Nov. 1956.

TREVELYAN, George Macaulay. *Clio, A Muse, and Other Essays Literary and Pedestrian.* London, 1913.
———. *English Social History: A Survey of Six Centuries, Chaucer to Queen Victoria.* London, Longmans, 1942; 2nd edn., 1947.

TREVOR-ROPER, Hugh Redwald. *Religion, the Reformation and Social Change, and Other Essays.* London, Macmillan, 1967; another edn., with title: *The Crisis of the Seventeenth Century. Religion, the Reformation and Social Change,* New York, Harper, 1968.
———. *The Past and the Present: History and Sociology.* London, London School of Economics and Political Science, 1969.

TRIFONOV, I. *Očerki istorii klassovoj bor'by v SSSR v gody NEP (1921–1937)* (= Essays on the History of the Class Struggle in the USSR during the Years of the NEP—1921–1937). Moscow, 1960.

TRIST, Eric L. 'The organization and financing of research.' In *Main Trends of Research in the Social and Human Sciences, Part I: Social Sciences,* Paris-The Hague, Mouton/Unesco, 1970, Chap. XI, pp. 693–811 (parallel publication in French version. 'Organisation et financement de la recherche,' in *Tendances principales de la recherche dans les sciences sociales et humaines, Ière Partie: Sciences sociales,* same ref., Chap. XI, pp. 825–980).

TROELTSCH, Ernst. *Gesammelte Schriften.* Vol. III. Tübingen, J. C. B. Mohr, 1920.
———. *Der Historismus und seine Probleme.* Tübingen, J. C. B. Mohr, 1922.

TUCHMAN, Barbara [WERTHEIM]. *The Guns of August.* New York, Macmillan, 1962; another edn., with title: *August 1914,* London, Constable, 1962.

TUDESQ, André-Jean. *Les grands notables en France (1840–1849): Etude historique d'une psychologie sociale.* Paris, Presses Universitaires de France, 1964.

TURNER, Victor. *From Ritual to Theatre: The Human Seriousness of Play.* New York, Performing Arts Journal Publications, 1982.

XIIth International Congress of Historical Sciences, Vienna, August 29–September 2, 1965 / XIIème Congrès international des Sciences historiques, Vienne, 29 août–2 septembre 1965: Reports / Rapports, Horn-Vienna, Berger & Söhne, 1965–68, 5 vols.: Vol. II; *History of the Continents / Histoire des continents* (1965); Vol. IV: *Methodology and Contemporary History / Méthodologie et histoire contemporaine* (1965); Vol. V: *Proceedings / Actes* (1968).

XX S'ezd KPSS (= XXth Congress of the Communist Party of the USSR): see *XX* [Dvadcatyj] *S'ezd KPSS*.

TWITCHETT, Denis C. *Land Tenure and the Social Order in T'ang and Sung China* (Inaugural Lecture). London, University of London, School of Oriental and African studies, 1962.

The University of Michigan History of the Modern World, series: see NEVINS & EHRMANN (eds.).

USTINOV, V. A. 'O primenenii èlektronnyh matematičeskyh mašin v istoričeskoj nauke' (= On the use of electronic mathematical machines in historical science), *Voprosy istorii*, 1962, No. 8, pp. 97–117 (French translation by Nina Godnev, 'Les calculateurs électroniques appliqués à la science historique.' *Annales*, 18th Yr., No. 2, Mar.–Apr. 1963, pp. 263–294, preceded by an introduction by J.-Cl. GARDIN, *op. cit.*, pp. 259–263).

———. *Primenenie vyčislitel'nyh mašin v istoričeskoj nauke* (= The use of computers in historical science). Moscow, 1964.

[See also DEOPIK, DOBROV. KAHK, KOVALCHENKO, PALLI & USTINOV.]

UTECHIN, S. V. 'Soviet historiography after Stalin.' In KEEP & BRISBY (eds.), *Contemporary History in the Soviet Mirror, op. cit.* (1964), pp. 117–129.

VAJNŠTEIN, O. L. *Istorija sovetskoj medievistiki* (= History of Soviet Mediaeval Studies). Leningrad, 1968.

VAN DER KROEF, Justus M. 'On the writing of Indonesian history.' *Pacific Affairs*, vol. XXXI, 1958, pp. 352–371.

VAN KIRK, Sylvia. *Many Tender Ties: Women in Fur-Trade Society, 1670–1870*. Winnepeg, Watson and Dwyer, 1980.

VANN, Richard T. 'History and demography.' In *Studies in Quantitative History, op. cit. (History and Theory*, Beiheft 9, 1969), pp. 64–78.

VANSINA, Jan. 'A comparison of African kingdoms.' *Africa*, vol. XXXII, 1962, pp. 324–335.

———. *De la tradition orale: Esai de méthode historique*. Tervuren (Belgium), Annales du Musée Royal de l'Afrique centrale, 1961 (English translation by H. M. Wright, *The Oral Tradition: A study in Historical Methodology*, Chicago, Aldine/London, Routledge & Kegan Paul, 1965).

VANSINA, Jan, MAUNY, Raymond & THOMAS, L. V. (eds.). *The Historian in Tropical Africa / L'historien en Afrique tropicale* (studies presented and discussed at the 4th International African Seminar, Dakar, 1961; texts in English or French with summaries in other languages; includes bibliographies). Published for the International African Institute. London, Oxford University Press, 1964.

The Varieties of History (1956): see STERN (ed.).

'Važnejšie dostiženija v oblasti istoričeskih nauk v 1967 g.' (= Outstanding achievements in historical science in 1967). *Voprosy istorii*, 1968, No. 5.

Veinticinco años de investigación histórica en México. Mexico City, 1966.

VELIZ, Claudio. *Obstacles to Change in Latin America* (sponsored by the Royal Institute of International Affairs and St. Antony's College, Oxford). London, Oxford University Press, 1965.

VERNANT, Jean-Pierre. 'Histoire et psychologie.' *Revue de synthèse*, Vol. LXXXVI, 1965, pp. 85–94.

VICENS VIVES, Jaime. *Historia social y económica de España y América.* Barcelona, Editorial Vicens-Vives, 5 vols. 1957–59 (sections on Latin America contributed by Guillermo CÉSPEDES del CASTILLO and Hernández SÁNCHEZ-BARBA).

――――. *Aproximación a la historia de España.* Barcelona, Universidad de Barcelona, Centro de Estudios Históricos Internacionales, 1960; 3rd edn., Barcelona, Editorial Vicens-Vives, 1962 (English translation by Joan C. Ullman, *Approaches to the History of Spain,* Berkeley, University of California Press, 1967; Cambridge, Cambridge University Press, 1968).

VIGARELLO, George. *Concepts of Cleanliness: Changing Attitudes in France Since the Middle Ages.* Translated by Jean Birell. New York, Cambridge University Press, 1988.

VILAR, Pierre. 'Pour une meilleure compréhension entre économistes et historiens.' *Revue historique* CCXXXIII/2 (474), Apr.–June 1965, pp. 293–312.

VJATKIN, R. V. & TIHVINSKIJ, S. L. 'O nekotoryh voprosah istoričeskoj nauki v KNR,' *Voprosy istorii,* 1963, No. 10, pp. 3–20 (English translation, VYATKIN, R. V. & TIKHVINSKY, S. L., 'Some questions of historical science in the Chinese People's Republic,' *The Current Digest of the Soviet Press,* XVI (4), 19 Feb. 1964, pp. 3–10; and in FEUERWERKER (ed.), *History in Communist China, op. cit.* (1968), pp. 331–355).

VOEGELIN, Eric. *Order and History.* Baton Rouge (La.), Louisiana State University Press, 1956– (6 vols. projected): Vol. I: *Israel and Revelation,* 1956; Vol. II: *The World of the Polis,* 1957; Vol. III: *Plato and Aristotle,* 1957; Vol. IV: *The Ecumenic Age,* 1975.

――――. 'Historiogenesis.' *Philosophisches Jahrbuch,* Vol. LXVIII, 1960, pp. 419–446.

VOGT, Joseph. *Geschichte des Altertums und Universalgeschichte.* Wiesbaden, Steiner, 1957.

VOLGIN, V. P., TARLE, E. V. & PANKRATOVA, A. M. (eds.). *Dvadcat' pjat' let istoričeskoj nauki v SSSR* (= Twenty-five Years of Historical Science in the USSR). Moscow, 1942.

Vsemirnaja istorija (1955–65): see ŽUKOV (ed.).

'Vsesojuznoe soveščanie istorikov' (report of the All-Union Historians' Conference on Measures to Improve the Training of Scientific and Pedagogical Personnel in Historical Sciences, held in Moscow on December 18–21, 1962). *Voprosy istorii,* 1963, No. 2, pp. 3–75.

VYATKIN, R. V. & TIKHVINSKY, S. L.: see VJATKIN, R. V. & TIHVINSKIJ, S. L.

WACHTEL, N. 'La vision des vaincus: la conquête espagnole dans le folklore indigène.' *Annales: Economies, Sociétés, Civilisations,* Vol. XXII, 1967, pp. 554–585.

WAGNER, Fritz. *Moderne Geschichtsschreibung.* Berlin, Duncker & Humblot, 1960.

――――. *Der Historiker und die Weltgeschichte.* Freiburg, Karl Alber, 1965.

WAHID, Zainal Abidin Z. A. (ed.). *History Teaching: Its Problems in Malaya.* Kuala Lumpur, 1964.

WALL, R. F. 'New openings: Asia.' In *New Ways in History, op. cit. (The Times Literary Supplement,* 1966), pp. 301–302.

WALLAS, Graham. *Human Nature in Politics*. London, 1908; republ., New York, Knopf, 1921; London, Constable, 1948.
WALLERSTEIN, Immanuel M. *Social Change: The Colonial Situation*. New York, Wiley, 1966.
WANG Gungwu. 'South.and Southeast Asian historiography.' In *International Encyclopedia of the Social Sciences, op. cit.* (1968), Vol. VI, pp. 420–428 (*sub* 'Historiography').
WATT, Donald Cameron, SPENCER, F. & BROWN, N. *A History of the World in the Twentieth Century*. London, Hodder-Fawcett, 1967; New York, Morrow, 1968.
WEBB, Walter Prescott. *The Great Frontier*. Boston, Houghton Mifflin/London, Secker & Warburg, 1951; rev. edn., Austin, University of Texas Press, 1964.
WEBER, Eugen Joseph. *Varieties of Fascism: Doctrines of Revolution in the 20th Century*. Princeton (N.J.), Van Nostrand, 1964.
———. 'Fairies and hard facts: the reality of folktales.' *Journal of the History of Ideas*, Vol. XLII (1), 1980, pp. 93–113.
WEBER, Max. 'Die Stadt.' In Max WEBER, *Wirtschaft und Gesellschaft*, Tübingen, J. C. B. Mohr, 1922; 2nd edn., 1925, Vol. II, pp. 735 sqq. (English translation and edition by Don Martindale & Gertrud Neuwirth, *The City*, Glencoe [Ill.], Free Press, 1958; republ., London, Heinemann, 1960).
WEBSTER, Sir Charles. 'Fifty years of change in historical teachings and research.' In *The Historical Association, 1906–1956, op. cit.* (1957).
WEHLER, Hans-Ulrich. Introduction to the collected edition of KEHR's essays, *Der Primat der Innenpolitik, op. cit. (1965).*
———. 'Zum Verhaltnis von Geschichtswissenschaft und Psychoanalyse.' *Historische Zeitschrift*, Vol. CCVIII, 1969, pp. 529–554.
WEHLER, Hans-Ulrich (ed.). *Moderne deutsche Sozialgeschichte*. Cologne, Kiepenheuer & Witsch, 1966.
WEISS, John. *The Fascist Tradition: Radical Right-Wing Extremism in Modern Europe*. New York, Harper, 1967.
WHEELER, Geoffrey E. & FOOTMAN, D. *Bibliography of Recent Soviet Source Material on Soviet Central Asia*, No. 1. London, 1960.
WHEELER, Sir Robert E. Mortimer. *The Indus Civilization (Cambridge History of India*, supplementary volume). Cambridge, Cambridge University Press, 1953; 2nd edn., 1960.
———. *Rome beyond the Imperial Frontiers*. London, G. Bell, 1954.
WHITAKER, Arthur Preston. *Nationalism in Latin America: Past and Present*. Gainesville (Fla.), University of Florida Press, 1962.
——— & JORDAN, D. C. *Nationalism in Contemporary Latin America*. New York, The Free Press, 1966.
WHITE, Hayden. *The Content of the Form: Narrative Discourse and Historical Representation*. Baltimore, Johns Hopkins University Press, 1987.
———. 'Historiography and Historiophoty.' *American Historical Review*, Vol. XCIII (5), December, 1988, pp. 1193–1199.
WHITE, Morton G. *Foundations of Historical Knowledge*. New York, Harper & Row, 1965.
WIDGERY, Alban G. *Interpretations of History from Confucius to Toynbee*. London, Allen & Unwin, 1961 (French translation by Serge Bricianer, *Les grandes doctrines de l'histoire: De Confucius à Toynbee*. 'Idées' series, No. 83. Paris, Gallimard, 1965).
WIETHOFF, Bodo. *Grundzüge der älteren chinesischen Geschichte*. Darmstadt, Wissenschaftliche Buchgesellschaft, 1971.
WILLIAMS, Charles Harold. *The Modern Historian*. London, Nelson, 1938.

WILLIAMS, Raymond. *Culture and Society, 1780–1850.* London, Chatto & Windus, 1958.

WINCHESTER, I. 'The linkage of historical records by man and computer.' *Journal of Interdisciplinary History,* Vol. I, 1970, pp. 107–124.

WIND, Edgar. 'Some points of contact between history and natural science.' In KLIBANSKY & PATON (eds.), *Philosophy and History, op. cit.* (1936), pp. 255–264.

WITTRAM, Reinhard. *Das Interesse an der Geschichte: Zwölf Vorlesungen über Fragen des zeitgenössischen Geschichtsverständnisses.* Göttingen, Vandenhoeck & Ruprecht, 1958.

———. 'Die Möglichkeit einer Weltgeschichte.' In WITTRAM, *Das Interesse an der Geschichte, op. cit.* (1958), pp. 122–136.

WOLF, Eric Robert. *Peasant Wars of the Twentieth Century.* New York, Harper, 1969.

WOLFF, Kurt H. 'Sociology and history: Theory and practice.' *American Journal of Sociology* LXV (1), July 1959, pp. 32–38.

WOOD, Herbert George. *Freedom and Necessity in History* (lectures delivered at King's College on 12, 13 and 14 March 1957), Riddell Memorial Lectures, No. 29. London, Oxford University Press, 1957.

WOODHAM-SMITH, Cecil [FITZGERALD], Mrs. *The Reason Why.* London, Constable/New York, McGraw-Hill, 1953; republ., London, Heinemann/New York, McGraw-Hill, 1971; paperback edns., Harmondsworth (Middx.), Penguin Books and New York, Dutton.

WOODWARD, C. Vann. 'History and the Third Culture.' *Journal of Contemporary History* III (2), Apr. 1968 (special issue: *Reappraisals*), pp. 23–35.

———. 'A Short History of American History.' *New York Times Book Review,* 8 August 1982.

WOOLF, Stuart J. (ed.). *European Fascism.* London, Weidenfeld & Nicolson, 1968.

———. *The Nature of Fascism* (proceedings of a conference held by the Reading Univ. Graduate School of Contemporary European Studies). London, Weidenfeld & Nicolson, 1968.

The World of Learning. 21st, 22nd and 23rd edns. London, Europe Publications, 1970–71, 1971–72 and 1972–73.

WOUDE, A. M. van der. 'De historische demografie in de ontwikkeling van de geschiedeniswetenschap.' *Tijdschrift voor Geschiedenis,* Vol. 82, 1969, pp. 184–205.

WRIGHT, Athur F. 'The study of Chinese civilization,' *Journal of the History of Ideas* XXI (2), Apr.–June 1960, pp. 233–255.

———. 'Symbolism and function: Reflections on Changon and other great cities.' *Association for Asian Studies,* 1963, pp. 667–679.

———. 'Viewpoints on a city.' *Ventures,* Vol. V, 1963, pp. 15–23.

———. 'Chinese historiography.' In *International Encyclopedia of the Social Sciences, op. cit.* (1968), Vol. VI, pp. 400–407 (*sub* 'Historiography').

WRIGLEY, Edward A. 'Family limitation in pre-industrial England.' *Economic History Review,* 2nd ser., Vol. XIX, 1966, pp. 82–109.

———. 'Population, family and household.' In BALLARD (ed.), *New Movements in the Study and Teaching of History, op. cit.* (1970), pp. 93–104.

WRIGLEY, Edward A., EVERSLEY, D. E. C. & LASLETT, P. (eds.). *An Introduction to English Historical Demography.* London, Weidenfeld & Nicolson, 1966.

WUSTEMEYER, M. 'Die "Annales": Grundsätze und Methoden ihrer "neuen" Geschichtswissenschaft." ' *Vierteljahrschrift für Sozial- und Wirtschaftsgeschichte,* Vol. LIV, 1967, pp. 1–45.

WYMAN, Walker D. & KROEBER, C. B. (eds.). *The Frontier in Perspective*. Madison (Wis.), University of Wisconsin Press, 1957.

YAMAMOTO, Tetsuro. Statement in Congress meeting of 26 August 1960, devoted to 'Discussion sur le rapport de M. E. M. ZHUKOV, "The periodization of world history" *(op. cit.)*, et sur les communications de M. Václav Husa . . . et de M. Branislav Djurdjev . . .' (summary), in *XIe* [Onzième] *Congrès international des Sciences historiques, Stockholm, 1960: Actes, op. cit.* (1962), p. 64 (the entire 'Discussion' occupying pp. 56–67).

YANG, Anand. 'A conversation of rumors: the language of popular *mentalités* in late nineteenth century colonial India.' *Journal of Social History*, Vol. XX, 1986–1987, pp. 484–505.

YEN Chung-p'ing. 'Yuan-yü Hsuan-ts'e Yen-chiu T'i-mu' (= On the selection of subjects for research), *Hung-ch'i* (= Red Flag), 16 June 1962 (available in English translation, U.S. Department of Commerce, Office of Technical Services, Joint Publications Research Service, JPRS: 14, 595, 24 July 1962, pp. 46–71; partially quoted in English by A. FEUERWERKER in 'China's modern economic history,' *op. cit.* (1965, 1968), p. 239 in FEUERWERKER (ed.), *History in Communist China, op. cit.*, 1968).

YOUNG-BRUEHL, Elisabeth. *Anna Freud: A Biography*. New York, Summit Books, 1988.

ZAPF, Wolfgang. *Wandlungen der deutschen Elite, 1919–1961*. Munich, Piper, 1965.

ZAVALA, Silvio A. 'A general view of the colonial history of the New World.' *American Historical Review*, Vol. LXVI, 1961, pp. 913–929.

——. *The Colonial Period in the History of the New World* (= *Program of the History of the New World*, Vol. 2), abridgement by Max SAVELLE. Mexico City, Instituto Panamericano de Geografía e Historia, 1962.

——. *El mundo americano en la época colonial*. Mexico City, Porrúa, 1967, 2 vols.

ZEA, Leopoldo, *El positivismo en México*. Mexico City, 1943.

——. *Apogeo y decadencia del positivismo en México*. Mexico City, 1945.

——. *América como conciencia*. Mexico City, 1953.

——. *The Latin-American Mind*. Translated from the Spanish by James H. Abbott & Lowell Dunham, Norman (Okla.), University of Oklahoma Press, 1963.

——. *América Latina y el mundo*. Buenos Aires, EUDEBA (Editorial Universitaria de Buenos Aires), 1965 (English translation by Frances K. Hendricks & Beatrice Berler, *Latin America and the World*, Norman (Okla.), University of Oklahoma Press, 1969).

Zeitschrift für Geschichtswissenschaft (periodical, East Berlin), 1952 sqq.

ZELDIN, Theodore. 'Personal History and the History of Emotions.' *Journal of Social History*, Vol. XV (3), Spring 1982, pp. 339–347.

ZEUNER, Friedrich Eberhard. *Dating the Past: An Introduction to Geochronology*. 4th edn., rev. and enl. London, Methuen, 1958.

ZHUKOV, E. M.: see ŽUKOV, E. M.

ZÍADAH, M. M. 'Modern Egyptian historiography.' *Middle Eastern Affairs*, Vol. IV, 1953, pp. 266–271.

ZINOV'EV, M. A. *Osnovnye voprosy metodiki prepodavanija istorii. Rukovodstvo dlja prepodavatelej istorii srednej školy* (= Main Questions relating to the Method of History Teaching. Instructions for the Teachers of History in Secondary Schools), Moscow, Izd. Akad. Nauk, 1948 (English translation by

Alexis Musin-Pushkin, ZINOVIEV, M. A., *Soviet Methods of Teaching History,* Russian translation project series of the American Council of Learned Societies, No. 12, Washington [D.C.]–Ann Arbor [Mich.], 1952).

ZINSSER, Hans. *Rats, Lice and History: Being a Study in Biography which, after Twelve Preliminary Chapters Indispensable for the Preparation of the Lay Reader, Deals with the Life History of Typhus Fever.* London, Routledge/ Boston, Little, Brown & Co., 1935.

ŽUKOV (ZHUKOV), E. M. 'The periodization of world history,' in *XIème Congrès international des Sciences historiques, Stockholm, 1960: Rapports, op. cit.* (1960), Vol. I, pp. 74–88 (Russian version published as 'O periodizacii vsemirnoj istorii,' *Voprosy istorii,* 1960, No. 8, pp. 22–23; English summary, p. 220).

ŽUKOV, E. M. (ed.). *Vsemirnaja istorija* (= World History). Moscow, 1955–65, 10 vols.

Zur Periodisierung des Feudalismus und Kapitalismus in der geschichtlichen Entwicklung des UdSSR (a selection of articles from *Voprosy istorii,* edited and translated for the Gesellschaft für Deutsch-Sowjetische Freundschaft by Karl-Eugen WÄDEKIN), Berlin, Verlag Kultur und Fortschritt, 1952 (= *Sowjetwissenschaft,* Beiheft 20).